Rethinking the Welfare State

Rethinking the Welfare State

The Political Economy of Pension Reform

Edited by

Martin Rein

Professor of Social Policy, Department of Urban Studies and Planning, Massachusetts Institute of Technology, USA

and

Winfried Schmähl

Professor of Economics and Director, Economics Department, Centre for Social Policy Research, University of Bremen, Germany

Edward Elgar
Cheltenham, UK • Northampton, MA, USA

© Martin Rein and Winfried Schmähl, 2004

Published by   Car
Edward Elgar Publishing Limited
Glensanda House
Montpellier Parade
Cheltenham
Glos GL50 1UA
UK

Edward Elgar Publishing, Inc.
136 West Street
Suite 202
Northampton
Massachusetts 01060
USA

A catalogue record for this book
is available from the British Library

Library of Congress Cataloguing in Publication Data

Rethinking the welfare state : the political economy of pension reform / edited by
    Martin Rein and Winfried Schmähl.
    p.   cm.
    Includes bibliographical references and index.
    1. Pensions. 2. Retirement income. 3. Social security. 4. Old age pensions.
    5. Welfare state. 6. Privatization. I. Title: Political economy of pension
    reform.   II. Rein, Martin, 1928–   III. Schmähl, Winfried.

    HD7091.R414   2003
    331.25′22—dc21   2003051611

ISBN 1 84376 102 5

Printed and bound in Great Britain by MPG Books Ltd, Bodmin, Cornwall

Contents

v

Contributors

David Blake, Birkbeck College London, UK

Giuliano Bonoli, Universities of Berne and Fribourg, Switzerland

Bernard H. Casey, London School of Economics, UK

Agnieszka Chłoń-Domińczak, Gdansk Institute for Market Economics, Poland

Barry L. Friedman, Brandeis University, US

Leny H. van der Heiden-Aantjes, Ministry of Social Affairs and Employment, The Netherlands

Yukiko M. Katsumata, National Institute of Population and Social Security Research, Japan

Katharina Müller, German Development Institute, Bonn

Edward Palmer, University of Uppsala and Swedish National Social Insurance Board, Sweden

Martin Rein, Massachusetts Institute of Technology, US

Michał Rutkowski, The World Bank and Warsaw School of Economics, Poland

Winfried Schmähl, University of Bremen, Germany

Heinz Stapf-Finé, German Trade Union Association (Deutscher Gewerkschaftsbund)

Júlia Szalai, Academy of Science, Hungary

John Turner, Public Policy Institute, AARP, US

Eskil Wadensjö, Swedish Institute for Social Research, Stockholm University, Sweden

R. Kent Weaver, Georgetown University and The Brookings Institution, US

Peter Whiteford, OECD and Department of Family and Community Services, Australia

Atsuhiro Yamada, Keio University, Japan

Introduction

Martin Rein and Winfried Schmähl

This book is about change in the political economy of pensions, what type of change took place, why and how it was realized and which outcome may be expected for the future. The chapters provide a detailed review of recent pension reforms in several countries, and offer institutional evidence of the extent to which these reforms suggest there has been something of a rethinking of the directions of the welfare state and, more specifically, whether the rethinking has taken the form of changing the public–private mix of policies. We have cast a wide net covering the experience of 15 western countries that have in the past decade or so launched a significant redirection of pension policy. The countries were selected to represent something of the great variety of new directions that mature industrial economies as well as economies in transition have taken. Two essays in this volume seek to provide a quantitative empirical foundation for examining the extent to which a change in the mix is evident in the income package of aged households. Finally, several chapters provide an overview of regional developments and emerging new patterns.

The question that we want to explore in this introduction is whether there are some general conclusions that can be drawn from the essays in this book. Is the thesis about change in the political economy of pension reform leading to new forms of the public–private mix justified? What are the general trends that have emerged from the reports presented in this volume? We propose five general themes. These are not exhaustive and they do not capture the subtle and detailed accounts presented in the country chapters. But our intention is to be selective in order to highlight what are the most important conclusions of this inquiry. The themes are interdependent rather than free-standing. The developments sketched out in each theme then proceed to influence the analysis in the following theme, forming something like an interlocking mosaic.

OVERLAPPING MODELS OF PENSION SYSTEMS

Traditional approaches to developing typologies of different welfare state regimes have assumed that it is possible to develop a classification of types that characterize the welfare state viewed as a whole embracing all the stages of the life course. Such schemes are assumed to be stable over time. Theories of path dependency seem to justify the assumption of relative stability, on the assumption that, once a pathway has been chosen, it is hard to reverse directions in any significant way that signals a shift in the underlying paradigm implied in the typology.

We believe that the evidence in the essays presented in this book suggest quite different general conclusions. We do not see examples of clear, unambiguous models of type A, B or C in the retirement domain that is the focus of this study. What emerges is hybrid forms rather than pure types. And if this conclusion is valid within a specific domain like retirement policy then it is hard to imagine that uniform patterns over the whole welfare state are faithful to the regime type that is posited.

Instead of focusing on stable, relatively unchanging and uniform types, we see a pattern of sequencing, changes in direction over time.[1] A specific form of overlapping models can be seen in particular in some of the countries in transition which implemented quite different new pension schemes compared to the already existing schemes. Here, different models are operating and sometimes covering identical persons. In most of the countries that we review in this book public sector pensions are available universally to virtually the entire population. But public schemes are under severe pressure in many countries. On the other hand, a feature of new pension policy initiatives is that in many countries there is a trend towards extending coverage in the private sector to the working-age population as a whole and by this changing the public–private mix in pension policy and in income packaging in the future.

THE MOVE TOWARD EXTENDING COVERAGE OF PRIVATE SECTOR PENSIONS

There has been a longstanding recognition that voluntary pensions in general as well as those sponsored by employers have the shortcoming that they only cover a segment of the working-age population. But the movement towards extending coverage of private sector schemes has emerged not only from several quite different and somewhat unexpected directions. Here we try only to bring together these disparate threads that are discussed in more detail in country chapters of this book.

Perhaps the earliest development was in the Netherlands, when, shortly after the Second World War, in 1946, legislation was passed which recognized that an adequate pension system requires the combination of a strong public system together with quasi-mandated private occupational pensions (see Chapter 5 of this book). So the Dutch started with a commitment, not to public dominance, but to a public–private mix. Over the years since the inception of this legislation occupational pension coverage grew to 90 per cent of the employed population. Then, in 1998, the government created a Pension Covenant, requesting that the private sector modernize its operation and lower the public franchise which is the method used for deciding the size of the public contribution to a consensually agreement replacement rate of 70 per cent of final wages. But then it also insisted that efforts be made to fill the 10 per cent gap in coverage and insisted on the development of additional schemes that would include the whole labour market. If the social partners could not reach an agreement, the government threatened to pass legislation that would ensure that these goals would be realized. So a new Covenant was created in 2002 to continue the pressure to realize this and other objectives. In the context of this discussion, the aim of universal coverage of occupational pensions is perhaps also based on the assumption that such a goal would also lower public pension costs in the long run, since the public–private schemes are tightly coupled, and a stronger private sector implies lower benefits in the public sector.

Another recent example of expanding private coverage and benefit levels came, surprisingly, from the Swedish pension reform of 1994 (see Chapter 8 of this book). Even though coverage in the Swedish occupational pension system is very extensive, the value of these pensions is relatively low, accounting for perhaps 10 per cent of the income package of aged households. The legislation called for the mandating of capital funding schemes in the market by setting aside 2.5 per cent of compulsory contributions for this purpose. Thus everyone receiving a public statutory pension system at the same time is enrolled in an individual financial accounts system. The collection and management of the contributions is organized by the public sector and the funds are then anonymously invested in a plan that is chosen by the worker. The managers of these plans do not know the identity of the investor, so this is clearly a public statutory programme with capital funds managed by the private sector.[2]

A very different pattern of extending coverage has its origin, not in the efforts to reform the pension system, but in the initiative of reforms introduced in the industrial relationship system of wage negotiations. The crucial assumption in these reforms is that an occupational pension is interpreted as being broadly equivalent to a postponed salary. Accepting this assumption, it follows that unions and employees would be willing to accept wage restraint and, in exchange for these deferred wages, an employment-provided pension benefit. This may support government policy in periods of an overheated economy. In Australia, the labour market tribunal refused to extend these labour agreements, since compliance with the agreements was weak and many firms failed to provide the pensions. As a result, the state decided to make the system mandatory and to use the power of taxation to impose uniform coverage. Over 80 per cent of wage and salary workers are covered by the legislation (see Chapter 3). A similar development occurred at very nearly the same time in the wage negotiations of 1991 in Denmark. In this situation public, mandatory statutory legislation was not necessary since in Denmark unionization was very strong. Most people over their lifetime will find themselves in jobs covered by collective contracts, hence this programme is referred to as one of labour market pensions.[3]

A similar expansion of coverage occurred when Switzerland mandated occupational pensions, but for very different reasons than that these developments occurred in the other countries. In part the expansion of the private sector by mandating was inspired by the fear that a referendum calling for an expansion of public pensions could be transformed into a legislative programme. Private mandating was designed to offset this development (see Chapter 4).

Taken together, these various developments have all contributed both to the extension of coverage and to increasing the value of these private occupational pensions. At the same time, the expansion of coverage has in some countries led to the partial substitution of private for public provision, a theme we discuss next.

SUBSTITUTION OF PRIVATE FOR PUBLIC

In the traditional employer-provided and financed occupational pension (discussed next) the relationship between public and private pension provision was based on the principle of supplementation. This meant that the private was paid on top of the public pension, whether the public system was resident-based and uniform or an earnings-related system. The exceptions to this generalization were discussed above, where we tried to show that, in those countries that introduced a transfer test as a condition for the receipt of a public pension, the principle of supplementation did not fully apply. Even here there were exceptions if, for example, rules for ensuring a minimum public guarantee were developed or a very high taper test was introduced so that the transfer test did not affect the benefit received from both systems.

But, in this section, we discern a new emerging pattern of substituting private for public pensions. The new design based on the principle of substitutions was introduced in the German pension reform of 2001, in the Swedish 1994 reform, and in the American debate about pension reform introduced by the President's Commission to Strengthen Social Security final report submitted in December 2001. The Swedish pension reform of 1994 created two defined contribution plans: a notional and a financial plan based on contributions made on lifetime earnings, an implicit rate of return more or less equal to per capita wage changes during the phase of lifetime savings, followed by an annuity based on life expectancy at retirement (see Chapter 8). A small part of the contributions made to public pension, 2.5 per cent of the total 16.5 per cent, was reassigned in the financial plan, so that individuals could create personal investment accounts in market equities with the freedom to select and invest in a plan of their choice. But the full implications of these market-driven investments are only evident when the changes in the contractual employer-provided supplementary pensions are considered. Sweden has an elaborate system of occupational pensions covering 90 per cent of the employed population. The Swedish contractual schemes are organized along four corporativist lines: white-collar, blue-collar, municipal and central government workers. These contractual schemes add about 10 per cent to the basic public pension.

The public pension reform (notional defined contribution, NDC) and the introduction of financial defined contribution (FDC) have led to the redefining of the role of private occupational pensions so that they can be better integrated into the new scheme based on lifetime earnings and defined contributions. But the contributions to these funds will be augmented in varying amounts from 2 to 4.5 per cent. The implications of this new scheme for pension replacement rates are very dramatic. They could lead to the substitution of private for public funding. The private contractual scheme, especially when it is placed in concert with the public FDC, would appear to be able not only to offset the decline in the value of the public pension system, but also to usher in an era where this combination of a public–private mix can come to dominate the Swedish pension scene. Perhaps this is an exaggeration for the population as a whole, but it may very well play an increasing role for many segments of the labour force, apart from those in the very highest income brackets.

Sweden has also moved towards investing the funds accumulated in collective investment buffer funds in a broader range of instruments than the traditional low-risk and low-return strategies relied on in the past. Kent Weaver's essay in this volume explores the Swedish experience with buffer funds, with a focus on the governance structure of default funds, which is the fund that accumulates the resources of those who do not make an active fund choice. He compares the politics of investing collective buffer funds in Sweden with that of a number of other countries, thus opening a new research agenda for the comparative study of public–private pensions.

Germany too is now changing the public–private mix through the reform of 2001 (see Chapter 6). The reform measures aim at a decline in public earnings-related pensions and to offset this by an increase of voluntary private or occupational pensions with tax incentives. Private pensions are even used as an instrument to reduce public pensions by introducing a notional contribution rate for private pensions into the formula for calculating public pensions. If employees are voluntarily saving in addition for old age, this leaves the retired person with about the same level of protection but with a partial substitution of private for public benefits.

If we accept the line of reasoning developed above, the reform in Sweden as well as in Germany see private pensions, not as an 'add-on', or a supplementary system, but one that 'carves out' a private segment that is designed to substitute for the decline in the public pension system. Thus the German voluntary private pension and the Swedish FDC share a strategy of carving out a private component to offset a faltering public system. In the United States, the substitution of private for public benefits will depend on whether the president proposes new legislation, on which plans are proposed in the legislation and on what action Congress might take in response. The details of these plans are reviewed by Friedman in Chapter 7.

'Contracting out and contracting in' is yet another way of substituting private for public provision. Several countries have encouraged with tax incentives, or simply permitted, the reduction of the public sector by a process of allowing individuals to contract out of the public system into an approved private plan that provides benefits and protection at least as good as that provided in the public sector. As Schmähl points out, such practice may actually occur in countries where one would least expect to find it. For example, in Germany, employees working in firms of professional groups of self-employed, for example medical doctors with an independent practice, architects or lawyers, can contract out of the public pension system. For all employees a special new scheme for a partial contracting out has been implemented in Germany, whereby employees gain the right to convert part of their earnings into an occupational pension. One of the possible ways of generating earnings for investment in the market is exempting the earning from both payment of tax and social insurance contributions. Thus the employer is not totally contracted out of the public scheme, but only that portion of the earning that would have been subject to tax and social security contributions.

On the other hand, there are at least two countries where contracting out is quite widespread: the United Kingdom and Japan. The essays in this volume (by Blake and Katsumata) describe the practice, and comment on some of the differences, in the two countries. In the UK contracting out is a widespread practice. Only about 15 per cent of wage and salary workers, mostly low wage workers, are in the earnings-related public statutory programme known as SERPS. Britain encouraged the practice, first into employer provide pensions, and then through tax subsidies that individuals switch to individual accounts. The government considered altogether eliminating the public social security programme but in the end decided against this radical action.

The development in Japan is particularly interesting. As firms fell on hard times with the economic recession, those that had contracted out of the public scheme found that they could not honour their commitments. The government, having required contracted-out firms to assume a rate of return on investments of 5 per cent, then lowered expectations to 2.5 per cent, but the actual rate of return was closer to zero. Under these persistent conditions, firms' pension systems will go bankrupt. To protect themselves, corporate pressure groups emerged which sought to convince the government to change the legislation and permit firms to contract back into the state programmes on favourable terms.

Such a contracting in was also allowed in the new Hungarian pension system introducing a mandatory funded pension scheme as second tier of the pension system. As the expected development in the new scheme was not forthcoming, contributors were offered the possibility to cancel their decision to join the new scheme.

What, then, are the long-term consequences of these different patterns that we have described: extending coverage of private pensions, the substitution of private for public, and the transition of employer-provided and financed pensions, at the same time introducing the flexibility of contracting out as well as moving in the opposite direction of contracting in? Of course, prediction is always difficult, but still some general conclusions seem beyond question. Instead of viewing the question as one of 'either or', it seems best to focus on the principle of 'both and'. The question that then emerged was to agree on what share of total income is to be provided from the contribution of both the public and the private spheres and what proportion of this total should come from each sector. But not all income groups have a public–private mix in the income package of aged households. Will the trends that we have described become dominant? That is, will wider shares of coverage in the private sector be accompanied by declining shares of the public sector? Partly the outcome will depend on the mechanisms that produce it. We have identified a wide range or mechanisms. The outcome could be brought about by the introduction of transfer testing in the basic public system; the tight harmonizing of public and private resources against a target replacement rate; the carving out of a portion of the public statutory pension for a mandatory investment in capital funds; encouragement of the carving out with a voluntary system with tax incentives; an additional consideration should the system be

designed is to permit the individual to contract back into the public sector
at some later point in time, as the British opted to do. Still other approaches
may emerge, since the list is by no means exhaustive. As always, the devil is
in the details of the mechanism that produces the outcomes.

There seems to be an overall development towards a closer contribution–benefit link. This can be realized in different ways:

- redesigning public defined benefit schemes, reducing intertemporal
  redistributive effects, extending the years of insurance taken into
  account for benefit calculation, financing interpersonal redistribution by tax instead of contribution revenue;
- introducing notional defined contribution schemes;
- shifting employer-provided occupational pensions from defined
  benefit to defined contribution plans;
- shifting from public to private pensions.

This is to be seen as a trend not only in mature Western pension schemes
but also in many of the countries in transition (see Chapter 11).

PERSISTENCE OF THE PUBLIC PENSION SYSTEM AND THE CONTINUOUS EVOLUTION OF THE PUBLIC–PRIVATE MIX

When we turn to the economies in transition it is obvious that the monopoly of public provided pensions is changing towards more diversity. There
is good evidence in Poland (see Chapter 12) as well as in Hungary (see
Chapter 13) that the systems are still evolving. The discussion of the
pension system can shape the public–private mix in the pension system that
is now implemented, when experience will have been made with its effects.
During the process of transforming pension schemes the disparity between
plans which set the ambitions of legislative intentions and practice which
defines what actually happens on the ground became obvious. So reform
leads to a process of continuous sequence of events whose direction
remains uncertain.

Rutkowski (in Chapter 11) tries to locate the Polish and Hungarian
development in the broader context of the actual experience of most transition economies. He also considers the development of the proposals for
reform made by the World Bank that have emerged from the experience of
the 1990s. The diversity of country conditions was more and more recognized and influenced the approach the bank was proposing in various countries for radical reform. The World Bank was an influential and perhaps

even a key actor in many countries that promoted the idea of the substitution of private for public provision. Müller (in Chapter 14) tries to associate the experience of transition economies in Europe with developments in Latin America, as the reforms made there were studied carefully in many countries in Central and Eastern Europe.

Of course the economies in transition in Central and Eastern Europe never had a developed private sphere, so any expansion of this sphere represents to some extent a substitution. But the question here is whether there has been an evolution towards private dominance, as in some Latin American countries. As the essays in this book clearly demonstrate, in Central and Eastern Europe a more or less full-scale replacement of public by private pensions has not taken place. Public pensions still predominate, but there is a continuously changing public–private mix. The new funded elements are far from mature. Their part in creating future pension benefits will increase over time. What the mix in retirement income from public and private schemes will be in the future we cannot tell.

TRADITIONAL EMPLOYER-PROVIDED PENSIONS IN TRANSITION

A simple meaning of traditional private employer-provided pension systems would be that of an employer who pays for, and provides a defined benefit for all employees who are eligible, in a fully funded pension programme whose main parameters were designed by the employer alone to address his need to attract, retain and motivate his employees. This simple scheme of pay, provide and decide is not a caricature, but a description of the private pension system offered by many large employers. Of course, many smaller firms do not directly provide, but delegate the administrative tasks to life insurance companies or to pension funds that administer several smaller schemes together, to benefit from economies of scale. But this account of the meaning of private does not imply that the public sector is absent from any active involvement. Besides its role as an employer, the state conventionally plays two traditional roles: it provides tax incentives and perhaps direct subsidies to pension plans to encourage the creation of plans that supplement the benefit levels provided under the public social security programme, and it also plays a regulatory role in protecting the money of contributors, preventing theft and the flagrant disregard of the conditions that were set in return for the resources offered to these tax qualified plans.

This model of employer-provided defined contributions, with the employer financing the scheme and bearing the risks of paying for the system when benefits are due, is almost everywhere in transition. The transition

takes many forms, but the clearest moves are in the direction of introducing
defined contribution plans, largely financed by the employee, but with
employer contributions in some schemes. The transition can take several
different forms: voluntary individual accounts based on personal savings
schemes with the individual paying for the accounts alone or with the help
of the employers. In the United States, 401 (k)[4] plans take both these forms.
But they can take the Danish form of a combination of forced savings and
contractual labour agreements that provide defined contributions financed
by deferred wages. They can also take the form of the 'carve-out' arrangements described above. We identify the transition and leave open the multiple pathways to move away from the voluntary agreements on traditional
defined benefit employer-provided and -financed plans.

A note of caution should be sounded here. Despite the shift in new plans,
employer-provided benefits may continue to rise for some time as generous
plans introduced in the past will reach maturity in the present. So once time
lags that are important in particular for old-age security are taken in
account, there can still be a rise in the importance of traditional plans as a
source of retirement income with the plans themselves in the process of
transition.

CONSEQUENCES OF THE EMERGING PATTERNS

If we allow for the twin outcomes of broader coverage and substitution of
private for public at least in mature welfare states, what might we expect as
a plausible emerging pattern? There are two possibilities. One scenario is
the growth of inequalities among the aged, on the assumption that private
pensions are more likely to be found among higher-income groups which
also benefit more from tax expenditure and other subsidies. In contrast to
public schemes, private schemes have no elements aiming at a reduction of
income inequality in old age. The evidence to support this claim is strong
(see Casey and Yamada in Chapter 15). But at the same time, if the focus
is on the total pension income from both sources it may not be the mix
per se that is crucial, but how the mix is designed. Some countries with
high mix, such as Sweden, Denmark, Norway, Holland, Switzerland and
Canada, have both low poverty rates and relatively low inequality. On the
other hand, countries like the UK and the USA have both high poverty and
high inequality. Design rather than the mix might in the end turn out to be
the more decisive factor in determining the wellbeing of people in retirement (see Chapter 16). To identify properly the emerging patterns in
income mix as well as regarding inequality, a cohort-specific approach is
needed, based on longitudinal data.

AMBIGUITIES IN THE CONCEPT OF PUBLIC AND PRIVATE

Now that we have developed our ideas about the recurrent themes that characterize recent pension reforms, we want to discuss some definitional issues about the meaning of a public–private divide and the extent to which quantitative data can help clarify these issues, or whether these issues must be resolved before empirical data can be usefully employed.

We have used the terms 'public' and 'private' throughout this discussion without calling attention to the blurring of the concepts and the substantial ambiguities surrounding these ideas. So it is important to make some of these difficulties more explicit. Nevertheless, this is not an argument for not using these concepts, but for recognizing that they are fuzzy. Fuzzy concepts play an important role in public policy debates, as witnessed by the widespread use of ideas such as sustainability or generational equity. But still it is useful to recognize and to identify some of the sources of the fuzziness.

The effects of the public–private mix on the economic wellbeing of the aged are difficult to pin down empirically. Some reasons for these difficulties warrant a brief discussion. As pensions systems have evolved over time it has become increasingly difficult to draw a clear and unambiguous boundary between public and private. The first complication arises because the state has a dual role as general provider of public social security programmes and as employer. These are two quite different roles. The state can establish its own employer-provided programme, for the same reasons that the private sector will establish supplementary pensions to the general public schemes.

The second complication involves, not a definitional change, but a change in practice. This change occurred in 2002 in Japan, with employees being able to opt out of the public sector pension into a private occupational pension. Japan and the UK have this possibility of officially contracting out of the public sphere and making private pension arrangements. In Japan, firms viewed the privatization of public pensions as an economic opportunity and they lobbied the government to facilitate the process of transition into private occupational pensions. The government established a condition for the transition, namely that the scheme had to be funded based on the assumption of a 5 per cent minimum rate of return on equity investments. This was attractive when the return rates were more than double this amount, but when there was an economic turnabout firms had a zero rate of return. In this new economic climate firms lobbied for a political change in legislation, passed in 2001, which makes it possible for firms to 'opt into' the public system. Although the process of transition took many years to achieve, this change from 'opting out' to 'opting in' of course also meant a change in the public–private mix (for details see Katsumata in Chapter 2).

The third complication concerns emerging practice, where a part of the public system is 'carved out' of the public statutory system and this separated portion is funded by direct investments in the equity market. In Germany, the carved out segment of the public pension is private and voluntary, although this may change in the future.

In Sweden, the carved out section of the public programme, which is called the premium pension, is a hybrid form since this is partly a public programme as the public sector handles the transfer of money to the equities market and the gains or losses in the financial account chosen by the individual reverts to them as a private investment. The investments are based on choices made by the individual with resources derived from the public contributory social insurance programme. The public component of this system is that of a notional account, since the money is not actually invested, but it is an accounting system which is only converted to actual resources at the time of retirement, whereas in the premium pension system, hard currency is actually invested in the market. (See the Swedish and German cases in this book.)

The fourth complication is that the use of the term 'private' does not imply that the public sector is totally absent from any active involvement. The state conventionally plays two traditional roles: it provides tax incentives and perhaps direct subsidies to pension plans to encourage the creation of plans that supplement the benefit levels provided in the public social security programme and to protect its investment; it also plays a regulatory role to insure compliance with the agreed upon rules for managing the system, to prevent direct theft or flagrant disregard of the agreed upon rules and norms of appropriate behaviour. In 1995, the Dutch Civil servant pension system was privatized, meaning that it was subject to the same set of regulations that private sector pensions were required to comply with. So we have a public agency defined as a 'private' agent. Many countries have such supplementary public sector pensions which are treated as private systems supplementing the general public social security programme. There is no completely satisfactory way to resolve these definitional questions (see Chapter 5). This note of caution regarding the fuzzy boundaries that demarcate our subject may be useful if it can cure the tendency to say more than what the data suggest.

NOTES

1.   Some analysts will concede the point about divergent paths, but still insist that there is nevertheless a common dimension in all the Nordic countries which is the unique model of a commitment to full coverage, universalism and to the principle of solidarity that justifies its having a unique Nordic commitment.

2. As early as 1960, Finland also created a hybrid earnings-related public statutory system that was partially funded but managed by private sector investors in conformity with tight public regulations. The basic public pension system is transfer-tested, so the larger the earning-related system, the lower the basic, uniform pension. Thus over time and over the income distribution, as this hybrid public–private system matures, the lower the level of aggregate public spending for the resident-based, flat rate public pension financed from general taxation. This, of course, follows a different logic than the Swedish financial accounts, but the Finnish design does involve the extension of coverage into the privately managed pension system by a public statutory programme with near universal coverage.

3. In Denmark, the public supplementary pension will decline as the labour market pensions grow, because these pensions are transfer-tested against the public scheme. In Australia, the nature of the relationship between the mandatory pension and the public means-tested programme has not yet been agreed upon. In Sweden and the Netherlands, coverage by the private occupational pension, which has traditionally been high, has continued to increase, but here the point is not so much extending coverage, but increasing the value of the pension for those that receive such benefits.

4. A set of rules in the tax code which allows employees to set up a defined contribution plan for individual employees who then decide on the options that they select for investment in market equities. See Chapter 7 in this volume.

PART I

The experience of mature welfare states in western economies

A

Contracting out: the experience in the United Kingdom and Japan

1. Contracting out of the state pension system: the British experience of carrots and sticks

David Blake

INTRODUCTION

The United Kingdom was one of the first countries in the world to develop formal private pension arrangements (beginning in the nineteenth century). First-pillar state pension provision began in the early twentieth century and the modern welfare state began in 1948. The UK operates its welfare state on the Beveridgean principle of providing just a minimum safety net, in contrast with the more generous Bismarckian principle that operates on the Continent. Second-pillar state pensions began in 1961 and the current second-pillar state pension scheme (S2P – the State Second Pension Scheme) began in April 2002. From the very beginning, individuals were offered a carrot in the form of very generous tax incentives to 'contract out' of the second-pillar state pension scheme into either occupational pension schemes or personal pension schemes. However, since 1980, a stick has also been in use: the UK became one of the first countries in the world to begin the process of reducing systematically unfunded state provision, thereby providing a different type of incentive to make private pension arrangements.

This explains why the UK is one of the few countries in Europe whose pension problem is manageable. The reasons for this are straightforward: state pensions (both in terms of the replacement ratio and as a proportion of average earnings) are amongst the lowest in Europe, the UK has a long-standing funded private pension sector, its population is aging less rapidly than elsewhere in Europe and its governments have taken measures to prevent a pension crisis developing. The UK is not entitled to be complacent, however, since there remain some serious and unresolved problems with the different types of private sector provision, such as poor portability in occupational pension schemes and variable investment returns, high charges, high-pressure selling and low persistence in personal pension schemes.

This chapter examines the key issues relating to the UK pension system. It reviews the current system of pension provision, describes and analyses the reforms since 1980, assesses the different types of risks and returns from membership of defined benefit and defined contribution pension schemes, and investigates the investment performance of pension fund assets.

THE CURRENT SYSTEM OF PENSION PROVISION

A flat-rate first-pillar pension is provided by the state and is known as the Basic State Pension (BSP). Second-pillar or supplementary pensions are provided by the state, employers and private sector financial institutions, the so-called three pillars of support in old age. The main choices are between a state system that offers a pension that is low relative to average earnings but which is fully indexed to prices after retirement; an occupational system that offers a relatively high level of pension (partially indexed to prices after retirement up to a maximum of 2.5 per cent p.a.), but, as a result of poor transfer values between schemes on changing jobs, only to workers who spend most of their working lives with the same company; and a personal pension system that offers fully portable (and partially indexed) pensions, although these are based on uncertain investment returns and subject to very high set-up and administration charges, often inappropriate sales tactics and very low paid-up values if contributions into the plans lapse prematurely.

Employees in the UK in receipt of earnings subject to National Insurance contributions (NICs) will build up entitlement[1] both to the BSP[2] and, on 'band earnings' between the lower earnings limit (LEL) and the upper earnings limit (UEL),[3] to the pension provided by the S2P; S2P was introduced in April 2002 and replaced the State Earnings-Related Pension Scheme (SERPS) which was introduced in 1978. These pensions are paid by the Department of Work and Pensions (DWP) (formerly the Department of Social Security (DSS))[4] from state pension age, which is 65 for men and 60 for women.[5] The self-employed are also entitled to a BSP, but not to a S2P pension. Employees with earnings in excess of the LEL will automatically be members of S2P, unless they belong to an employer's occupational pension scheme or to a personal or stakeholder pension scheme that has been contracted out of S2P. In such cases both the individual and the employer contracting out receive a rebate on their NICs (1.6 per cent of earnings for the employee and 3.5 per cent for the employer, unless it operates a COMPS, in which case the employer rebate is 1.0 per cent[6]) and the individual forgoes the right to receive a S2P pension. However, there is no obligation on employers to operate their own pension scheme, nor, since 1988, is there any contractual requirement for an employee to join the employer's scheme if it has one.

There is a wide range of private sector pension schemes open to individuals. They can join their employer's occupational pension scheme (if it has one), which can be any one of the following:

- contracted-in salary-related scheme (CISRS),
- contracted-in money purchase scheme (CIMPS),
- contracted-out salary-related scheme (COSRS),
- contracted-out money purchase scheme (COMPS),
- contracted-out mixed benefit scheme (COMBS),
- contracted-out hybrid scheme (COHS).

A CISRS is a defined benefit scheme that has not been contracted out of S2P and so provides a salary-related pension in addition to the S2P pension. A CIMPS provides a defined contribution supplement to the S2P pension. A COSRS must satisfy a 'reference scheme test' in order to contract out of S2P, namely provide a pension for life from age 65 which is indexed to inflation up to a maximum of 5 per cent p.a. where the starting pension is calculated by taking a minimum of 1/80th of the average salary over the three years prior to retirement for each year of service in the scheme up to a maximum of 40 years' service. A COMPS must have contributions no lower than the contracted-out rebate. A COMBS can use a mixture of the reference scheme test and the minimum contributions test to contract out of S2P, while a COHS can provide pensions using a combination of salary-related and money purchase elements. Individuals can also top up their schemes with additional voluntary contributions (AVCs) or free-standing additional voluntary contributions (FSAVCs) up to limits permitted by the Inland Revenue.

As an alternative, individuals have three individual pension choices that are independent of the employer's scheme: a personal pension scheme (PPS), a group personal pension scheme (GPPS) or a stakeholder pension scheme (SPS). A PPS is divided into two components. The first is an appropriate personal pension scheme (APPS) which is contracted out of S2P and provides 'protected rights' benefits that stand in place of S2P benefits: they are also known as minimum contribution or rebate-only schemes since the only contributions permitted are the combined rebate on NICs with the employee's share of the rebate grossed up for basic rate tax relief (at 22 per cent). The second is an additional scheme, also contracted out, that receives any additional contributions up to Inland Revenue limits. A GPPS is a scheme that has been arranged by a small employer with only a few employees: it is essentially a collection of individual schemes, but with lower unit costs because of the savings on up-front marketing and administration costs. An SPS is a low-cost PPS with charges capped at 1 per cent p.a. of the fund value and into which contributions of up £3600 p.a. can be made, irrespective of whether the SPS member has made any net relevant earnings during the year.[7]

In 1996, the UK workforce totalled 28.5 million people, of whom 3.3 million were self-employed.[8] The pension arrangements of these people were as follows:[9]

- 7.5 million employees in SERPS (now S2P),
- 1.2 million employees in 110000 contracted-in occupational schemes,
- 9.3 million employees in 40000 contracted-out occupational schemes (85 per cent of such schemes are salary-related, although 85 per cent of new schemes started in 1998 were money purchase or hybrid),
- 5.5 million employees in personal pension schemes,
- 1.7 million employees without a pension scheme apart from the BSP,
- 1.5 million self-employed in personal pension schemes,
- 1.8 million self-employed without a pension scheme apart from the BSP.

These figures indicate that 72 per cent of supplementary pension scheme members in 1996 were in SERPS or an occupational scheme and 28 per cent were in personal pension schemes.[10]

Table 1.1 shows the sources of retirement income in 1997–8. A single person had total retirement income averaging 43 per cent of national average earnings (NAE). Nearly two-thirds of this came from state benefits and another quarter came from occupational pensions: personal pensions provided only about 5 per cent of total retirement income for the average person.[11]

THE REFORMS SINCE 1980

Thatcher–Major Reforms to the Pension System

The Thatcher Conservative government that came into power in 1979 became the first government in the developed world to confront head on the potential crisis in state pension provision. The reforms were continued by the succeeding Major government. These governments introduced a number of measures. First, they linked the growth rate in state pensions to prices rather than national average earnings, thereby saving about 2 per cent p.a. (Social Security Act 1980). Second, they raised the state pension age from 60 to 65 for women over a 10-year period beginning in 2010, thereby reducing the cost of state pensions by £3bn p.a. (Pensions Act 1995). Third, they reduced the benefits accruing under SERPS (which had only been set

Table 1.1 Sources of retirement income in 1997–8

Source	Single person			Married couples		
	£per week	% of total	% of NAE	£per week	% of total	% of NAE
State benefits[a]	95	64	27	133	44	38
Occupational pensions	33	22	10	90	30	26
Investment income[b]	14	9	4	48	16	14
Earnings[c]	7	5	2	33	11	9
Total	149	100	43	304	100	87

Notes:
[a] Includes incapacity benefit, housing benefit, council tax benefit etc.
[b] Includes income from personal pensions.
[c] Women in the age range 60–65 and men in the age range 65–70.

Source: Department of Social Security (2000a, Table 1).

up in 1978) in a number of ways: (a) the pension was to be reduced (over a 10-year transitional period beginning in April 1999) from 25 per cent of average revalued band earnings over the best 20 years to 20 per cent of average revalued band earnings over the full career (Social Security Act 1986); (b) the spouse's pension was cut from 100 per cent of the member's pension to 50 per cent over an eight-year transitional period beginning in October 2002 (Social Security Act 1986); (c) the revaluation factor for band earnings was reduced by about 2 per cent p.a. (Pensions Act 1995); the combined effect of all these changes was to reduce the value of SERPS benefits by around two-thirds.

Fourth, they provided a 'special bonus' in the form of an extra 2 per cent National Insurance rebate for all PPSs contracting out of SERPS between April 1988 and April 1993 (Social Security Act 1986) and provided an incentive between April 1993 and April 1997 in the form of a 1 per cent age-related National Insurance rebate to members of contracted-out PPSs aged 30 or more to discourage them from recontracting back into SERPS. Age-related National Insurance rebates continued in a revised form after April 1997 (Social Security Act 1993).

Fifth, they relaxed the restriction on PPSs that an annuity had to be purchased on the retirement date, by introducing an income drawdown facility which enabled an income (of between 35 and 100 per cent of a single life annuity) to be drawn from the pension fund (which otherwise remains invested in earning assets) and delaying the obligation to purchase an annuity until age 75 (Finance Act 1995). Sixth, they enabled members of occupational pension schemes to join personal pension schemes (Social Security Act 1986).

Seventh, they simplified the arrangements for occupational schemes to contract out of SERPS by abolishing the requirement for occupational schemes to provide guaranteed minimum pensions (GMPs): since April 1997, COSRSs have had to demonstrate only that they satisfy the reference scheme test (Pensions Act 1995).

Eighth, they ended their commitment to pay for part of the inflation indexation of occupational schemes (Pensions Act 1995). Until April 1997, COSRSs had to index the GMP up to an inflation level of 3 per cent p.a. and any additional pension above the GMP up to an inflation level of 5 per cent p.a. Since the GMP replaced the SERPS pension which was itself fully indexed to inflation, the government increased an individual's state pension to compensate for any inflation on the GMP above 3 per cent p.a. But the 1995 Act abolished the GMP altogether and required COSRSs to index the whole of the pension that they pay up to a maximum of 5 per cent p.a. (this is known as limited price indexation). This was later reduced to 2.5%.

Finally, they improved the security of the assets in private sector schemes through the creation of the Occupational Pensions Regulatory Authority (OPRA), a compensation fund operated by the Pensions Compensation Board (PCB), a minimum funding requirement (MFR) and a statement of investment principles (SIP) (Pensions Act 1995); OPRA, the PCB and the MFR are examined in more detail below.

Defects in the Thatcher–Major Reforms

The main defects of the Thatcher–Major reforms were as follows. First, they removed the requirement that membership of an occupational pension scheme could be made a condition of employment. Membership was made voluntary and new employees had to take the active decision of joining their employer's scheme: barely more than 50 per cent of them did so.

Second, there was no requirement to ensure that transferring from an occupational to a personal pension scheme was in the best interests of the employee, leading directly to the personal pensions mis-selling scandal that erupted in December 1993. Between 1988 and 1993, 500 000 members of occupational pension schemes had transferred their assets to personal pension schemes following high-pressure sales tactics by agents of PPS providers. As many as 90 per cent of those who transferred had been given inappropriate advice. Miners, teachers, nurses and police officers were amongst the main targets of the sales agents. Many of these people remained working for the same employer, but they switched from a good occupational pension scheme offering an index-linked pension into a PPS towards which the employer did not contribute and which took 25 per cent of the transfer value in commissions and administration charges. An example reported in the press concerned a miner who transferred to a PPS in 1989 and retired in 1994 aged 60. He received a lump sum of £2576 and a pension of £734 by his new scheme. Had he remained in his occupational scheme, he would have received a lump sum of £5125 and a pension of £1791. As a result of a public outcry, PPS providers have had to compensate those who had been given inappropriate advice to the tune of £13.5bn.

Third, no restriction was placed on the charges that could be imposed in personal pension plans, in the hope that market forces alone would ensure that PPSs were competitively provided. Finally they gave personal pension scheme members the right to recontract back into SERPS. This option has turned out to be extremely expensive for the government because of the backloading of benefits in defined benefit pension schemes such as SERPS: benefits accrue more heavily in the later years than the earlier years.[12] Despite the financial incentives given to contract out of SERPS into PPSs, it turned out to be advantageous for men over 42 and women over 34 to contract back into SERPS once the period of the special bonus had ended in 1993. To discourage this from happening the government has been forced to offer additional age-related rebates to PPS members since 1993. Far from saving the government money, the net cost of PPSs during the first ten years was estimated by the National Audit Office to be about £10bn.

The Blair Reforms to the Pension System

The Blair New Labour government came into power in 1997 with a radical agenda for reforming the welfare state. In the event, Frank Field, appointed the first Minister for Welfare Reform at the Department of Social Security (DSS) and charged with the objective of 'thinking the unthinkable', proved to be too radical for the traditional Old Labour wing of the Labour Party and was soon replaced. The eventual DSS Green Paper proposals, 'A New Contract for Welfare: Partnership in Pensions' (December 1998), turned out to be much less radical than initially anticipated, but nevertheless continued with the Thatcher government's agenda of attempting to reduce the cost to the state of public pension provision and of transferring the burden of provision to the private sector through the introduction of stakeholder pension schemes. Nevertheless, there was much greater emphasis on redistributing resources to poorer members of society than was the case with the Conservatives. Shortly after the publication of the Green Paper, the Treasury issued a consultation document on the type of investment vehicles in which stakeholder pension contributions might be invested. We will examine these proposals in turn.

The Department of Social Security proposals
The key objectives of the DSS Green Paper were as follows:

1. to reduce the complexity of the UK pension system, by abolishing SERPS;
2. to introduce a minimum income guarantee in retirement linked to increases in national average earnings on the grounds that people who work all their lives should not have to rely on means-tested benefits in retirement; the first-pillar BSP will remain indexed to prices, however, and over time will become a relatively unimportant component of most people's pensions;
3. to provide more state help for those who cannot save for retirement, such as the low-paid (those on less than half median earnings), carers and the disabled, via the unfunded state system;
4. to encourage those who are able to save what they can for retirement, via affordable and secure second-pillar pensions: (a) provided by the state for those on modest incomes (via a new unfunded state second pension), and (b) provided by the private sector for middle- and high-income earners, with the option of new low-cost defined contribution stakeholder pensions which are likely to replace high-cost personal pensions. But there will be no extra compulsion to save for retirement at the second pillar and no additional incentives over those already existing at the second pillar.

The Green Paper proposals formed the basis of the Welfare Reform and Pensions Act which received the Royal Assent in November 1999. The Act deals with state pensions, stakeholder pensions, occupational pensions and personal pensions.

State pensions   A Minimum Income Guarantee (MIG) of £75 per week was introduced for pensioners in April 1999: it is means-tested on a weekly basis (and tapers off if the claimant's capital exceeds a specified limit) and is indexed to earnings. The MIG significantly increased the benefit income of the poorest pensioners, creating a new, higher income threshold below which pensioners with no or little savings should not fall.

In April 2003, the government introduced the Pension Credit (PC),[13] the aim of which is not just to end the penalty on savings, but, for the first time, to reward savings. The PC, which is untaxed, is designed to make up the difference between the income a pensioner receives from *all* existing sources (including private pensions and savings) and the MIG. The PC will (a) reward work and savings in retirement, by abolishing the capital limits and introducing a cash reward for modest savings, earnings or second-pillar pensions; (b) modernize the system, by abolishing the weekly means test, and moving more into line with the tax system which is based on an annual cycle, thus paving the way for further tax and benefit integration in the future.

SERPS was replaced by a new State Second Pension (S2P) in April 2002: the S2P was initially earnings-related but, from April 2007, becomes a flat-rate benefit, even though contributions are earnings-related, a feature that is intended to provide strong incentives for middle- and high-income earners to contract out. The S2P

- ensures that everyone with a complete work record receives combined pensions above the MIG;
- gives the low-paid earning below £9500 p.a. twice the SERPS pension at £9500 p.a. (implying that the accrual rate is 40 per cent of £9500 rather than the 20 per cent under SERPS);
- gives a higher benefit than SERPS between £9500 and £21 600 p.a. (average earnings in 1999);
- leaves those earning over £21 600 p.a. unaffected (with an accrual rate of 20 per cent);
- uprates these thresholds in line with national average earnings;
- provides credits for carers (including parents with children under five) and the disabled.

Stakeholder pensions New Stakeholder Pension Schemes (SPSs) were introduced in April 2001, and are principally intended for middle-income earners (£9500–£21 600) with no existing private pension provision. They can be used to contract out of S2P. They are collective arrangements, provided by an employer, a representative or membership or affinity organization, or a financial services company.

They are defined contribution schemes, with the same restrictions as for personal pensions, namely that, on the retirement date, up to 25 per cent of the accumulated fund may be taken as a tax-free lump sum, while the remaining fund may be used to buy an annuity or to provide a pension income by way of a drawdown facility until age 75, when an annuity must be purchased with the remaining assets.

They have to meet minimum standards, known as CAT (charges–access–terms) marks concerning (a) the charging structure and level of charges (a maximum of 1 per cent of fund value p.a.), (b) levels of contractual minimum contributions (£20), and (c) contribution flexibility and transferability (no penalties if contributions cease temporarily (up to five years) or if the fund is transferred to another provider).

The main provisions of the Pensions Act 1995 apply to SPSs, covering the annual report and accounts, the appointment of professional advisers and the Statement of Investment Principles. They are regulated principally by OPRA, although the selling of schemes and the supervision of their investment managers is regulated by the Financial Services Authority (FSA), with the Pensions Ombudsman for redress. Employers without an occupational scheme and with at least five staff must offer access to one 'nominated' SPS and provide a payroll deduction facility.

There is a new integrated tax regime for all defined contribution pension plans. SPSs, personal pension plans and occupational DC plans will attract tax relief on contributions up to a maximum of 17.5 per cent of earnings (below age 36), rising to 40 per cent (above age 61). But contributions up to £3600 p.a. can be made into any DC plan regardless of the size of net relevant earnings. Contributions in excess of £3600 p.a. may continue for up to five years after relevant earnings have ceased. Thereafter, contributions may not exceed £3600 p.a. All contributions into DC plans will be made net of basic rate tax, with providers recovering the tax from the Inland Revenue and with higher rate tax, if any, being recovered in the self-assessment tax return.

Occupational pensions   Occupational schemes can contract out of the S2P. Employers can again make membership of an occupational scheme a condition of employment, and employees are only allowed to opt out if they have signed a statement of rights being given up, certified that they have adequate alternative provision, and have taken advice that confirms that the alternative is at least as good as the S2P. The compensation scheme established by the 1995 Pensions Act was extended to cover 100 per cent of the liabilities of pensioners and those within ten years of normal pension age (NPA).

Personal pensions   PPS can contract out of the S2P. They receive protection in cases of the bankruptcy of the member.

HM Treasury proposals
The Treasury proposals were contained in 'Helping to Deliver Stakeholder Pensions: Flexibility in Pension Investment' (February 1999). They called for the introduction of more flexible investment vehicles for managing pension contributions, not only those in the new stakeholder pension schemes, but also those in occupational and personal pension schemes. These investment vehicles were given the name Individual Pension

Accounts (IPAs). The main IPAs are authorized unit trusts (AUTs or open-ended mutual funds), investment trust companies (ITCs or closed-ended mutual funds), and open-ended investment companies (OEICs).

In comparison with the individual arrangements of existing personal pension schemes and the poor transferability of occupational pension schemes, IPAs offer lower charges, since collective investment vehicles have much lower overheads than individual investments, and greater flexibility, since IPAs are easy to value and transfer between different stakeholder, personal and occupational pension schemes, allowing employees to move jobs without having to change pension schemes, thereby encouraging greater labour market flexibility.

Assessment of the Blair Reforms

The Welfare Reform and Pensions Act, while containing some significant improvements on the existing system, does not fully meet the Green Paper's own objectives.

Reforms to state pensions

While the abolition of SERPS helped to simplify the UK's extremely complex pension system, the proposal to have a MIG (of £75 per week) that differed from the BSP (£67.50 per week at the time) reintroduced substantial complexity at the starting point for state pension provision, especially when the difference between the two amounts (£7.50 per week) was initially so small. It would have been far simpler to set the MIG equal to the BSP and to link the latter to earnings. Now the government explicitly rejected this on the grounds of both cost[14] and the fact that it would benefit the high-paid as well as the low-paid, whereas the government's emphasis was on helping the low-paid. But the problem with keeping the BSP linked to prices rather than to earnings is that it will continue to fall relentlessly as a proportion of national average earnings (NAE): it is currently just 17 per cent of NAE and will fall to well below 10 per cent by 2025. While the government admits that this will save substantial sums of money, it implies the government is effectively abandoning the first pillar of support in old age and obliging everyone to rely on the second and third pillars. The Green Paper talked about building on the BSP, but this implies building on a sinking ship.

If the government is genuinely concerned about security at the minimum level for all, it should consider funding the first pillar appropriately by establishing an explicit fund (like the Social Security Trust Fund (SSTF) in the USA) into which it places the NICs of those who are in work, while the government itself funds the contributions of the low-paid, carers and the disabled.[15] The contribution rate could be actuarially set to deliver the

MIG for all when they retire. It could be a hypothecated part of NICs. In other words, the contributions would accrue 'interest' equal to the growth rate in NAE. The state could explicitly issue NAE-indexed bonds which the SSTF would buy. This is the only honest way of both preserving the value of and honouring the promises under the first pillar. The second and third pillars could then be formally integrated with the first pillar; that is, the second pillar being used to deliver the tranche of pension between the MIG and the Inland Revenue limits, while the third pillar is used for voluntary arrangements above the IR limits. If the first pillar remains unfunded, there is nothing to prevent future generations reneging on an agreement which they are expected to keep but did not voluntarily enter into.

The fact that membership of private pension schemes at the second pillar remains voluntary is highly worrying for reasons of myopia and moral hazard. Compulsory contributions are seen as one way of dealing with individual myopia and the problem of moral hazard. Myopia arises because individuals do not recognize the need to make adequate provision for retirement when they are young, but regret this when they are old, by which time it is too late to do anything about it. Moral hazard arises when individuals deliberately avoid saving for retirement when they are young because they calculate that the state will feel obliged not to let them live in dire poverty in retirement. Inevitably, this will lead to substantial means testing in retirement.

In short, while the Welfare Reform and Pensions Act has some good points, it fails three tests set by Frank Field for a good state pension system: it is not mandatory, it is not funded and it remains means-tested (Field, (1996a; 1996b)). Field argued that means testing turns honest, thrifty citizens into dishonest citizens, since they have a strong incentive to conceal the true extent of their savings from the authorities in order to avoid having their state benefits cut. The spendthrift tend to end up with higher state benefits than the thrifty, to the annoyance of the latter. However, the Pension Credit was specifically designed to overcome this problem, by rewarding rather than penalizing retirement savings.

Reforms to private pensions
The government's proposal to have a maximum annual charge of 1 per cent of fund value on SPSs will have two dramatic effects on private sector pension provision, especially PPSs. The first is that it will help to force economies of scale in DC pension provision. This is because stakeholder pensions will be a retail product with wholesale charges. To deliver this product effectively, providers will need to exploit massive economies of scale. Charges for personal pension schemes, which prior to the introduction of stakeholder pension schemes averaged 1.4 per cent p.a. and rose to as much

as 2.2 per cent p.a. of fund value for 25-year policies,[16] are much higher than the 1 per cent p.a. CAT-marked limit on SPSs. There may be a range of providers of SPSs to begin with, but the only way for a provider to survive in the long run will be for it to operate at low unit cost on a large scale. This will inevitably lead to mergers amongst providers and a final equilibrium with a small number of very large providers.

Existing personal pension providers and distribution channels face a number of challenges:

- PPSs face massive competition from SPSs for future NIC rebates;
- SPSs could be better than PPSs for middle-income groups, leaving PPSs as a choice only for those on high incomes who require and are willing to pay for a bespoke product;
- new affinity-based SPSs with gateway organizations linking up with pension providers (for example, the Amalgamated Engineering & Electrical Union with 720000 members and Friends Provident);
- the Treasury's IPAs provide a low-cost alternative investment vehicle to the high-cost managed funds of most PPSs;
- Individual Savings Accounts (ISAs), introduced by the Treasury in April 1999 to encourage greater personal sector savings, also provide an important alternative to PPSs. Contributions into ISAs of up to £7000 per annum are permitted and the investment returns are free from income and capital gains tax. While not intended as pension savings vehicles (they do not attract tax relief on contributions, for example, unlike standard pension savings products), ISAs can be used in retirement income planning, since they enjoy the big advantage that they can be cashed in tax-free at any time, thereby avoiding the need to purchase a pension annuity on the retirement date.

The second benefit is that the government's proposal will effectively force stakeholder pension funds to be passively managed, since active management would result in a charge higher than 1 per cent. As demonstrated below, active fund managers have not demonstrated that they can systematically deliver the superior investment performance that justifies their higher charges. Further, passively managed mutual funds in the USA, such as Vanguard (which are similar investment vehicles to IPAs), have charges below 0.3 per cent.

The Political Economy of Pension Reform

How has it been possible for UK governments to reduce the size of state pension provision without significant political protest, when similar attempts to do so on the Continent have led to street protests and strikes (for example, in Italy in November 1994 and France in November 1995)?

Consider the SERPS pension. When it was first introduced in 1978, it offered a pension of 25 per cent of the best 20 years of band earnings revalued to the retirement date by increases in national average earnings, with a 100 per cent spouse's pension. Within a quarter of a century, the value of these benefits had been reduced by two-thirds, before the scheme was abandoned altogether. How has this been achieved so peaceably? There are three main explanations. First, SERPS had only been established a few years before changes to it started being made, so very few people were drawing the pension and little loyalty to the scheme had accumulated. Second, SERPS was an incredibly complex pension system that very few pensions professionals fully understood, let alone members of the general public. While there was comment in the media at the time of these changes to SERPS, very little of this seems to have permeated the consciousness of the mass of the population and the extent of the changes was little understood. Third, the changes were introduced with a lag of 15 to 20 years, so it was easy for everyone to forget about them.

Even when changes were introduced immediately, as with the switch in the uprating of the state pension from earnings to prices, the immediate difference was relatively small and most people failed to realize how, over time, small differences can build up into large amounts.[17]

A final explanation lies in the fact that state pension provision is much less important for most people in the UK than it is on the Continent, and those for whom it is important, namely the low-paid, have little political influence. The situation on the Continent is rather different. State pensions provide a much higher replacement ratio than in the UK and social solidarity appears to be a more important objective than it is in the UK. As a consequence, it is much harder to alter pension arrangements on the Continent, even if the political will to do so is strong, which it clearly is not. The British may look with envy on their Bismarckian cousins across the English Channel but are still prepared to accept Beveridgean minimalism when it comes to their own social security system.

THE RISKS AND RETURNS IN FUNDED SCHEMES

There are two main types of funded scheme: the defined benefit (DB) scheme and the defined contribution (DC) scheme.[18] With a DB scheme, it is the pension benefit that is defined. In the UK, for example, most DB schemes are arranged by companies and are known as occupational final salary schemes, since the pension is some proportion of final salary, where the proportion depends on years of service in the scheme. A typical scheme in the UK has a benefit formula of one-sixtieth of final salary for each year of service up to a maximum of 40 years' service, implying a maximum pension in retirement of two-thirds of final salary, and with the pension indexed to inflation up to a maximum of 2.5 per cent p.a. (that is, limited price indexation or LPI). In contrast, with a DC scheme, what is defined is the contribution rate into the fund, such as 10 per cent of earnings. The resulting pension depends solely on the size of the fund accumulated at retirement. Given that the contributions are invested in financial assets, the accumulated fund and hence the pension will be subject to investment risk. Such schemes are also known as money purchase schemes and in the UK they are better known as personal pension schemes. The accumulated fund must be used to buy a life annuity from an insurance company (although, in the UK, up to 25 per cent of the fund can be taken as a tax-free lump sum on the retirement date).

Defined Benefit Schemes

Defined benefit and defined contribution schemes have different costs and benefits. Defined benefit schemes offer an assured (and in many cases a relatively high) income replacement ratio in retirement. People in retirement can expect to enjoy a standard of living that is related to their standard of living just prior to retirement. But this is the case only for workers who remain with the same employer for their whole career. Fewer than 5 per cent of workers in the UK do this: the average worker changes jobs about six times in a lifetime.[19]

Every time workers switch jobs they experience a 'portability loss' in respect of their pension entitlement. This is because DB schemes are generally provided by specific employers and when a worker changes jobs they have to move to a new employer's scheme. When they do so, they will either take a transfer value equal to the cash equivalent of their accrued pension benefits with them or leave a deferred pension in the scheme that they are leaving. Accrued benefits are valued less favourably if someone leaves a scheme than if they remain an active member of the scheme. This is because scheme leavers (whether they choose a transfer value or a deferred pension) have their years of service valued in terms of their leaving salary (although this is uprated annually to the retirement date by the lower of the inflation rate or 2.5 per cent), whereas continuing members will have the same years of service as the early leaver valued in terms of their projected salary at retirement which is likely to be higher. Long stayers are therefore subsidized at the expense of early leavers. In the UK, the portability loss is more commonly known as a 'transfer value loss' or 'cash equivalent loss'.

For a typical worker in the UK changing jobs six times during their career, Table 1.2 shows that the portability loss lies between 25 and 30 per

Table 1.2 *Portability losses from defined benefit schemes (percentage of full service pension received at retirement)*

Worker type	Job separation assumptions[1]	Transfer value[2]	Deferred pension[3]	Defined contribution pension (employer-run)[4]	Personal pension (employer contributions)[5]	Personal pension (no employer contributions)[6]
Average UK worker (MFR assumptions realized)[7]	A	75	75			
	B	71	71			
	C	84	84	71	61	37
Average UK manual worker	A	75	88			
	B	71	86			
	C	84	96	78	66	45
Average UK non-manual worker	A	75	86			
	B	71	83			
	C	84	94	79	68	44

Notes:
1. This table presents estimates of the size of the portability losses experienced by three different types of UK workers (based on typical lifetime earnings profiles) under three different sets of job leaving assumptions: A, leaves at ages 28, 29, 30, 40 and 57; B, leaves at 26, 27, 30, 31, 38, 44 and 55; C, leaves at 45. The loss is expressed in the form of a reduced pension compared with what each of the three workers would have received had they remained in a single scheme for their whole career.
2. Leaving worker takes transfer value to new scheme.
3. Leaving worker leaves deferred pension in leaving scheme.
4. Leaving worker transfers into employer-run DC scheme.
5. Leaving worker transfers into personal pension scheme where the employer also contributes.
6. Leaving worker transfers into personal pension scheme where the employer does not contribute.
7. The MFR (minimum funding requirement) assumptions are the assumptions specified in the 1995 Pensions Act concerning future inflation, earnings growth and investment returns that must be used by UK pension funds from April 1997 to determine the minimum contribution level needed to meet projected pension liabilities.

Source: Blake and Orszag (1997, Appendix E, Table 5.8, p. 74).

cent of the full service pension (that is, the pension of someone with the same salary experience but who remains in the same scheme all their working life). Even someone changing jobs once in mid-career can lose up to 16 per cent of the full service pension. It is possible to reduce portability losses by, for example, indexing leaving salaries between the leaving and retirement dates to the growth in real earnings or by providing full service credits on transfers between jobs, but this is not common in the UK (except on transfers between different public sector occupational pension schemes).

Defined Contribution Schemes

With DC schemes, it is important to distinguish between the accumulation and distribution stages.

The accumulation stage
Defined contribution schemes have the advantage of complete portability when changing jobs. However, individual DC schemes (such as personal pension schemes) tend to have much higher operating costs than occupational DB schemes (although occupational DC schemes may have lower operating costs than occupational DB schemes on account of their much simpler structure). Individual DC schemes in the UK take around 2.5 per cent of contributions in administration charges and up to 1.5 per cent of the value of the accumulated assets in fund management charges. The Institute of Actuaries has estimated that all these costs are equivalent to a reduction in contributions of between 10 and 20 per cent; in contrast, the equivalent costs of running an occupational scheme work out at between 5 and 7 per cent of annual contributions.[20] On top of this, most of the costs associated with an individual DC scheme relate to the initial marketing and set-up. To reflect this, charges are also frontloaded; that is, they are extracted at the start-up of a scheme rather than spread evenly over the life of the scheme. In many schemes, much of the first two years of contributions is used to pay sales commissions. This has a dramatic effect in reducing the surrender value of a scheme if contributions cease early on and it is transformed from a continuing to a paid-up basis. The cumulative effect of these charges in respect of DC schemes is shown in Table 1.3. Over a 25-year investment horizon, the average scheme with a full contribution record takes around 19 per cent of the fund value in charges, while the worst scheme provider takes around 28 per cent.[21] There is also evidence of a substantial absence of persistency in regular premium personal pension policies. Table 1.4 shows that the estimated average lapse rate is 27 per cent after two years and 53 per cent after four years: it is 84 per cent after 25 years

Table 1.3   Percentage of DC fund value represented by charges

	5 years	10 years	15 years	20 years	25 years
Regular premium scheme (£200/month)					
Best commission-free fund	3.1	4.1	7.2	8.5	9.8
Best commission-loaded fund	4.0	4.1	7.4	8.9	10.6
Industry average	11.6	13.0	14.8	17.7	19.0
Worst fund	19.2	22.0	24.6	28.2	27.8
Single premium scheme (£10000)					
Best commission-free fund	3.8	7.1	9.2	10.6	10.4
Best commission-loaded fund	3.8	7.1	9.2	10.6	10.4
Industry average	9.6	13.3	16.3	19.1	21.9
Worst fund	17.4	20.5	27.0	32.9	38.2

Source: Money Management (October 1998).

Table 1.4   Persistency rates for regular premium personal pension plans (percentages)

	Company representatives: after				Independent financial advisers: after			
	1 Year	2 Years	3 Years	4 Years	1 Year	2 Years	3 Years	4 Years
1993	84.1	72.3	63.6	56.7	91.5	83.3	76.6	70.5
1994	83.7	72.8	64.4		91.3	82.1	74.5	
1995	85.5	75.0			90.8	81.6		
1996	86.6				90.2			

Source: Personal Investment Authority (1998, Table 1).

(assuming a 6.5 per cent annual average lapse rate after four years). The lapse rate-adjusted reduction in contributions for a 25-year policy is 62 per cent: the effective contributions into this scheme for a typical policy holder are just 38p in the pound.[22]

Further, although individual DC schemes are portable between jobs, they are not fully portable between scheme providers or even between different investment funds operated by the same provider. Transfers between personal pension scheme providers, for example, can incur charges of between 25 and 33 per cent of the value of the assets transferred. Transfers from DB schemes into DC schemes can cost even more than this. Table 1.2 shows that, even if a worker changes jobs only once in mid-career and moves out of a DB scheme, he will receive a reduced pension of 71–9 per cent of the full service pension if he moves to an employer-run DC pension (with the same total contribution rate as the DB scheme and no extra charges), 61–8 per cent if he moves to a personal pension scheme (where the employer also contributes), and only 37–44 per cent if he moves to a personal pension scheme (without employer contributions). Moving to a DC scheme involves a 'backloading loss' in addition to the cash equivalent loss incurred when leaving a DB scheme. The backloading loss arises because benefits are backloaded in final salary schemes but not in DC schemes; this follows because salary and therefore accrued benefits generally *increase* with years of service. Individuals transferring to a DC scheme (with age-independent contributions) forgo these backloaded benefits: the marginal benefit from an additional year's membership of a DC scheme is simply that year's contributions (plus the investment returns on these) which are usually a *constant* proportion of earnings. If the DC scheme happens to be a personal pension scheme then there are also initial and annual charges to pay, plus the possible loss of the employer's contribution. The impact of these factors can be extensive, as the above portability losses indicate.[23]

Another problem with DC schemes, in practice, is that total contributions into them tend to be much lower than with DB schemes. In a typical DB scheme in the UK, the employee's contribution is about 5–6 per cent of employee earnings, while the employer's contribution is double this at about 10–12 per cent.[24] The size of the employer's contribution is not widely known amongst employees; and, to an extent, the size of the employer's contribution is irrelevant from the employee's viewpoint, since the pension depends on final salary, not on the level of contributions. This is not the case with DC schemes, where the size of the pension depends critically on the size of contributions. When personal pension schemes first started in the UK in 1988, most employers refused to contribute anything towards these schemes and many workers were not fully aware of the penalty in terms of the reduced pension they were incurring as a result of forgoing the employer's contribution.

However, most (about 85 per cent) of the new occupational schemes being established in the UK are DC schemes. The average employee contribution into such schemes is 3 per cent, while the average employer contribution is again double at 6 per cent (although some employers only match the employee's contribution).[25] Total contributions into occupational DC schemes are therefore around 9 per cent of employee earnings compared with 15–18 per cent for occupational DB schemes. Nevertheless, administration costs are much lower with occupational DC schemes than with personal pension schemes, so even if employers made the same contribution into an

Table 1.5   Contributions needed to achieve a pension of two-thirds final salary

Age at commencement (male)	Required contributions (% of salary)	Maximum contributions (% of salary)
25	10.90	17.5
30	13.41	17.5
35	16.81	17.5
40	21.66	20.0
45	28.92	20.0
50	40.81	25.0
55	64.15	30.0
60	129.83	35.0

Note:
The following assumptions apply: male retiring at age 65; no previous contributions into any other pension scheme; salary increases by 3% p.a.; investment return 6% p.a.

Source: Blake (1997, Table 10.2).

employee's personal pension scheme as into their own DC scheme, the final pension would still be lower in the personal pension scheme.

Investment risk is not the only risk borne by DC scheme members and their dependants. They also bear some of the other types of risk, namely, ill-health, disability and death-in-service. In DB schemes, these risks exist, but are typically carried by the scheme sponsor. In DC schemes, protection against these risks has to be purchased directly by the member as additional insurance policies.

Nevertheless, Table 1.5 shows that, so long as individuals join a DC scheme at a sufficiently early age and maintain their contribution record over a sufficiently long investment horizon (and so get the benefits of compounded returns), a decent pension in retirement can be achieved for a modest contribution rate. The table indicates that a 25-year-old male can expect a pension of two-thirds of final salary (the maximum available from a DB scheme in the UK) with a total net contribution rate of just under 11 per cent of earnings. The required contribution rate rises sharply with age, however. Someone joining at 35 would need a contribution rate of around 17 per cent, and by the age of 40, the required contribution rate is above the maximum permissible under the regulations establishing such schemes.

The distribution stage: annuities
The weak tail of DC pension provision lies in the distribution stage and relates to the annuities market. The market for immediate annuities is

highly concentrated: of around 200 authorized life companies in the UK, only about ten are serious providers of life annuities at any given time.[26] There are a number of problems facing both annuitants and annuity providers.[27] First, there is an adverse selection bias associated with mortality risk. This is the risk that only individuals who believe that they are likely to live longer than the average for the population of the same age will wish to purchase annuities. Second, mortality tends to improve over time and there can be severe consequences if insurance companies underestimate mortality improvements. Insurance companies add substantial cost loadings to cover these risks, something of the order of 10–14 per cent of the purchase price.[28] Third, there is inflation risk, the risk that, with level annuities, unanticipated high inflation rapidly reduces the real value of the pension. Fourth, there is interest rate risk. Annuity rates vary substantially over the interest rate cycle. They are related to the yields on government bonds of the same expected term; and since these yields vary by up to 150 per cent over the cycle,[29] annuity rates will vary by the same order of magnitude. Finally, there is reinvestment or mismatch risk arising from an inadequate supply of long-maturing assets, such as government fixed-interest and indexed-linked bonds, to provide an income stream that can be used to pay the annuity.[30]

Even worse, the market for deferred annuities is extremely thin, particularly at distant starting dates (where the market is virtually non-existent). Where deferred annuities are available, they are very poor value for money. Deferred annuities are particularly important in the case where a DB scheme is wound up, say, as a result of the insolvency of the sponsoring company. The assets of the scheme, which is often in deficit at the time (since the company, recognizing its serious financial position, usually ceases making contributions into the scheme some time before the insolvency is formally declared) are insufficient to pay the current and future pension liabilities in full. In the past, the residual assets in the scheme were used to buy non-profit policies for current pensioners and deferred annuities for deferred pensioners. But fewer and fewer insurance companies are willing to sell deferred annuities because of the uncertainties attached to forecasting mortality improvements.

Insurance companies use the government bond market to protect themselves against both interest rate and inflation risk. When an insurance company sells a level annuity it uses the proceeds to buy a fixed-income government bond of the same expected term as the annuity (typically 15 years) and then makes the annuity payments from the coupon payments received on the bond. Similarly, when an insurance company sells an indexed annuity, it buys an index-linked bond of the same expected term as the annuity; few, if any, insurance companies sell indexed annuities with expected maturities beyond that of the most distant trading indexed-linked gilt. As a consequence, interest and inflation risk are transferred to the annuitant. If a DC scheme member retires during an interest rate trough (as happened in the mid-to-late 1990s), he can end up with a very low pension. Similarly, if a 65-year-old annuitant chooses an indexed annuity, he will receive an initial cash sum that is about 30 per cent lower than a level annuity, and, with inflation at 3 per cent p.a., it would take 11 years for the indexed annuity to exceed the level annuity.[31] Since retired people tend to underestimate how long they will continue to live, most prefer to buy a level annuity and thereby retain the inflation risk. In 1995, as a result of falling interest rates, the UK government was pressed into allowing income draw-down: it became possible to delay the purchase of an annuity until annuity rates improved (or until age 75, whichever was sooner) and in the interim take an income from the fund which remained fully invested.

However, until very recently, the insurance industry (especially in Europe) has been reluctant to offer products that help annuitants hedge the risks, especially interest rate risk, that they have been forced to assume. Yet a whole range of financial instruments and strategies is available to enable them do this. The simplest strategy, based on the principle of pound cost averaging, involves a planned programme of phased deferred annuity purchases in the period prior to retirement which must be of sufficient length to cover an interest rate cycle (say, five to seven years). A more sophisticated solution for the pre-retirement period is protected annuity funds which employ derivative instruments. One example places a part (for example, 95 per cent) of the funds on deposit and the rest in call options on bond futures contracts: if interest rates fall during the life of the option, the profit on the options will compensate for the lower interest rate. Another example places a fraction of the funds in bonds and the rest in call options on an equity index, thereby gaining from any rise in the stock market over the life of the options. However, there are very few providers of these products in the UK.

A possible solution for the post-retirement period is provided by variable annuities. These were first issued in 1952 in the USA by the TIAA-CREF.[32] In the UK, they are better known as unit-linked or with-profit annuities, but only a few insurance companies offer them. A lump sum is used to buy units in a diversified fund of assets (mainly equities) and the size of the annuity depends on the income and growth rate of assets in the fund. The annuity can fall if the value of the assets falls substantially, so there is some volatility to the annuity in contrast to a level annuity. But since the pension from a level annuity is based on the yield on gilts, it is likely that the pension from a variable annuity, based on the return on equities, will generate a higher overall income (assuming that the duration of the annuity is sufficiently great).

The government could also do more to ameliorate these market failures in the private sector provision of annuities which arise, in part, from aggregate risks that are beyond the abilities and resources of private insurance companies to hedge. A number of proposals have been suggested recently. For example, in order to help the private sector hedge against inflation risk more effectively, the Goode Report (1993, sec. 4.4.44) suggested that the government introduce a new type of bond, with income and capital linked to the retail price index, but with payment of income deferred for a period. Such bonds were given the name 'deferred income government securities' (DIGS): they could be introduced with different starting and termination dates and would allow all deferred pensions to be indexed to prices. DIGS were never officially introduced, but the introduction of the gilt strips market in 1997 could help insurance companies construct them synthetically. Similarly, the introduction of limited price index (LPI) bonds would allow post-retirement inflation risk to be hedged more effectively.

But the main causes of market failure are the risks associated with adverse selection and mortality. Making second pensions mandatory rather than voluntary would do much to remove the adverse selection bias in the demand for annuities.[33] The government could also help insurance companies hedge the risk associated with underestimating mortality improvements by issuing 'survivor bonds', a suggestion made in Blake and Burrows (2001). These are bonds whose future coupon payments depend on the percentage of the population of retirement age on the issue date of each bond who are still alive on the date of each future coupon payment. For a bond issued in 2000, for instance, the coupon in 2010 will be directly proportional to the amount, on average, that an insurance company has to pay out as an annuity at that time. The insurance company which buys such a security bears no aggregate mortality risk and, as a consequence, cost loadings fall. There is therefore much that could be done by both government and the insurance industry to improve the market for annuities which remain the weak tail in DC pension provision.

THE INVESTMENT PERFORMANCE OF PENSION FUND ASSETS

Good or bad investment performance by DB and DC pension schemes have very different consequences for scheme members. With DB schemes, the investment performance of the fund's assets are of no direct relevance to the scheme member, since the pension depends on the final salary and years of service only and not on investment performance. The scheme member can rely on the sponsoring company to bail out the fund with a deficiency payment if assets perform very badly. In extreme circumstances, however, it is possible for a firm and possibly the scheme to become insolvent.[34] Of course, if the assets perform well, the surplus is retained by the sponsor.

However, investment performance is critical to the size of the pension in the case of a DC scheme: scheme members bear all the investment risk in such schemes. Scheme members, especially personal pension scheme members, can find themselves locked into a poorly performing fund, facing very high costs of transferring to a better performing fund. In addition, the type of funds in which personal pension scheme members invest can and do close down and then the assets do have to be transferred to a different fund. In this section, we examine the investment performance of pension scheme assets, beginning with those of DC schemes.

Investment Performance of DC Schemes

The anticipated return in a high-risk investment vehicle must be greater than that in a low-risk investment vehicle, but there can be wide differences in realized returns, even for schemes in the same risk class. Blake and Timmermann (1998) conducted a study of the investment performance of unit trusts in the UK, one of the key investment vehicles for DC schemes. Table 1.6 shows the distribution of returns generated by unit trusts operating in the four largest sectors. These figures indicate enormous differences in performance, especially over the long life of a pension scheme. For

Table 1.6   Distribution of returns generated by UK unit trusts, 1972–95

Sector	Top quartile	Median	Bottom quartile	Ratio of fund sizes
UK Equity Growth	16.0	13.6	11.9	3.2
UK Equity General	14.3	13.4	13.1	1.4
UK Equity Income	15.4	14.0	12.4	2.3
UK Smaller Companies	18.7	15.5	12.8	5.3

Note:
The first three columns are averages measured in percentages per annum for the sample period 1972–95; the last column gives the ratio of fund sizes after 40 years, based on the top and bottom quartile returns. The formula is (assuming the same contribution stream):

$$\frac{(1+r_T)^T - 1}{r_T} \div \frac{(1+r_B)^T - 1}{r_B},$$

where $r_T = 0.160$, $r_B = 0.119$ and $T = 40$, etc.

Sources: Blake and Timmermann (1998) and Lunde *et al.* (1999).

example, the 4.1 percentage point per annum difference between the best and worst performing unit trusts in the UK Equity Growth sector leads, over a 40-year investment horizon, to the accumulated fund in the top quartile being a factor of 3.2 times larger than the accumulated fund in the bottom quartile for the same pattern of contributions. The 5.9 percentage point per annum difference between the best and worst performing unit trusts in the UK Smaller Companies sector leads to an even larger fund size ratio after 40 years of 5.3.

So personal pension scheme members can find themselves locked into poorly performing funds.[35] But should it not be the case in an efficient capital market that systematically underperforming funds fail to survive and are taken over by more efficient fund managers? Lunde *et al.* (1999) investigated this possibility. They found that underperforming trusts are eventually merged with more successful trusts, but that on average it takes some time for this to occur. The modal duration is 4.25 years (51 months), but the average duration is about 16 years. Across the unit trust industry, the average return on funds that survived the whole period was 13.7 per cent per annum, while the average return on funds that were wound up or merged during the period was 11.3 per cent per annum. This implies that a typical personal pension scheme member might find him or herself locked into an underperforming trust that is eventually wound up or merged into a more successful fund, experiencing an underperformance of 2.4 per cent p.a., over a 16-year period. This translates into a fund value that is 19 per cent lower after 16 years than a fund that is not wound up or merged. So it seems that, in practice, personal pension scheme members cannot rely on the markets to provide them with a painless way of extricating them from an underperforming fund. They have to do it themselves, paying up to one-third of the value of their accumulated fund in transfer charges.

The Investment Performance of DB Schemes

There are about 120 000 small defined benefit pension schemes in the UK, most with fewer than 100 members in each. Virtually all these schemes are managed on a pooled basis by insurance companies. There are about 2000 large schemes, including 70 or so with assets in excess of £1bn each.[36] The investment performance of these funds is much more important for the scheme sponsor than for the scheme member. The recent history of the UK pension fund industry embraces a period of substantial deficiency payments in the 1970s (arising from the UK stock market crash in 1974–5), the build-up of huge surpluses during the bull markets of the 1980s and 1990s, and the sudden ending of those surpluses as a result of the collapse of the bubble in technology stocks at the beginning of the 2000s. The surpluses enabled sponsors to reduce their contributions into their schemes (that is, to take employer's contribution holidays). In other words, during the 1980s and 1990s, UK pension scheme sponsors benefited enormously from the investment successes of their fund managers.

The investment performance of UK defined benefit pension fund managers between 1986 and 1994 has been investigated in Blake *et al.* (1999; 2002).[37] The data set used covers the externally appointed active fund managers of more than 300 medium-to-large pension funds with a mandate agreement to 'beat the market'. The UK pension fund industry is highly concentrated and most of these active fund managers come from just five groups of professional fund managers (Deutsche Asset Management, Merrill Lynch Investment Management, UBS Asset Management, Schroder Investment Management and Gartmore Pension Fund Managers).

While the average or median performance has been very good over the sample period, important implications concerning the behaviour of fund managers can be derived from an examination of the distribution of this performance about the median. Table 1.7 shows the cross-sectional distribution of returns realized by the pension funds in the sample over the period 1986–94 in the most important individual asset classes as well as for the total portfolio. The semi-interquartile range is quite tight, below two percentage points for most asset classes and only just over one percentage point for the total portfolio return. This suggests evidence of a possible herding effect in the behaviour of pension fund managers: fund managers, although their fee is determined by their *absolute* investment performance, are appointed and evaluated on the basis of their *relative* performance against each other and therefore have a very strong incentive not to underperform the peer group.[38] The fund managers in the sample are active managers who have won mandates on the basis of promises to beat the market: they are not passive managers attempting to match the market. If they were genuinely pursuing active strategies, there would be a wide dispersion in performance, as is observed in the USA. What we find is a tight dispersion of performance about a median. From this we may conclude that the active fund managers are herding to avoid delivering poor relative performance (which puts their mandate at risk). Despite this, the difference between the best and worst performing funds is very large, as the last row of Table 1.7 indicates.

Table 1.8 shows how well UK pension funds have performed in comparison with other participants in the market. The fourth column shows that the average UK pension fund underperformed the market average by 0.45 per cent p.a.; and this is before the fund manager's fee is taken into account. Further, only 42.8 per cent of funds outperform the market average. The main explanation for this is the relative underperformance in UK equities,

Table 1.7 Fractiles of total returns by asset class for UK managed funds, 1986–94 (average annualized percentages)

	UK equities	International equities	UK bonds	International bonds	UK index bonds	Cash/other investments	UK property	Total
Min.	8.59	4.42	6.59	−0.64	5.59	2.67	3.05	7.22
5%	11.43	8.59	9.44	2.18	7.20	5.46	5.07	10.60
10%	11.85	9.03	9.95	7.56	7.81	7.60	6.58	10.96
25%	12.44	9.64	10.43	8.30	7.91	8.97	8.03	11.47
50%	13.13	10.65	10.79	11.37	8.22	10.25	8.75	12.06
75%	13.93	11.76	11.22	13.37	8.45	11.72	9.99	12.59
90%	14.81	12.52	11.70	14.55	8.80	14.20	10.84	13.13
95%	15.46	13.14	12.05	18.15	8.89	16.13	11.36	13.39
Max.	17.39	14.68	17.23	26.34	10.07	19.73	13.53	15.03
Max.–Min.	8.80	10.26	10.64	26.98	4.48	17.06	10.48	7.81

Note:
The table shows the fractiles of the cross-sectional distribution of returns on individual asset classes as well as on the total portfolio.

Source: Blake *et al.* (2002, Table 1).

45

Table 1.8 Performance of UK pension funds in comparison with the market, 1986–94 (percentages)

	Average portfolio weight (%)	Average market return (%)	Average pension fund return (%)	Average outperformance (%)	Percentage of outperformers
UK equities	53.7	13.30	12.97	–0.33	44.8
International equities	19.5	11.11	11.23	0.12	39.8
UK bonds	7.6	10.35	10.76	0.41	77.3
International bonds	2.2	8.64	10.03	1.39	68.8
UK index bonds	2.7	8.22	8.12	–0.10	51.7
Cash/other investments	4.5	9.90	9.01	–0.89	59.5
UK property	8.9	9.00	9.52	0.52	39.1
Total		12.18	11.73	–0.45	42.8

Note:
International property is excluded since no market index was available.

Source: Blake *et al.*, (1999; 2002).

the largest single category with an average portfolio weighting of 54 per cent over the sample period; the average underperformance is −0.33 per cent per annum and only 44.8 per cent of UK pension funds beat the average return on UK equities. To be sure, relative performance is better in other asset categories, especially UK and international bonds, but the portfolio weights in these asset categories are not large enough to counteract the relative underperformance in UK equities.

Tables 1.7 and 1.8 together indicate how close the majority of the pension funds are to generating the average market return. The median fund generated an average total return of 12.06 per cent p.a., just 12 basis points short of the average market return, and 80 per cent of the funds are within one percentage point of the average market return. This suggests that, despite their claims to be active fund managers, the vast majority of UK pension fund managers are not only herding together, they are also closet index matchers.

There are some other features of UK pension fund performance worthy of note. First, there is some evidence of short-term persistence in performance over time, especially by the best and worst performing fund managers. For example, we found that UK equity fund managers in the top quartile of performance in one year had a 37 per cent chance of being in the top quartile the following year, rather than the 25 per cent that would have been expected if relative performance arose purely by chance. Similarly, there was a 32 per cent chance of the fund managers in the bottom quartile for UK equities for one year being in the bottom quartile the following year. There was also evidence of persistence in performance in the top and bottom quartiles for cash/other investments, with probabilities of remaining in these quartiles the following year of 35 per cent in each case. However, there was no evidence of persistence in performance for any other asset category or for the portfolio as a whole. Nor was there any evidence of persistence in performance over longer horizons than one year in any asset category or for the whole portfolio. This suggests that 'hot hands' in performance is a very short-term phenomenon.

Second, there was some evidence of spillover effects in performance, but only between UK and international equities. In other words, the funds that performed well or badly in UK equities also performed well or badly in international equities. This suggests that some fund managers were good at identifying undervalued stocks in different markets. This result is somewhat surprising since the world's equity markets are much less highly integrated than the world's bond markets, yet there was no evidence of spillover effects in performance across bond markets.

Third, there was evidence of a size effect in performance. Large funds tended to underperform smaller funds. We found that 32 per cent of the

quartile containing the largest funds were also in the quartile containing the
worst performing funds, whereas only 15 per cent of the quartile containing the smallest funds were also in the quartile of worst performing funds.
These results confirm the often-quoted view that 'size is the anchor of performance': because large pension funds are dominant players in the
markets, this severely restricts their abilities to outperform the market.

The final result concerns the abilities of UK pension fund managers in
active fund management, that is, in their attempts to beat the market in
comparison with a passive buy and hold strategy. The most important task
of pension fund managers is, as we have seen above, to establish and maintain the strategic asset allocation. This is essentially a passive management
strategy. However, fund managers claim that they can 'add value' through
the active management of their fund's assets. There are two aspects to active
management: security selection and market timing (also known as tactical
asset allocation). Security selection involves the search for undervalued
securities (that is, it involves the reallocation of funds within sectors) and
market timing involves the search for undervalued sectors (that is, it
involves the reallocation of funds between sectors). We decomposed the
total return generated by fund managers into the following components:

	(%)
Strategic asset allocation	99.47
Security selection	2.68
Market timing	−1.64
Other	−0.51
Total	100

We found that 99.47 per cent of the total return generated by UK fund
managers can be explained by the strategic asset allocation, that is, the
long-run asset allocation specified by pension scheme sponsors on the
advice of their actuaries following an asset-liability modelling (ALM) exercise. This is the passive component of pension fund performance. The
active components are security selection and market timing (or TAA). The
average pension fund was unsuccessful at market timing, generating a negative contribution to the total return of −1.64 per cent. The average
pension fund was, however, more successful in security selection, making a
positive contribution to the total return of 2.68 per cent. But the overall
contribution of active fund management was just over 1 per cent of the
total return (or about 13 basis points), *which is less than the annual fee that
active fund managers charge* (which ranges between 20 basis points for a
£500mn fund to 75 basis points for a £10mn fund).[39]

CONCLUSION

Over the last quarter century, governments have had two major impacts on pension provision in the UK. First, they have reduced the cost of providing state pensions by reducing the level of benefits from the state schemes (the stick). Second, they have encouraged greater private sector provision (the carrot), although the Conservative and Labour governments have done this in quite different ways. The Thatcher–Major governments made private supplementary pension arrangements voluntary and used tax incentives to encourage consumers to join personal pension schemes, but they left it to the market to determine the structure and efficiency of these schemes. The result was schemes that exhibited very high front-loaded charges, because retail customers tend not to be skilled at assessing the cost-effectiveness of retail financial products.[40] In contrast, the Blair government, recognizing the market failure arising from poorly informed consumers, imposed restrictions on the structure of stakeholder pension schemes that helped to enforce economies of scale and hence lower charges. It also helped to encourage pension savings by introducing the Pension Credit and so helped to reduce the disincentive effects of means-tested benefits.

The suitability of the two key types of private funded scheme, defined benefit or defined contribution, to particular workers depends on both individual behaviour and characteristics, for example how often someone changes jobs and their attitude to risk. The more frequently someone changes jobs and the more risk-tolerant they are, the more appropriate it will be for them to choose a DC scheme.

However, even if someone has chosen the appropriate pension scheme in principle, weaknesses in the design of their scheme can lead to lower pensions than otherwise need be the case. One illustration of this concerns investment performance: it affects the net cost to the sponsor of a DB scheme and the net pension benefit to the member of a DC scheme. We showed that, on average, UK pension funds have underperformed the market and, while there has been a wide dispersion of performance by individual fund managers, most of them appear to herd around the median fund manager. Furthermore, we found that fund managers have not been especially successful at active fund management: virtually the same or better returns could have been generated if pension funds had invested passively in index funds. In addition, fund management costs would have been lower and the dispersion in returns across fund managers would have been reduced. Another example concerns charges. It is most unlikely that good investment performance can compensate for high charges, and we have seen that it is equally unlikely that above-average investment performance can be sustained for a significant period of time. Well-designed pension schemes would take these factors into account.

Some important policy conclusions emerge from this analysis. First, if governments want to see well-designed pension schemes in the private sector, they must provide an infrastructure that helps the private sector offer these. The regulatory framework should be kept as simply as possible in order to minimize compliance costs, and charging structures should be made simple and transparent to enable consumers to identify the most competitive providers more easily. Governments could also help keep costs down or improve benefits in other ways: for instance, by enabling economies of scale to be exploited more fully (such as establishing a central clearing house to channel contributions in the case of DC schemes) or by introducing a common set of actuarial assumptions, as in Holland, which would enable full service credits to be transferred between schemes when workers change jobs, thereby improving the portability rights of members of DB schemes. Governments could help the private sector cope with the market failures that prevent or at least make it difficult for individuals to hedge certain risks; for example, mortality risk could be hedged through the introduction of survivor bonds.

Second, if governments wish to promote the efficient investment management of pension assets, they should not put in place regulations that distort pension fund asset allocations, as is likely to happen under the European Pension Fund Directive. They should also encourage the introduction of appropriate incentives, such as greater transparency in published performance data and the adoption of performance-related fund management fees.[41] This would encourage the less talented fund managers to invest in index funds, with consequential benefits in terms of lower fund management charges and a lower dispersion of performance.[42] There is evidence that governments are becoming more aware of at least some of these issues. For example, the new stakeholder pension schemes have an upper limit placed on the charges that can be imposed and this will effectively rule out the active management of the assets in such schemes; and, in the USA, the government is considering a range of options for dealing with the growing burden of social security, including the establishment of individual privatized accounts and the investment of part of the Social Security Trust Fund in equities.

However, the greatest impediment to having a decent pension in retirement is inadequate pension savings made during the working lifetime. Voluntary arrangements tend to lead to low initial participation and low subsequent persistence. There is a strong case for arguing that only with sufficient mandatory minimum contributions into a funded pension scheme (with credits given to those on very low earnings) can a decent pension be achieved, but few governments seem willing to confront this issue: the UK mandatory minimum for the state second pension (equal to the contracted-out rebate on national insurance contributions of 4.6 per cent of earnings) is not sufficient to build to an adequate pension (as Table 1.5 showed) and the Welfare Reform and Pensions Act explicitly ruled out additional compulsory contributions.

NOTES

1. NICs also build up entitlement to health service, sickness, disability and incapacity benefits, and the job seeker's allowance.
2. Worth £75.50 per week for a single person in 2002–3, while national average earnings were £450 per week, suggesting a replacement ratio of about 17 per cent.
3. The LEL was £75 per week and the UEL was £585 per week in 2002–3.
4. The Department of Social Security (DSS) was renamed the Department of Work and Pensions in June 2001.
5. The state pension age for women is being progressively raised to 65 over the period 2010–20.
6. The non-contracted-out National Insurance contribution rate in 2002–3 for employees was 10 per cent of earnings between £89 per week and the UEL, while for employers it was 11.8 per cent of all earnings above £89 per week.
7. UK private pension schemes benefit from an Exempt, Exempt, Taxed (EET) system of tax breaks: the contributions into schemes are exempt from tax, the investment returns (with the exception, since 1997, of dividend income on UK equities) are exempt from tax, and the pension is taxed (with the exception of a tax-free lump sum equal to 1.5 times the final salary in the case of a defined benefit scheme and 25 per cent of the accumulated pension fund in the case of a defined contribution scheme).
8. *Economic Trends Annual Supplement 1999* (Table 3.2).
9. Department of Social Security (1998, Table 1.0), National Association of Pension Funds (1997) and estimates by the Government Actuary's Department.
10. For more details of the UK pension system, see Blake (1997; 2003), Fenton *et al.* (1995), Reardon (2002), Pensions Provision Group (1998).
11. This is partly because personal pension schemes have only been around since 1988.
12. Although the backloading effect is lower in average salary schemes (such as SERPS) than in final salary schemes (such as a typical occupational scheme).
13. Department of Social Security (2000b).
14. An additional £3bn per year (*Daily Telegraph*, 31 July 1999).
15. In fact, the Conservative government in the UK announced in March 1997 plans to privatize the entire state pension system from the turn of the century and to end its unfunded nature. All individuals in work would receive rebates on their NICs which would be invested in a personalized pension account. The initial costs in terms of additional taxation were estimated to be £160mn in the first year, rising to a peak of £7bn a year in 2040. However, the long-term savings to the taxpayer from the end of state pension provision were estimated to be £40bn per year (all in 1997 prices). The proposals were put on hold as a result of the Conservative government's defeat in the May 1997 general election (see *Basic Pension Plus*, Conservative Central Office, 5 March 1997).
16. *Money Management*, October 1998.
17. Had the indexation of the BSP to the growth rate in national average earnings been preserved since 1980, the BSP would have been £95 per week in 1999 rather than £66.75 (*Daily Telegraph*, 31 July 1999).
18. However, there is an increasing number of hybrid schemes being introduced which

combine features of both DB and DC schemes. It is also possible to have unfunded DB and DC schemes.

19. Burgess and Rees (1994) and Gregg and Wadsworth (1995).
20. Blake (1995, sec. 7.34).
21. It is the high costs associated with individual personal pension schemes in the UK that has led many small companies without the resources to run either occupational DB or occupational DC schemes to establish group personal pension schemes (GPPs) which have lower unit costs than personal pension schemes.
22. The lapse rates come from Personal Investment Authority (1998), while lapse rate-adjusted reductions in contributions are estimated in Blake and Board (2000).
23. There are other costs which are more difficult to quantify, the most important of which are search and information costs. The Office of Fair Trading's (1997a) *Inquiry into Pensions* found (on the basis of a survey it conducted) that most people in the UK did not regard themselves as being financially literate and also they did not tend to shop around (80 per cent of the survey's respondents had little or no interest in financial matters and 85 per cent of respondents who had sought advice on pensions had used only one source). Traditional providers of pensions (such as insurance companies) were regarded as offering complex products that were difficult to understand and therefore required additional training by sales staff. Newer providers (such as direct-selling pension providers) were regarded as offering pension products that were easy to understand and therefore to sell. The tax rules were also regarded as a major source of confusion.
24. National Association of Pension Funds (1997), Government Actuary's Department (2000).
25. National Association of Pension Funds (1997).
26. Financial Services Authority Returns, 2002. The top five providers account for about 60 per cent of sales.
27. Blake (1999).
28. MacDonald (1996) found that mortality forecast errors of 15–20 per cent over intervals of ten years are not uncommon. US studies (for example, Mitchell *et al.*, 1999; Poterba and Warshawsky, 1998) found that the deduction from the actuarially fair value of an annuity for a 65-year-old US male was 15 per cent if the male was a typical member of the population as a whole (calculated using the mortality tables for the whole US male population) and 3 per cent if the male was typical of the population buying annuities voluntarily (calculated using the select mortality tables for male annuity purchasers), implying a 12 per cent deduction for the greater mortality risk. Finkelstein and Poterba (2002), using UK data, estimated cost loadings for 65-year-old males of 10 per cent.
29. CSFB (2002).
30. This was recently a serious issue in the UK on account of recent government budget surpluses and the consequential absence of new gilt issues; see Bishop (1999).
31. Khorasanee (1996).
32. Teachers Insurance and Annuity Association of America – College Retirement Equity Fund.
33. There is a growing body of support for mandatory contributions into second pensions, including Field and Owen (1993), Borrie (1994), World Bank (1994), Dahrendorf (1995) and Anson (1996), as well as surveys of customers conducted by NatWest Bank and Coopers & Lybrand (reported in Field, 1996b, pp.52–3). Compulsory contributions are seen as one way of dealing with individual myopia and the problem of moral hazard. The first issue arises because individuals do not recognize the need to make adequate provision for retirement when they are young. The latter problem arises when individuals deliberately avoid saving for retirement when they are young because they know the state will feel obliged not to let them live in dire poverty in retirement.
34. To avoid this risk, nearly 70 per cent of companies in the UK had closed their DB schemes to new members by 2003, while 10 per cent of companies had closed their schemes to additional contributions from existing members (FT.com, 12 June 2003).

35. This is despite the fact that, as we have seen above, there are investment management techniques available to reduce the dispersion of realized returns.
36. Pension Schemes Registry and Government Actuary's Department (2003).
37. Very similar results have been found for the USA: see Lakonishok *et al.* (1992).
38. Davis (1988) reports a survey of UK and US fund managers in which they acknowledge the existence of a herding effect.
39. *Pensions Management*, September 1998.
40. Office of Fair Trading (1997b, 1999).
41. The fund manager benefits by sharing some proportion of the outperfromance of the benchmark index; there is also a penalty for underperformance, although it comes in the form of a credit against the future fee rather than as a cash refund in the quarter in which the underperformance occurs.
42. Even though there was no evidence that fund managers could systematically outperform the market, it would be difficult for the government to require pension fund managers to use index matching. There would be no clear consensus on which index to match (the FTSE100 index, the FT A All Share index, a European index or a global index). Also there is a risk that market inefficiencies could emerge if large institutional investors such as pension funds were prevented from searching for under- and over-valued stocks: the evidence indicates that the only source of value-added in active fund management is security selection.

REFERENCES

Anson, Sir J. (Chairman) (1996), *Pensions 2000 and Beyond*, Report of the Retirement Income Enquiry, London.

Bishop, G. (1999), 'Why are Long Gilts the Richest Bonds in the World, and Getting Richer?', SalomonSmithBarney, London, October.

Blake, D. (1992), *Modelling Pension Fund Investment Behaviour*, London: Routledge.

Blake, D. (1997), 'Pension Choices and Pensions Policy in the United Kingdom', in S. Valdés-Prieto (ed.), *The Economics of Pensions: Principles, Policies and International Experience*, New York: Cambridge University Press, pp.277–317.

Blake, D. (1999), 'Annuity Markets: Problems and Solutions', *Geneva Papers on Risk and Insurance*, 24, 358–75.

Blake, D. (2000), *Financial Market Analysis*, Chichester: Wiley.

Blake, D. (2003), *Pension Schemes and Pension Funds in the United Kingdom*, 2nd edn, Oxford: Oxford University Press.

Blake, D. and Board, J. (2000), 'Measuring Value Added in the Pensions Industry', *Geneva Papers on Risk and Insurance*, 25, 539–67.

Blake, D. and Burrows, W. (2001), 'Survivor Bonds: Helping to Hedge Mortality Risk', *Journal of Risk and Insurance*, 68, 339–48.

Blake, D. and Orszag, J.M. (1997), *Portability and Preservation of Pension Rights in the UK*, Report of the Director-General's Inquiry into Pensions, vol.3, London: Office of Fair Trading, July.

Blake, D. and Timmermann, A. (1998), 'Mutual Fund Performance: Evidence from the UK', *European Finance Review*, 2, 57–77.

Blake, D., Lehmann, B. and Timmermann, A. (1999), 'Asset Allocation Dynamics and Pension Fund Performance', *Journal of Business*, 72, 429–47.

Blake, D., Lehmann, B. and Timmermann, A. (2002), 'Performance Clustering and Incentives in the UK Pension Fund Industry', *Journal of Asset Management*, 3, 173–94.

Borrie, Sir G. (Chairman) (1994), *Social Justice – Strategies for National Renewal*, Report of the Commission for Social Justice, London: Vintage.
Burgess, S. and Rees, H. (1994), *Lifetime Jobs and Transient Jobs: Job Tenure in Britain 1975–91*, London: Centre for Economic Policy Research.
Crédit Suisse First Boston (2002), *Equity-Gilt Study*, London: CSFB.
Dahrendorf, Lord R. (Chairman) (1995), *Wealth Creation and Social Cohesion in a Free Society*, Report of the Commission on Wealth Creation and Social Cohesion, London: Xenogamy.
Davis, E.P. (1988), 'Financial Market Activity of Life Insurance Companies and Pension Funds', Economic Paper No.21, Bank for International Settlements, Basle.
Department of Social Security (1998), *A New Contract for Welfare: Partnership in Pensions*, Cm 4179, December, London: Department of Social Security.
Department of Social Security (2000a), *The Pensioners' Income Series 1997–98*, Analytical Services Division, London.
Department of Social Security (2000b), *The Pension Credit: A Consultation Paper*, Cm 4900, November, London: Department of Social Security.
Fabozzi, F. and Konishi, A. (eds) (1991), *Asset-Liability Management*, Chicago: Probus.
Fenton, J., Ham, R. and Sabel, J. (1995), *Pensions Handbook*, Croydon: Tolley Publishing.
Field, F. (1996a), 'Stakeholder Welfare', Choice in Welfare Series no. 32, Institute of Economic Affairs, London.
Field, F. (1996b), 'How to Pay for the Future: Building a Stakeholders' Welfare', Institute of Community Studies, London.
Field, F. and Owen, M. (1993), 'Private Pensions for All: Squaring the Circle', Fabian Society Discussion Paper no. 16, London.
Finkelstein, A. and Poterba, J. (2002), 'Selection Effects in the United Kingdom Individual Annuities Market', *Economic Journal*, 112, 28–50.
Goode, R. (1993), *Pension Law Reform: Report of the Pension Law Review Committee*, Cm 2342-I, London: HMSO.
Government Actuary's Department (2003), *Occupational Pension Schemes 2002 – Eleventh Survey by the Government Actuary's Department*, London: The Stationery Office.
Gregg, P. and Wadsworth, J. (1995), 'A Short History of Labour Turnover, Job Tenure and Job Security, 1973–93', *Oxford Review of Economic Policy*, 11, 73–90.
Khorasanee, M.Z. (1996), 'Annuity Choices for Pensioners', *Journal of Actuarial Practice*, 4, 229–55.
Lakonishok, J., Shleifer, A. and Vishny, R. (1992), 'The Structure and Performance of the Money Management Industry', *Brookings Papers: Microeconomics*, 339–91.
Lunde, A., Timmermann, A. and Blake, D. (1999), 'The Hazards of Mutual Fund Underperformance', *Journal of Empirical Finance*, 6, 121–55.
MacDonald, A. (1996), 'United Kingdom', in A. MacDonald (ed.), *The Second Actuarial Study of Mortality in Europe*, Brussels: Groupe Consultatif des Associations D'Actuaires des Pays des Communautés Européennes.
Mitchell, O.S., Poterba, J.M., Warshawsky, M.J. and Brown, J.R. (1999), 'New Evidence on the Money's Worth of Individual Annuities', *American Economic Review*, 89, 1299–1318.
National Association of Pension Funds (1997), *Annual Survey*, London.

Office of Fair Trading (1997a), *Report of the Director General's Inquiry into Pensions*, London, July.

Office of Fair Trading (1997b), 'Consumer Detriment under Conditions of Imperfect Information', Research Paper 11, London.

Office of Fair Trading (1999), 'Vulnerable Consumers and Financial Services', Report 255, London.

Pensions Provision Group (1998), *We All Need Pensions: Prospects for Pension Provision*, London: The Stationery Office.

Personal Investment Authority (1998), 'Survey of Persistency of Life and Pension Policies', London, October.

Poterba, J.M. and Warshawsky, M.J. (1998), 'The Cost of Annuitising Retirement Payouts', Working Paper, Economics Department, Massachusetts Institute of Technology, Cambridge, MA.

Reardon, A.M. (2002), *Pensions Handbook*, London: Zurich.

HM Treasury (1999), 'Helping to Deliver Stakeholder Pensions: Flexibility in Pension Investment', February, London.

World Bank (1994), *Averting the Old-Age Crisis*, Oxford: Oxford University Press.

2. The relationship between the role of the corporate pension and the public pension plan in Japan

Yukiko M. Katsumata

INTRODUCTION

Two bills, the Defined Contribution Corporate Pension Plan Act and the Defined Benefit Corporate Pension Plan Act, were passed in the 151st session of the Diet on 29 June 2001. The two bills had already been introduced to the Diet on 14 November 2000 and on 24 February 2001, respectively, and since then deliberations on both bills have been carried over to the next session. The reason why both bills related to the corporate pension plans have been introduced to the Diet one after another in 2001 is that corporate debt has been rising, owing to the introduction of new corporate accounting standards, and corporate profits have decreased as a result of long-term Japanese economic stagnation. This chapter examines the role of the corporate pension in the context of the relationship between the history of the retirement allowance system and the public pension plan.

Changes in the corporate pension in Japan resulted from internal and external corporation changes. The changes happening inside corporations suggest the end of the Japanese style lifetime employment system, as indicated by the high rate of actual unemployment, which is the highest since 1945. One of the external changes is the structural stagnation of the Japanese economy as represented by ultra-low interest rates and sluggish stock markets. Another external change is the current condition of the public pension plan, which is facing a lowering of benefit levels from mid- and long-term perspectives, because of a drop in the premium income due to an aging population, fewer births and a decrease in earned income.

To carry out administrative and financial reforms under the conditions described above, the Council on Economic and Fiscal Policy was organized by the new Cabinet (Koizumi Cabinet) in 2001. This Council prepared the draft 'Structural Reform of the Japanese Economy: Basic Policies for Macroeconomic Management' (approved by the Cabinet meeting on 26 June 2001). In this draft, earlier implementation and promotion of reforms to the corporate pension plan and the Defined Contribution Corporate Pension were expressed as means to support 'self-help measures'. The schedule of administrative and financial reforms was officially announced on 21 September. For the corporate pension, it declared that execution and promotion of the Defined Benefit Corporate Pension Plan Act should be carried out smoothly from 1 April 2002.

Discussions on the reform of the next Japanese public pension are expected after the announcement of the population projection in January 2002 with the results of a recalculation of financial resources. However, it is not clear at this time (May 2003) that the relationship between the public pension plans and the private pension plans, including the corporate pensions, will be fully discussed in the concrete plan. Considering the background of the corporate pension plan acts set forth later in this chapter, corporate pensions have been introduced and developed on the initiative of employers, and the idea that public pensions should be supplemented by private pensions might not be on the table for discussion in the processes of policy making.

POSITIONING OF THE CORPORATE PENSION IN JAPAN

Scale and Scope of Application

The sum of pension benefits paid as the income security after retirement in Japan is estimated. The estimated sum of public pensions and private pensions including corporate pension, life insurance and postal insurance is 40 159.8 billion yen (1998) (Table 2.1).

Assuming this is the total amount of pension benefits paid in Japan, the amount paid by corporate pensions is only 7.8 per cent of the total.[1] Furthermore, the quality of corporate pensions provided is substantially different among corporations, depending on corporate scale. Corporations with a retirement allowance system account for 50 per cent of all corporations and 90.4 per cent of large corporations with more than 1000 employees, while only 43.9 per cent of small corporations with more than 30 and fewer than 100 employees provide retirement allowances.[2] Furthermore, from statistics on the distribution of employees in Japan, 42.1 per cent of all regular employees are employed by small and medium-sized corporations with fewer than 100 employees, while 29.5 per cent of all regular employees are employed by large corporations with more than 1000 employees.[3] In other words, about half of all employees are employed by small and medium-sized corporations with no provision for corporate pensions, while only about 30 per cent of all employees are employed by large

Table 2.1   Japan's pension estimates in 1998

	Unit: 100 mill ¥	Per GDP (%)	Share of the total (%)
Total	401 598	7.8	100.0
Public	351 186	6.8	87.4
Employees'	193 379	3.8	48.2
Other (national pension)	157 807	3.1	39.3
Private	50 412	1.0	12.6
Corporate pension	31 443	0.6	7.8
Employees' fund[1]	9 267	0.2	2.3
Tax qualified	20 421	0.4	5.1
Farmers' fund	1 755	0.0	0.4
Individual	18 969	0.4	4.7
Life insurance	10 303	0.2	2.6
Postal saving	8 666	0.2	2.2
Severance pay[2]	386	0.0	

Notes:
[1] Deducted the opting-out for employee's pension insurance.
[2] The data taken from National Tax Bureau, where only including rich employees' whose annual income above 10 million yen. Most of audinal employees' data for severance pay is not available due to the withholding system.

corporations with corporate pensions. About 30 per cent of all employees are provided with corporate pensions, which is low compared with the 48 per cent in the UK and 45 per cent in both Germany and the USA.[4]

Corporate Pension and Retirement Allowance

The retirement allowance system and tax advantages for employees employed for a long period have been developed by Japanese corporations in line with the lifetime employment practice. As a result, in many cases, a part of the retirement allowance is paid as a corporate pension. According to research, 52.5 per cent of corporations with the retirement allowance system provide retirement pension plans.[5] In Japan, corporate pensions have grown out of the retirement allowance. The retirement allowance has been considered a part of welfare for employees. Therefore, even today, employers think that differences between the retirement allowance and corporate pensions are unclear.

I prepared and submitted the estimated expenditure of social security in Japan to the OECD as an assignment. However, when corporate pensions were appropriated for the voluntary private social expenditure, I was requested by the OECD to list the retirement allowance separately. Many Japanese feel it is wrong to consider the retirement allowance to be the same as a corporate pension. The reason why Japanese employees feel that way is that they regard the retirement allowance as a reward from employers. However, as a result of this research on the history of the development of corporate pensions, it becomes clear that the retirement allowance was the origin of corporate pensions, and it is difficult to draw a clear line between them. Japanese pension plans are composed of three tiers, with public pensions occupying the first and second, while private pensions occupy the third tier to supplement public pensions, as shown in Figure 2.1.

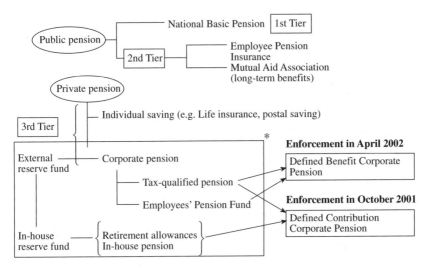

* Area indicates retirement allowance

Figure 2.1   The relation between the public and private pensions

The corporate pension also includes the external reserve fund. Before adopting corporate pensions and external reserve funds, corporations put all pension funds into a booking account to pay retirement allowances and pensions. Therefore the corporate pension has its roots in the booking account, which overlaps the retirement allowance in its functions. The Corporate Pension Acts passed in June 2001 function to promote the transition from the booking account to a more reliable external reserve fund.[6]

Many Japanese corporate pensions with their roots in the retirement allowance provide short-term benefits. In terms of payment method, 32.2 per cent of retirement pensions are combined with the retirement allowance and, if it is not paid as a lump sum, the corporate pension is paid for a limited period, so it differs from the public whole life annuity.[7] Particularly in the case of the tax-qualified pension plan, which accounts for 5.1 per cent of the corporate pension of 7.8 per cent described above, most recipients choose to receive a lump sum payment. Research found that, in 1998, 63.1 per cent of all recipients of the tax-qualified pension received their pension as a lump sum, and 1.7 trillion yen, which accounts for 82 per cent of all pension benefits, was paid as a lump sum.[8]

Japanese Corporate Pensions Developed on the Initiative of Employers

Examining the characteristics and the development processes of the corporate pension in Japan, it becomes clear that immature industrial relations and labour movements did not result in social policies. As described above, the origin of the corporate pension is the retirement allowance. On the other hand, it is reported that the first corporate pension in Japan was started in 1905.[9] However, the corporate pension plan contributed by both employer and employees did not become popular, and it remained in an embryo state until 1945. The conventional retirement allowance paid when an employee retires was considered to be a kind of reward paid to the employee by an employer by reserving funds as a booking account for the retirement allowance.[10] The restrictions on free speech and labour movements represented by the Maintenance of Public Order Act deterred the growth of labour union movements in Japan, while it helped the growth of the retirement allowance as a reward for long-term service under paternalistic industrial relations.

The retirement allowance is simply a compensation system developed on the initiative of employers. The tax revisions of 1951 and 1952 were the turning point for the postwar development of the corporate pension, from the benevolent retirement allowance to the corporate pension. The former revision applies separate taxation on the retirement allowance as retirement income. The latter revision raised corporate income tax from 35 per cent to 42 per cent. The reserve fund for retirement compensation was introduced to reduce the tax burden. Thus the payment of the retirement allowance acted as an effective legal means of reducing taxes.

The spread of employees' pensions and the rise of the level of benefits supported the development of the corporate pension out of the retirement allowance. That is, the spread of the employees' pension insurance brought about a rise in labour costs, because of the increased contribution by employers, and management had to review the conventional retirement allowance system. The relationship between the corporate pension and the public pension is shown in Table 2.2.

Table 2.2   *A chronological table of Japanese corporate vs public pension schemes*

Corporate schemes	Public schemes
	1942 Labour pension insurance
	1944 Employees' pension insurance enforced (formerly known as Workers' Pension Act)
– – – – – – – – – – – – – – *End of WWII* – – – – – – – – – – – – – –	
1952 Income deduction for corporate tax on reserve fund to cover retirement payment	1954 New Act of **Employees' Pension Insurance**
1956 Increasing numbers of corporations introduced pension plans	
1960 Seamen's retiremen pension founded	1961 Implemented universal pension system **National pension insurance** enforced
1962 **Tax qualified retirement pension** enforced	1965 **Employees' pension insurance** 10000 yen pension benefit (36%)
1966 **Employees' pension fund** established	1969 **Employees' pension insurance** 20000 yen pension benefit (45%) **National pension insurance** 8000 yen per person
	1985 **National Basic Pension** enforced
1989 National pension fund established	1994 **Employees' pension insurance** Pensionable age for the first tier amended to 65 years, gradually implemented during the period 2001 to 2013 Indexation by net disposable income introduced
	2000 **Employees' pension insurance** Reduced 5% of benefit of employees' pension insurance Pensionable age for the second tier amended to 65 years, gradually implemented during the period 2013 to 2030
2001 June **Defined Benefit Corporate Pension Law** passed **Defined Contribution Corporate Pension Law** passed	Indexation by earnings abolished

Note: ( ) in 1965 and 1969 indicates approximate replacment ratio.

If we consider a chronology of the development of the corporate pension and the public pension in Japan, the establishment of the public pension dates back to 1942. The Workers' Pension Act was enacted in 1942, and its name was changed to the Employees' Pension Act in 1944. The main purpose of the introduction of this pension was to collect money for war expenditure. Therefore actual implementation of the public pension that served as social insurance had to be postponed until a comprehensive revision of the Employees' Pension Act was made in 1954, when the Japanese economy recovered as a result of the special demands of the Korean War. The number of corporations that adopted the retirement pension benefit as a substitute for the retirement allowance, which required an enormous reserve fund, increased. In those days the level of a retirement allowance was determined on the basis of the salary paid just before retirement. The amount of a retirement allowance increased with the annual increase of salary in those high-growth days of the Japanese economy. It was necessary for corporations to reserve funds in advance for the retirement allowance, but it was difficult to reserve enough funds because this increased production costs.[11] Because only large corporations could adopt the retirement allowance system, employers were almost alone in contributing to the reserve fund, with most employees not making contributions. Originally, the retirement allowance had the characteristic of a reward from the employer, and employees made no objection to the change of the benefit system from retirement allowance to pension.

In 1961, the public pension plan for the whole population, including not only employees but also self-employed persons, was established under the slogan of 'a public pension for the whole population'. Accordingly, the number of employees joining the employees' pension rapidly increased. As a result, many employers were forced to increase their production costs because of the increase in contributions which they had to bear.

The purpose of introducing the tax-qualified pension in 1962 was to arrange a tax system to meet the shift from a retirement allowance to a pension.[12] Management organizations put pressure on the tax system council of the government to introduce the tax-qualified pension backed by the introduction of the public pension for the whole population and the radical reform of pensions. Miyajima analyses this process as follows:

> A report of the financial policy council sees the tax-qualified pension plan as a tax arrangement for the pension plan not as a special preferential measure in order not to deter the further development of the employees' pension plan. Concretely, a tax system that includes contributions to pensions in the loss of corporation tax, makes the paid contribution exempt from income tax, and imposes an income tax on the pension received, which is the same as the tax system for corporate pensions in England and the United States which were

referred to, but the special corporation tax equivalent to overdue interest on tax applied to operating profit and corporate contributions in connection with the income tax deferred until the time a pension is received is different from the tax system in England and the United States. However, the discussion on the tax system council saw that the corporate pension is an American and British style of pension, and the lump-sum benefit might not be taken into account. (Miyajima, 1991, pp.30–31)

However, more than 80 per cent of the tax-qualified pension has been paid as a lump-sum benefit, as mentioned above, and the tax-qualified pension functioned differently from the initial object of the tax system council. In other words, 'management acquired the means to balance retirement costs and employees got the preferential income tax treatment by accepting a lump-sum benefit' (ibid.).

New corporate pension and employees' pension funds were established in 1966. This was an adjustment pension plan intended to adjust for the increased burden on the corporation for employees' pension insurance due to the introduction of the pension for the whole population and the cost of corporate retirement allowances, and this was introduced at the request of corporations. Corporations that established employees' pension funds made contributions to the earnings-related benefits of the employees' pension, and the earnings-related component was exempted from the application of the employees' pension (exempted contribution) and was put into the fund. This is the so-called 'British-style' opting out system, but the method of making contributions for employees is different, as described below.

Miscalculation of Corporate Pension (Employees' Pension Fund) as an Adjustment Pension

The financial conditions of the employees' pension fund, which was established with high expectations of playing the role of an adjustment pension for the public pension, have recently been very difficult. According to the financial conditions of the employees' pension fund examined by the Ministry of Health, Labour and Welfare, 44 per cent of the funds did not hold enough reserves to pay the promised benefits to members at the end of 1999.[13] The establishment of the employees' pension fund as an adjustment pension was permitted on the condition that more than 30 per cent of its funds were considered to be a contracted-out portion of the employees' pension. The contracted-out portion is different from the opting out system in the UK (see Figure 2.2). In the latter case, the earnings-related component exempted from application of the public pension and the component of the pension added by corporations are operated in the same account to pay benefits. However, in the case of Japan, the contracted-out portion is operated by assigning the employees' pension, so the interest rate of the investment has to be the same as the rate of the employees' pension. This difference has to do with the scope of responsibility of a corporation. For instance, when the expected interest rate is not attained, in the case of the UK, it has to be operated within the corporate pension, that is, the level of the corporate pension fund including the exemption of application changes, and it directly affects the level of employees' pensions. In the case of Japan, however, as for the contracted-out portion, a corporation has to supplement the operating profit up to the expected interest rate designated for the employees' pension (state). As a result, the corporate pension depends on the corporation's judgment. Exemption of application in Japan does not influence the scale of the corporate pension on the third tier. In the UK, the benefit for individuals exempted from application on the second tier may be decreased, depending on the conditions of fund operation.

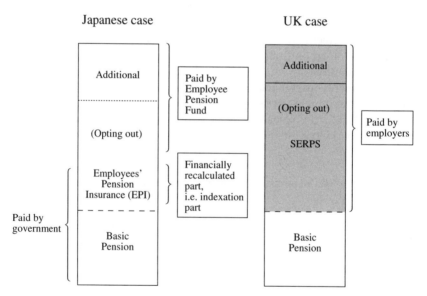

Figure 2.2   The difference between the Japanese and the UK contracted-out portion

In the case of Japan, the earnings-related component of the second tier is the contracted-out portion to be operated by the assessment method for the employees' pension. The financial calculation by the assessment method is affected by population dynamics such as the mortality rate. However, because the corporate pension plan is a system to provide defined

benefits by operating reserve funds, some experts point out that it is difficult for the corporate pension to operate two different funds.[14]

After the collapse of the bubble economy in 1992, the performance of
pension funds has been stagnant owing to low interest rates and low stock
prices, presenting a serious problem. For instance, the expected operating
interest rate of the contracted-out portion of the employees' pension fund
has been set at 5.5 per cent, which is the same as that of the employees'
pension, but the performance has been unstable since the latter half of the
1980s, as shown in Figure 2.3.

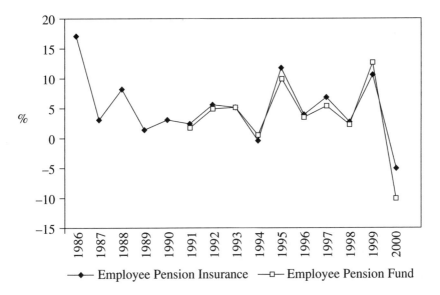

Source: White Paper on Corporate Pension (2000).

Figure 2.3   Average rate of return

For this reason, each fund has been able to set its own expected interest
rate since fiscal 1997, but many funds could not overcome financial problems and the number of dissolved funds has been increasing since 1996.
Twenty-four funds, a record high, were dissolved during fiscal 1999. Not
only could the employees' pension fund not achieve the expected performance because of the low interest rates, but also the employees' pension has
been seriously influenced by poor profit rates.

In the case of the employees' pension fund, if the expected operating
interest rate is not attained, the shortfall in benefits has to be supplemented
by corporations. Under the conditions of poor performance, the 'return of

the contracted-out portion' and the method of paying the contracted-out portion with stock were requested by corporations. To respond to these requests, an agreement-type corporate pension based on an agreement between labour and management, and the fund-type corporate pension without a contracted-out portion were introduced as a new type of corporate pension plan according to the Corporate Pension Plan Act to execute the policy to approve the shift from the employees' pension fund to the agreement-type corporate pension or the fund-type corporate pension without a contracted-out portion.[15]

The Shift from the Tax-qualified Pension to the Defined Benefit Corporate Pension

Among corporate pensions the tax-qualified pension pays the biggest benefit today. The reason why the tax-qualified pension has survived with lump-sum benefits regardless of the intention of the tax system council is its relation with the Japanese tax system. The rate of corporation tax was raised during the 1980s to procure financial resources for a reduction in individual income tax. As a result, corporations took measures to reduce tax and used the retirement allowance reserve system positively as a means to do so. The current corporation tax rate as a national tax is 30 per cent following the tax revision of 1999, while the business tax rate as a local tax is 9.6 per cent and the inhabitants tax rate is 17.3 per cent of the corporation tax. The tax rate executed in 1999 in Japan was 40.87 per cent.[16] The characteristics of the Japanese structure of tax revenue since 1945 are heavily dependent on corporation tax revenues as compared to the member countries of the OECD. In the case of Japan, the structure of tax revenues being dependent on direct tax has been maintained for a long time. However, after the introduction of the consumption tax it has gradually been shifting to indirect tax revenues. But the structure of tax revenues is still dependent on income tax and corporation tax. However, the maximum retirement allowance reserve transferred will be reduced by stages from 40 per cent to 20 per cent, starting in April 1998 and ending in April 2003, because of a recent revision of corporation tax. Accordingly, the merits of using it as a means of reducing tax have been decreased.[17] Furthermore, the introduction of the International Accounting System (IAS) in April 2001, based on international standards, has changed the way the retirement allowance reserve is treated, decreasing its use as a means of reducing tax.

ENACTMENT OF NEW CORPORATE PENSION ACTS AND THE INTRODUCTION OF NEW ACCOUNTING STANDARDS

Two bills for new corporate pension Acts were passed on the same day. The Defined Contribution Corporate Pension Plan Act, which referred to 401K in the United States, was introduced first. The Defined Benefit Corporate Pension Plan Act, introduced next, was designed to provide legal arrangements for the tax-qualified pension. The tax-qualified pension was determined to stop making new contracts from April 2002 and to exist until March 2012, thereafter to transfer to a new system because even the defined benefit pension has demerits regarding the tax exemption compared to the employees' pension fund and problems in protecting benefit rights owing to insufficient provision.[18]

There was a reason for introducing the Defined Contribution Corporate Pension Plan Act first: because the International Accounting System (IAS) would be introduced from April 2001, and the future obligations of the retirement allowance and the corporate pension, which had been dealt with as off-balance-sheet by the former corporate accounting, have to be included in the new corporate accounting under Projected Benefit Obligation.[19] Therefore, in many corporations, large future obligations have to be made clear in corporate accounting, and there are concerns that this has a direct negative impact on the evaluation of corporate performance.[20] To avoid this negative impact, many corporations started to take into consideration the shift to the Defined Contribution Corporate Pension, which does not bring about any operating risk, resulting in the introduction of the Defined Contribution Corporate Pension Plan Act (see Figure 2.4).

Because implementation of the Defined Contribution Corporate Pension Plan Act started in October 2001, it is too early to see the impact on existing corporate pensions, but labour unions such as the Japanese Trade Union Confederation have been against the introduction of the Defined Contribution Corporate Pension Plan, saying that it jeopardizes income security after retirement.[21] Some experts are cautious about its introduction on the ground that, in the case of introducing the Defined Contribution Corporate Pension Plan, where individuals choose the method of operation, it is necessary for individuals to have a thorough understanding and training regarding the system, citing experiences in the UK where many individuals received reduced benefits owing to the expansion of the exemption of application. On the other hand, the government approached the introduction of the Defined Contribution Corporate Pension Plan Act positively, for four major reasons: (1) portability of the corporate pension can meet the rising demands for labour mobility, (2) a

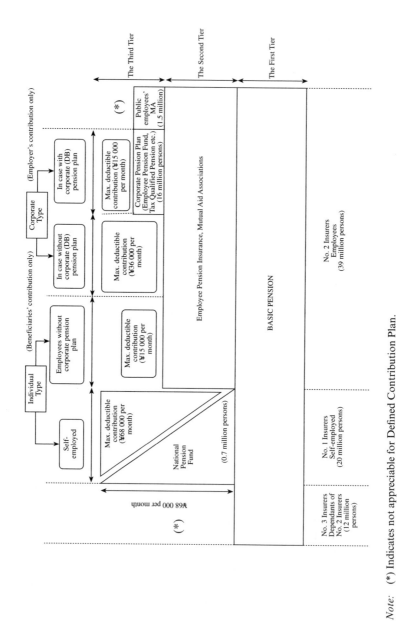

Note: (*) Indicates not appreciable for Defined Contribution Plan.

Figure 2.4   Outline of Japan's Defined Contribution Corporate Pension Plan

68

trend of design liberalization of corporate pension is established, (3) reduction of public pension benefit resulted in the increased importance of self-help, and (4) individuals' assets flowing into stock markets through the new type of pensions would result in the re-vitalization of the markets, as seen in the United States where the model was born.

The Defined Contribution Corporate Pension Plan Act enacted in June 2001 includes two types: the corporate-type pension and the individual-type pension. The individual-type pension is designed for the insured covered by category No.1 (self-employed), and the insured under employees' pension insurance who are less than 60 years old, who are not the target of the corporate pension. Provisions of the individual-type pension are prepared by the existing National Pension Fund Federation. An employer or a group of employers of the corporation to which the employees' pension is applied manages the corporate-type pension. Public employees covered by a mutual aid association cannot be covered by any type of defined contribution pension. Furthermore, the insured covered by category No.3 (spouse of employee without earnings) cannot be qualified for any pensions. With regard to the maximum contribution accorded tax incentives, in the case of the individual type, self-employed persons must pay the maximum monthly contribution, 68 000 yen (an annual sum of 816 000 yen) minus the contribution for other pensions such as a national pension fund, and individuals covered by the employees' pension fund insurance and not covered by the corporate pension must pay 15 000 yen per month (an annual sum of 180 000 yen). In the case of the corporate type, corporations that do not provide the defined benefit corporation pension must pay 36 000 yen per month (432 000 yen a year), and corporations providing the corporate pension must pay 18 000 yen per month (216 000 yen a year). Furthermore, in the case of the corporate type, the contribution is limited only to corporations, while in the case of the individual type, the contribution is limited only to the insured.

It is said that the Japanese defined contribution pension plan was influenced by the 401K plan in the United States. However, there are many differences between them. In the case of 401K in the United States, both employers and employees contribute, while, in Japan, in the case of the corporate type, only employers contribute, and in the case of the individual type, only the insured contribute, and they cannot be covered by two pensions at the same time. This is because emphasis was laid on the fairness of the pension system as a whole. In Japan, large corporations provide corporate pensions, while many small and medium-sized corporations do not. Because employees of large corporations covered by corporate pensions are already receiving tax incentives, the government seemed to judge that additional tax incentives from the defined contribution corporate pensions might adversely affect the fairness of the pension as a whole.[22] Another difference is related to the tax system. In the United States, 401K is not liable for taxation in the cases of contribution and operation, while in the case of payment of benefits it is liable for taxation, as with tax incentive pension systems in almost all developed countries. However, in Japan it is liable for taxation in the case of both operation and payment of benefits. One per cent of the amount outstanding is imposed as a special corporation tax in the case of operation. The purpose of the taxation is to collect the interest while allowing the corporation to postpone its tax payment on its contribution until the payment of benefits. In practice, however, the imposition is postponed until 2003 owing to the influence of the suspension of imposition of the special corporation tax for tax-qualified pensions.

Tax incentives are accorded not only to the contribution but also to the payment of benefits. If a benefit is received as a lump sum, it qualifies for the retirement income deduction, and the more seniority, the less tax is imposed (Figure 2.5).

Furthermore, if the benefit is received as a pension, it qualifies for the public pension reduction, and the taxable minimum amount is set very high.

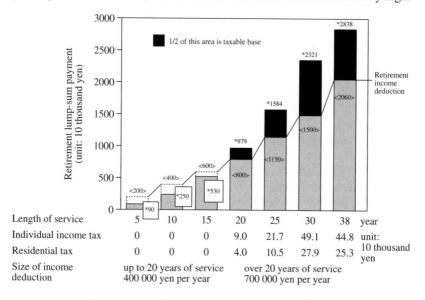

Note: The model employee is assumed to be a university graduate, engineer, male, involuntarily retired; * indicates amount of retirement payment; <> indicates the scale of deduction under the assumption of indicated length of service.

Figure 2.5 *Retirement income deduction, individual tax, residential tax: a model retirement lump-sum payment*

Thus the tax incentives work for both cases of contribution and benefit, a more effective way of saving tax than deposits and savings. The defined contribution pension, however, has both positive and negative aspects. In the case of poor performance, both individual-type and corporate-type pensions have to bear risk to the principal. Operating profits depend on market conditions. However, considering the fact that the yield of a ten-year national bond, a typical financial instrument with principal guaranteed, is 1.2 per cent and the yield of a ten-year time deposit of postal savings and banks is 1 per cent at best, actual profits after deducting commission for a life insurance company and so on are very small. Stock markets in Japan have been sluggish, particularly since 2001, and corporations are reluctant to shift to the defined contribution corporate pension, although they previously intended to make the change.[23]

PENSION REFORM MIX LEARNED FROM OTHER COUNTRIES

Recent public pension reform policies introduced by other countries include policies emphasizing private pensions such as the corporate pension and the public pension with the partial introduction of a reserve fund. In Japan, in the process of discussions on public pension reform policies, an expectation grew that corporate pensions can play a supplementary role in public pension reform, as seen in the paper prepared by the Council on Economic and Fiscal Policy, wherein the Council recommended corporate pension reform and earlier implementation and promotion of the defined contribution pension as means to support self-help. So far, however, in the discussion on public pension reform, the role of corporate pensions as a supplementary pension system (third tier) for the public pension has not been discussed actively. This has to do with the fact that Japanese corporate pensions grew out of an in-house welfare entity. In other words, the corporate pension is a form of retirement allowance from the perspective of the employee. The Japanese Trade Union Confederation took it as deferred compensation in the context of opposing the defined contribution corporate pension. Furthermore, many employees see the retirement allowance as a means to purchase their own houses, using it for repayment of housing loans. Therefore it is very hard for them to take the corporate pension as a long-term benefit like the public pension.

In the UK, under the Blair leadership of the Labour Party, compulsory participation in a private pension plan has been proposed. The establishment of the stakeholder pension, the establishment of secondary public pension and the lifting of a ban on compulsory participation were proposed in the

Green Paper published in 1998. The role of the public pension, which was reduced by the Thatcher administration, was re-evaluated. A gold standard and a rationalization of public pension benefits were discussed at the same time, and the private pension was promoted as a government policy. Promotion of the compulsory participation in the public pension as a policy has to do with the anticipated population structure change in the UK. From 2020 to 2040, the population aged over 65 years is expected to increase sharply, although the ratio of worker households will stay almost same (Criss Daykin, 1999).

A two-tier pension plan was restructured into a single-tier earnings-related pension system in Sweden, while other countries with social in-surance systems were trying to overcome financial problems by promoting participation in private pensions while maintaining two- or three-tier pension plans. The contribution rate for the earnings-related pension is fixed permanently at 18.5 per cent. As regards the 16 per cent part of the 18.5 per cent contribution rate, the earnings-related pension is financed by an amended levy system that has a reserve fund like the previous additional pension. However, as regards the 2.5 per cent part, a new funding method was introduced. This fund is contributed to by individuals and is operated in the market. Contributions and operation of the fund are handled by the national pension fund or private operating organizations, according to individual choice. The defined contribution pension plan was adopted as a system to design the earnings-related pension, and the operation risk is borne by pension recipients.[24]

The reasons why the reserve fund system was adopted in Sweden are first, that the conservative party and the middle-of-the-road parties (Moderate Party, Central Party, Christian Democratic Party and The Swedish Liberal Party) propose freedom to choose, and introduction of the principle of com-petition, strongly supporting the introduction of the reserve fund system; second, internationally, the saving rate in Sweden is low, so it is necessary to secure resources to invest by institutionalizing compulsory savings to promote economic growth. In terms of saving, Japan is a special case, having maintained a high saving rate for a long time (Inoue, 2000) (Figure 2.6).

Both public pension reforms and private pension plans are discussed below in the context of the rationalization of benefits of the public pension, and promotion policies of private pensions. Examples of these policies can be seen in the UK, Sweden and Germany.

In a Green Paper published in 1998, the Blair government proposed the establishment of a stakeholder pension, establishment of a secondary public pension and the lifting of the ban on compulsory participation. The role of the public pension, which was reduced by the Thatcher adminis-tration, was re-evaluated. The stakeholder pension plan is intended to

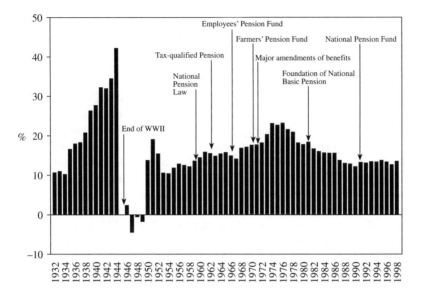

Figure 2.6   Trend of the household saving rate in Japan

provide a cost-reduced defined contribution-type individual pension for the middle-income stratum. The secondary public pension is a public income security with reinforced functions of income redistribution taking the place of the former earnings-related public pension by taking into account the fact that the basic pension is guaranteed only by consumer price indexation. A lower-income stratum can be provided with income security by applying a different benefit multiplier, depending on the income stratum.

The biggest difference from the Thatcher government is the proposal to lift the ban on compulsory participation, intended to force people to participate in private pensions. Employers are forced to make stakeholder pensions available to employees. Compulsory participation is, at first sight, against liberalization and restricts choice. Criss Daykin (1999) explains why the Blair government proposed the policy change for compulsory participation as follows.

> Policies carried out by the Thatcher administration show the approach of taking care of people of many classes, rather than providing individual freedom. There were limited options to choose within insufficient arrangements for the occupational pension plan, although options to choose were freely expanded. Furthermore, people took their options because of canvassing by sales persons from insurance companies. In many cases, because they tried to increase benefits in the short term, they did not think about long-term consequences. When employees are covered by an occupational pension, it is better to use it.

The policy to promote compulsory participation in the private pension is influenced by the anticipated population structure change in the UK. From 2020 to 2040, the population aged over 65 years is expected to increase sharply, while the ratio of worker households will stay almost the same (Criss Daykin, 1999).

In Germany in May 2001, as a part of pension reform, a new subsidy for the preferential treatment of savings was established. The new subsidy plan that became effective in January 2002 is borne by the federal government as a part of the voluntary, capital-funded provision for old age. This plan is effective from 1 January 2002, and 10 billion Euros will be paid for this subsidy up to 2008. The plan was designed to promote safe individual savings for lower-income people, and preferential fiscal treatment such as income reduction through strict checks. Basically, qualification is up to 60 years of age or until receipt of the benefits of the old age pension. The amount of the subsidy is determined by age, regardless of income. However, an additional subsidy will be paid per child according to the number of dependent children and it will be tax-deductible. Because this plan is a measure to promote savings, people are obliged to pay the minimum contribution and they are not allowed to receive only the subsidy itself.

Other reforms were also introduced to reinforce the corporate pension. For example, the vesting of occupational pension credits guarantees pension benefits during the working period, even if employees change their jobs before the pensionable age. Furthermore, employees are able to change their jobs more easily than before because the qualifying age has been lowered from 35 years to 30 years and the participating period in the corporate pension was shortened from ten years to five years by the reform. Corporations are able to manage the fund in conformity with American accounting standards by holding sufficient corporate pension reserve funds to meet the standard. Furthermore, the contribution by employers is tax-exempt and, in the case of insolvency, the corporate reserve fund is protected by the Mutual Benefit Association for Pension Security for the pension funds if the corporate pension fund is established.

CONCLUSION: THE JAPANESE 'PENSION' AND ITS DESTINATION

According to the latest report, entitled 'Population Projection for Japan: 2001–2050' (January 2002), the total population will reach its peak in 2006, and then will start decreasing, and during the projected period (until 2050) the aging rate will increase sharply. It is projected that the rate will reach 28.7 per cent by 2025 and 35.7 per cent by 2050. The population projection is based on data from a census carried out every five years. As shown in Table 2.3 the projected aging rate has been modified upwards every time.[25]

According to figures in 'Recalculation of Public Pension Financing' (1999) based on the population estimate of 1997, the contribution to the national basic pension will be 26 400 yen by 2025, assuming no change in the plan. Thereafter, without raising the contribution, the fund can be financed using a reserve fund until the introduction of a full assessment. As for the employees' pension plan, the contribution rate based on the same assumption as that mentioned above is estimated to be 34.5 per cent by 2025 (contributed equally by labour and management). The public pension reform mentioned above was designed to raise the pensionable age from 60 to 65 years by stages, and the public pension including both first and second tier will start payment of benefits from 65 years.[26] The public pension reform reduces the burden of premiums by changing the pensionable age. To respond to the aging population, there is no effective means to reduce expenditure other than to reduce the number of pensioners and the average amount of benefits.

An actuarial revaluation of public pension financing based on the population projection for Japan, January 2002, will be published in 2003. The next pension reform plan in 2004 will be discussed on the basis of this result. People are worried about increased burdens and reduction of benefits in a period of accelerated aging. However, the younger generation are aware of the end of the 'Good Old Days' in which retired employees were able to live on benefits from the public pension. Therefore the number of young people who do not pay their contributions to the national pension with full conviction is increasing. Such an unfavourable situation cannot be ignored.[27] The government and the bureaucrats in Japan insist on maintaining the national pension for all people. Officially, they would not admit the fact that the national pension plan had been devoid of substance until recently. Because the national pension is social insurance, four million pensioners who are the low-income stratum and are exempted from contributions receive only one-third of the full benefits that are contributed by the state. To be qualified as a recipient of the benefits of the national pension, it takes a minimum 25 years of participation, and the full amount of benefits is about 56 000 yen per month, while the pensioners mentioned above receive only 18 700 yen per month.

What kind of quality of life for retired old-age recipients can be expected? Before becoming the national pension for all people, the pension was called a 'welfare old-age pension' and there were many recipients of the public pension who did not make contributions. But they could receive 34 333 yen per month, while the recipients exempted from contributions will receive much lower benefits.[28] Quite contrary to the original intention

Table 2.3 *Aging rate by year, based on population projections (per cent)*

	Feb. 1960	Aug. 1969	Feb. 1975	Nov. 1981	Dec. 1986	Sep. 1992	Jan. 1997	Jan. 2002
1960	5.7	–	–	–	–	–	–	–
1965	6.3	–	–	–	–	–	–	–
1970	7.0	7.0	–	–	–	–	–	–
1975	7.5	7.9	7.9	–	–	–	–	–
1980	8.2	8.9	8.8	9.1	–	–	–	–
1985	8.7	9.5	9.6	10.1	10.3	–	–	–
1990	9.6	10.5	10.8	11.6	11.9	12.1	–	–
1995	11.1	12.0	12.4	13.6	14.2	14.5	14.6	–
2000	12.8	13.4	13.9	15.6	16.3	17.0	17.2	17.4
2005	14.1	14.4	15.0	17.1	18.0	19.1	19.6	19.9
2010	15.6	15.4	16.1	18.8	20.0	21.3	22.0	22.5
2015	17.7	16.9	17.7	21.1	22.5	24.1	25.2	26.0
2020	–	17.2	18.0	21.8	23.6	25.5	26.9	27.8
2025	–	16.4	17.4	21.3	23.4	25.8	27.4	28.7
2030	–	–	16.9	20.9	23.1	26.0	28.0	29.6
2035	–	–	–	–	–	–	30.4	30.9
2040	–	–	17.3	22.0	24.1	28.0	31.0	33.2
2045	–	–	–	–	–	–	34.3	34.7
2050	–	–	18.1	21.1	23.5	28.2	32.3	35.7

Note: Aging rate = ratio of 65 years old and over to the total population.

Source: Population projections by National Institute of Population and Social Security Research.

of maintaining the national pension plan for all people based on the idea of social insurance, many people receive fewer pension benefits than those receiving the welfare pension without having made a contribution, whereas more people pay into the livelihood protection scheme which is supposed to secure a minimum standard of living.

The next pension reform, for implementation in 2004, has just started. Based on the new population estimate, a further reduction of benefits and raising of the pensionable age are on the agenda. How to secure jobs up to 65 years old for retired people who are still not eligible to receive pension benefits is a difficult issue. The standard of partial benefits for early receivers must be high on the agenda. Contrary to the aged in European countries, those in Japan tend to work longer.[29] It is hard to predict whether this tendency will continue or if the number of aged employees will decrease as a result of a change in their life cycles and their values. It is naïve to assume that the behaviour patterns of the aged Japanese 25 years and 50 years ahead would be the same as those today. It is hard to forecast where the Japanese 'pension plan' is heading and whether corporate pensions in Japan may or may not take the path of pensions that supplement the public pension plan, as is the case in other countries.

NOTES

1. Here I have included employees' pension fund, farmers' pension fund and tax-qualified pension in the scope of corporate pension. As for the amount of the benefit of the employees' pension fund, the benefit of the contracted-out portion of the employees' pension mentioned later is excluded in the recalculation. Furthermore, the total retirement income is shown in Table 2.1. These data are based on the annual statistical report of the National Tax Administration Agency. The figure is drawn from the retirement income of employees who earn more than 10 million yen per year and are exempted from withholding tax and submitted a final return. Therefore, it cannot be seen as the sum of retirement income of all employees in Japan. The total retirement income including the withdrawing tax is not disclosed.
2. Policy Planning and Research Department, Minister's Secretariat, Ministry of Labour, Japan, *Survey on Retirement Allowances System and Payments*, 1997.
3. Recalculated on the basis of data from the Statistics Bureau, Management and Coordination Agency, Japan, 1999, *Establishment and Enterprise Census of Japan, Vol. 3, Results of Incorporated Enterprises.*
4. Pension Fund Association, Corporate pension in the 21st century, 1998, p.195.
5. Ministry of Labour, *Research on Wage and Working Hours of 1997* (1998).
6. Among corporations with the retirement allowance, the in-house reserve fund accounts for 68.3 per cent (1997), the small and medium-scale corporation retirement allowance mutual aid system accounts for 30.2 per cent, and the specified retirement allowance mutual aid system accounts for 11.1 per cent (Ministry of Labour, *Report on the Retirement Allowance System and Its Payment*, 1997). The retirement allowance mutual aid system and the specified retirement allowance mutual aid system are external reserve fund systems that are the same as the tax-qualified pension plan and employees' pension fund. The former is executed by the worker's retirement allowance mutual aid organization, a government-related

judicial person under the control of the Ministry of Health, Labour and Welfare, and the latter is handled by the Chamber of Commerce and Industry and Association of Commerce and Industry. All contributions are borne by employers and it is tax-exempt. As for the payment of benefits, preferential tax measures are taken for retirement allowance, and partial benefit is treated as a public pension reduction.

7. According to *Research on Wage and Working Hours of 1997*, conducted by the Ministry of Labour (1998), in the case of the tax-qualified pension, the whole life annuity is only 13.1 per cent and most are limited to 10 years. Period of limited payment depends on corporate scale.

8. Mitsubishi Trust and Banking Corp., Mitsubishi Pension Documents, 1999.

9. It is said that Kanebo, Ltd, introduced the first corporate pension plan in 1905. The employees contributed 3 per cent of their pay, while the employer contributed more than half of the total contributions. Use of this corporate pension did not spread and a similar pension was not adopted until the introduction of a corporate pension plan by Mitsui & Co. in 1914. However, these corporate pension plans born in private corporations did not develop during the Taisho period (1912–26) owing to neglect by the government and the Diet. See Yoshiaki Hirano, *Defined Contribution Corporate Pension Plan, Defined Benefit Corporate Pension Plan, 401 K of the Hybrid Pension Plan and Taxation*, Taxation Symposium Press, 1999, pp.75–81.

10. Tomitaro Hirata, *Retirement Allowance and Pension*, Taxation Symposium Press, 1956, pp.20–21.

11. General Council of Trade Unions of Japan, *Expert Committee for Spring Wage Negotiations by Neutral Labor Federation, Retirement Allowance and Pension: Its Essence, Reality and Struggle*, Rodo Keizai Sha, 1996, p.172.

12. Under the former tax system, the retirement allowance reserve plan was applied to the amount of money contributed to the pension plan like a retirement allowance. However, under this reserve plan based on the standard for the required payment for voluntary retirement, only a small reserve is applied, and almost all of the contributions are excluded from non-taxable expenses because they are considered to be voluntary contributions. Japan Federation of Employers' Associations asked the government to reduce the tax on corporate pensions in August 1956 on the ground that the tax system was preventing the development of the corporate pension. The qualified retirement allowance plan was introduced by fiscal reform in April 1962 under pressure from Japan Federation of Employers' Associations, Trust and Bank Association and Life Insurance Association (General Council of Trade Unions of Japan, *Expert Committee for Spring Wage Negotiations by Neutral Labor Federation, Retirement Allowance and Pension: Its Essence, Reality and Struggle*, Rodo Keizai Sha, 1996, p.172).

13. Ministry of Health, Labour and Welfare, documents disclosed in August 2001.

14. Kiyoshi Murakami, *Choice of Pension Plan: Bureaucrats' Scenario or People's Will?*, Toyo Keizai Sha, 1998, p.135.

15. Life Design Research Institute, 2001 Version of White Paper on Corporate Pension, p.17.

16. International comparison of taxes for different systems is very difficult and has to be carried out very carefully. The data comparing national tax and local tax in terms of effective tax rate are drawn from documents of the Ministry of Finance. As of 1999, the tax rates were 40.87 per cent for Japan, 40.85 per cent for the USA, 30.00 per cent for the UK, 48.55 per cent for Germany and 36.67 per cent for France. The Japanese tax rate is almost the same as that in other advanced countries. See International tax comparison (2) Corporation tax
    (http://www.mof.go.jp/jouhou/syuzei/memo/memo02.ht).

17. Ito, S. and T. Kotani (eds), *Corporate Management and Pension Issue*. Taxation Symposium Press, 2000, p.206.

18. A tax-qualified pension has fewer regulations than the employees' pension fund, and all corporate contributions are included in non-taxable expenses. However, the only preferential tax measure for the employee's contribution is the insurance premium reduction (about 50000 yen per year). In addition, because there is a levy of a special corporation tax of 1 per cent and inhabitant tax of 0.173 per cent on the currently frozen pension

fund, it has been pointed out that there are non-taxable merit differentials between the tax-qualified pension and the employees' pension fund.

19. Ito, S. and T. Kotani, *Corporate Management and Pension Issue*, Taxation Symposium Press, 2000, pp.85–90.

20. Reserve shortfall for the contracted-out portion of the employees' old-age pension can be included in the retirement allowance obligation. The amount of the reserve shortfall for the retirement allowance obligation is 14.4 trillion yen in total and 421 000 yen per person when calculated on the basis of data for 1388 corporations with information disclosed by corporations listed in the quarterly, *Nikkei Corporation Information of 2000* (III summer edn), Life Design Institute, 2001 Version of White Paper on Corporate Pension, p.49.

21. Tadayuki Murakami, the group chief of policy making of the Japan Trade Union Confederation stated: 'Because the Japanese corporate pension is a deferred payment of the retirement allowance, it has to be a defined benefit. It is not reasonable to say that, because corporations cannot take the operating risk, employees have to take it' (*Weekly Social Security*, no.2155, p.43). When the employees' pension fund was set up as an adjustment pension, the trade union was against it. The reasons for this objection were that, because the amount of benefits paid by the employees' pension was small, it was necessary to upgrade the public pension plan, and some large corporations with the capacity to contribute might upgrade their own corporate pension plan, and thereafter might withdraw from the public pension plan, damaging the public pension. Unions were cautious about the strategies of management; namely, the retirement allowance would be terminated by the introduction of the adjustment pension, and ultimately this introduction would be used as a means of cost reduction. See General Council of Trade Unions of Japan (1996), p.225.

22. 'The 401 K in the United States, the model plan for the defined contribution corporate pension plan, has the two characteristics of pension and savings, but a saving function is excluded and it is specified to function as a pension in Japan.' (Presentation at the symposium of the Ministry of Health, Labour and Welfare, *Weekly Social Security*, no. 2155, p.41.)

23. According to the *Yomiuri* newspaper dated 22 September 2001, Hitachi, Ltd. decided to introduce the defined contribution corporate pension plan first among major Japanese manufacturing companies. Hitachi, Ltd. contributes 60 per cent of its corporate pension fund to the employees' pension fund, and contributes 40 per cent of its corporate pension fund to the retirement allowance. Thereafter, however, half of the retirement allowance is to be transferred to the defined contribution corporate pension. According to the *Asahi* newspaper dated 2 October, in reality, the majority of corporations are reluctant to introduce the new plan. The corporations that decided to introduce this plan are newly developing corporations that do not have corporate pension plans or have a short history of corporate pension plans. On the other hand, only large corporations can introduce the conventional corporate pension plan because of its heavy burden, while the defined contribution corporate pension plan is affordable for small and medium-sized corporations to introduce. Some people point out this advantage.

24. As regards the levying system in the Swedish new earning-related pension plan, a very special design for levying and yet defined contribution system has been adopted. Documents of the Swedish government call this a Notional Defined Contribution (NDC) system. Inoue, ibid, 2000

25. The main cause of the revision is a decline in the fertility rate. The fertility rate in 1960 was 2.00, but it dropped sharply to 1.36 in 2000. The population estimate in 2002 assumes the long-term total fertility rate to be 1.39.

26. A pensionable age of 65 years for public pensions will be applied to men born after 2 April 1961 and to women born after 2 April 1966.

27. An increase in the number of people who do not pay contributions to the national pension has become a serious issue, damaging the foundations of the national pension system as a whole. According to a publication of the Ministry of Health, Labour and Welfare, non-participants in the national pension number 990 000 (1.38 per cent of the

total), and defaulters 1 720 000 (2.41 per cent of the total), with 4 000 000 exemptions (5.6 per cent of the total). The percentage of non-participants and defaulters together is thus about 4 per cent of the total. However, it accounts for 33 per cent of all persons covered by Pension No.1 (self-employed persons and employees of small and medium-sized enterprises).

28. In principle, those who were more than 50 years old (persons more than 90 years old in April 2001) when the national pension plan was started are eligible to receive the benefits of the old-age welfare pension from a pensionable age of 70 years. The amount of the benefit is 412 000 yen per year (34 333 yen per month). However, if the income of the person or his/her dependants exceeds a specified amount, all or a part of benefits will be suspended.

29. See Yukiko Katsumata, 'Japanese Social Security Measures to Support the Retiring Aged – From employment insurance and public pension', The Year 2000 International Research Conference on Social Security, 'Social Security in the Global Village', September, Helsinki, pp.25–7.

REFERENCES

Daykin, Chris (1999), 'Lecture Notes', presented at the 22nd Pension Financing Seminar, 24 August, Pension Fund Association of Japan.

General Council of Trade Unions of Japan (1996), *Expert Committee for Spring Wage Negotiations by Neutral Labor Federation, Retirement Allowance and Pension: Its Essence, Reality and Struggle*, Rodo Keizai Sha.

Hirata, Tomitaro (1956), *Retirement Allowance and Pension*, Romukenkyusyo.

Ito, S. and T. Kotani (2000), *Corporate Management and Pension Issue*, Zaimukenkyukai.

Inoue, Seichi (2000), *Introduction of Swedish Public Pension Reform*, no. 1403, Nenkin Jitsumu.

Katsumata, Yukiko (2000) '*Japanese Social Security Measures to Support the Retiring Aged – From employment insurance and public pension*', The Year 2000 International Research Conference on Social Security, 'Social Security in the Global Village', September, Helsinki.

Life Design Research Institute (2001), *White Paper on Corporate Pension.*

Ministry of Labour (1998), *Research on Wage and Working Hours of 1997.*

Mitsubishi Trust and Banking Corp. (1999), *Mitsubishi Pension Documents.*

Miyajima, Hiroshi (1991),*Corporate Welfare and Taxations*, Nihon Zeimukenkyu Center.

Murakami, Kiyoshi (1998), *Choice of Pension Plan: Bureaucrats' Scenario or People's Will?* ,Toyo Keizai Sha.

Pension Fund Association (eds) (1998), *Corporate Pension in the 21st Century*, Pension Fund Association.

Policy Planning and Research Department, Minister's Secretariat, Ministry of Labour, Japan (1997), *Survey on Retirement Allowances System and Payments.*

Statistics Bureau Management and Coordination Agency (1999), *Establishment and Enterprise Census of Japan, Volume 3, Results of Incorporated Enterprises*, Government of Japan.

Yoshiaki, Hirano (1999), *Defined Contribution Corporate Pension Plan, Defined Benefit Corporate Pension Plan, 401 K of the Hybrid Pension Plan and Taxation*, Zaimukenkyukai.

B

Mandating of contractual agreements: Australia, Switzerland and the Netherlands

3. Reforming pensions: the Australian experience

Peter Whiteford

INTRODUCTION

The Australian social security system differs from that in most other countries.[1] Using World Bank (1994) terminology, Australia can be described as having a three-pillar model. The first pillar is a flat rate, means-tested pension financed from general government revenue. The second pillar involves compulsory savings through an employment-based system known as the Superannuation Guarantee. The third pillar encourages individuals to supplement the first two pillars, through either voluntary superannuation assisted by tax concessions or other private saving, particularly housing.

Public spending on age pensions is low compared to that of most other OECD countries. Nevertheless, coverage is comprehensive, and the system appears highly redistributive to groups often poorly served by social insurance systems, such as women, those with long-term disabilities, low-wage earners and others with marginal or incomplete attachment to the labour force. Indeed, the Australian pension system has been described as 'radically redistributive' (Aaron, 1992).

Australia's retirement income arrangements are also of interest for the example of the second-tier, compulsory, funded pension scheme. In a relatively short period, coverage has expanded to cover the great majority of the employed population, although this system will take many years to mature.

This chapter discusses the Australian system of provision for retirement incomes, and some of the lessons that might be learned from Australian experience operating a targeted income support system and developing a compulsory private second pillar. The second and third sections of the chapter provide details of the public income support system, and the private superannuation system. The concluding sections discuss a range of issues relevant to an assessment of Australian arrangements.

THE AUSTRALIAN SYSTEM OF INCOME SUPPORT FOR RETIREMENT

Means testing has long been a fundamental feature of the Australian system of income support, although its history has been chequered.[2] Like the early pension systems of New Zealand and Scandinavia, age pensions in Australia were selective from their inception. Means-tested pensions were introduced in the two most populous colonies at the end of the nineteenth century, and by the Commonwealth government in 1909. Despite the means test, a third of the eligible population were receiving benefits within five years.

Consideration had been given to a social insurance system, but this approach was explicitly rejected as being administratively costly and providing insufficient coverage (Neild, 1898). A Royal Commission in 1905–6 also rejected social insurance on the German model as inappropriate in Australia. Pensions for war widows were introduced in 1914, again on a non-contributory basis. A social insurance plan was proposed in 1928, but the government lost office in 1929. In 1938, Federal Parliament actually passed legislation introducing such a scheme, but the legislation lapsed at the outbreak of the Second World War. The system of benefits for people of workforce age introduced in the 1940s was also non-contributory, financed from general revenue, and, with the exception of child endowment, payments were means-tested. The Commonwealth Government took sole responsibility for income tax in 1942, and in 1943 it notionally split income tax into two components, one of which was a special social security levy paid into the 'National Welfare Fund', but benefits remained non-contributory, flat-rate and means-tested. The Levy was remerged with income tax in 1950, but the National Welfare Fund remained as an accounting device, until it was abolished in 1985.

During the 1960s and 1970s, there was electoral pressure to abolish the means test on age pensions, although the two major political parties adopted different paths towards this objective. From 1909 to 1969, the withdrawal rate on age pensions had been 100 per cent, although the threshold (or 'free area') after which this withdrawal rate was applied was high, at times being equal to the basic pension rate. The first step towards a universal age pension was made in 1969 by the Coalition (Conservative) government, with the introduction of the 'tapered means test' with a 50 per cent rather than 100 per cent withdrawal rate. In 1972, the pension free areas were doubled by the Coalition government, just before it lost office. In 1973, the newly elected Labor government abolished the means test for those aged 75 years and over, and in 1975 for those aged 70 to 74 years. In 1976, the returned Coalition government replaced the remaining means test with a test on income alone, and introduced price indexation of basic pension rates. A National Superannuation Inquiry set up earlier by the Labor government reported in 1976, and recommended the introduction of a free of means test basic pension, supplemented by earnings-related pensions, and supplementary pensions for those below a specified minimum, to be financed by compulsory contributions. These proposals were formally rejected by the Coalition in 1979.

The move towards a universal age pension in the first half of the 1970s was accompanied by substantial increases in real payment rates and the introduction of new benefits (for example, for sole mothers). Tax rebates for children were cashed out in the form of increased family allowances. These initiatives also coincided with substantial increases in unemployment. Together, all these factors produced a large increase in social security spending. From the second half of the 1970s, attention focused on reducing the Federal budget deficit.

The rates of income test-free pension for those over 70 years of age were frozen by the Coalition government in 1978, at a time when inflation averaged 8 to 14 per cent. This rapidly reduced the value of the universal payment, although people could apply for the same payment available to those under 70, but had to satisfy the income test.

A Labor government was re-elected in 1983 and, as part of its programme to reduce the budget deficit, the pension for those aged 70 years and over was again subjected to the income test. In 1985, the assets test on pensions was reintroduced amidst considerable controversy. Thus, in little more than a decade, the movement towards universality was reversed, and targeting became the preferred government approach.

The current public pension system (and the occupational superannuation system) is very much a product of reforms introduced by the Labor government between 1983 and 1996. Since the reintroduction of the assets test there have been significant reforms, but the basic structure of the system has remained broadly the same. These policy initiatives include the introduction of 'deeming' of a minimum rate of return on financial assets, to counter the practice where people sought to minimize income to maximize pension entitlement. Deeming on bank deposits was introduced in 1990 and extended in July 1996. Labor also announced the phased increase in the pension age for women from 60 to 65 years.

A Coalition government was re-elected in 1996, and has since made further reforms. One of the first of these was to introduce legislation to index pensions to male total average weekly earnings, in addition to prices. It had long been the objective of the Labor Party to set pensions at 25 per cent of average earnings. While this was largely achieved from 1990 onwards, this was because real average earnings fell as a result of wage restraint (see below), and the standard had not been legislated.

A second reform was the introduction of the Deferred Pension Bonus Scheme from July 1998. Under this scheme, persons who defer retirement and access to the age/service pension accrue a tax-exempt bonus (9.4 per cent of basic entitlements) for each year of additional employment, up to a maximum of five years, when the bonus reaches 47 per cent of entitlement. At current rates, the maximum bonus would be a lump sum of around A$25 000 for a single person and A$42 000 for a couple.

A further change in July 2000 was the reduction of the pension withdrawal rate to 40 per cent, as part of a package to compensate low-income groups for the introduction of a broad-based Goods and Services tax (a VAT).

Table 3.1 shows the parameters of the pension system at September 2003. The pension is flat-rate, and financed from general revenue on a pay-as-you-go (PAYGO) basis. Eligibility is primarily determined by residence, and entitlements are then calculated using the income and assets test parameters shown.

The age pension is received by around two-thirds of the population of pensionable age. Veterans' pensions give a combined coverage of around 80 per cent of the aged population. A small number of people receive other benefits, but the bulk of the remainder are excluded from payments by their level of private incomes or assets. Coverage of the pensionable population has fluctuated, reflecting changes in policy towards income and assets testing. The percentage of pensioners receiving a reduced rate has fluctuated, but increased from 10–15 per cent in the 1960s to roughly one third in the 1990s. Correspondingly, the proportion completely dependent on pensions has fallen from more than a quarter in the early 1970s to less than one in ten, reflecting increasing access to private income and assets.

Overall, the Australian public pension system can be considered to be closer to a demogrant than to the means-tested social assistance payments in other OECD countries. The assets test is not intended to restrict benefits only to the very poor. Rather, it is designed to ensure that pensions are not payable to very wealthy people who could otherwise arrange their affairs to qualify under the income test – 'tall poppies' in Australian jargon.

OCCUPATIONAL AND PRIVATE RETIREMENT PROVISIONS

The first employer-sponsored occupational superannuation scheme, covering public servants, was introduced in South Australia in 1854, while the Bank of NSW established the first private scheme in 1862. The Commonwealth Government in 1915 provided concessions for superannuation when

Table 3.1 Parameters of the Australian age pension system, September 2003

Parameters of age pension system	Value in $A at September 2003	Value in $US at 2002 PPPs
Standard (single) pension rate	452.80 per fortnight	727 per month
Married pension rate (each)	378.00 per fortnight	607 per month (each)
Supplementary rental assistance	Up to	Up to
	94.40 per fortnight single,	152 per month single,
	89.20 per fortnight couple	143 per month couple
Free areas (disregards)		
Single	120.00 per fortnight	193 per month
Combined married	212.00 per fortnight	340 per month
Withdrawal rate	40% for single and 20% for each of a couple	—
Cut-out points		
Single	1266.50 per fortnight	2003 per month
Combined married	2116.50 per fortnight	3397 per month

Assets test	Allowable assets	No rate paid above	Allowable assets	No rate paid above
Single home owners	149 500	302 500	110 740	224 070
Single non-home owners	257 500	410 500	190 740	304 070
Married home owners	212 500	466 500	157 410	345 560
Married non-home owners	320 500	574 500	237 410	425 560

Note: Uses 2002 purchasing power parities (PPPs) of $US 1.00 equal to $A 1.35.

income taxation was introduced. There was little development of superannuation prior to the Second World War. Occupational schemes were largely confined to white-collar public servants and employees of financial organizations and large manufacturing concerns (Borowski *et al.*, 1986).

Superannuation coverage gradually expanded, with 32 per cent of employees covered by 1974 and 42 per cent by 1982. But superannuation was still concentrated in the public sector (69 per cent of government employees) and in higher-income private sector employment (39 per cent of those in private employment). There was little regulation to ensure that superannuation savings were preserved to deliver income in retirement. There was limited portability of benefits between schemes. Superannuation mainly served to provide higher-income earners with concessionally taxed termination payments. Only 5 per cent of benefits taken as a lump sum were included in a person's taxable income and taxed at marginal tax rates, providing strong incentives to take benefits as lump sums rather than income streams.

A reform process commenced in 1983, following the election of the Labor government. The tax on that component of lump sums relating to employment after June 1983 was increased to encourage taking benefits as annuities and pensions. A higher tax was imposed on benefits taken before age 55 to encourage preservation of savings until retirement after that age. Rollover vehicles (approved deposit funds and deferred annuities) were created to provide people still in the workforce with opportunities to preserve benefits within the concessionally taxed environment until retirement, and to facilitate portability of superannuation when people changed jobs.

Subsequent developments cannot be understood without appreciating the distinctive role of Australian workplace relations institutions. After repeated industrial disputes in the 1890s, colonial governments established machinery to address issues of conciliation and arbitration of disputes, and wage rates (in some states). A Commonwealth Court of Conciliation and Arbitration was established in 1904. The basic legal character of the federal conciliation and arbitration system remained unchanged over the subsequent 85 years. The system involved the use of a permanent and independent tribunal funded publicly to exercise the conciliation and arbitration function. The system was compulsory in that either party could be compelled by the other to submit differences for resolution, with the court's resolutions being legally binding. The system developed into a mechanism for establishing and implementing minimum labour standards, including wage rates, hours of work, annual leave, sick leave, allowances and notice of termination and payments. Among the most visible manifestations were national wage cases to determine the adjustment of wages in relation to inflation and productivity changes. The most famous example was the

Harvester case in 1907, where, in a case concerned with tariff protection, Justice Higgins set out the principle of the basic wage, essentially a (more than) minimum wage for an unskilled adult male labourer (with a dependent wife and three children). This system gave considerable influence to trade unions. In the mid-1980s, the basic terms and conditions of around 83 per cent of the employed workforce were governed by the awards and determinations of the state and federal tribunals, even though union membership was less than 40 per cent of employees.[3]

Just before the 1983 election, the Labor Party and the union movement reached an 'Accord', emphasizing a consensual approach towards economic and social policy. The union movement promised wage moderation, and the Labor Party pledged tax cuts and social policy measures (the 'social wage') to maintain living standards. Significant social reforms introduced under the Accord included the reintroduction of universal national health insurance (largely phased out by the Coalition government between 1976 and 1983), taxation reforms, improved family assistance and increased funding for social services, including child care.

The move to compulsory superannuation had its origin in centralized wage negotiations in 1985–6, as part of this Accord. In 1986, the government sought to increase superannuation coverage by agreeing to support the Australian Council of Trade Unions in seeking through the Industrial Relations Commission a universal 3 per cent employer-provided superannuation benefit in lieu of an equivalent productivity-based general wage rise. Award superannuation was to be fully vested in the member and subject to preservation until retirement after age 55. Following endorsement by the Industrial Relations Commission, award superannuation played a key role in extending access, with coverage increasing from 42 per cent in 1982 to 72 per cent of employees by 1991. However, it suffered a number of problems, including non-compliance by some employers. In addition, awards did not cover all wage and salary earners, and there were difficulties in ensuring award superannuation provisions were reflected in all state and federal award jurisdictions.

Recognizing that a voluntary private system could not be relied upon to deliver a secure retirement other than for the wealthy, the government moved to introduce a form of compulsory superannuation through the Superannuation Guarantee (SG) in 1992. The SG was intended to reduce (but not replace) reliance on the PAYGO approach to funding the age pension system.

The SG is a compulsory, occupation-based, superannuation system. Under the SG, employers are required to make prescribed minimum contributions to complying superannuation funds. The required minimum contribution was set at 3 per cent of employee earnings in 1992, rising in steps to 9 per cent in 2002–3. The mandatory aspect of the scheme relies on the fact that employers failing to make prescribed minimum contributions to a complying fund must pay a tax, namely the Superannuation Guarantee Charge (SGC). The charge requires employers to pay to the Australian Taxation Office an amount equivalent to the contributions (plus interest) that they should have paid directly to a superannuation fund on behalf of their employees, plus administrative and any late payment penalty charges. The SGC is not tax-deductible for employers, whereas direct payments to complying funds generally are.

In 1995, the Labor government announced that it would boost superannuation by requiring employee contributions. It was intended to phase in a requirement for employees to contribute 3 per cent of earnings to superannuation by the year 2000. In addition, the government was to match employee contributions up to a maximum of 3 per cent by redirecting tax cuts originally announced in 1992. Together with employer contributions required under the Superannuation Guarantee, the measures would have resulted in employees having the equivalent of up to 15 per cent of their earnings directed towards their retirement savings from 2002. These planned arrangements lapsed with the election of a Coalition government in 1996.

The Coalition government, while generally endorsing Australia's three-pillar retirement incomes policy, introduced further changes. Retirement Savings Accounts (RSAs) were introduced to provide a simple, low-cost, capital guaranteed product suited to those with small superannuation amounts. RSAs yield relatively modest returns. Accounts are fully portable, owned and controlled by the RSA holder, and are subject to the retirement income standards applying to other superannuation products, including preservation, contributions eligibility and disclosure rules. By 1999, RSAs accounted for only 1 per cent of total assets.

The government also legislated for a phased increase in the preservation age from 55 to 60 by the year 2025. Consequently, the preservation age for someone born after 30 June 1964 will rise to 60 years. The government also simplified and tightened the preservation rules, with effect from 1 July 1999. All contributions and earnings accruing after this date will be preserved until retirement. From July 1998, people earning A$450 to A$900 per month (or A$1800 over two months where the person is under 18 years of age) were allowed, with the employer's agreement, to choose to receive wages or salary in lieu of employer SG contributions. (Those with earnings below A$450 per month were already exempt.)

The government also introduced legislation in 1997 to give employees greater choice of funds or RSAs into which compulsory contributions could be made. It was argued that this measure would lead to improved returns and lower administration charges, and give employees greater control over their superannuation. However, this legislation was blocked in the upper house (the Senate) and has not yet been implemented.

By June 2002, there were more than 240 000 superannuation funds with assets totalling around A$520 billion. However, some 98 per cent of all member accounts are held in approximately 8000 funds, and nearly two-thirds of assets are in 100 funds. Currently, 86 per cent of fund members belong to a defined contribution fund, while 14 per cent belong to a defined benefit or a hybrid fund.

Superannuation funds operate as trusts with trustees solely responsible for the prudential operation of their funds and for formulating and implementing investment strategies. Duties and obligations are codified and trustees are liable under civil and criminal law for breaches of obligations. Superannuation funds face few investment restrictions. The main exceptions are a ceiling of 5 per cent of assets in in-house investments, and there is a 'no borrowing' rule. Apart from this, there are no asset requirements or floors, no minimum rate of return requirements, nor a government guarantee of benefits. As a result, funds tend to invest in a wide variety of assets with a mix of duration and risk/return characteristics.

Table 3.2 summarizes data on developments in superannuation. Coverage of the workforce has increased substantially, from around 40 per cent in the mid-1980s to 91 per cent of all public and private sector employees in 1998. Most employees with no superannuation fall below the income threshold for the Superannuation Guarantee. However, only 36 per cent of employers and the self-employed were covered, giving a coverage rate across all workers of 81 per cent.

Coverage is below average in retail trade, agriculture, cultural and recreational services, accommodation, cafes and restaurants, and personal and other services. These industries tend to have lower wages and significant numbers of part-time employees and juniors. Those with higher coverage include utilities, mining, finance and insurance, and communication services. These sectors are characterized by both full-time employment and high unionization (utilities and mining) or by high wages and greater familiarity with the benefits of superannuation (finance, insurance and communication).

Superannuation assets increased from only 3 per cent of GDP in 1972, to 19 per cent in the early 1980s, and around 75 per cent by 2002. Government estimates suggest that, by 2020, fund assets could approach 120 per cent of GDP (Tinnion and Rothman, 1999). Assets of superannuation funds increased at an average annual rate of 12.5 per cent in the 1990s (and by over 20 per cent over 1996–7, and again in 1999–2000). This rapid growth was partly attributable to high earnings rates. For example, total superannuation assets grew by 16.6 per cent in the year to December 1999,

Table 3.2 Developments in superannuation, 1983 to 2003

Year	Benefits ($ million) Pensions	Benefits ($ million) Lump sums	Contributions ($ million) Member	Contributions ($ million) Employer	Assets ($ billion)	Assets (% of GDP)	Net investment income ($million)	Operating expenses ($ million)	Members (000)	Number of funds (000)	Coverage (%) Employees	Tax concessions ($m)
1983	–	–	–	–	32	19	–	–	–	n.a.	–	2 180
1984	–	–	–	–	36	19	–	–	–	n.a.	–	2 370
1985	–	–	–	–	40	19	–	–	–	66	39	2 610
1986	–	–	–	–	51	21	–	–	–	54	39	2 970
1987	–	–	–	–	73	28	–	–	–	127	42	3 230
1988	–	–	–	–	95	29	–	–	–	122	42	3 715
1989	–	–	–	–	108	30	–	–	–	105	48	3 825
1990	–	–	–	–	124	33	–	–	–	87	53	3 615
1991	–	–	–	–	135	37	–	–	–	73	72	4 455
1992	–	–	–	–	165	41	–	–	–	74	80	4 765
1993	–	–	–	–	183	43	–	–	–	81	87	5 780
1994	–	–	–	–	203	45	–	–	–	88	87	7 665
1995	–	–	–	–	228	48	–	–	15 471	105	90	5 770
1996	1 026	3 359	2 411	5 617	260	54	3 854	465	16 335	131	–	8 315
1997	3 977	14 534	10 156	19 122	320	62	32 525	2 052	17 240	153	–	8 650
1998	4 530	17 624	13 766	21 643	358	64	22 572	2 192	18 230	178	91	9 920
1999	4 988	18 706	17 759	30 378	406	69	25 264	2 505	19 720	198	–	9 510
2000	5 095	21 959	20 362	25 961	490	78	39 563	3 276	21 880	214	(88)	10 210
2001	6 458	23 734	22 989	27 683	527	79	20 795	3 581	23 238	226	–	9 065
2002	6 980	25 748	21 658	29 917	520	75	–9 857	4 032	24 278	243	–	9 770
2003	7 273	27 661	16 800	33 583	508	–	–15 707	4 112	25 479	260	–	–

Note: Figures for contributions and benefits and income and expenses for 1995–6 refer only to the June quarter of that year. Corresponding figures for 2003 are extrapolated from the first three quarters of the year.

Source: Australian Prudential Regulatory Authority, Superannuation Trends, 2001; Insurance and Superannuation Commission Bulletin, Insurance and Superannuation Commission, Canberra, various years; Department of the Treasury, *Tax Expenditures Statement*, various years; Bateman and Piggott, 2000.

and of this 78 per cent was provided by net earnings. Total assets fell in 2002 and 2003, as a result of the stock market slump.

Between 1990 and 2002, the earnings rate on assets provided average annual real rates of return of over 8 per cent. Movements in share markets were a major influence on these earning rates, with around half of all super-annuation fund assets invested in Australian and overseas equities. In March 2003, 44 per cent of assets were held in equities and units in trusts, 17 per cent in interest-bearing securities, 18 per cent overseas, 8 per cent in cash and deposits, 4 per cent in loans and placements, and 6 per cent in direct property.

Gross contribution rates to funds have risen rapidly. In 1998–9, 58 per cent of employer contributions were made under the Superannuation Guarantee. Mandated employer contributions have meant that contribu-tions are now more than double the level of the early 1980s. Contributions were A$51.6 billion in 2001–2002, then some 13 per cent of GDP. The main factors behind this growth were the increase in the contribution rates, plus increased employment and wage growth over the period.

In 2002, more than A$32 billion in benefits were paid out, which is nearly twice as great as combined public spending on age and service pensions. However, more than three-quarters of benefits were paid as lump sums, and nearly three-quarters of these are from private sector schemes. The public sector employs just under 20 per cent of all wage and salary earners, but public sector schemes pay out about one-third of all benefits and nearly 60 per cent of superannuation pensions.

The taxation treatment of superannuation is both complex and contro-versial. Taxation applies at all three possible stages – contributions, fund earnings and benefits (and benefits can also reduce the level of public pension received). However, the income of complying funds (which includes earnings, employer contributions and deductible member contri-butions) is generally subject to concessional taxation at a rate of 15 per cent, compared to the standard tax rate of 30 per cent, and the highest mar-ginal rate of 47 per cent. In addition, a superannuation surcharge of up to 15 per cent applies to employer and deductible member superannuation contributions of higher-income earners where their taxable income plus total tax-deductible superannuation contributions is greater than specified thresholds (A$81 493 in 2000–2001). Superannuation pensions and lump sums (within specified thresholds) are also subject to concessional taxation. Additional voluntary contributions (up to a prescribed reasonable benefit limit) also receive concessional treatment. In 2001–2002, tax expenditures on superannuation were estimated at some A$9.8 billion (Treasury, 2002), although there is considerable debate about the valuation of these conces-sions.

DEMOGRAPHIC PROSPECTS, FISCAL PRESSURES AND NATIONAL SAVINGS

Concerns about population aging have influenced the reforms adopted in Australia, even though, by European standards, Australia appears to have very modest expenditure on public pensions. The age pension is the largest income support programme in Australia. Total outlays in 1998–9 were roughly 2.4 per cent of GDP, and about one-third of total social security outlays, which are themselves the largest spending programme of the Commonwealth Government. Pensions for veterans cost a further 0.8 per cent of GDP. Consequently, increased spending on pensions is of considerable economic significance.

Nevertheless, Australian spending on retirement pensions is only just over half the OECD average. In part this reflects Australia's relatively young age structure. Standardizing for age structure increases Australian spending on the aged from half to two-thirds of the OECD mean. But even on this basis, only Ireland, Korea, Mexico and Turkey spend less on age pensions than Australia.

Like other developed countries, Australia is experiencing a process of demographic aging, associated with increases in life expectancy and past reductions in fertility rates. In addition, rates of income support receipt rise rapidly after age 50. Population aging will result in higher proportions of the population being over pension age, and also and more immediately, higher proportions in the 'mature age' bracket where rates of other benefits are high.

The proportion of the population over 65 is projected to increase slowly over the next decade, not reaching 15 per cent until 2009, but then is expected to rise more rapidly. In absolute terms, the projected population 65 and over will increase by 29 per cent between 1997 and 2010. Thereafter, it is estimated that those aged 65 years and over will rise to about 23 per cent of the total population by 2051, compared to around 12 per cent currently.

A number of concurrent demographic and social changes have the potential to affect the sustainability of the retirement income system. These include sustained levels of high unemployment, a trend to early retirement, and a high proportion of people (mostly women, but increasingly men) experiencing broken work patterns or low incomes during their working lives. On the other hand, the increased labour force participation of women has increased the ability of many to accumulate some retirement savings

Expenditure on age and service pensions is projected to rise to 4.7 per cent of GDP in 2050 after taking into account reduced pension outlays resulting from superannuation savings accumulated under SG arrangements. Without the SG, pension outlays are estimated to increase by a further 0.3 per cent of GDP in 2050. The Guarantee will not substantially reduce the proportion of older people receiving a pension, but with the increase in private income over the free area the average rate of payment will fall. It can be noted that at the same time higher proportions of the older population will be directly exposed to the high effective tax rates caused by income testing.

Concerns about national savings rates have also influenced the reform process. Successive governments have taken the view that, to achieve higher levels of sustainable economic growth, Australia must increase domestic savings and reduce reliance on borrowing from overseas. The development of superannuation funds has been one part of this strategy, one that appears to be successful given the growth in assets described earlier. It is estimated that the reformed superannuation arrangements and the schedule of increasing SG contribution rates will have a positive impact on national savings of 1.5 per cent of GDP in 2001–2002, rising to 3.6 per cent of GDP in 2019–20 (Costello and Newman, 1997, pp.9–10).

Both political groupings also have had a broad commitment to a strategy of maintaining underlying fiscal balance, on average over the course of the economic cycle. Labour was more successful in this in the 1980s than in the 1990s. The Coalition government, in particular, undertook significant fiscal consolidation measures in the 1996–7 and 1997–8 Budgets. Australia now has one of the lowest levels of gross government debt in the OECD: 26.9 per cent of GDP in 2001 compared to an OECD average of 70.5 per cent of GDP.

It can be noted that the modest level of pension spending in Australia does not necessarily mean that even relatively small increases in spending are easy. Future government health spending is also likely to increase significantly, and Australian spending on health is already around the OECD average. The difficulty facing Australian governments is that there are no social security contributions and, until 2000, there was no broad-based consumption tax, and even now this is at a comparatively low level. Increased spending therefore is likely to imply higher direct income taxes. While total tax revenue in Australia is 20 per cent below the OECD average, income taxes as a percentage of GDP are about 30 per cent above the OECD average. The income tax structure is also very progressive, making it difficult to raise revenues further without exacerbating problems of avoidance or evasion. Alternatively, across-the-board income tax increases are likely to be politically unpopular.

ADEQUACY OF PAYMENTS AND INTERNATIONAL COMPARISONS OF LIVING STANDARDS

A longstanding area of concern with Australian retirement income arrangements relates to the adequacy of payments. This is not surprising

given that the public transfer system is selective, and is apparently dominated by the objective of reducing poverty, rather than providing income
replacement for the majority of the population.

While Australia operates what is almost certainly the most targeted
public pension system in the developed world, it is not a 'residual' system
restricted only to the very poor. What is most distinctive about Australia is
the very low share of transfers received by the richest income groups. As
noted earlier, the Australian system is closer to a 'citizen's pension' or a
demogrant than a social assistance scheme, with benefits being reduced for
the well-off, rather than only restricted to the very poor.

Nevertheless, the level of pensions certainly appears low in terms of
replacement rates. However, this is not a fully accurate picture of the generosity of the Australian system, for a range of reasons. The details of this
argument are set out in Whiteford and Kennedy (1995) and Whiteford and
Bond (2000). Put briefly, comparisons of replacement rates can be misleading, when countries differ in the ways they finance benefits, particularly in
the use of employer social security contributions. Further, comparisons of
income distributions in countries that differ in the way they finance benefits may not be comparing like with like. In fact, when the purchasing
power of benefits is compared, rather than their replacement rates, the
Australian public pension system proves to be significantly more generous
to the poor than the OECD average (Whiteford, 1995).

Whiteford and Kennedy (1995) found that the Australian distribution of
pensioners' disposable incomes was more compressed than that of any
other of 11 OECD countries. More than 30 per cent of the older Australian
population fell between 40 and 60 per cent of average income, compared
to around 20 per cent in other countries with basically flat-rate pensions,
and under 15 per cent in the continental European welfare states and the
United States. Johnson (1998) also found that Australia had the highest
concentration of older people in the third and fourth income deciles of
seven countries.

Moreover, the mix of resources of older Australians differs in significant
ways from other countries. Disney *et al.* (1998) estimate that at age 67 the
financial wealth to income ratio in Australia is between 5 and 6.2 (for
couples and singles, respectively) compared to ratios of 1.3 to 1.4 in the
United Kingdom, and even lower ratios in Germany, the Netherlands and
Sweden. If financial wealth were converted to an annuity it would raise the
incomes of older Australians by between 14 and 18 per cent. In the United
Kingdom, Sweden, the Netherlands and Germany, the effect of annuitization would be to raise incomes by less than 4 per cent.[4]

Again, housing wealth is both more significant and more equally distributed in Australia than in many other countries. Around 80 per cent of the

poorest 20 per cent of older people in Australia are owner-occupiers, compared to 54 per cent in the UK, 44 per cent in the Netherlands and 37 per cent in Germany. One estimate is that imputed income from housing is equal to 27 per cent of cash disposable income for older people in Australia, compared to about 10 per cent in the United Kingdom and Germany (Whiteford and Kennedy, 1995).

The means test reinforces the Australian bias towards home ownership. Owner-occupied homes, no matter their value, are exempted from the assets test (and from capital gains tax). The income test leverages imputed income from housing by a factor between 2 and 2.5. That is, given the effects of the income test and income tax, a pensioner who rents, and with other income over the free area, would need an income from other sources of $250 a week for each $100 of net imputed income they could receive from home ownership.

Overall, the Australian situation is one where older people have relatively low incomes compared to the population average, but very much higher levels of financial and housing wealth. This, plus the concentration of people around statutory pension levels, suggests that there has been a very strong behavioural response to the incentive structure implied by a flat-rate and means-tested system. This does not mean that older Australians have impoverished themselves in order to qualify for pensions. What appears to have happened is that older Australians have structured their package of resources in retirement in order to maximize the combination of private income and entitlements to public pensions, while keeping their wealth intact as far as possible.

CONCLUSIONS

It is apparent that the motivations for reform of retirement income arrangements in Australia differ significantly from those in many other countries. The introduction of a mandatory second pillar preceded the publication of the World Bank report, *Averting the Old Age Crisis* (1994). If anything, Australian experience may have influenced that report, rather than the reverse. But, unlike the other well-known example of early reform – Chile – and also unlike a number of subsequent reformers, it is difficult to say that the Australian pension system was in crisis in any significant way, or even unsustainable in the long run. The one area where there could be argued to be an important underlying problem is in relation to national savings. Overall, the major motivations for reform were to improve future retirement incomes, to contribute to macroeconomic management of wages growth, and to increase national savings.

It also seems reasonable to argue that, even in the area of improving the adequacy of future retirement incomes, the need for this was not so great as in the United Kingdom, for example. In addition, because there was no immediate crisis of funding, and because the introduction of employer contributions was initially financed by explicitly forgone wage increases, there were no significant transitional financing problems, as there may be in other countries. In summary, the Australian reform appears to have been relatively successful precisely because reform was not essential.

One should not be over sanguine, however. An assessment of the Australian reform experience might conclude 'so far, so good'. To date, the introduction of the second pillar has not run into any major problems. There have been no significant scandals (as in the United Kingdom).[5] Assets have grown rapidly, and earnings have maintained fairly high levels of real growth, albeit fluctuating at times. However, the system is still in the accumulation phase, and people will not be receiving the benefits of mandatory superannuation for many years to come. Any problems are much more likely to become obvious when the system is mature.

Nevertheless, the first pillar public age pension is likely still to be able to provide a modestly adequate basic income even when the second pillar is mature. The nature of the income test also means that the public pension system can partly compensate for adverse market outcomes for individuals quite high up the income distribution. It is also interesting to note that the introduction of a funded second pillar has not (yet?) been used as a reason for reducing the generosity of the first pillar. If anything, the first pillar has become more generous, now being legislatively linked to average earnings and with a lower withdrawal rate.

This assessment does not mean that there are not many significant issues to be resolved, or that it will be easy to resolve these issues. For example, there are claims that the 9 per cent employer contribution is insufficient to guarantee an adequate income in retirement. The current government is not disposed to increase employer contributions, arguing that this would reduce employment growth. This may be more true now than in the past, as changes to workplace relations policies towards a more decentralized system mean that it is not possible to engineer a reduction in wage claims to finance this, as was the case under the Accord.

The earlier discussion of pensioner living standards suggests that there may well be important future issues in relation to the way superannuation benefits are paid. Annuities are an extremely small component of the total market at present (Knox, 2000). There is an obvious policy interest in encouraging income streams or annuities, when the first pillar is income-tested. Given the Australian predilection for lump sums, it may be politically difficult to achieve such a shift. Moreover, mandatory purchase of annuities is an unpopular policy in a number of countries. There are also arguments that individuals should have the choice of how they structure their resources in retirement, so long as they do not arrange their affairs simply to maximize government support.

A further area of continuing controversy relates to the tax treatment of superannuation, with welfare lobby groups arguing that it is overgenerous and industry lobby groups arguing that it is punitive. Whichever perspective one takes, it is difficult to escape the conclusion that current arrangements are extremely complex and appear motivated mainly by concerns with current revenue.

There is also debate about the administrative costs of the second pillar. Ingles (2000) noted that, while the system has provided high real rates of return, administrative and investment costs were about 1.3 per cent of assets, which is equivalent to a tax of 19 per cent on real income earned. Subsequent estimates by Bateman (2001) were of costs of 1.7 per cent of assets. Bateman's estimates are criticized by Clare (2001), who estimates average costs at 1.3 per cent of assets, with the bulk of members in funds with cost ratios below 1 per cent. All of these papers canvass a range of measures to reduce operating costs, which, as Ingles (2000) points out, could raise benefits by up to a quarter.

A final issue relates to the continuing tension between universality and selectivity in public pension provision. Earlier discussion has made it clear that the balance between these two approaches has swung over time, although the recent reduction in the withdrawal rate has moved towards reduced selectivity. This is also linked to proposals for the abolition of superannuation tax concessions to finance a universal pension. The difficulty with this is of course that the immediate beneficiaries of universality would be current high-income retirees, while those who pay would be current workers, including some with low incomes. Universality might reduce some of the incentive problems that appear to be associated with current means-testing arrangements, with positive implications for economic efficiency. On the other hand, it is difficult to see that a universal pension could be maintained as generously in the long run as are current arrangements.

Any policy change is possible, of course, as shown by the many reforms and reverses that governments have introduced over recent decades. The public system can be changed relatively easily, precisely because it is non-contributory. It is quite common in Australia for people to argue that they have paid taxes all their lives and are entitled to a pension. But the force of this argument is certainly not as strong as in an explicitly contributory system, and is also undercut by the even more common argument that benefits should go to those 'most in need'. In a sense, this suggests that

Australian public pension arrangements are particularly susceptible to political risks. But one person's political risks are another's fiscal flexibility. These continuing tensions are unavoidable, and seem likely to be a feature of Australian retirement income arrangements in the foreseeable future.

NOTES

1. The views expressed here are my own and should not be taken to represent those of either the OECD or the Department of Family and Community Services. I am grateful for comments received from David Stanton. A significant number of sources of information on the Australian system are available online. Papers and statistics on the public pension system can be found at http://www.facs.gov.au/ and at http://www.dva.gov.au/. The Australian Prudential Regulation Authority has statistics on the private superannuation system at http://www.apra.gov.au/. Details of the Commonwealth public servants' scheme are at http://www.comsuper.gov.au/. Papers from the Retirement Income Modelling Taskforce can be found by following links from http://www.treasury.gov.au/. Some government inquiries into superannuation can be found at http://www.aph.gov.au/senate/committee/super_ctte/. The Association of Superannuation funds, an industry grouping, is at http://www.superannuation.asn.au/home/rpm.cfm?page=main. The Centre for Pensions and Superannuation is at http://www.economics.unsw.edu.au/. Papers from the Centre for Actuarial Studies at the University of Melbourne can be found at http://www.economics.unimelb.edu.au/actwww/wps1994.html. Useful papers by Ingles and related links can be found at http://www.anu.edu.au/pubpol/Discussion%20Papers/dp_77.htm.
2. For a more detailed history of developments, see Kewley (1973) and Unikoski (1989).
3. Since the late 1980s, there have been substantial changes in industrial relations, including a shift in the level at which bargaining takes place, towards a hybrid system that emphasizes agreements at the enterprise and workplace level. Trade union membership declined from around 50 per cent of the workforce in 1976 to 25 per cent in 2000, concentrated in a small number of large industry and multi-industry unions. Under the 1997 Workplace Relations Act, for the first time, agreements could be struck directly between employers and workers, without union intervention if desired, and would be recognized as legally binding before the Industrial Relations Commission.
4. The poorest income quintile of older people in Australia have liquid assets equivalent to more than two years of disposable income, compared to the poorest quintile in the Netherlands, for example, whose liquid assets are estimated to approximate one week's worth of income (Whiteford and Kennedy, 1995, p.80).
5. In 2001, a large health insurance company, supervised by the same regulatory authority as supervises superannuation, did collapse. This is currently the subject of a Royal Commission, which is also investigating the role of the auditor (Andersen). However, as pointed out by APRA (http://www.apra.gov.au/speeches/The-Challenges-of-Regulating-Superannuation.cfm), the combined losses over the past year from the failure of HIH and the handful of superannuation funds involved is in the order of less than half a per cent of total financial sector assets. The combined losses from failures over the past decade would be unlikely to bring the total to much more than 1 per cent.

REFERENCES

Aaron, H. (1992), 'The economics and politics of pensions: evaluating the choices', in *Private Pensions and Public Policy*, Paris: OECD.

Bateman, H. (2001), 'Disclosure of Superannuation Fees and Charges', paper prepared for the Australian Institute of Trustees, Melbourne.

Bateman, H. and Piggott, J. (2000), 'Australia's Mandatory Retirement Saving Policy: A View from the New Millennium', Research Paper no. 19, Retirement Economics Group, University of New South Wales, Sydney.

Borowski, A., Schulz, J. and Whiteford, P. (1986), 'Providing adequate retirement income: What role occupational superannuation?', *Australian Journal on Ageing*, 6(1), February.

Clare, R. (2001), 'Are administration and investment costs in the Australian superannuation industry too high?', ASFA Research Centre, Sydney.

Costello, P. and Newman, J. (1997), *Savings: Choice and Incentive*, Statement by the Treasurer and Minister for Social Security, Canberra: Australian Government Publishing Service, 13 May.

Dawkins, J. (1992), *Security in Retirement: Planning for Tomorrow Today*, Statement by the Treasurer, Canberra: Australian Government Publishing Service, 30 June.

Disney, R., Mira d'Ercole, M. and Scherer, P. (1998), 'Resources During Retirement', Ageing Working Paper, no. 4.3, OECD, Paris.

Ingles, D. (2000), 'Reducing Administrative Costs in the Australian Superannuation System', Discussion Paper no. 77, Public Policy Program, Australian National University, Canberra.

Johnson, P. (1998), 'Older Getting Wiser', Institute of Chartered Accountants, Sydney.

Kewley, T.H. (1973), *Social Security in Australia 1900–72*, Sydney: Sydney University Press.

Knox, D. (2000), 'The Australian Annuity Market', Policy Research Working Paper No. 2495, Development Research Group, World Bank, Washington, DC.

Neild, J.C. (1898), *Report on Old Age Pensions, Charitable Relief and State Insurance in England and on the Continent of Europe*, Sydney: Government Printer.

Newman, J. (Minister for Social Security) (1997), 'The Government's Vision for Retired Australians', ASFA Annual Conference, 30 October.

Tinnion, J. and Rothman, G. (1999), 'Retirement Income Adequacy and the emerging Superannuation System – New Estimates', Retirement Income Modeling Unit, Department of the Treasury, paper presented to the 7th Colloquium of Superannuation Researchers, University of Melbourne.

Unikoski, I. (1989), 'Veterans of Labour, Veterans of War', Policy Research Paper no. 44, Department of Social Security, Canberra, January.

Whiteford, P. (1995), 'The Use of Replacement Rates in International Comparisons of Benefit Systems', *International Social Security Review*, 48 (2/95), 3–30.

Whiteford P. and Bond, K. (2000), 'Trends in the incomes and living standards of older people in Australia', Policy Research Paper no. 6, Department of Family and Community Services, Canberra.

Whiteford, P. and Kennedy, S. (1995*), Incomes and Living Standards of Older People: A Comparative Analysis*, UK Department of Social Security, Research Report no. 34, London: HMSO.

Willis, R. (1995), *Saving for Our Future*, Statement by the Treasurer, Canberra: Australian Government Publishing Service, 9 May.

World Bank (1994), *Averting the Old Age Crisis: Policies to Protect the Old and Promote Growth*, Oxford: Oxford University Press.

4. The institutionalization of the Swiss multi-pillar pension system

Giuliano Bonoli

INTRODUCTION

Amidst worldwide concern over the 'demographic time bomb' and heated debates on 'pension crises' and pension reforms, Switzerland stands out, with a few other industrial countries, as one whose pension system is unlikely to experience major disruption as a result of population aging. Its three-pillar pension system, which comprises a pay-as-you-go universal basic pension, a tier of fully funded compulsory occupational pensions and fiscal incentives to buy personal pensions, seems particularly well suited to withstand demographic pressures while at the same time guaranteeing reasonable pension coverage on a universal basis.

This positive assessment of the Swiss approach to old age income security is found in the international literature on pensions. Switzerland's multi-pillar pension system closely resembles the ideal type put forward by international agencies such as the World Bank (for example, 1994). Moreover, in projections of public pension expenditure, Switzerland stands out for a comparatively low expected increase in the proportion of GDP that will be needed to finance retirement in 20–30 years (Bonoli 2000, p.18). Finally, an extremely positive view of the Swiss system is also found in what is probably the most comprehensive study on Swiss pensions carried out by international observers, which goes as far as suggesting that the system may be seen as the 'triumph of common sense' (Queisser and Vittas, 2000).

Such favourable evaluations of the Swiss pension system may come as a surprise to those who know well Swiss political institutions and the hurdles that policies need to clear before they are adopted. Switzerland has one of the most fragmented political systems among democratic countries, characterized by the sharing of power among a large number of actors, both on a formal and on an informal basis. Switzerland is a federal country, it has a bicameral parliament, a fairly strict separation of powers between the executive and the legislative branches of government and, most notably, it allows legislation to be initiated and challenged directly by voters through referendums. Its political system, in order to function properly, requires extensive agreement, generally achieved through encompassing compromises and negotiation.

The result is that rational and goal-oriented policy making is often difficult. Typically, legislation that gets adopted contains many elements, not necessarily consistent with one another, but that respond to the requests made by the individual actors involved in the policy-making process. This system allows the integration into decision making of the many minorities that make up the country (see, for example, Lehmbruch, 1993). Its key casualties, however, are coherence, speed and innovation in legislation. Viable compromises tend to deviate as little as possible from the status quo, but still need lengthy negotiations. Yet, with regard to the establishment of a comprehensive pension system, an issue that in other European countries proved to be one of the most intractable political problems of the 1960s and 1970s, the Swiss political system did remarkably well.

This chapter provides an account of the way in which, notwithstanding institutional fragmentation, veto points and forced compromises, Swiss legislators were able build what is today regarded as one of the best pension systems in the world. Ironically, the key independent variable in this story of policy making is the Swiss political system itself, which has forced actors to compromise and adopt moderate solutions, from the point of view both of responding to social needs and of financial affordability. If given more power, any of the actors involved would probably have chosen a different solution, either more costly or less able to provide adequate pension coverage on a universal basis. Pressure to compromise was instrumental in developing a system that turns out to be suitable in the current context.

The chapter is structured in the following way. It starts with a brief presentation of some key elements of the Swiss political system, paying special attention to those that played an important role in the setting up of the current pension system. Next comes a presentation of the current pension system's key features. The third section provides a historical account of the way this system developed, and the last one focuses on key current issues.

MAKING POLICY IN SWITZERLAND

The Swiss political system contains many features that are rather unusual by international standards and that tend to result in a substantial degree of power fragmentation and generate a high number of veto points in the law-making process (Immergut, 1992).[1] These features are both formal, like written constitutional rules, and informal, such as amicable agreements among key parties, and tend to support each other in generating inclusive-but-slow decision-making procedures (Lane, 2001). Among the key institutions of Switzerland, a few are worth mentioning because of the impact they have on policy making, and because of the role they played in the decision to make occupational pensions mandatory.[2]

First, the government (Federal Council) is a collegial institution. This means that, unlike the situation in other democracies, there is no single individual head of government or head of state,[3] these two functions being fulfilled jointly by the seven members of the Federal Council. Decisions within the Federal Council are taken through majority voting, and individual ministers are expected to conform to the majority view, regardless of their initial opinion. The party composition of the Federal Council has remained unchanged since 1959, and consists of two Free-Democrats, two Christian-Democrats, two Socialists and one member of the Swiss People's party (a former farmer party). The Federal Council, because of its politically encompassing character and because of the need to speak with one voice, is a typical locus of compromise seeking and consensual policy making.

Second, Switzerland has a symmetric bicameral parliament: every piece of legislation needs to be accepted by each chamber. The upper chamber, the Council of States, represents the member states of the confederation, or cantons. Each canton, irrespective of its size, has two members in the Council of States, elected through majority voting. In contrast, in the lower chamber, the National Council, cantons have a number of MPs which is proportional to the size of their population, and elections are fought with a proportional representation system. Because the two chambers are elected with different systems, their political orientation can be different. Typically, in the Council of States, the larger right-of-centre parties are overrepresented, giving way to a more conservative political orientation.

Third, the Swiss constitutional order is characterized by a relatively strict separation of powers between the government and parliament. Members of the federal government are elected by parliament for a four-year term. During this period of time, however, parliament cannot bring down a government, nor can the executive dissolve parliament. The result is a lack of governmental control over parliament, as the executive lacks the key instruments that in parliamentary democracies allow it to secure the vote of parliamentarians belonging to the same party coalition. This means that the executive has comparatively little control over decisions taken by parliament. As a matter of fact, party discipline among Swiss MPs is nowhere near that observed in Europe's parliamentary democracies (Kriesi, 2001, p.62).

Finally, and probably most importantly, the Swiss constitution makes provision for various types of referendums (Kobach, 1993). Constitutional change as well as accession to supranational organizations are automatically subjected to a referendum. Constitutional change can also be put forward by voters by means of a 'popular initiative', if they are able to back their proposal with 100 000 signatures. The vast majority of popular initiatives are rejected by voters (about 90 per cent), but they can still have a substantial indirect effect on policy (Papadopoulos, 2001, p.44). First, popular initiatives put on the national political agenda issues that would otherwise remain marginal, thereby generating debate, and opening new opportunities for coalition building. Second, initiatives can also push the government to take pre-emptive action to dissuade voters from backing radical proposals, by putting forward a more moderate alternative. Referendums can also intervene at the end of the law-making process, as voters can challenge at the polls any Act passed by parliament, if they are able to produce 50 000 signatures to that effect.

This set of political institutions has had a fundamental impact on the policy-making process. Because of the high degree of power fragmentation it generates, a large number of actors have the opportunity to veto the adoption of legislation they regard as unsatisfactory. As a result, Swiss authorities have traditionally dealt with institutionally induced power fragmentation by developing all-inclusive policy-making procedures. First, the governing coalition has been gradually expanded over the twentieth century, to include the country's four largest parties that currently account for over 80 per cent of all votes. Second, it has developed consensus-building instruments such as the so-called 'expert commissions', where organized interests are represented, or highly structured consultation procedures, which allow the government to 'test' the political feasibility of given policy options. Typically, legislation is presented in parliament after going through expert commissions and consultation procedures, so that substantial backing from political parties and relevant interests is ensured.

Notwithstanding these inclusion-based strategies, the policy-making process contains a substantial element of unpredictability. Carefully crafted compromises can be overhauled by parliament, or simply rejected by voters. What is more, unpredictability seems to be on the increase. While in the 1950s and 1960s the compromises drafted jointly by the relevant interest groups were generally accepted by parliament, in more recent years, legislators have played a much more active role in shaping policies. This has been particularly the case in pension policy, including the preparation of the law that made occupational pension coverage compulsory.

THE SWISS PENSION SYSTEM TODAY

The Swiss pension system is best described as a three-pillar system, where each pillar caters for a distinct level of provision. The first pillar (AVS –

Assurance Vieillesse et Survivants) covers the basic needs of retirees. It is moderately earnings-related and includes a means-tested pension supplement. The second pillar has the task of providing retirees with a standard of living close to the one they experienced while in work and consists of mandatory occupational pensions. Finally, the third pillar allows people to tailor pension coverage to their individual needs through non-compulsory personal pensions supported by tax concessions. The functional division between three levels of pension provision is upheld by the federal constitution, and it is widely regarded as an important constraint with regard to policy change in the area of pensions.

The first pillar was introduced in 1948, and has been reformed several times in the postwar years. It provides universal coverage and a fair degree of vertical redistribution, due to a compressed benefit structure: the highest pension is worth only twice as much as the lowest one. Contributions, in contrast, are proportional to earnings without a ceiling. Even though its benefits are moderately earnings-related, the Swiss basic pension is a scheme of Beveridgean inspiration, geared towards poverty prevention rather then income maintenance. As a matter of fact, in international comparisons, AVS is often considered as a flat-rate pension scheme (for example, Schmähl, 1991, p.48). As far as financing is concerned, the AVS works on a pay-as-you-go basis, but has accumulated funds equal to roughly one year of outlays. It is financed through contributions (4.2 per cent of salary each for employees and employers; up to 7.8 per cent for the self-employed) and receives a subsidy equal to 19 per cent of expenditures.[4] Coverage is universal: those who are not working (for example, students) are required to pay flat-rate contributions or, if providing informal care, are entitled to contribution credits. Unemployed people pay contributions on their unemployment benefit, which is treated as a salary (the unemployment insurance fund contributing on their behalf 4.2 per cent of the unemployment benefit). As in Bismarckian systems, AVS has its own separate budget. The social partners do take part in the management of the scheme by running some branch funds. The central fund, however, is managed by the federal administration.

The second pillar, occupational pensions were first granted tax concessions in 1916.[5] They developed substantially throughout the twentieth century, but coverage remained patchy. In 1970, some 50 per cent of employees were covered by an occupational pension. For women, the proportion was a much lower 25 per cent. Since 1985, however, occupational pension coverage has been compulsory for all employees earning at least twice the amount of the minimum basic pension (just over CHF24000 per annum, or about 35 per cent of average earnings). Today, the rate of coverage approximates 100 per cent for male employees, but reaches only 80 per cent in the case of women (OFAS, 1995, p.10). Benefits vary according to the type of pension fund, though the law prescribes minimum requirements. As far as financing is concerned, occupational pensions are funded schemes. They are financed by employer/employee contributions, the former contributing at least as much as the latter.

When compulsory occupational pensions were introduced, many employees were already covered by voluntary arrangements of this kind. Just before the coming into force of the new law in 1985, some 80 per cent of all employees already had access to occupational pension coverage, though for a quarter of them the level of provision was lower than the compulsory minimum (Conseil Fédéral, 2000b, p.6). The situation was such that legislation needed to take into account the existence of a relatively developed system of occupational pension provision. As a result, it was decided to introduce a compulsory minimum level of provision (known as the *Obligatorium*) which is calculated on the basis of notional contributions,[6] leaving relatively wide room for manoeuvre to existing pension funds regarding how to deliver and finance that minimum level of provision. Many pension funds (especially in the public sector, or those sponsored by large employers) still offer better conditions than the *Obligatorium* (Vontobel 2000).

The objective of the new law was a replacement rate of 60 per cent of gross earnings up to a ceiling equal to three times the maximum AVS benefit. For low-paid workers, this goal could be achieved by the moderately earnings-related benefits provided by AVS. As a result, insured earnings are those comprised between the lower limit (CHF24000) and the ceiling (CHF72000). Minimum compulsory benefits are calculated on the basis of notional contributions. Depending on the employee's sex and age, individual accounts must be credited with a percentage of insured earnings, ranging from 7 to 18 per cent (Table 4.1). Pension funds are free to finance the set amount as they wish, with the proviso that contributions must at least be equally split between workers and employers (the latter can contribute more than half of the contribution bill, if they so wish). For instance, a pension fund could decide to apply an age-neutral contribution rate of 12.5 per cent, or alternatively to charge employees on the basis of their age, thus reflecting the pre-set notional contributions.[7] Because notional contribution rates are age-related, pension funds with an unfavourable demographic structure are disadvantaged. As a result, it was decided to introduce a demographic compensation mechanism whereby funds with more young employees subsidize those with a less favourable risk structure. De facto, because of the way notional contributions are calculated and financed, the system is not purely funded but includes some intergenerational redistribution, or a pay-as-you-go (PAYG) element. The rationale for this was to guarantee adequate coverage to workers who were already in employment before the 1985 law came into force, and thus were not going to have a full contribution record. In theory, this pay-as-you-go element should disappear once (and if) every worker spends her whole working life in the system.

Table 4.1   Notional contribution rates for mandatory occupational pensions (percentage of insured earnings)

Men		Women	
Age	Rate	Age	Rate
25–34	7	25–31	7
35–44	10	32–41	10
45–54	15	42–51	15
55 -64	18	52–62	18

Source: Loi fédérale sur la prévoyance professionnelle, 1982.

Besides notional contributions, the occupational pension law also prescribes a minimum nominal interest rate of 4 per cent per year that must be credited to individual accounts. As a result, even though the system is technically of the defined (notional) contribution kind, it de facto includes a defined benefit minimum level, based on career earnings, of approximately 36 per cent of relevant earnings (the actual amount depends on how earnings increase throughout the working life of an individual).

When a worker reaches retirement age, or decides to take early retirement (possible from the age of 60, but with an actuarially determined benefit reduction), the capital resulting from the notional contribution credited and the compound interest of 4 per cent (or more) is converted into a pension, on the basis of a conversion rate set by the government (currently 7.2 per cent). The rate is used to convert the capital into an annual pension. There is no annuity market for (compulsory) occupational pensions, as the price of annuities is de facto determined by the government in the shape of the conversion rate, which does not take into account sex-based differences in life expectancy.[8] A large number of pension scheme members enjoy more favourable conditions than those guaranteed by the occupational pensions law. In 1996, about 29 per cent of insured persons were covered by standard defined-benefit plans, though the figure was down from 33 per cent in 1994 (OFS, 1999).

The third pillar of the pension system, private provision, consists of tax concessions for payments made to personal pension schemes. Employees who are already covered by an occupational pension can deduct from their taxable income contributions paid into a third pillar pension up to approximately CHF5700 per year. Tax concessions are more substantial for people who are not covered by an occupational pension (self-employed). Personal pensions play a relatively small role in the Swiss pension system. The size of this industry, however, is expanding fast. Between 1996 and 1997, assets held by third pillar pension providers increased by almost CHF10 billion, to CHF78 billion (or 20 per cent of GDP).

Readers who are familiar with the approach to pension policy supported by international agencies like the World Bank will certainly have recognized many of its features in the above description of the Swiss multi-pillar system. The origins of the present structure, however, go back to the late 1960s/early 1970s, long before the World Bank began to popularize the multi-pillar model as the best institutional design for old age income transfers. The adoption and implementation of the current arrangement in the mid-1980s was delayed by several obstacles, many of which are to be found in Switzerland's political institutions. The overall impact of the political system on the establishment of a multi-pillar pension system, however, has been bidirectional. The process that eventually led to the adoption of a multi-pillar system, in fact, was set off by initiatives sponsored by external, marginal groups, whose political influence was temporarily amplified by Switzerland's direct democracy institutions.

THE WINDING ROAD TO MANDATORY PENSIONS

The political origins of the decision to make occupational pension coverage compulsory for employees go back to the early 1960s. After the Second World War, Switzerland had adopted a poverty prevention approach in pension policy. State intervention was not intended to provide former workers with income replacement but was aimed at guaranteeing everyone a minimum income level: hence the compressed benefit structure and universal character of the basic pension. The approach was similar to the one adopted by countries like the UK or Sweden, and can be qualified as Beveridgean in its inspiration.

In all three countries, the 1960s saw the emergence of new expectations among wage-earners in relation to pension policy. Rapidly rising wages for blue-collar workers and the expansion of the middle classes made the original postwar settlement look increasingly inadequate. The security of a poverty-free retirement was to be supplemented by provision guaranteeing retirees access to income levels that would allow them to maintain the living standards to which they had become used as workers. The pressure on governments to include income replacement as an objective of pension policy was exacerbated in all three countries by the existence of visible inequalities in pension coverage between those whose who had access to occupational pension coverage and those who had not. The issue, which in Britain received the label of 'superannuation', proved to be politically problematic in all three countries.

First, new legislation needed to take into account the existence of a fairly large number of pension funds, generally very popular with both employees and employers. This meant that, politically, legislators were forced to develop a second pillar of pension provision in a way that permitted the maintenance of existing pension funds. The shift to a Bismarckian approach, where public schemes provide generous earnings-related benefits for all workers, was, as a result, out of the question. Second, policy makers had to overcome employers' resistance to occupational pension coverage being made compulsory. Employers have traditionally been quite happy to provide this kind of fringe benefit to highly valued staff, but have always resented the imposition of rules that generate higher labour costs.

As a result, the expansion of second pillar pensions remained a key political issue throughout the 1960s and 1970s in countries which had initiated a pension policy with a Beveridgean approach. Sweden was the first to settle the issue, with the introduction of the ATP (*Allmaean Tillagspension*) scheme in 1959, which de facto replaced existing pension funds. In Britain, the extension of second pillar pension coverage had to wait until 1978 and the introduction of a state earnings-related pension scheme (SERPS) which was made available to workers without occupational pension coverage. In Switzerland, the settlement of the 'superannuation' issue took somewhat longer, but, interestingly, the solutions adopted by both Britain and Sweden featured in the Swiss political debate that led to the adoption of a multi-pillar system. Policy, though, took a different course.

The first important step in establishing mandatory occupational pensions was a popular initiative sponsored by the Federation of Christian Unions in 1966, which, if accepted by voters in a national referendum, would have required the government to make occupational pensions mandatory. The government's position in relation to this proposal was rather sceptical. In its official bulletin it argued that to make occupational pensions compulsory would have been 'extremely difficult, both legally and practically'. In addition, it maintained that such a measure was not really needed, as voluntary occupational pension coverage had expanded rapidly in the previous two decades (FF, 1968, I, 1, p.682). In parallel, and possibly in partial response to the Christian Unions' initiative, the government adopted a reform of the basic pension, which led to a 30 per cent benefit increase. Satisfied with this result, the unions withdrew their popular initiative before the referendum had taken place.

Things were to change in the following years. By the late 1960s/early 1970s, the pension issue had regained momentum and the left-wing parties were busy putting forward policy proposals. Socialist Party policy at the time was to favour the Swedish solution, with the introduction of an ATP-style second pillar pension, and a gradual abandonment of the existing pension funds. This solution, however, was opposed by the trade unions, and was soon dropped (Binswanger, 1987, pp.208–9). During the same period, the Communist Party, a rather marginal but at the time vociferous political grouping, was able to collect the 100000 signature needed for a popular initiative that would have changed the benefit structure of the basic pension in the direction of a Bismarckian scheme. According to the proposal, AVS would have paid benefits equal to 60 per cent of average gross earnings during the best five years.

A few months later, the Socialist Party also managed to obtain sufficient support for a popular initiative, which essentially put forward the British solution to the superannuation problem. A state second pension, delivering earnings-related benefit, was to be introduced. Workers covered by occupational pensions, however, were to be allowed to contract out of the state scheme and remain members of their employer-sponsored plans. At the time, the saliency of the superannuation and the political climate were such that the success at the polls of one of these two initiatives could not be ruled out. As a result, the right-of-centre parties joined forces to put together a third popular initiative, which had the objective of promoting a solution to the superannuation issue that was more acceptable to employers. It contained the proposal of making occupational pensions compulsory.

Faced with three different policy proposals that had a common goal, the government charged an expert commission (AVS Federal Commission) with the task of finding a suitable compromise between these different positions. Rather than a compromise, however, the result of the expert commission's work was simply to support the proposal made by the right-of-centre parties (with some minor changes): no state intervention as a provider of second pillar pensions, but mandatory occupational coverage for all employees. This solution satisfied the Socialists, who withdrew their initiative, but not the Communists, who maintained theirs.

The government accepted the reform plan agreed by the expert commission, and turned it into a proposal for constitutional change, automatically subjected to a referendum. Of course, it included mandatory occupational pension coverage for employees. In the documentation that accompanied the proposal (*Message*) there was no mention of the fact that only three years earlier the government's position on mandating occupational pensions had been that it was both unnecessary and unfeasible. The introduction of compulsory occupational pension coverage was justified on the basis of the large consensus that there seemed to be on this policy option (FF, 1971, II, 2, p.1624).

In the following year, on 3 December 1972, Swiss voters were asked in a national referendum to choose between the government-backed proposal and the Bismarck-type scheme favoured by the Communist Party. The outcome was unequivocal. The Communists' initiative was rejected by 83 per cent of voters, whereas the government solution was accepted by a large majority (73 per cent). The principle of compulsory occupational pensions was now enshrined in the federal constitution, which more precisely stated that 'the federal government requires employers to insure their staff with a pension fund . . . [and] establishes the minimal requirements that must be satisfied by such pension funds' (Swiss Federal Constitution, Art. 34[quater]; my translation). Under the pressure of more interventionist and radical solutions to the superannuation problem, the key political actors, including peak employers' associations, agreed to make occupational pension coverage compulsory. The details of how to achieve this goal, however, still needed to be worked out with a new law on occupational pensions, and with substantial technical and political problems.

An occupational pensions bill was submitted to parliament in December 1975. It already embodied the overall spirit of the present legislation. For example, it made provision for a compulsory minimum, but it allowed funds which offered better benefits to maintain them. It coordinated occupational and basic pension provision, by exempting earnings insured by the latter from occupational pension coverage. It also contained the idea of notional contributions, although these were to be used only to calculate the transfer value of the pension, or to calculate benefits in defined contribution schemes. The bill allowed funds to decide whether they wished to provide defined-benefit or defined-contribution benefits, and imposed different minimal conditions depending on the option chosen. In defined-benefit schemes, the benefit needed to be at least equal to 40 per cent of average insured earnings over the three years prior to retirement. In defined-contribution schemes, the minimum requirements were based on notional contributions and a minimum interest rate. As in the present system, notional contributions were age-related, but set at a higher average rate.

In addition, the government was to set up a central fund, jointly financed by pension schemes, that was to provide the funds needed to improve the pensions paid to middle-aged workers, who did not have enough working years left to accumulate a capital sufficient to finance the prescribed benefits. This central fund also had the task of financing the indexation of pensions after the age of retirement. Funds for each task were to be provided by occupational schemes on a PAYG basis. Contribution rates diverted to the central funds in order to offer older workers better retirement conditions were expected to increase gradually and reach their peak in 1996 at 4.13 per cent of insured earnings. The rate needed to finance inflation proofing of pensions was expected to reach 2.5 per cent of insured earnings by the year 2000 (FF, 1976, I, pp.299–302).

The proposal was accepted with minor changes in the lower chamber, the National Council, and was subsequently debated in the more conservative Council of States, where substantial criticism was levelled against what were perceived to be excessive levels of guaranteed benefits. In addition, the introduction of a central fund was attacked by the majority right-of-centre MPs for being too costly for employers (Pfitzmann-Boulaz, 1981). As a result, the bill was profoundly modified in the upper chamber. First, the minimum requirement (*Obligatorium*) was to be established only on a notional defined-contribution basis. Funds providing defined-benefit pensions were to be subjected to the same minimum requirements as defined-contribution funds. Second, notional contributions rates were reduced from a career average of 14.625 per cent of insured earnings to 12.5 per cent. Finally, the revised bill did not include plans to set up a central fund, or to provide full benefit indexation. Older workers, who would not have been able to accumulate sufficient capital to finance a full pension, were to be favoured by the age-related structure of notional contributions. In addition, pension funds were required to set aside 1 per cent of all contributions to finance measures to improve the benefits of older workers. Indexation, instead, was to be provided at the discretion of individual funds (BO.CdE, 1980, pp.241–301).

Back in the National Council, the bill as amended by the upper chamber was accepted by a majority of members, with minor changes. Even though many, especially on the left, felt that the new version of the occupational pensions bill did not provide sufficient income protection for many workers, it was decided that it was not in their interest to delay further the adoption of this long-awaited piece of legislation. In addition, there was a general agreement that the law did not completely fulfil the constitutional mandate, but that it was to be considered as a first step towards a more generous occupational pension system such as the one put forward by the Federal government in its 1975 bill. The law was finally approved in June 1982. Despite the criticisms, there were no attempts to challenge the pension law with a referendum, so that the new legislation came into force on 1 January 1985.

Of the three European countries that in the 1960s were confronted with the superannuation problem, Switzerland has been the only one to introduce mandatory occupational pensions. It is also one of very few OECD countries to have adopted this approach in pension policy. The idea of mandating occupational pensions did of course surface in other countries, but was generally strongly and successfully opposed by employers.[9] Its adoption in a country like Switzerland, where employers are extremely influential political actors is thus particularly striking, and can only be understood with reference to the country's peculiar political institutions, and in particular the popular initiative. It is very difficult to imagine that the government U-turn on mandatory pensions that took place between 1968 and 1971 would have come about in the absence of the pressure exerted by the popular initiatives of the Communist and Socialist parties.

CURRENT PRESSURES AND REFORM PLANS

Notwithstanding international praise, the Swiss pension system is facing two important challenges: to adapt to population aging and to respond to changes in the labour market. Current pension debates focus predominantly on these two issues, although the elaboration of policy is considerably more advanced in relation to the former. A pension reform which is currently being debated in parliament has the explicit objective of adapting the pension system to demographic change, and concerns both the first and second pillars. In contrast, the issue of improving pension coverage for precarious and atypical workers, whose numbers are increasing at a fast pace, has not been picked up in the current reform proposal, in spite of the demands expressed by the left and by the trade unions. At the time of writing (August 2001), a parliamentary commission in the National Council is re-examining the issue, and may come up with a proposal to improve coverage for low-paid, part-time and intermittent workers.

The adaptation of the pension system to population aging concerns the first two pillars. Being financed on a PAYG basis, the basic pension will see expenditures rising faster than receipts over the next decade (see Table 4.2). Demographic aging, however, will also have an impact on occupational pensions, even though these are fully funded schemes. Because of increases in life expectancy, the conversion rate which is used to determine the amount of a pension on the basis of the accumulated capital needs to be reduced. The result, unless some corrections are adopted, will be lower than expected benefits for future retirees.

With regard to the basic pension scheme, the current pension reform includes measures that will reduce expenditure and increase receipts. In the long term (that is, after a transition period) the reform is expected to generate combined annual savings and additional receipts of approximately CHF1.2 billion. Among the most important measures it is planned to abolish widows pensions as these have in most cases become redundant, given the adoption of a contribution sharing system between spouses in the 1995 reform (see Bonoli, 2000, pp.86–117); to increase the retirement age for

*Table 4.2 Current and projected receipts, outlays and balance of AVS
pension scheme (CHF millions)*

	With current legislation			With proposed legislation		
	Receipts	Outlays	Balance	Receipts	Outlays	Balance
1998	25322	26715	−1393			
2000	27622	27662	−40			
2005	29127	30791	−1664	30601	29968	+403
2010	30056	33900	−3844	34768	33900	+1198

Source: Conseil Fédéral (2000a, Annexes 1 and 2).

women to 65 (currently at 62 but rising to 64 as a result of the 1995 pension
reform); and the slowing down of benefit adaptation which will take place
every three years instead of every two. The reform will also increase contribution rates for the self-employed and require AVS recipients who are still
in employment to pay pension contributions (Conseil Fédéral, 2000a).

Together with these austerity measures, the reform will also introduce
early retirement, which will be possible from the age of 59, with a reduction
in the benefit. The reduction will be actuarially determined, but low-paid
workers will enjoy lower-than-actuarial benefit reductions. The reform bill,
currently being discussed in parliament, presents many of the features that
are typical of Swiss compromises. In particular, it includes both savings
measures and improvements in provision. In the past, reforms that comprised these two elements have been rather successful in gaining the necessary level of approval, both in parliament and with voters when challenged
by a referendum (Bonoli, 1999b). However, it is possible that, as has happened in the past, this carefully crafted compromise may be overhauled in
parliament, which might make it unable to attract the necessary level of
popular consensus.

The reform is supposed to guarantee the solvency of the basic pension
until 2010 (Table 4.2). The task is facilitated by a previously adopted
measure consisting of the increase by one percentage point of the VAT rate,
entirely assigned to the AVS pension scheme. VAT-raised funds were first
paid into the AVS budget in 1999 and explain the improvement in the
balance between 1998 and 2000. The projections presented in Table 4.2
assume a further increase of the VAT rate by 2.5 percentage points. After
2010, additional measures will arguably be needed in order to guarantee the
solvency of the scheme, as the proportion of the population aged 65 and
over is expected to continue increasing from the projected 17.5 per cent for
2010 to 25 per cent in 2040.

Together with the basic pension, the current reform will also modify the occupational pensions law. Here its main objective is to adapt the parameters that define the minimum requirements to current and future increases in life expectancy at age 65. Longer lives for retirees means that pensions will need to be paid out for longer periods and as a result will either have to be lower or to be financed by a higher level of capital. The government proposal in this respect is to gradually reduce the conversion rate used to determine the amount of an annual pension on the basis of the accumulated capital from the current 7.2 per cent to 6.65 per cent in 2016. In order to avoid a reduction in benefits, the notional contribution rates that are used to determine the amount of the capital available to employees will also be increased, as shown in Table 4.3. Because of retirement age equalization between men and women, the reform will also abandon gender-based rate differentiation. The result should be neutral in terms of benefit levels, but during the transition period some male employees will see a reduction in their replacement rate of up to 2 percentage points. Because the contribution rates that are increased are notional rates, this measure will not necessarily result in higher actual contributions. Some schemes have been able to achieve higher than expected returns to capital in recent years, which can be used, for some time at least, to finance higher notional contribution rates.

Table 4.3   *Notional contribution rates for compulsory occupational pensions, current and proposed*

Age	Current rates (men)	Proposed rates (either sex)
25–34	7	7
35–44	10	11
45–54	15	18
55–64	18	18

Source: Conseil Fédéral (2000b).

The current reform is not expected to address the issue of pension coverage for low-paid, atypical and part-time workers, who are often unable to reach the earnings limit that would entitle them to occupational pension coverage (approximately CHF24000 a year, or 35 per cent of average earnings). This threshold was introduced in order to reduce the administrative problems and non-wage labour costs associated with casual employment, but also because the first pillar of provision guarantees a replacement rate of 60 per cent or more to workers with average career earnings below the lower limit. In this respect the exclusion of low-paid workers from the second pillar pension seems consistent with the division of labour between the first and the second pillar, upheld by the Federal Constitution.

Over the years, however, a number of problems have been identified in relation to this situation. First, although a replacement rate of 60 per cent can be considered adequate for someone on an average wage, this cannot be said in relation to low-paid workers, whose earnings are barely above the social assistance minimum. A 30–40 per cent income reduction as a result of retirement will put them below the poverty line (Rechsteiner, 1987). Second, workers often spend only a few years in atypical employment, and subsequently manage to enter better-paid and more stable forms of work. However, the fact of having a second pillar pension with missing contribution years can result in low benefits, and in replacement rates lower than the 60 per cent target. Third, there is anecdotal evidence that some employers take advantage of the opportunity they have to reduce non-wage labour costs by carving up full-time jobs into part-time ones which are paid less than the lower limit for compulsory affiliation to an occupational pension.

Because of lack of research in this area, there is very little knowledge of the size and the extent of this development. The suspicion is strong, however, that there is in Switzerland a generation of low-paid, mainly (female) part-time workers, who are heading towards pensionable age without adequate pension provision and who face retirement on means-tested benefits. Flückiger estimates at 270000 (or 7.1 per cent of the working population) the number of workers who are not covered by an occupational pension because of earnings below the lower earnings limits. Of these, 82 per cent are women (Flückiger, 1999, data for 1996).

In order to deal with this situation and to include this section of the working population in occupational pension coverage, the Socialists and the trade unions support the abolition of the lower limit for the compulsory affiliation to a pension fund. This measure is opposed by employers, on grounds that it will engender unreasonable administrative costs, especially in relation to casual, temporary employment, and that it will inhibit job creation for low-skill workers. The government has so far decided not to take up the issue, even though it has in the past acknowledged the existence of a coverage problem for low-paid workers in the Swiss pension system (OFAS, 1995). This issue was among those the current pension reform was supposed to address, but it has been dropped from the agenda, possibly because of its cost implications. The consultation procedure has revealed strong employer resistance to the inclusion of all employees in the system of compulsory occupational pensions, because of the additional expenditure this would represent on low-skill, low-paid employment, but also because of the administrative burden this would create.

As in the 1960s, the main obstacle to an expansion of occupational pension coverage is employer resistance. Perhaps, as then, direct democracy will put pressure on them to make concessions. It is not difficult to imagine that the left will negotiate its support for the lowering of the conversion rate (see above), against a reduction in the earnings limit needed to qualify for occupational pension coverage. Recent experience has shown that, for a social policy reform to survive a referendum challenge, the support of the left is essential (Bonoli, 1999b). The inclusion of retrenchment and expansion measures within a single piece of legislation constitutes an important strength in the referendum arena, as these compromises are generally able to attract support from the whole political spectrum.

CONCLUSION

The impact of Switzerland's political institutions on policy making has been the subject of extensive research, and many of the effects that characterized the process leading to the adoption of the 1982 law on occupational pensions are well known to political scientists. Popular initiatives have led indirectly to innovative policy making on various occasions, often by prompting the Federal government to respond with alternative proposals with similar aims (see Werder, 1978; Kriesi, 1995; Papadopoulos, 2001, p.44). In relation to social policy, the standard view found in the literature is that direct democracy has had an overall negative impact on the expansion of the Swiss welfare state. On many occasions, carefully drafted compromises have been blown away by sceptical voters. Without direct democracy, Switzerland would probably have developed a fully-fledged Bismarckian welfare state, in line with other continental European countries (Armingeon, 2001; Bonoli, 1999a; Obinger, 1998). This view, however, focuses on one particular instrument of direct democracy, the 'optional referendum', or the opportunity to challenge at the polls any piece of legislation passed by parliament, provided 50000 signatures are collected.

The introduction of compulsory occupational pensions highlights a different relationship between direct democracy and the development of a welfare state, though this time the independent variable is the popular initiative. Thanks to this instrument, marginal groups like the Communist Party, or more influential minorities like the Socialists, were able to put substantial pressure on the government and on right-of-centre parties. Here direct democracy amplified the otherwise meagre political influence of the Swiss left, with the result that an unusually interventionist reform was eventually adopted.

This welfare-expanding effect of popular initiatives, however, has not been a frequent occurrence. On most occasions, left-sponsored initiatives aiming at improving levels of social protection were simply rejected by voters, thus reflecting the left–right balance of power within the electorate. This suggests that other factors must have played a role in making compulsory pensions politically feasible. Arguably, these pertain to the existence of a genuine social demand for better pension coverage which spanned party lines. This would be consistent with the developments observed in other European countries, and would explain why the government and the right-of-centre parties came to accept the idea of compulsory pensions. Possibly, for these actors, compulsion represented not only a burden on employers, but also an opportunity to respond to expectations that were widespread among their constituencies.

ACKNOWLEDGEMENT

I would like to thank for comments on a previous version of this chapter Werner Nussbaum and Herbert Obinger.

NOTES

1. For good overviews of the Swiss political system, see Lane (2001) or Kriesi (1995).
2. This short presentation of key Swiss political institutions does not include federalism, because it did not play any significant role in the law making process that led to the 1982 pension reform.
3. There is in Switzerland a 'President of the Confederation'; however, this position has an exclusively representative function. The Presidency is assumed by each Federal Council member, by yearly rotation.
4. The Federal government provides a subsidy of 17 per cent of outlays, while the Cantons jointly provide an additional 2 per cent.
5. On Swiss occupational pensions (LPP), see Helbling (2000) or Hepp (1990). For a comparative analysis including Switzerland, see Lusenti (1990).
6. Typically, the concept of notional contribution is used with reference to PAYG pension schemes (for example in Italy or Sweden). In the Swiss case, pensions are fully funded, but the calculation method for the compulsory minimum is based on contributions determined by law that do not necessarily reflect actual payments. The use of the term 'notional contributions/accounts' here is consistent with other English-language publications on Swiss pension policy (see, for example, Queisser and Vittas, 2000).
7. In 1996, 36 per cent of pension fund members were paying fixed rate contributions, 58 per cent paid age-related contribution, and for the rest some other method was used (OFS, 1999, p.28).
8. It should be noted that, even though the law prescribes that the notional capital must be converted into a pension, it also makes it possible for pension funds to pay out benefits as lump sums. In the government's view this practice is consistent with the spirit of the law, which is to set minimum requirements but to allow pension funds to offer better conditions. However, the risk of adverse selection is strong, as bad risks (who would find it expensive to buy an annuity) are more likely to opt for the government set pension, making it more difficult for pension schemes to meet their liabilities. The nightmare

scenario would be to have all men choosing a lump sum payment and all women opting for an annuity.

9. This has been the case in Britain on various occasions. In the 1980s, the government did consider the adoption of the Swiss multipillar model, but the idea was apparently dismissed by Thatcher, saying that it could only work in a country like Switzerland, where everything is '. . . either compulsory or forbidden' (BBC, 1996).

REFERENCES

Armingeon, K. (2001), 'Institutionalizing the Swiss welfare state', *West European Politics*, **24**(2), 145–68.
BBC (1996), *Consequences: Personal Pensions*, Radio 4, broadcast on 27 January 1996.
Binswanger, P. (1987), *Histoire de l'AVS*, Zurich: Pro Senectute.
BO.CdE (Bulletin Officiel du Conseil des Etats), various issues.
Bonoli, G. (1999a), 'Pension Policy in Switzerland: Institutions and the Politics of Expansion and Retrenchment', in U. Klöti and K. Yorimoto (eds), *Institutional Change and Public Policy in Japan and Switzerland*, Zurich: IPZ, 165–78.
Bonoli, G. (1999b) 'La réforme de l'Etat social en Suisse. Contraintes institutionnelles et opportunités de changement', *Swiss Political Science Review*, **5**(3), 57–78.
Bonoli, G. (2000), *The Politics of Pension Reform. Institutions and Policy Change in Western Europe*, Cambridge: Cambridge University Press.
Conseil fédéral (2000a), *Message relatif à la révision de la loi fédérale sur l'assurance vieillesse et survivants (LAVS)*, Berne.
Conseil fédéral (2000b), *Message relatif à la révision de la loi fédérale sur la prévoyance professionnelle (LPP)*, Berne.
FF (Feuille Fédérale), various issues.
Flückiger, Y. (1999), '*Inégalité, bas salaires et working poor en Suisse*', unpublished manuscript, University of Geneva.
Helbling, C. (2000), *Personalvorsorge und BVG*, Berne: Haupt.
Hepp, S. (1990), *The Swiss Pension Funds, An Emerging New Investment Force*, Berne: Haupt.
Immergut, E. (1992), *Health Politics. Interests and Institutions in Western Europe*, Cambridge: Cambridge: University Press.
Kobach, Kris (1993), *The Referendum. Direct Democracy in Switzerland*, Aldershot: Dartmouth.
Kriesi, H. (1995), *Le système politique suisse*, Paris: Economica.
Kriesi, H. (2001), 'The Federal parliament: the limits of institutional reform', *West European Politics*, **24**(2), 59–76.
Lane, J.-E. (2001), 'Introduction – Key Institutions and Behavioural Outcomes', *West European Politics*, **24**(2), 1–18.
Lehmbruch, G. (1993), 'Consociational Democracy and Corporatism in Switzerland', *Publius: The Journal of Federalism*, **23**, 43–60.
Lusenti, G. (1990), *Les institutions de prévoyance en Suisse, au Royaume Uni et en Allemagne Fédérale*, Geneva: Georg.
Obinger, H. (1998), 'Federalism, direct democracy, and welfare state development in Switzerland', ZeS-Arbeitspapier Nr. 8/98, Bremen.
OFAS (Office Fédéral des Assurances Sociales) (1995), *Rapport du Département*

fédéral de l'intérieur concernant la structure actuelle et le développement futur de la conception helvétique des trois piliers de la prévoyance vieillesse, survivants et invalidité, Berne: OFAS.

OFS (Office Fédéral de la Statistique) (1999), *La prévoyance professionnelle en Suisse. Aperçu des principales données de la statistique des caisses de pensions*, Neuchâtel: OFS.

Papadopoulos, Y. (2001), 'How does direct democracy matter? The impact of referendum votes on politics and policy-making', *West European Politics*, **24**(2), 35–58.

Pfitzmann-Boulaz, H. (1981), 'Le futur régime obligatoire de la prévoyance professionnelle', *Schweizerische Zeitschrift für Sozialversicherung*, **25**, 81–93.

Queisser, M. and Vittas, D. (2000), 'The Swiss multipillar pension system. Triumph of common sense?', World Bank, Development Research Group, Washington.

Rechsteiner, R. (1987), 'Stärken und Schwächen des BVG – 16 Reformvorschläge aus der Sicht der Versicherten', in Schweizerische Vereinigung für Sozialpolitik (ed.), *Sozialpolitische Auswirkungen des BVG*, Zurich, 63–84.

Schmähl, W. (ed.) (1991), *The Future of Basic and Supplementary Pensions Schemes in the European Community – 1992 and beyond*, Baden-Baden: Nomos.

Vontobel, W. (2000), 'Die Säulen- Scheinheiligen – Pech hat, wer in einem Kleinbetrieb arbeitet: Die Versicherung behält die Zinsen zurück', *CASH*, 1 December, 44.

Werder, H. (1978), *Die Bedeutung der Volksinitiative in der Nachkriegszeit*, Berne: Franke.

World Bank (1994), *Averting the Old Age Crisis*, Oxford: Oxford University Press.

5. The quality of the Dutch pension system: will it be sustainable in the twenty-first century?

Leny H. van der Heiden-Aantjes

INTRODUCTION

In this chapter I want to give my perspective on the question whether the Dutch pension system should be considered sustainable or not. After a short review of the birth of the system, the development over the last decades of the past century will be described. The question is: does the Dutch system need further reform in the twenty-first century? The chapter begins with a brief outline of the three pillars of the Dutch pension system. Subsequently, recent developments and the developments to be expected in the future will be described. Finally, the question whether the Dutch pension system is sustainable in the twenty-first century is answered.

THE SYSTEM

The Dutch old age pension system in its broadest sense is a three-pillar system. The first pillar is the AOW: a basic pension under a statutory national insurance scheme, providing an equal pension for all residents at a level related to the net minimum wage level. The second pillar is formed by the occupational non-statutory pension schemes supplementary to the general old age pensions Act (AOW). Occupational pension schemes are part of (collective) labour agreements. They can differ widely from each other, depending on each different agreement. Most prominent within the range of occupational pension schemes are the company pension schemes and the branch pension schemes. Participation in a branch (or industry-wide) pension fund can be made mandatory for all employers and employees in a branch of industry. This can be done at the request of organizations of employers and employees which are considered sufficiently representative for their branch of industry. There is no general obligation for employers to make a pension commitment.

The third pillar consists of the private provisions that are neither statutory nor part of (collective) labour agreements.

History

The introduction of the Invalidity Act in 1913 marked the first step towards a statutory social security system. It consisted of a mandatory insurance, exclusively designed to cover workers. Under this Act, workers who had become disabled or who had reached retirement age were entitled to a benefit, and so were the widows and orphans of deceased workers. Contributions were paid by the employers in the form of insurance stamps which were affixed to a stamp card. The rate of the benefit depended on the number of stamps affixed: in other words, on the employment history. However, as benefits were not index-linked, inflation soon rendered them all but worthless.

In 1919, a statutory scheme was set up which offered self-employed people the possibility to make arrangements for old age provisions on a voluntary basis. This, however, did not put an end to the discussion about a state pension and extension of coverage. Instead, this discussion continued up to the Second World War. At the beginning of the twentieth century the first non-statutory pension plans were set up, on the initiative of employers. The coverage of these plans was sometimes extended if they formed part of a collective labour agreement which was later declared binding.

In 1949, the instrument for declaring a collective labour agreement binding was, as far as pension schemes are concerned, replaced by the Act on mandatory participation in a branch pension fund (Act Bpf). In January 2001, the new Act on mandatory participation in a branch pension fund (Act Bpf 2000) came into effect, replacing the old one. In 1952, the Pension and Savings Fund Act (PSW), designed to secure pension commitments, became effective. In 1972, the Act on mandatory participation in a pension scheme for professional groups (Act Bpr) took effect.

After the Second World War, there was a renewed call for a national old age provision. This ultimately resulted in the introduction of the general old age pensions Act (AOW), which took effect on 1 January 1957. The AOW coverage is intended not only for employed persons but also for self-employed and non-working people: actually, for all residents of the Netherlands. At the outset, in 1957, there were almost 750000 AOW beneficiaries. By 2000, there were more than 2.2 million.

Around 1950, the level of cover provided by supplementary pension plans was very low. During the period in which the statutory system was built up, more and more non-statutory pension plans were created as well.

Both employers' organizations and trade unions set great store by creating supplementary pension plans for employed people. The level of cover slowly increased, to no less than 91 per cent in 1996. In many cases, plans provide not only for old age pensions, but also for survivor's pensions and disability benefits.

THE THREE PILLARS

First Pillar (AOW)

Entitlement and transitional arrangement

The AOW is the only statutory pension scheme of the Netherlands. It provides a flat-rate pension benefit, which is related to the net minimum wage, for all inhabitants of the Netherlands from the age of 65. The AOW is a mandatory scheme, financed on a 'pay-as-you-go' basis. On the benefit side, there is no means test; other forms of income have no influence on the AOW benefit.

In principle, all residents of the Netherlands between the age of 15 and 65 are insured for the AOW. There is no distinction between men and women, between civil servants, employees, self employed persons, agrarians or housewives. During the above-mentioned period of insurance, entitlement is being built up by steps of 2 per cent for every insured year. This leads to a 100 per cent entitlement to the relevant pension benefit upon reaching the age of 65, provided there are no gaps in the period of insurance. For every year a person was not insured, for instance because of residence and work outside the Netherlands, entitlement to the pension benefit is reduced by 2 per cent. This is the case for most of the migrant workers living in the Netherlands. Certain provisions apply:

- people who are not entitled to the full AOW benefit and have, together with other sources of income, a total income below the subsistence level, can receive social assistance;
- insured people, leaving the country to work or live abroad, can insure themselves optionally while residing abroad.

When this system was introduced, one problem had to be solved: only those who reached the age of 15 after 1 January 1957 would be able to build up to a full pension. The intention of the AOW, however, was to entitle all people aged 65 or older to a full AOW old age pension right from the start. For this purpose, a transitional arrangement was needed. Even today, this arrangement is still of great importance to pensioners. It will not be until

2007 (50 years after the introduction of the AOW) that AOW pensions can be awarded which are not partly based on the transitional arrangement. The transitional arrangement includes the following provisions:

- claimants who were aged between 15 and 65 on 1 January 1957 are considered to have been insured for the period between their fifteenth birthday and 1 January 1957 if they have lived in the Netherlands for a total of six years after their 59th birthday;
- claimants who had already reached the age of 65 before 1 January 1957 are entitled to a full AOW old age pension if they have lived in the Netherlands for a total of six years after their 59th birthday.

Only Dutch nationals living in the Netherlands are covered by this transitional arrangement. In this respect, however, nationals of countries with which a treaty on social insurance is effective are considered equal to Dutch nationals. Around 10 per cent of all current beneficiaries receive a reduced pension because they do not meet, or fully meet, the conditions of the transitional arrangement. The transitional arrangement applies to Dutch nationals only (or people with equal status) living in the Netherlands. However, the accrual of pension rights is not limited to Dutch nationals but is open to all residents of the Netherlands, regardless of their nationality, and to those who live outside the Netherlands but are liable to Dutch taxation on the basis of employment in the Netherlands.

Benefits

The AOW provides a benefit from the age of 65. Early retirement or deferment of the benefit is not possible. The AOW benefit is a flat rate, based on the net statutory minimum wage. The amount of the benefit does not depend on any former income or on contributions paid in the past. Housewives who have never paid contributions are also entitled to an AOW old age pension when they turn 65. Only the composition of the household is normative for the level of the benefit. These levels are as follows:

- 50 per cent of the net minimum wage for a married person or a person living together with a partner,
- 70 per cent of the net minimum wage for a single person,
- 90 per cent of the net minimum wage for a single parent with an unmarried child under 18.

In the case of an AOW beneficiary having a partner younger than 65, he is entitled to a supplementary benefit of 50 per cent of the net minimum wage on top of his regular AOW benefit of 50 per cent of the net minimum wage. However, most of the work-related income of the younger partner is to be deducted from the supplementary benefit.

From 2015, the AOW will no longer provide these supplementary benefits. People reaching the age of 65 after 2014, living with a younger partner without income, are expected to take private measures to cover this 'gap'.

Minimum wage   The statutory minimum wage is related to the average development of collective labour agreement (CAO) wages. AOW benefits are linked to the statutory net minimum wage. Following the development of the statutory minimum wage, AOW benefits are adapted twice a year, on 1 January and on 1 July. However, the Indexing Conditional Suspension Act (WKA) provides the statutory possibility to rule out this adaptation and 'freeze' the AOW benefits for any period of time. This was the case in the early 1990s, because of unfavourable economic conditions. However, from 1996, the link between the AOW benefits and the statutory minimum wage was fully restored.

Pay-as-you-go system

The system of funding led to much debate when the AOW was introduced. Two systems of funding can be distinguished: pay-as-you-go and capital funding. In order to finance the AOW scheme, a pay-as-you-go system was selected. In fact this was the only option available, as people over 65 were directly entitled to a pension when the AOW took effect on 1 January 1957. Since no provisions had been made for these pensions, there was no alternative but to pay them from contributions levied from 1 January 1957.

Collection of contributions

AOW pensions are paid from contributions levied on income. Income earners pay a certain percentage of their income in contributions. The AOW contribution rate for 2001 was set at 17.9 per cent on incomes of up to 27 009 Euros a year. Depending on the economic situation, the percentage may rise, up to a statutory limit in the years to come. The statutory limit is 18.25 per cent. Possible future deficiencies as a result of this statutory limit will be balanced by a government grant.

Contributions are collected from a person's salary by the employer and subsequently remitted to the tax authorities. Self-employed people receive a tax assessment from the tax authorities and must pay contributions directly to the tax authorities, who see to it that the money is transferred to the Social Insurance Bank (SVB), which is responsible for payments to AOW beneficiaries. People who have no income are not required to pay contributions. They do, however, accrue AOW pension rights.

In cases where people receive an income but refuse to pay contributions, and the tax authorities are unable to collect the contributions in another way, the future pension of the people concerned will be reduced. This reduction comes to 2 per cent for each year for which contribution was not paid. The SVB keeps a record of all those who have at any time defaulted on payment of contributions.

Aging provisions
Both the capital funding system and the pay-as-you-go system have their advantages and disadvantages. A pay-as-you-go system is very sensitive to demographic changes such as aging of the population. A capital funding system is hardly affected by aging of the population but is sensitive to inflation. However, since the AOW benefit is a flat rate and not linked to former wages, the disadvantage of the aging of the population is far from being the problem it is in most other countries. Nevertheless, the approaching aging of the population led to much public debate and studies in the Netherlands as well. The key question was whether the Dutch pension system (the first pillar as well as the second) would still be affordable in the future. An additional question raised (again) by some was whether the AOW scheme should continue to be based on a pay-as-you-go system and whether people receiving an AOW old age pension should also be required to pay towards the increasing costs resulting from the aging of the population. The following decisions were finally made:

- AOW beneficiaries will not be required to pay AOW contributions;
- an upper limit for the AOW contribution percentage (18.25 per cent) was introduced;
- deficits in the AOW fund due to insufficient income from contributions will be balanced by a government grant. This government grant will be paid from tax revenues (to which pensioners contribute as well);
- an AOW savings fund was established. By law, the fund receives annual deposits from general tax revenue. Thanks to these, and the interest earned, its capital is expected to reach about 135 billion Euros in 2020. From that year on, it will be possible to use the capital to help cover AOW spending. Given a cautious prognosis of economic growth, when demographic aging reaches its peak around 2030, the AOW Savings Fund will be covering about 12 per cent of AOW spending. The ceiling on AOW contributions and the money from the AOW Savings Fund should provide a solid guarantee against the forecast rise in AOW spending.

A variety of other measures were proposed as well but were ultimately rejected for various reasons. The most important precondition in this respect was that labour costs were not allowed to go up. The argument goes as follows: the AOW scheme will remain affordable if sufficient people participate in the labour market and pay contributions. An increase in the cost of labour, for example through a higher premium, is therefore not a desirable option. For a higher cost of labour will lead to less participation in the labour market and, consequently, to a narrower financial basis for the AOW scheme.

In the end, the AOW Savings Fund proved to be the solution which had wide-ranging political and public support.

Administration: Social Insurance Bank (SVB)

The administration body for the AOW is the Social Insurance Bank (SVB). The SVB is an independent body, which means that it is not a part of the Ministry of Social Affairs and Employment (SZW) or any other government department. The SVB is also the administration body for two other national insurance schemes, the General Surviving Relatives Act (ANW) and the General Child Benefits Act (AKW).

The SZW is not authorized to interfere directly with the implementation of the AOW or any other scheme administered by the SVB. The SVB is subject to supervision by the Inspection for Work and Income (IWI). The IWI is a part of the SZW, but the inspector-general is allowed to publish his control reports himself, without involvement of the SZW Minister.

Second Pillar (Occupational Pensions)

Basic principles

Occupational pensions are regarded as a form of wages. They are therefore subject to negotiations on labour conditions between the social partners (employers and employees). There is no general statutory obligation for employers to make pension commitments to employees. However, once pension commitments have been made, they must be upheld. The Pension and Savings Fund Act (PSW) holds essential safeguards to this end. The most essential of these is that pension contributions must be placed outside the employer's company. This must be done by concluding an insurance agreement with an insurance company (direct insurance), or establishing a company pension fund, or joining a branch (industry-wide) pension fund.

As indicated above, occupational pension schemes are created through negotiations between employers and employees. The strength of the trade union(s) involved often determines where pensions are administered. If the trade union is weak it is more likely that a pension scheme will be administered by an insurance company or a company pension fund. In the case of a strong trade union, it is more likely that a pension scheme for a whole branch of industry will be created, administered by a branch pension fund. A pension scheme forms part of the terms of conditions of employment, which are laid down in a (possibly collective) labour agreement. In principle, employees are obliged to participate in this pension scheme. Occupational pension schemes differ on many details, for instance in the way payment of contributions is shared between employer and employee. In general, two-thirds of the contribution are paid by the employer and one-third is paid by the employee, but there are many variations. The aim of most schemes is an old age pension of 70 per cent of the final salary after 40 years of participation (final pay system), but a number of schemes aim at 70 per cent of the average career salary (career average system). Occupational (or supplementary) pension schemes are also called 'second-pillar' schemes. They are considered supplementary to the AOW state pension. The AOW benefit – the first pillar – is therefore a factor included in the calculations of second pillar pension schemes in order to arrive at the aforementioned 70 per cent aim. This is known as the AOW franchise.

Statutory framework: Pension and Savings Fund Act (PSW)
Once an employer has made a pension commitment to his employees, this commitment must be implemented in the way prescribed in the PSW. Thus the commitment is subject to the protection of the PSW. The foremost safeguard is the rule that pension contributions must be placed outside the employer's company either by joining a branch pension fund, or establishing a company pension fund, or concluding an agreement with an insurance company. Other protective measures laid down in the PSW are as follows:

- in the case of termination of participation owing to termination of employment, workers are entitled to a pension proportionate to the full-term duration of employment;
- the legal right of transfer of pension rights in the event of a change from one employer to another;
- the fact that indexation rights applied to pensioners must also be applied to early leavers (indexation itself is customary but not mandatory);
- a ban on surrendering pension rights of the beneficiary (exchanging the entitlement to a lump sum payment would undermine the purpose of accrual and safeguarding of pensions);
- an obligation to inform participants annually on the status of their pension rights and an obligation to inform participants at least once a year of changes in their pension scheme;
- as from 2002, participants who are building up a survivor's pension become entitled to exchange this pension on the pension date for a

higher or earlier old age pension. Effective from 2002, the outcome of these and other choice modules in pension schemes must lead to equal benefits for men and women. As from 2005, benefits in defined contribution schemes must also be equal for men and women;

- prohibition of the distinction between part-time workers (the majority of whom are women) and full-time workers; equal treatment of men and women is prescribed in the Non-discrimination Act for men and women;
- rules governing the separation of pension rights in the event of a divorce.

Rules especially meant to safeguard pensions

The PSW also lays down the institutional framework of a pension scheme. For pension schemes implemented by pension funds, there are requirements on the following:

- articles of association and regulations;
- the composition of the board of a pension fund (equal representation of employers and employees or organizations of employers and employees);
- the possibility for participants to set up a participants' council;
- day-to-day management by at least two people;
- expertise and integrity of the board;
- the Actuarial and Technical Business Memorandum. As from 1 January 2001, all pension funds must operate in accordance with an Actuarial and Technical Business Memorandum. On the basis of this document, the Pensions and Insurance Supervisory Board (PVK) will decide whether or not a pension fund is allowed to be self-administrative;
- registration of the pension fund with the supervisory body (PVK);
- reinsurance (unless the PVK permits self-management);
- supervision of pension funds by the PVK. The PVK also supervises insurance companies, but this is done, not on the basis of the PSW, but on that of the Insurance Industry Supervision Act;
- Code of Conduct. As from 1 January 2001, a pension fund is obliged to draw up a Code of Conduct. This Code must contain rules for the prevention of conflicts of interest and abuse of information at hand. The Code applies to employees as well as board members of pension funds;
- informing the PVK. As soon as possible, the auditor as well as the actuary must inform the PVK about any relevant circumstances regarding legal stipulations and the obligations of the fund. At its

request, they also must inform the PVK about their activities. Furthermore, they are obliged to submit all information which may be necessary for the task of the PVK to be carried out.

For pension schemes implemented by both insurance companies and pension funds, there are requirements on sound investments, reporting to the Pensions and Insurance Supervisory Board and pension fund records being kept in the Netherlands. As for insurance companies, this requirement can only be made with respect to Dutch insurance companies and insurance companies based outside the European Union.

Pension commitments to a managing director of a company may be exempted from the obligation, prescribed by the PSW, to place the pension contributions either in a branch pension fund, in a company pension fund or with an insurance company. Exemption is only granted if the managing director holds at least 10 per cent of the shares of that company.

Supervision: Pensions and Insurance Supervisory Board (PVK)
The PVK is an independent body. It is not a part of the SZW or any other government department. The governing board of the PVK is appointed by the government. Its management is appointed by the governing board. Currently, the following instruments of supervision are at the disposal of the PVK. The PVK may raise objections against an Actuarial and Technical Business Memorandum (ATBM). In that case, a pension fund may be forced by the PVK to reinsure its commitments. The PVK may raise objections against an actuary whose proper functioning with a pension fund is questioned by the PVK. It is authorized to ask board members and employees of a pension fund for information and to summon witnesses and experts (actually also the board members of a fund), who are obliged to obey the summons. The PVK is authorized to have access to the books and records of a pension fund or an employer and may make its remarks on articles of association and regulations, as well as on the state of affairs of a pension fund, known to the board of a pension fund. The PVK is also allowed to inform representative organizations of employers, employees, and other parties concerned, of its remarks to the board of a pension fund.

When the board of a pension fund fails to comply with the demands of the PVK, the PVK is authorized to bring its observations into the open through the press or otherwise. It may request the Enterprise Division of the Court of Justice in Amsterdam to appoint a conservator to the pension fund. It may raise objections to collective or individual value transfers. Finally, the PVK may determine that the auditor is not authorized to draw up the annual report when he does not (or does no longer) meet the necessary requirements regarding the way in which he fulfils his task.

The Act on mandatory participation in a branch pension fund (Act Bpf 2000)

When a collective labour agreement is declared binding, competition with respect to terms and conditions of employment can be prevented. The problem, however, is that collective labour agreements have a duration of two to three years, while the accrual of a pension may take up to 40 years. In 1949, therefore, pensions were removed from the scope of the Collective Labour Agreements Act. The Act on mandatory participation in a branch pension fund (Act Bpf) was introduced. From January 2001, this Act was replaced by the Act on mandatory participation in a branch pension fund (Act Bpf 2000).

When employers' organizations and trade unions together set up a branch pension fund, they may ask the government to impose an obligation to participate in this fund on all employers and employees within their particular branch of industry. In this way, agreements between the social partners are made binding for everyone within the branch. For participation in a pension fund to be declared mandatory, however, the employers and employees affiliated to it must form an adequate representation of their branch of industry. As for employers' organizations, the employers supporting the request must at least employ 60 per cent of the employees in their particular branch of industry. For the organized employees, no supporting percentage is prescribed.

Taxation

Contributions from the employer and employee are tax-deductible. Pension benefits received by the beneficiaries are taxed as income. In the case of a collective scheme provided by an employer, the pension scheme has to comply with the definition of collective pension schemes as laid down in the Wages and Salaries Tax Act in order to enjoy tax relief. The tax definition of a pension is as follows. A collective pension scheme is an arrangement whose exclusive or almost exclusive purpose is to provide for employees and former employees in the event of their becoming disabled or in their old age and for their spouses (or unmarried partners under certain conditions) and children (under 30 years), whether natural or adopted, by means of a pension.

On 29 April 1999, the Taxation of Pensions Act was approved by parliament. This Act was based on the recommendations of the 'Witteveen Commission'. This commission advised on what can be seen as a reasonable pension, regarding more diversified labour patterns, household compositions (single or dual earners) and greater differences in needs. The new Act specifies under what conditions pensions are reasonable pensions. In line with the present social standards, the new Act on taxation of pensions allows an accrual of 2 per cent per year of the final salary, taking into account a 'franchise' of at least the level of the individual state pension. This means that an employee can build up a pension of 70 per cent of his final salary in 35 years. So even a person who (partially) leaves the labour market for a few years, for instance to take care of children, can build up a full pension. If an employee works for more than 35 years, an additional accrual of pension entitlement is allowed, up to a maximum of 100 per cent of his salary. The date on which the old age pension may become payable is no longer fixed. The usual date on which it may become payable is that of the employee's 65th birthday, but it can also become payable at an earlier or later date. In the case of an earlier date, the pension payments will be reduced proportionately. In the case of a later date, the pension will be maximized to 100 per cent of the final salary.

Since pension funds do not make profits, they are exempt from corporation tax which is levied on profits. Insurance companies are liable to pay corporation tax if they make profits.

Sorts of pension administration

Branch pension funds (Bpf)   A pension scheme is administered by a branch pension fund when it applies to a whole branch of industry. Like company pension funds, branch pension funds are subject to the articles of the PSW. Additionally, however, they are also subject to the articles of the Act Bpf 2000, when participation was made mandatory on the basis of this Act. The trade unions and the employers' organizations must be equally represented on the administration board of a branch pension fund.

Civil Servants' Pension Fund (ABP)   The largest bpf in the Netherland is ABP. With an invested capital of 150 billion Euros, the Dutch Civil Servants' Pension Fund, administered by the ABP, is one of the largest pension funds in the world, second only to the California Public Employees' Retirement System (CalPERS). Until recently, the ABP fund was subject to separate legislation. However, since 1996, the ABP is treated as a 'private' pension fund and therefore subject to the PSW. The obligation for civil servants to participate in the ABP fund is laid down in their collective labour agreement and regulated by the Act on Privatization of the ABP. At this moment, there exists no mandatory participation on the basis of the Act Bpf 2000. Barring unforeseen developments, however, the ABP will become subject to this Act in a few years.

Since the ABP fund became subject to the PSW, the Pensions and Insurance Supervisory Board (PVK) is also supervising the administration of civil servants' pensions by the ABP. In general, negotiations between employers and employees determine who should pay what share of the contribution. The same applies to the general government and the civil servants' trade union. The latter is the largest trade union in the Netherlands.

Unlike the situation in many other European countries, Dutch civil servants' pension benefits are not paid at the expense of the national budget. The ABP fund, just like every other bpf, is based on the principles of capital funding.

Company pension funds (Opf)　Where larger enterprises are concerned, pension schemes are usually administered by a company pension fund, provided the company is not obliged to participate in a branch pension fund. Although company pension funds have natural ties with the employer's company, they are separate legal entities and not liable for debts of the employer. Company pension funds are not allowed to invest more than 5 per cent of their assets in the employer's company. The administration board of the company pension fund must include a number of employees' representatives, at least equal to the number of employers' representatives.

Insurance companies　An employer may conclude a group life insurance contract with an insurance company for the benefit of his employees. In accordance with the description in the PSW, such a contract is referred to as a 'B-contract'. An employer may also enable an employee to conclude an individual contract with an insurer. This is called a 'C-contract'. Life insurance companies are also involved in occupational pensions through reinsurance, fully or partly, of company pension funds and branch pension funds.

Pension funds for professional groups　A pension scheme for professional groups is based on an agreement between self-employed professionals within a particular profession. Through a procedure based on the Act on mandatory participation in a pension scheme for professional groups (Act Bpr), the government can make participation in a pension scheme for a professional group mandatory for the profession as a whole. This will occur at the request of an organization or organizations representing an adequate majority of the professionals concerned. Because pension schemes for professional groups are not based on pension commitments made by employers, such a pension scheme is subject only to the Act Bpr and not to the PSW. At present, there are 11 pension funds for professional groups based on the Act Bpr.

Parties involved in occupational pensions
Directly involved in occupational pensions are (organizations of) employers and employees, primarily responsible for occupational pension

schemes; the national government, responsible for creating favourable conditions; and pension providers (pension funds and insurance companies), which implement and administrate the schemes agreed by the employers and employees.

In addition, there are interest groups, such as the organizations of pension providers – the Association of Branch Pension Funds, the Foundation for Company Pension Funds and the Dutch Association of Insurers – and combined organizations for the elderly (CSO).

The role of the government is (a) to lend support and create conditions (also fiscal facilities); (b) to safeguard compensation for inequality (protection of the weaker party); (c) to ensure a balanced economic development (the development of labour costs is important, but so is the income position of the elderly); and (d) to impose mandatory participation in a branch pension fund at the request of representative organizations of employers and employees in the branch of industry (there exists no general obligation for an employer to make a pension commitment to his employees).

Representation of pensioners

In June 1998, recommendations to the pension funds were made by the Joint Industrial Labour Council (*Stichting van de Arbeid*) and by organizations of old age pensioners, to stimulate the creation of participants' councils, strengthen the influence of these councils, and increase the possibilities for pensioners to have direct membership of administration boards. The government has endorsed these recommendations and has promised to change the PSW with regard to the influence of the participants' councils. The recommendations were evaluated in July 2001. Involved parties are still considering whether further steps or legal measures are wanted or even necessary. The government has already announced that further recommendations will be looked at positively.

Third Pillar (Private Pensions)

Annuity insurance and endowment insurance

All individuals have the opportunity to enter into a private pension arrangement with an insurer. This can be done by annuity insurance as well as by endowment insurance. Income from both forms of insurance can be used as an old age supplement to the AOW state pension alone or to the combination of the AOW state pension and an occupational pension.

Annuity insurance as an old age provision

Annuity insurance is an agreement giving entitlement, during a person's life, to a fixed, consistent and periodical (possibly indexed) payment, which as a rule cannot be lowered or raised. Profit sharings related to the annuity insurance are also considered part of the entitlement. Annuity insurance premiums can be deducted from taxable income up to various limits, depending on a number of indicated situations. In 2000, the basic deductible premium amount for every taxable person was at least 2839 Euros.

Endowment (lump sum) insurance
Endowment insurance is an agreement aimed at the payment of a lump sum in connection with (in the context of old age provisions) the life of a person. Under specific conditions, the interest components of life insurance-benefits remain, up to certain limits, free from taxation. The principal conditions are that yearly premiums must have been paid over an unbroken period of at least 15 years and that the highest (year) premium may not exceed ten times the lowest (year) premium.

In 2000, the amounts free from taxation were up to 28 134 Euros after 15 years of premium payments and up to 95 293 Euros after 20 years of premium payments.

A fiscal old age umbrella for the twenty-first century
With its 'Tax Plan for the Twenty-first Century', the Cabinet has in fact presented an old age umbrella. This umbrella establishes maximums for the eligibility for individual pension schemes on an annuity basis (third pillar) for tax facilities. Contributions are tax-deductible up to a maximum of an annuity system that allows the accrual over a period of 40 years, including state old age pension (AOW) and any other pension provisions, of an old age pension of 70 per cent of one's final pay, taken from the age of 65. This means that pension rights accrued within the second pillar have to be deducted from this maximum level of ambition.

RECENT DEVELOPMENTS

Early Retirement: Transition from VUT Schemes to Pre-pensioning

VUT schemes for early retirement are separate from pension schemes and came into existence in the early 1980s. They were the result of collective negotiations and were introduced as a means of curbing youth unemployment. They are now in effect in many branch and employer-sponsored plans. VUT schemes are based on a pay-as-you-go system and can be financed through book reserves or separate VUT funds. Conditions may vary from scheme to scheme, but in general all VUT schemes provide for retirement over a number of years (in some schemes less than five years, in other schemes more than five years) before the normal retirement age, with a gross benefit level of 70–85 per cent of the final salary, often up to a stipulated maximum, until the normal retirement age.

Participation in the regular pension plan usually continues as if the person were still employed. Benefit payments will not be allowed or will cease if the retiree is paid full disability benefits, or if the retiree becomes unemployed. Although implemented as a means of combating youth unemployment in the early 1980s, the VUT has grown into a quasi-retirement scheme with a considerable number of beneficiaries. As a result, expenditures for VUT payments have risen steeply. Escalating cost is creating increasing pressure on the VUT schemes. Not surprisingly, employers have started looking for ways to curb this development.

Pre-pension schemes are now looked upon as a more actuarially fair and affordable alternative to the outdated VUT schemes. Many companies and branches of industry are already in the process of transition from VUT to pre-pensioning. The main difficulty is the transition of the financing system from pay-as-you-go to capital funding, required for pre-pensioning (on pre-pensioning, the articles of the PSW are applicable, including the prescription of capital funding). Depending on the scheme, pre-pensioning may result in a lifelong lower old age pension than one would receive on retirement at the age of 65. On the other hand, retirement at an age older than 65 may yield a lifelong higher old age pension.

Promoting Participation of Older Workers in the Labour Process

The fact that the number of older people will increase considerably over the coming years means that the burden of financing pensions is becoming heavier to bear. Therefore it is desirable that the level of participation in the labour process by older workers be raised.

A structural increase in participation calls for a structural approach. The social partners are to a significant extent responsible for this. By adopting an age-awareness personnel policy, by improving the employability of their employees, by converting their early retirement schemes to pre-pension or flexible pension schemes, and by pursuing a sound policy on working conditions, both employers and employees have many instruments available to them to limit the number of retiring older workers and to promote the number of entrants into the labour market.

The government is developing a general policy and a series of measures based on the following considerations:

● the main target group are workers between 40 and 55 years of age; it is important that this group be prevented from retiring from the labour process in numbers similar to those of the present group of employees aged between 55 and 56;

- participation among 55–65-year-olds will need to be raised annually by approximately 0.75 per cent for several years;
- it is essential that a change in mentality be achieved among individual employers and employees;
- it must be possible and (more) attractive for elder workers to go on working;
- policies that encourage early retirement must be reviewed;
- involuntary retirement must be prevented wherever possible;
- voluntary retirement must continue to be an option, but must be accompanied by an individual price tag; if at all possible, the costs must be prevented from being passed on to the community.

In connection with the foregoing considerations, the government has decided to propose the following concrete measures:

- abolishment of tax facilities for early retirement schemes that are realized from 1 January 2003;
- establishment, from 1 January 2003, of a statutory regime for the fiscal treatment of early retirement schemes and pre-pension schemes, and transitional arrangements to be drawn up for the conversion of early retirement to pre-pension schemes;
- the planned statutory regime implies that, from 1 January 2009, all existing early retirement schemes will cease to be eligible for tax concessions unless they are transitional arrangements that were finalized prior to 1 January 2009 for the purpose of converting an early retirement scheme to a pre-pension scheme;
- provision will be made for a maximum transitional period for transitional arrangements starting on 1 July 2002. This means that, from 1 July 2022, no more early retirement schemes will be eligible for tax concessions;
- the fiscal regime for pension schemes realized before 1 January 2009 as a result of converting an early retirement scheme will remain unchanged. Accelerated build-up over at least ten years for a pre-pension of 85 per cent at 60 years of age will therefore still be possible. The social partners will need to examine whether it is necessary to make full use of this option for each individual scheme.

Pension covenant

In 1997, the government argued in favour of cost control, modernization and increasing the rate of participation. The Social and Economic Council

(SER: the advisory body to the government on social and economic affairs) advised that a covenant should be reached between social partners and government. Why did the Dutch, both government and social partners, opt for a covenant in the field of pensions?

To understand this choice, one must realize that, in the Netherlands, the primary responsibility for occupational pension schemes belongs to the social partners. Social partners decide whether there will be an occupational pension scheme and what the elements in this scheme are, including, of course, some legal conditions. Therefore a government that wants (major) changes in occupational pension schemes is, at least partly, dependent on the social partners.

On the other hand, social partners always want a sufficient and flexible regime for the taxation of occupational pension schemes in legislation. For a few years, 1994 to 1996, there was a discussion between government and social partners about new, more flexible, fiscal legislation for pension schemes. In that situation both parties, government and social partners, had something to gain from a pension covenant. Therefore a pension covenant was achieved in December 1997. The main elements of this covenant were cost control, modernization (of pension schemes and of fiscal legislation) and increasing the rate of participation. The evaluation of the covenant in 2001 showed that it was successful; all targets were achieved.

On 22 July 2002, a new Cabinet came into force. Strategic Agreement of this new Cabinet determined that a new pension covenant be made. There are several possible reasons for having a new pension covenant. One of these is the problem of developments on the (international) stock markets and the low, sometimes even negative, returns for pension funds. Another reason may be the statement that the former Cabinet sent to the parliament in March 2002 about the basic principles of a new pension law, the main elements being more transparency and better information for participants; confirmation of the primary responsibility of the social partners; the need for the rate of participation to be further increased before 2006; pension funds not being permitted to carry out activities other than administrating pension schemes; and the need to modernize the system for financial supervision, but with the confirmation of the basic principle that the assets of a pension fund must always be at least 100 per cent of liabilities.

Social partners do not agree with all these basic principles and in particular they have different opinions on the way some of the targets can be best achieved. Furthermore, the Strategic Agreement also declared that the fiscal regime for pension schemes will be cut down, in favour of new to make financial arrangements that should make it easier to combine labour and care over a lifetime.

As social partners are not very fond of these new ideas, it is perhaps a good idea to have a new pension covenant between government and social partners. Both parties have something to gain. The coming months promise to be very interesting: do both parties want a new pension covenant and, if so, what will be the main elements of this covenant? It seems likely that the following aspects will be the most important. There will be a large increase in the rate of participation, but up to what level exactly? Pensioners will have more influence on the boards of pension funds, but should this be supplemented by legislation or not? There will be more transparency and better information for participants, but is legislation necessary? Will the fiscal regime for occupational pension schemes be maintained at the present level? For now, we just have to wait and see.

CONSEQUENCES OF AGING AND THE SUSTAINABILITY OF THE DUTCH OLD-AGE PENSION SYSTEM

Introduction

A study entitled 'Aging in the Netherlands' (see www.cpb.nl/eng/pub/bijzonder) by the Netherlands Bureau for Economic Policy Analysis (CPB) describes important trends that are affecting and will continue to affect pensions and how these trends affect each other. The study heavily influenced a report entitled 'An exploration of long-term debt policies' by a working group of civil servants drawn from the Budget Margin Study Group. The CPB study focuses on the budgetary impact of demographic aging, and has a wide reach, which includes developments affecting first and second pillar pension provisions. It also includes explicit projections for the long run, and the grounds on which they are based. The CPB projects developments in the field of demographics and labour market participation. These projections are used when predicting the financial consequences of aging.

Demographics

Demographic aging is linked not only to the aging of the baby-boom generation, but also to the falling birth rate and rising life expectancy. Demographic aging is thus both a temporary and a long-term problem. Given the population prognosis of Statistics Netherlands (CBS), life expectancy at birth will continue to rise from 2000 to 2050: for men, from 75 to 80 years, and for women, from 81 to 83 years. The future fertility rate will remain at the current historically low rate of 1.7 children per family. The result will be an increase in the elderly dependency ratio from 22 per cent in 2000 to a peak of 43 per cent around 2040. After a small dip, it will sta-bilize at around 40 per cent. Immigration is expected to decrease gradually in net terms, from 38000 people in 2000 to 24000 in 2040.

Labour Market Participation

The upward trend in labour market participation is expected to continue over the next 20 years, increasing by 5–6 per cent; 77–8 per cent of the 20–65 age group are expected to be in work in 2020. Men's average participation in the labour market is not expected to increase. The 5–6 per cent rise will therefore be entirely due to increasing participation by women. Since part-time working is also expected to increase, the growth in labour market par-ticipation in terms of full-time equivalents will only be around 2 per cent. The standard working week is expected to shrink by around 6 per cent in the next 20 years. The structural unemployment rate among the working-age population is expected to be 4 per cent. Use of the early retirement schemes will increase from 2.5 per cent to 3.5 per cent.

Financial Consequences

Given the projections for demographic changes and trends in labour market participation, the CPB expects that the government expenditures on the first pillar pensions will rise from 4.7 per cent GDP to 9.0 per cent of GDP. In addition, it examines the second and third pension pillars and the extent to which the growth expected in them (especially the growth in income once policies have matured) will boost tax revenue, not only because direct tax is payable on supplementary pension payments, but also because revenue from indirect tax will increase, owing to a growth in con-sumer spending by older people. All in all, the picture shown in Table 5.1 will emerge for the first and second pillars.

Since it combines a pay-as-you-go system in the first pillar with capital funding in the second, the Dutch pension system will be fairly resistant to the impact of demographic aging in the next few decades. The financial impact of demographic aging can also be largely absorbed by future tax claims on current pension entitlements. One concern, however, is the rela-tively low labour market participation, especially among older people. Only one in three of the 55–65 age group works. To strengthen the eco-nomic base and the sustenance of the pension system, therefore, the government has launched a policy aimed at increasing the labour market participation of older people for the long term. The social partners will have to make an important contribution to this objective. Some important measures, in the areas of training, age-aware personnel policy, workplace

*Table 5.1   Gross pension payments and tax revenue from income from
             pensions*

		2001	2020	2040
I	Gross pension payments (payments to pensioners)			
	First pillar (% GDP)	4.7	6.8	9.0
	Second pillar (% GDP)	4.1	7.3	12.9
	Total pension payments (% GDP)	8.8	14.1	21.9
II	Tax revenue from pensions			
	Direct taxes on pension payments	1.8	2.9	4.9
	Indirect taxes on pension payments	1.5	2.3	3.5
	Total taxes on pension payments	3.3	5.2	8.4
III	Pension contributions & pension fund assets (2nd pillar)			
	Contributions (% of wages)	6.8	6.8	7.2
	Pension fund assets (% GDP)	121	172	195

Source: 'Ageing in the Netherlands', Netherlands Bureau for Economic Policy Analysis, The Hague, 2000, p.53.

conditions and part-time working, will have to be taken, especially in the business sector.

Future Tax Claims on Supplementary Pensions

The importance of future tax claims for the problems being discussed here can be illustrated as follows. The CPB expects pension payments to rise from 8.8 per cent of GDP now to 21.9 per cent in 2040 (see part I of Table 5.1). The impact on government finances will be largely mitigated by the rise in the tax revenue from these pension payments. While first-pillar pension payments will rise to 5.3 per cent of GDP, tax revenue levied on older people will rise to 5.1 per cent of GDP (see part II of the table).

In the case of supplementary pensions, contributions may rise only from 6.8 per cent of gross pay now to 7.2 per cent in 2040 (see part III of the table). But the invested assets of the pension funds – in 2001 about 120 per cent of GDP – will grow to 195 per cent of GDP by 2040. The growth in income from investments will be a growing source of financing for the supplementary pension payments. Crucial to these estimates is the expected return of 5.75 per cent if pay rises at 1.75 per cent per year.

Another important point is that income from investments will largely come from abroad. Net assets invested abroad are expected to grow from 2 per cent of GDP in 2000 to 178 per cent of GDP in 2040. Income from investments abroad will then be 10 per cent of GDP as against 1 per cent now.

CONCLUSION: THE QUALITY OF THE DUTCH PENSION SYSTEM

The quality of a pension system can be looked at from various angles, with three being the most important:

1. the level of income protection offered (related to pre-retirement income);
2. the level of guarantee that the accrued pension benefits will actually be paid out after retirement; and
3. the amount of say members have over their own pension arrangements.

This conclusion will concentrate on the first of these three, the level of income protection the Dutch system offers now and in the future. Table 5.2

Table 5.2   Pension result accrued after maximum number of years of participation

Gross old-age pension as % of income just before pensioning	Occupational pension incl. 1 × AOW pension* (couples)	Occupational pension incl. single person AOW**	Ocupational pension incl. 2 × AOW pension*** (couples)
<50%	6	—	—
50–60%	36	2	—
60–70%	52	29	1
70–80%	7	54	19
80–90%	—	15	46
90–100%	—	—	25
>100%	—	—	9
Total	100	100	100

Notes:
* Net 50% of the net minimum wage.
** Net 70% of the net minimum wage.
*** Net 100% of the net minimum wage.

shows how gross pension results compare with the gross final salary. The figures are based on an individual who has contributed to the scheme for the maximum number of years possible. Generally speaking, this is 35 to 40 years. The level of state pension available in the first pillar has also been taken into account. Since supplementary pensions are additional to the state pension, the level of supplementary pension in the second pillar depends partly on the amount of state pension available. As can be seen, the overall pension one can build up in the first and second pillars is higher on average for couples than for single people. This is because couples receive 100 per cent of the net minimum wage by way of state pension, and single people receive only 70 per cent. Where only one member of a couple receives a state pension – 50 per cent of the minimum wage – this is only temporary, until the partner also reaches the age of 65.

An important instrument to keep pension benefits at an acceptable level is indexation. This can be applied to the pension as it is being accrued, as in the case of career average schemes, or to pensions already being paid out. This is important for the most common types of pension scheme in the Netherlands, the final salary schemes. Table 5.3 shows how current pensions in the second pillar are indexed.

Table 5.3   Indexation of pension rights in the second pillar

Basis for indexation	Participants in %
No indexation	—
Decision by pension board/employer (every year)	23
Wage movements (upward)	56
Similar to branch pension fund	3
General price movements	12
Other	7
Total	100

Another matter which must be mentioned is the level of the AOW franchise (Table 5.4). The AOW franchise is the amount deducted from the supplementary pension to ensure that, together with the first pillar pension, beneficiaries receive a maximum of 70 per cent of their final salary. The level of the AOW franchise varies widely from one supplementary pension scheme to another. The higher it is, the less supplementary pension is accrued in the second pillar. Supplementary pension schemes without any AOW franchise usually have a lower build-up factor than the normal 1.75 per cent per year and are based on the career average salary. Many supplementary pension schemes still use the 'breadwinner's model' in calculating the level of the AOW franchise. This means that it is assumed that individual employees will receive a state pension equivalent to 100 per cent of the net minimum wage, even though they are entitled to only 50 per cent when they reach the age of 65. The Dutch government's policy is to reduce the average level of the AOW franchise in supplementary pension schemes.

Table 5.4   The AOW franchise in the second pillar

Level of AOW franchise in % of participants	
No franchise	13
Less than 1 × AOW (couples)	11
More than 1 × AOW (couples), but less than 1 × single AOW	30
More than 1 × single AOW, but less than 2 × AOW (couples)	45
More than 2 × AOW (couples)	1
Total	100

Note:
The AOW franchise is the build in factor used in calculations in occupational pension schemes to arrive at the aimed pension level of 70% of the last salary or career average salary (incl. AOW)

A law introduced in 1994 gave people the right to transfer their accrued pension rights when they change jobs. This put an end to the situation where employees lost some of their pension, as the value already built up would remain in the old employer's scheme and therefore did not continue to grow along with their new salary. Allowing rights to be transferred preserves the employee's accrued pension benefits in the new scheme.

What can be expected in the years ahead? Figure 5.1 shows that the number of elderly people with no supplementary pension is set to fall over the next 15 years. The number of households with a supplementary pension will rise from the current 85 per cent to 90 per cent in the year 2020. This change will be accompagnied by a decline in the number of elderly people with only a small supplementary pension. As a result, the first pillar pension will decrease as a proportion of overall pension income. This is illustrated in Figure 5.2. Among low, middle and high income groups over the age of 65, the significance of supplementary pensions is set to increase at the expense of the state pension.

As well as the level of pension benefits, the question of who is participating in an occupational pension scheme is an important aspect in evaluating the quality of pension systems. The continuation of pension build-up is arranged in situations where employees are not participating in the labour process. Three situations are relevant: disablement, unemployment and

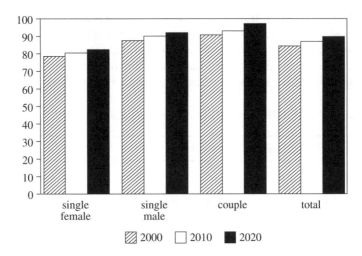

*Figure 5.1   Percentage of households, 65+, with occupational pension
            benefits (second pillar)*

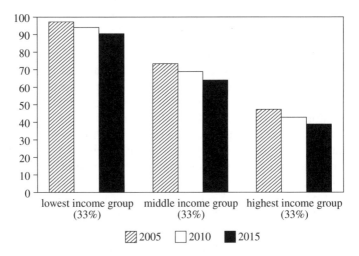

*Figure 5.2   Part of AOW (first pillar) in total income out of pension
            benefits (all three pillars)*

(protracted) leave. In all situations, the continuation of pension build-up is
arranged and set up by the social partners and therefore it is their responsibility. Most pension schemes include coverage for the non-contributory
continuation of pension build-up in the event of disablement. In that case,
continuation is usually at the level of one's previously earned salary. So

pension build-up will not be reduced compared to the situation before disablement.

In the event of unemployment, certain employees can continue their pension build-up. An employee aged 40 or over who becomes unemployed can be awarded a financial contribution to allow him to build up his pension while receiving his income-related unemployment benefit. This unemployment benefit is provided on a temporary basis and dependent on one's employment history. Unemployed aged 57.5 years and over are entitled to continuation of their pension build-up until the age of 65.

Most occupational pension schemes also include coverage for the continuation of pension build-up in the event of protracted leave. For about three-quarters of the participants in such schemes, accrual of pension benefits is continued during the period of leave, which may include, for example, maternity leave and educational leave.

Of all employees who are members of an occupational supplementary pension scheme in the second pillar: 91 per cent are currently paying into a supplementary pension. There are two possible reasons why the other 9 per cent have made no provision: either their employer has not set up a supplementary pension scheme (about 2 per cent) or their employer has attached certain conditions to participation in the scheme (this applies to 7 per cent). The most common conditions exclude employees on a temporary contract (4.7 per cent) and cleaners (1.6 per cent).

The last aspect of quality which should be mentioned is the equal treatment of women and men, which takes an important place in the second pillar of the Dutch pension system. The Netherlands took an important step towards gender equality not only by laying down the right to opt for a retirement pension instead of a surviving dependant's pension, but also by declaring that pension payments for women and men must always be equal. Differences in life expectancy should no longer lead to differences in pension payments between women and men. This is with regard both to options within the plan and to the pension eventually paid out, regardless of whether the pension plan is based on defined benefits or defined contributions. For defined contribution plans, the relevant Act will apply from 2005.

Our conclusion about the Dutch pension system therefore is as follows: it is a good system and, because the discussion on modernizing and on the sustainability of the system started on time, this system, in principle, will be sustainable in the twenty-first century. Further major reforms of the system will not be necessary, but of course all parties involved should constantly be aware of needs for adjustment. Since pension policy in the Netherlands is put on the political as well as the social agenda, we can be sure that there will always be some party available to start the necessary discussion.

APPENDIX

Table 5A.1   Pension system in the Netherlands: key figures (2002)

Population/labour market participation	mn persons	% total population	% working population
1. actually working (>12 hrs/week)	6.9	42.8	100
2. sick	0.4		
3. unemployed/social assistance	0.6		
4. disabled	0.9		
5. early retired	0.2*		
6. survivors	0.2		
7. pensioners (65+)	2.4*	14.9	34.7
8. without income	1.5		
9. children (0 to 14)	3.0*		
Total population	16.1	100	
Employment (>12 hrs/week)	7.3		
Labour force (15–64)	7.7		
Inactive population with income (2 to 7)	4.7	29.1	66.7
Population without income (8+9)	4.5		
Labour share 55–64 (in % total population 55–64)		37.0	
Dependency rate 65+ (in % total population 15–64)		20.2	
Financial figures	bn Euros	% GDP	
GDP	445.5	100	
Budget balance collective sector		–1.1	
National debt		52.4	
Public expenditure (gross)		47.7	

	bn Euros	% GDP
Social security expenditure		11.9
Public health expenditure		8.4
Yearly expenditure 1st pillar (AOW)	21.4	4.8
Yearly expenditure 2nd pillar (funds)	14.0*	3.1
Yearly expenditure 2nd pillar (insurers)	5.9*	1.3
Yearly expenditure 3rd pillar (life insurers)	7.9*	1.8
Pension savings 2nd pillar (funds)	456.2*	102.4
Pension savings 2nd & 3rd pillar (insurers)	251.2*	56.4

Contributions	bn Euros	% GDP
Public social security (including health)	66.5	14.9
1st pillar (AOW)	17.7	4.0
2nd pillar (occupational pensions)	9.5*	2.1

Incomes (per year)	Euros	% average wage
Gross average wage	36400	100
Gross minimum wage	15800	43
Net average wage (single)	24252	100
Net minimum wage (single)	12547	52
Net AOW (single)	9844	41
Net average wage (single earner)	25900	100
Net minimum wage (single earner)	14195	55
Net AOW (couple)	13871	54
2nd + 3rd pillar assets (average per capita)	15600*	

Notes.
* 2001 figures
** 2000 figures

C

Carve-outs: Germany, USA and Swedish financial accounts

6. Paradigm shift in German pension policy: measures aiming at a new public–private mix and their effects

Winfried Schmähl

INTRODUCTION

Germany has one of the oldest public pension schemes in the world. When in 1889 the political decision on the design of the statutory (social) pension insurance was made, a number of structural elements were introduced that more than one hundred years later still influence pension schemes.[1] However, since the late nineteenth century a lot of changes have taken place in the process of adapting pension arrangements to changing conditions in the environment of pension schemes, such as demography, economy, household structures and living conditions, but also in political objectives and dominating normative positions in the country. Nevertheless, there has also been some continuity. Several attempts or proposals to abolish the social insurance scheme that is mainly based on contribution payments were not successful.[2]

Pension reform has been a topic debated worldwide for many years and also has a high ranking on the political agenda in Germany. Pension reform was also of great importance in several election campaigns to the Federal Parliament after the Second World War. One of the central questions in recent debates is the role of the state in general as well as in pension policy. Pay-as-you-go (PAYGO)-financed public schemes in particular are under severe political pressure in Germany. Often a radical shift towards capital funding is proposed, which is in general linked to proposals for privatizing at least major parts of public old age security. It is not surprising that the insurance industry, banks and investment funds are proposing to perform old age provision more via capital markets instead of PAYGO financing and thus using (pre-)funding.

In Germany, pension reform has been at the centre of political debate for many years. Decisions have been made rather frequently over the last few years. The most recent political decisions from 2000 and 2001 (in the following referred to as '2001 pension reform') are aiming at a major shift in the structure of Germany's pension provision by reducing PAYGO-financed public pensions[3] and replacing public pensions partially with sub-sidized private (including occupational) pensions that up to now have been voluntary. These decisions will have far-reaching consequences for pension policy in Germany. A transformation process has started that affects not only public pension schemes but also occupational pensions in the private and the public sector, as well as additional private old age provision.

There are numerous reasons for recent pension reform debates in Germany. Many are similar to those in other industrialized countries, such as demographic aging, resulting from a low fertility rate (which in Germany for a long time has been only two-thirds of the replacement level) and from increasing life expectancy. The growing number of elderly people (in abso-lute and relative terms) is labelled primarily as a burden on the economy and especially on the younger generation. 'Generational equity' became one of the catchphrases most often used in the German pension debate.

There are many other factors affecting pension schemes, such as changes in the labour market and in the life cycle of adults between employment and retirement. In the German public debate, effects of an intensified inter-national competition (and in general of 'globalization') were and are an important topic. In particular the reduction of non-wage labour costs – and here above all of employers' contributions to social insurance – are high on the agenda of politicians, employers and industry organizations.

Some challenges in Germany are different from those of other countries, such as the economic consequences of German unification, which include, among other things, high unemployment rates in general and especially in East Germany. This increased the contribution rate to social pension in-surance. In recent years, there has also been an additional effect from the process of integration within the European Union which has important consequences at the national level in framing the pension debate. Obviously there exists a very complex set of influencing factors. And there is also a great number of active players in the 'pension arena'. Here some changes in the comparative influence of these players took place. For example, banks and also the mass media gained more influence in recent years.

The main focus of this chapter is on the most recent pension reform (2001 reform) and its implications for future development. In order to understand what has changed it is necessary to broaden the picture and to put the '2001 reform' into context. Therefore this chapter begins with a short overview of the institutional structure of the pension arrangements in Germany, its major concepts and distributional objectives prior to the '2001 reform'. It will be shown that, after the Second World War, there were already some important paradigm shifts in pension policy. This informa-tion about the past gives a better understanding of the conceptual changes that may result from the recent political decisions for old age security and the new public–private mix in this area.

The major structural decisions in postwar German pension policy were based for a long time on a broad political consensus between the major political parties as well as trade unions and employers' organizations (both also working together in self-administration bodies of social insurance). This consensus was lost, however, a few years after German unification. Regarding the recent decisions (2001 pension reform) the underlying concepts, interests and goals are outlined as well as the major instruments to realize these goals. Then an analysis is given of some short-term as well as long-term effects resulting from the measures implemented. Although it is too early to have empirical data on major economic effects – especially on income distribution – some consequences seem to be obvious. Finally, some information is given on topics that will soon be on the political agenda as well as some reflections regarding the question of which type of pension arrangements may develop in Germany in the future.

THE INSTITUTIONAL STRUCTURE OF PENSION ARRANGEMENTS IN GERMANY BEFORE AND AFTER THE '2001 PENSION REFORM'

Before the '2001 Reform'

Germany has complex, highly diversified and fragmented pension arrangements, which becomes obvious from Figure 6.1. This fact is mainly the result of the historical development because, for example, the mandatory schemes were not developed to cover the whole population but separate pension schemes were established for several groups of the population, depending on the type of employment, such as civil servants, white-collar and later also blue-collar workers, and several groups of self-employed: professional associations and farmers.[4] Germany therefore has no uniform and universal first tier as a basis of old age security for the whole population, as in its neighbouring countries of Denmark, Holland or Switzerland.

In Germany, three tiers (often labelled 'pillars') of old age security have existed for a long time.[5] There are mandatory basic pension schemes for different groups of the population as the first tier, supplementary occupational schemes as the second tier and additional private voluntary arrangements for old age provision as the third tier. In the following, the situation up to the 2001 pension reform is briefly described first. Then some changes resulting from the recent reform are mentioned. They will be discussed later.

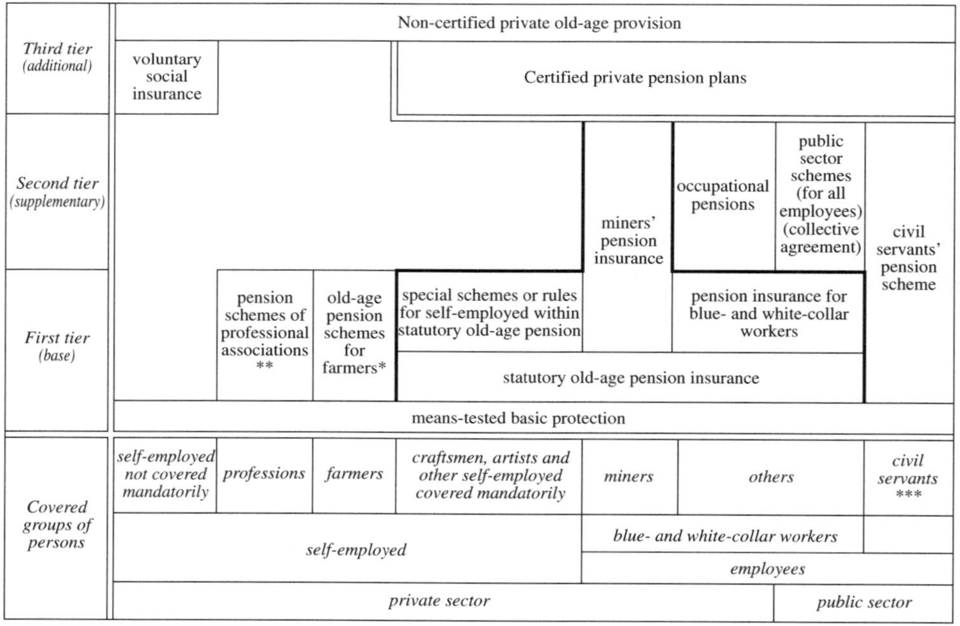

Third tier (additional)	Non-certified private old-age provision							
	voluntary social insurance	Certified private pension plans						
Second tier (supplementary)		pension schemes of professional associations **	old-age pension schemes for farmers*	special schemes or rules for self-employed within statutory old-age pension	miners' pension insurance	occupational pensions	public sector schemes (for all employees) (collective agreement)	civil servants' pension scheme
							pension insurance for blue- and white-collar workers	
First tier (base)				statutory old-age pension insurance				
				means-tested basic protection				
Covered groups of persons	self-employed not covered mandatorily	professions	farmers	craftsmen, artists and other self-employed covered mandatorily	miners	others	civil servants ***	
						blue- and white-collar workers		
		self-employed				employees		
		private sector					public sector	

Figure 6.1 *Old-age pension schemes for various groups of the population in the Federal Republic of Germany*

Notes:
* Including family workers. This scheme is designed as partial old-age security beside income from the former farm.
** Partly also for employees of the respective branches.
*** Including judges and professional soldiers.

156

Regarding the first tier, statutory social pension insurance is the dominating element. It is also the most important part of the whole German pension system. It covers in principle all blue- and white-collar workers (including miners) but also some groups of self-employed. The major source of revenue is contributions paid in equal parts by employees and employers, but there is also revenue from the federal public budget. The rules for miners,[6] as well as for the self-employed, differ from the general rules relevant for employees (civil servants have a separate scheme). Further information concerning the design of the statutory pension scheme will be given below. A major part of the paradigm shift of the '2001 reform' is linked to this scheme.

A special pension scheme exists for civil servants. It is a final salary scheme based on a combination of a first-tier pension and a supplementary occupational pension. It is integrated into general public budgets (at federal, state and local level) and financed from general (tax) revenue. Separate pension schemes exist for several groups of self-employed. They differ in many respects from statutory pension insurance and civil servants' pensions. There are schemes for farmers and for professional associations, like those of doctors, lawyers, architects, tax consultants and pharmacists.

It is not well known in Germany that, on average, only 50 per cent of the members of these schemes for professional associations are self-employed – 50 per cent are employees. This means that, for employees working in these branches, there is the possibility of contracting out from the general scheme for blue- and white-collar workers – the statutory (social) pension insurance.

Regarding old-age protection of the self-employed, the statistical data are far from being sufficient. We only know that about half of the self-employed are not mandatorily covered (Fachinger and Oelschläger, 2000, p.165), but we do not know how much and by which instruments they are saving for their own old age.

Most of the first-tier schemes are pay-as-you go (PAYGO)-financed (statutory pension insurance, schemes for civil servants and farmers). Schemes for professional associations are capital-funded.

Supplementary occupational pension schemes are the second tier of the German pension system. In the private sector they are generally voluntary, with a great variety in design. Only about 50 per cent of all employees are covered and coverage varies widely according to the branch and size of the firm. Pensions are mainly defined benefit and employer-financed. Occupational schemes in the private sector are based on capital funding.

In Germany, four different types of occupational schemes existed already before the '2001 reform': direct pension commitments, pension insurance funds, support funds and direct insurance.

Direct pension commitments were made by the employer in favour of his employees and financed within the firm, based on book reserves. This type is of special importance in Germany. More than half of all accumulated reserves in occupational schemes in the private sector are based on book reserves. In the period of reconstructing the German economy after the Second World War this was an important instrument of self-financing. But it remains attractive today. It is used especially by big firms. The firm itself is the pension institution. This type of occupational pension is under severe attack from actors in the financial markets because the money does not flow via capital markets. It is argued that the efficient allocation of capital is reduced if self-financing is used. We will see, later, that the '2001 reform' gives incentives for firms to outsource capital and thereby to reduce the quantitative impact of this specific way of organizing occupational pension arrangements.

The pension insurance funds (*Pensionskassen*) are legally independent institutions in the form of mutual insurance associations. Financing is by the employer, but the employee can also contribute. Support funds (*Unterstützungskassen*) are also legally independent institutions, mostly registered associations, financed only by the employer. In the case of direct insurance, the employer is the policy holder and takes out individual or group life insurance for the employee. Financing is by the employer and/or the employee.[7] By the '2001 reform' a fifth type was introduced, namely pension funds (for details, see below).

During the 1990s, a decline in occupational pension arrangements took place, because of less favourable conditions being given for new employees or the closing of schemes for newly hired employees. Several reasons were mentioned for this development, among other things costs of occupational pensions as part of labour costs. It is argued that high labour costs are a severe disadvantage in periods of intensified international competition. Tax conditions are also mentioned by firms as a reason for a downward trend in occupational pensions. It can be also assumed that (employer-financed) occupational pensions as an instrument of attracting qualified labour have lost their importance because of the labour market conditions (high unemployment). Collective agreements were an exception in the private sector up to the '2001 reform',[8] in marked contrast, for example, to the Netherlands. Following the '2001 reform', a process of change has been under way.

It is important to note that taxation of saving for old age and of pension benefits differ within the first as also between first and second and within the second-tier schemes. This has to be taken into account when comparing, for example, the pension benefits of different schemes. Occupational pension schemes for wage and salary earners in the public sector are based on collective agreements, in contrast to the private sector. Financing is mainly by public employers and PAYGO financing dominates. The supplementary pensions in the public sector are fully integrated with the statutory insurance pensions, which means that a reduction in social insurance pension will be compensated by higher supplementary pensions – if the collective agreement is not changed. From both types of pensions, wage and salary earners in the public sector will receive a pension benefit that is aimed at the level of civil servants' pensions. That means that a final salary scheme (as a combination of first and second tiers) exists also for blue- and white-collar workers in the public sector. After the '2001 reform', trade unions and public employers agreed upon a new collective contract that will abolish this integrated approach. It will separate the supplementary pension from the development of the first-tier schemes – that is, from the development of civil servants' pensions as well as statutory pension insurance.[9] It will also be changed from defined benefit to defined contribution.

As a third tier, there exists a great variety of voluntary and capital-funded additional types of saving for old age, some with risk pooling (life insurance), others without such insurance elements, while some types are tax-privileged. Empirically it is very difficult to identify which part of the saving of households is for old age. Even tax-privileged life insurance benefits can be used for other purposes. In order to get the tax privileges, only a life insurance contract for at least 12 years is required. Tax treatment differs for different types of voluntary saving.

The borderline between the second and the third tier became more and more blurred over time because of using models of deferred compensation and, especially, earnings conversion financed only by employees but with the support of the employer, for example by negotiating group insurance contracts with a life insurer resulting in better conditions compared to individual contracts. Time saving accounts are used as well. Several collective agreements are tailored to maximize net labour income by avoiding tax and social insurance contributions on that part of labour income that is deferred for old age security. The '2001 reform' is extending the concept of earnings conversion and introduces new possibilities for taking up subsidies for voluntary old age provision.

Summing up the situation before the '2001 reform', the first tier is mandatory, the biggest part is public and the majority of benefits is defined benefit and PAYGO-financed. The second tier of occupational pensions is mainly employer-financed, voluntary in the private sector, but based on collective agreements in the public sector. Defined benefit dominates.

In Germany, at the end of the 1990s, about 80 per cent of all pension expenditure for old age, invalidity and survivors was PAYGO-financed (around 68 per cent social insurance, 12 per cent civil servants' pension scheme). Some 10 per cent of all pension expenditure came from the second tier (occupational pensions) and, at a rough estimate, another 10 per cent from the third tier.[10] It is an explicit goal of the '2001 reform' to change these ratios towards more capital funding.

Social pension insurance covers by far the most of all gainfully employed people in Germany: in 1999, 93 per cent of those covered by mandatory first-tier schemes were members of this scheme (see Table 6.1). Almost 69 per cent of total pension expenditure was from this scheme. This was almost 10.6 per cent of GDP.

Table 6.1   Persons covered by pension schemes in Germany at the end of 1999

Pension scheme	1000s	As % of total first tier
Mandatory first tier		
Statutory (social) pension insurance in total	33 250	92.9
White- and blue-collar workers	32 166	
Miners	147	
Self-employed		
(voluntarily and mandatorily insured)	755	
Artists	96	
Craftsmen	86	
Civil servants' pension scheme	1 587	4.3
Professional associations	546	1.5
Farmers' pension scheme	417	1.2
Total of first tier	35 800	100.0
Second tier: occupational pension schemes		
Private sector	12 000[1]	
Public sector	4 864	

Note: [1] Estimate

Source: Data from Sachverständigenrat (2001, p.159).

It is not surprising that social insurance pensions were (at least on average) by far the most important source of (monetary) income in old age in Germany (Table 6.2).[11] In 1998 in West Germany gross income of pensioner households (the head of the household aged 60 years or more) was about 80 per cent from public transfer payments (mainly from social pension insurance). In East Germany, this percentage was even higher, resulting from the fact that, in the German Democratic Republic, in principle no supplementary occupational pensions existed and also private saving for old age (for example by life insurance) was not very common. It

*Table 6.2   Income of pensioners¹ from different sources, Germany 1998
(percentage of gross household income)*

Income (gross) from	Single-person households		Two-person households	
	West	East	West	East
Public transfer payments	82.3	95.8	77.8	93.4
Private transfer payments (incl. occupational pensions)	8.9	1.6	9.2	1.6
Employment	2.2	0.9	4.4	3.1
Private life insurance	1.7	0.4	3.3	0.4
Assets²	4.9	1.3	5.4	1.6

Notes:
[1] Pensioner = person age 60 and over; dominating income source not from employment; in two-person households: the first person with these characteristics.
[2] Without imputed income from living in own house or flat.

Source: Income and Expenditure Survey 1998, own calculations.

is obvious that the introduction of funded elements of pension provision will need a long time before income from these schemes can become a notable source of income in old age.

On average, income from assets was only of minor importance for German pensioner households: about 5 per cent of gross income in West Germany was from this source (about 1.5 per cent in East Germany). However, there exist great differences in the income packaging within the group of pensioner households. This cannot be discussed here.[12] This heterogeneity of household income is often neglected in public, including scientific debates. The important microeconomic as well as macroeconomic role of social insurance pensions illustrates why in Germany so much attention is focused on this part of the pension scheme. The majority of the people in Germany are affected by this scheme during most of their lives, either as contributors or as pensioners. And, for the majority of the elderly, social insurance pensions are the most important element of their income in old age.

Germany had no general minimum pension. If household income is lower than a certain amount, means-tested social assistance can be claimed. Fewer than 2 per cent of all elderly people received (at the end of 1998) social assistance. If those persons are added to the number who may be eligible for social assistance but do not claim this payment, even the most pessimistic estimates state that no more than about 4 per cent of pensioners are living in 'poverty': that is, with income below the social assistance level.[13]

New Institutional Elements Introduced by the '2001 Reform'

The '2001 pension reform' introduced two new elements into the German pension system. The first is a means-tested transfer payment in the case of insufficient income for those aged 65 and older, as well as for disabled persons. The benefit amount, however, is calculated in the same way as the already-mentioned means-tested social assistance. But there is one major difference: children are not obliged to pay back the whole sum or part of it (as in the case of social assistance – depending on their own financial resources) if their parents claim this new means-tested benefit and if the income of the children does not exceed 100 000 Euros per year.

The second new element is a subsidy for contributions for a private pension that fulfils certain criteria in order to get a certificate which is a prerequisite for subsidies. This approach (subsidizing private pensions) is labelled as the 'heart' of the 2001 pension reform by the ruling coalition government (Social Democratic and Green Party).[14] These new elements changed the structure of the German pension scheme because social assistance was not a specific element of the scheme and already existing subsidized private saving for old age is not aimed at pension provision in particular. The two new elements are integrated in Figure 6.1.

In the above, the organizational setting of the German pension system especially was described as regards its basic elements. We now turn to the design of the pension system and particularly the social pension insurance which is the cornerstone of the German pension system. This PAYGO scheme has been under severe political pressure for a number of years. Many actors have been and still are trying to scale down the scheme fundamentally and to change its structure. In recent decades several remarkable changes have taken place in German pension policy and in particular in the social pension insurance, and there have already been paradigm shifts. This will be outlined in what follows and can be contrasted to the new paradigm shift the '2001 pension reform' is based upon.

SOME PARADIGM SHIFTS AND MAJOR STRUCTURAL DECISIONS IN GERMAN POSTWAR PENSION POLICY BEFORE THE '2001 PENSION REFORM'

The design of German pension policy is linked above all to the scope and design of the social pension insurance. Only a few elements can be highlighted here to illustrate the development of its basic features and the consequences for supplementary and additional pension schemes. These schemes are highly influenced by the level and structure of the most important public pension scheme.

From 1889, when the political decisions on the social pension insurance were made, up to 1956, social insurance pensions were based on a flat rate amount, financed from general tax revenue, and an earnings-related part, mostly financed from contribution revenue. The level of pensions was very low and often, after a long working life, not sufficient to finance one's living in old age. This was in part due to the fact that the individual pension amount was calculated on the absolute amount of former nominal earnings. It was a static scheme. This structure in principle remained effective even after the collapse of the Nazi regime, although there were attempts to change the scheme towards flat-rate benefits. After the Second World War, and up to 1956, there were only few ad hoc increases in the pension amount. A major paradigm shift in pension policy took place in 1957 in West Germany (Federal Republic) which changed social insurance pensions fundamentally regarding distributional objectives, benefit level and financing method. In East Germany, however, the previous type of pension calculation remained in principle effective up to July 1990, when the Deutschmark was introduced in East Germany,[15] together with the pension law of West Germany.[16]

The Paradigm Shift of 1957: Introducing a 'Dynamic Pension' in West Germany

In 1957, the flat-rate amount in the pension formula was abolished in West Germany and pensions were linked to actual earnings. Pension calculation was no longer based on former nominal earnings but on the relative earnings position (individual earnings compared to average earnings during all the years of insurance). Pensions were increased on average by 65.3 per cent (blue-collar) and 71.9 per cent (white-collar) in 1957.[17] The introduction of a rule for regular pension adjustment linked in principle to the growth rate of average gross earnings was important. It was the distributional objective that pensioners should participate in the economic development and that pensions should replace former earnings to a certain extent. Financing now was based mainly on the PAYGO principle,[18] while, before, the official concept was capital funding for social insurance pensions.[19] This shift towards PAYGO made it possible to increase the pension benefits for present pensioners as well – not only for future pensioners in about 20 or more years.

This pension reform, like some other important decisions in the years to come, was based on a broad consensus of the major political parties, although there was much resistance even within the government, in particular by the Ministry of Finance, the labour and industry organizations, banks (including the Federal Reserve Bank) and the insurance industry. In spite of fears of banks, employer organizations and other actors, the pension reform had no negative effect on private saving. The saving rate of pensioners even increased. And there was a remarkable growth in new life insurance contracts.

Based on highly optimistic expectations for future economic development at the beginning of the 1970s, calculations for pension financing showed remarkable budget surplus for the coming years. In the political arena, a real race in proposing additional expenditure took place. The result was a package of decisions in 1972. This included the introduction of a flexible retirement age: it became possible to claim a pension before the standard retirement age (of 65) without any deductions from the full pension.[20] This became very popular with employees and was used later by firms in combination with other measures of early retirement to restructure and rejuvenate their workforce. The average retirement age decreased.[21]

Early retirement imposed a heavy financial burden for social pension insurance because of the increase in pension expenditure. After the first oil price shock in the mid-1970s, economic conditions changed. A great number of ad hoc measures were taken to reduce the development of pension expenditure. In addition, demographic aging in the years to come and the effects on PAYGO pension schemes had been a much discussed topic in Germany for many years. All this stimulated a more fundamental pension reform debate in Germany.

At the centre of the debate there was the question of how to distribute the increasing economic burden in public pension schemes resulting from population aging. An increase in the contribution rate (as well as the expected increase in income tax) would reduce the development of net earnings of employees, while on the other hand the development of pensions was linked to the growth rate of (average) gross earnings. Most of the social insurance pensions were not burdened by income tax. Therefore the ratio of pensions to net earnings would increase more and more. This development (as well as the increase in non-wage labour costs in the case of rising contribution rates) stimulated proposals for a new pension adjustment formula aiming at a reduction in the growth rate of pension expenditure and a new distribution of economic burden resulting from demographic aging.

The Paradigm Shift of 1989: Stabilizing the Pension Level and Introducing an 'Expenditure-oriented Revenue Policy' within a Self-regulating Mechanism

On 9 November 1989 (the very day that the Berlin Wall was opened) a reform Act was decided in parliament, based on a clear distributional objective and the idea of constructing the social pension insurance scheme according to a self-regulating mechanism.[22] Among the measures to realize this was a new pension adjustment formula: individual pensions were now linked to the development of the growth rate of average net earnings. This was an important instrument to realize an explicit distributional objective: pensioners with a specific number of pension claims (earnings points) should always be entitled to a pension benefit equivalent to a specific percentage of actual average net earnings of all employees. This should be realized not only at the time of retirement but also throughout the phase of receiving a pension benefit. Therefore a constant net pension level (pension compared to net average earnings) was aimed at and realized by adjusting individual pension benefits to the growth rate of net average earnings. This underlines the character of the social pension insurance as a defined benefit scheme.

The pension scheme was constructed according to the idea of an 'expenditure-oriented revenue policy': the contribution rate was the dependent variable as well as the grant from the federal budget to pension policy. Federal grant was linked not only – as before – to the development of earnings but also to the development of the contribution rate in pension insurance. Contribution rate and federal grant would be calculated in such a way that they were sufficient to finance the pension expenditure that were expected according to demographic, economic and other assumptions. An increase in the contribution rate as well as in other direct burdens of the employees, however, would also reduce the increase of pensions via the net adjustment formula.

The new adjustment formula was an important instrument in reducing the future development of pension expenditure. In addition, it was also decided to introduce a deduction from the full pension in the case of early retirement.[23]

BASIC FEATURES OF THE SOCIAL PENSION INSURANCE SCHEME BEFORE THE '2001 PENSION REFORM' IN COMPARATIVE PERSPECTIVE

The social pension insurance is income-related with a high degree of intertemporal income redistribution over the life cycle. In recent years, a reduction of elements aiming at interpersonal income redistribution in social pension insurance has been realized, either by reducing such expenditure or by financing this expenditure increasingly in an adequate manner from general tax revenues. Pension claims based on contribution payment are looked upon as property rights protected by the constitution.

The whole insurance period is taken into account for calculating pensions. Individual pension claims of the insured person from earnings or other activities are accumulated within an individual account managed by social insurance pension administration. Income and consumption smoothing over the life cycle is the main distributional objective of the statutory pension scheme, and not primarily avoiding poverty. For pensioners – at least for those with a longer insurance record – the pension is sufficient to maintain to a certain specified percentage during retirement the level of living that was financed before retirement from earnings. Social pension insurance is a defined benefit scheme.

These few characteristics of the German pension system already allow us to categorize it within a simple typology. With regard to mandatory public pension schemes, this typology is based on the dominating distributional objective and dominating type of income redistribution (see Table 6.3). As regards the main basic pension scheme in Germany (social pension insurance) its place in this typology is obvious.

A remarkable finding from international comparisons is that, in general, in countries with earnings-related pension schemes, the need for additional means-, income- or asset-tested (social assistance) benefits is lower than in countries with a public pension scheme aimed at avoiding poverty in old age.[24] For example, in Switzerland, the number of pensioners receiving means-tested benefits (*Ergänzungsleistungen*) additional to the basic AHV

Table 6.3   Mandatory public pensions, first tier

Dominating objective \ Dominating type of redistribution	Interpersonal redistribution	Intertemporal redistribution (close contribution–benefit link)
Avoiding poverty in old age	flat-rate pension; means- or income-tested transfer payments; low pension level	minimum pension based on contribution payments
Income and consumption smoothing over the life cycle (income-related)	social insurance with weak contribution–benefit link	social insurance with strong contribution–benefit link (Germany)
	← defined benefit	defined contribution →

Source: Own chart (based on Schmähl, 2002b, p.18).

pensions in the case of insufficient income in old age is relatively higher than in Germany[25] a fact often neglected in German discussions, where often the 'Swiss model' is mentioned as a guideline for pension policy.

If we look at countries with a low public pension level or with flat-rate or almost flat-rate pensions (like Holland and Switzerland) or with income-tested transfer payments in old age like Australia, those countries sooner or later introduced mandatory income-related second tiers to top up low public pensions and to realize an income-related pension provision in old age by two income sources. However, countries with a more generous public pension level in general have voluntary supplementary schemes, as in Germany or the United States (Table 6.4).[26]

Table 6.4   Combinations of mandatory public first tier and mandatory or voluntary supplementary second tier

Supplementary 2nd tier (capital-funded) ⟍ Mandatory 1st tier (PAYGO)	Mandatory or collective agreement	Voluntary

Flat-rate
  Means-tested
  (low pension level)
	Netherlands
	Switzerland
	Australia	

Income-related (higher pension level)		USA Germany

These lessons from international development are of special interest regarding future development in Germany as it may take place after the '2001 pension reform'. Before describing and discussing this point, some facts will be outlined which were important in the German debate that finally resulted in the '2001 pension reform'.

SOME MAJOR BACKGROUND FACTS IN RECENT DEBATES ON PENSION REFORM IN GERMANY

The Growing Economic Burden in PAYGO-Financed Schemes

In the 1980s, as well as in the years following German unification in the 1990s, debates on further reform measures, especially regarding the PAYGO-financed social pension insurance and – to a minor extent also civil servants' pensions – were based on projections showing an increasing future economic burden of social security: increasing expenditure, rising contribution rates and rising non-wage labour costs. The topic of labour costs was important in the public debate and mainly focused on assumed negative effects regarding competitiveness. This had two dimensions: (1) a national one – expected negative incentive effects on the official labour market competitiveness of the official sector compared to shadow work activities and (2) one focused on international competitiveness of German industry. Whether and how far the assumed effects are empirically well-founded, the arguments were and are important in the political debate.

If we look at the relative economic 'burden' of expenditure of statutory pension insurance, the development at least up to the end of the twentieth century does not look 'dramatic': the expenditure has remained more or less unchanged in West Germany since the end of the 1980s (see Figure 6.2). Up to German unification, even a reduction in the ratio occurred. It is obvious that the German unification had a ratio-increasing effect. Such a ratio is influenced not only by the development of expenditure, but also by the growth rate of the GDP. The (moderate) recession in 1966/7 in West Germany and the difficult economic conditions, especially in East Germany, after unification are examples.

If the ratio is calculated separately for East and West Germany,[27] at the end of the 1990s the ratio of GDP was below 10 per cent in West Germany and increased to more than 20 per cent in East Germany.

However, this macroeconomic picture hides a development which is at the centre of the political debate, namely the development of contribution rates. Here, not only contribution rates in pension insurance were discussed as relevant, but the total of contribution rates of pension, health, long-term care and unemployment insurance. The contribution rates in social insurance were increasing over time (Figure 6.3). For some years, it has been a political target to reduce the total contribution rate of the social insurance schemes to below 40 per cent.

The assessment basis for social security contributions is labour income of insured employees (not exceeding the upper contribution limit).[28] Because of a decline in the share of labour income in total factor income, the basis for contribution financing was declining, too.[29] The reduction in the labour income share subject to contributions, together with relatively rising expenditure, made higher contribution rates necessary.[30] And, for the future, demographic aging especially is seen as a major factor for rising contribution rates in social insurance that are expected and the main argument for demanding expenditure cuts, particularly in pension insurance.

This past development, and in particular the expected negative economic effects of population aging, stimulated the development of crisis scenarios.

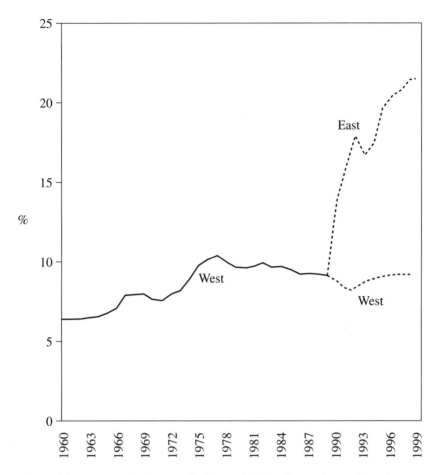

Note: * Statutory pension insurance for blue- and white-collar workers and for miners

Figure 6.2   Total expenditure of statutory pension insurance in per cent
of GDP, 1960–99, Germany*

Here an interaction of many economists, actors in the financial market, politicians and the mass media took place. Rolling back the welfare state became a much-recommended strategy to cope with future economic problems.[31] Cutting back PAYGO-financed expenditure was demanded and above all an increase in capital funding. The already mentioned present ratio of 80 per cent PAYGO-financed pension expenditure and 20 per cent based on capital funding should be changed, for example to 60:40 as some economists have proposed. This would make it necessary to reduce the level of public pension expenditure remarkably. Capital funding – some economists

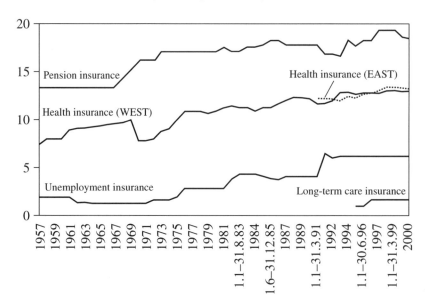

Source: Data from VDR (2001).

*Figure 6.3   Contribution rates, statutory pension, health and long-term
            care insurance*

declared – is dominating PAYGO financing in nearly all aspects.[32] Therefore
it was argued that such a shift towards funding would improve the wellbeing
of the population, at least in the long run.

   In the German public debate the future contribution rates are often calculated according to the development of the old age dependency ratio
(number of persons above retirement age compared to number of persons
of working age). Because the old age dependency ratio was expected to
double until the year 2030, a doubling of the contribution rates also was
often predicted. This can be highly misleading because, for financing, the
pensioner ratio (number of pensioners compared to contributors) is decisive, which may develop differently, for example if labour force participation rates are changing. And also the effects of already implemented
political decisions affecting revenue and expenditure of the pension scheme
are neglected.

   If we compare, for example, the projected contribution rates for the year
2030 that were officially calculated in 1989 and take into account the
changes already decided in the statutory pension scheme before the '2001
pension reform', we see that remarkable changes took place over time. In
1989, it was projected that contribution rates for West Germany would rise

to more than 36 per cent until 2030. That means a doubling of the contribution rate compared to the rate that existed at that time. In 2000, the projection which is the basis for political decisions of the '2001 pension reform' gave a different picture: an increase of the contribution rate up to 'only' 23.6 per cent in 2030 for West and East Germany (Schmähl, 1998b, p.261).

To evaluate such contribution rates there should be taken into consideration, among other things, that German unification increased the overall contribution rate in pension insurance by about one percentage point. This situation will not change for a long time. And not only PAYGO but capital-funded schemes as well will become more expensive in the process of demographic aging, especially if life expectancy is increasing.

The public debate about the coming demographic crisis and almost daily reports in the mass media prepared the ground for a major paradigm shift based (this is my interpretation) on a coalition (often informal) aiming in the same direction: reducing the public PAYGO-financed scheme and replacing this with private capital-funded elements. The actors have different motives. The minister of finance became a major actor in the pension policy arena. He is particularly interested in reducing the burden for public budgets and public debt in line with the Maastricht convergence criteria. A lower contribution rate also means a lower federal grant to social pension insurance.

Many mainstream economists are arguing in favour of only minimum protection which should mainly be for interpersonal redistributive purposes. This view is also supported by those who recommend more interpersonal redistribution (often labelled 'solidarity') in pension policy instead of a close contribution–benefit link. Employers' organizations are in favour of a reduction of the PAYGO public scheme because of lower contribution rates. And, of course, the actors in the financial market such as banks, pension funds and insurance companies are highly interested in a reduction of the benefit level in public PAYGO schemes. The activities of banks and so on in the pension arena were much increased compared to former times. The total sum of pension money is increasing in an aging population and makes this field more attractive for companies. It is argued that the rate of return of funded schemes would by far exceed the low rate of return of the PAYGO scheme.[33] These calculations are often based on highly optimistic assumptions and are not very transparent, neglecting costs in general as well as transition costs when replacing PAYGO with capital funding. These calculations are only for capital funded old-age pensions, while in the statutory pension insurance disability pensions and expenditure for rehabilitation are also covered, which reduces the rate of return.[34]

Many, especially younger, people were convinced by the argument that, only by saving in capital-funded schemes, is one doing something for oneself, while contributing to a PAYGO scheme is paying for others (the present pensioners). Although this is a highly biased argument, in particular if the PAYGO scheme has a strong contribution–benefit link, it was an argument that influenced the view of many regarding the need for a reform that (at least) reduces the PAYGO scheme and gives the opportunity for more capital funding.

The political debate was finally framed by the new government (Chancellor Schröder) which came into power in autumn 1998, in such a way that a contribution rate of about 24 per cent in 2030 in social pension insurance would be unbearable and would burden the 'younger generations' too much.[35] This became a cornerstone in the reform agenda. The development of the contribution rate became the decisive indicator. Therefore cuts in the pension level would be unavoidable. To compensate such cuts, additional private saving is necessary for living in old age. The 'stick' was the cut in the public pension level and the 'carrot' was a subsidy for private pension saving ('government makes you a gift'). This looked especially attractive during the boom period of the stock markets.

Attempts to reduce the level of statutory pension insurance had, however, already been decided by the former government (chancellor Kohl), together with measures to strengthen the contribution–benefit link in social pension insurance. This was done by reducing elements aiming at interpersonal redistribution (such as crediting pension claims for years of schooling without contribution payments) and financing those redistributive elements more from general tax revenue. Meanwhile this approach was also supported by the Social Democratic Party, at that time the biggest opposition party in Parliament.[36] The Social Democrats, however, were strictly against lowering the pension level, which the former Kohl government had decided upon, by introducing a so-called 'demographic factor' into the pension formula.[37]

A NEW PARADIGM SHIFT BY THE '2001 PENSION REFORM'

The main elements of the new political strategy will be mentioned in the following. Thereafter, the most important instruments implemented to realize the new approach will be identified.[38]

Main Elements of the New Paradigm Shift

As has already been pointed out, the main objectives and characteristics of the social insurance pension scheme as realized by decisions in 1989 (1992 pension reform) and based on the 1957 reform are as follows:

- an explicit distributional objective: an individual pension should be a fixed percentage of average net earnings (the percentage depending on the accumulated sum of pension claims);
- a defined benefit scheme;
- a constant pension level maintained over time by linking the development of pensions to the development of average net earnings;
- financing (by social insurance contributions and federal grant) as a dependent variable, a strategy that can be labelled 'expenditure-oriented revenue policy';
- occupational pensions as a supplement to social insurance pensions. Financing by employers predominates, pensions are mainly of the defined benefit type. Occupational pensions in the private sector are voluntary;
- voluntary private saving for old age (for example by life insurance contracts) as an additional means of old age protection.

The '2001 reform' changed several of these characteristics:

- A 'revenue-oriented expenditure policy' in social pension insurance was established by declaring the development of the contribution rate to be the main objective. The benefit level becomes the dependent variable.
- Employees now have a right of earnings conversion. Collective agreements are favoured. (New) occupational pensions become quasi-mandated. Instead of financing by the employer, financing by employees will predominate. Therefore it seems justifiable to speak no longer of 'occupational pensions' – in Germany these were identified as being employer-financed – but of 'firm- (or employer-) based pensions'.
- Subsidized private saving becomes an explicit substitute for social pensions.[39] This is realized by a direct link of contribution rates for private pensions to the formula for adjusting social insurance pensions aiming at a reduction of the level of public pensions.
- Capital funding will replace PAYGO financing.

Main Instruments in Social Pension Insurance to Realize the Paradigm Shift and Some of the Effects

A major instrument to reduce the benefit level in social pension insurance was a reformulation of the pension (adjustment) formula. Besides this, changes in disability pensions and widow(er)s' pensions were decided.

Changing the pension adjustment formula to reduce the benefit level in general

Changing the formula for adjusting pensions affects all pensioners, those who claimed a pension in the past as well as those who will claim it for the first time. It affects insurance pensions (retirement and disability) as well as survivors' pensions (for widow(er)s' and orphans' pensions).[40] This becomes obvious if one takes into consideration the basic structure of the social insurance pension formula. The calculation of the individual (insurance) pension (P^i) is based on two elements. The first is the sum of individual earnings points (EP^i) the insured person accumulates during his/her whole life. In the case of employees covered by social insurance, the earnings point in one year is the ratio of individual gross wages (W^i) to average gross wages of all employees (W^a): W^i/W^a. If $W^i = W^a$ then EP in this year is one. There is also a crediting of earnings points for activities like child caring, caring for the frail elderly, in the case of unemployment[41] and for non-contributory periods like schooling. At the time of retirement the sum of earnings points of the whole insurance period is accumulated and multiplied by the second factor, the actual pension value (ARW), which gives the amount in DM (now in Euros) per month for one EP.

$$P^i = \sum_{t=1}^{n} EP^i_{\ t} \cdot ARW_t,$$

where $n =$ years of insurance. If the pension is claimed before the reference retirement age for the full pension, the already mentioned deduction from the full pension becomes effective (3.6 per cent per year).

The growth rate of ARW is the rate for adjusting those pensions which were calculated in former years. Therefore all pensioners with the same sum of EP have an identical pension benefit irrespective of the year of retirement. For a so-called 'standard pension' with $EP = 45$, according to the rules implemented in 1992, the target value of the pension is 0.7 multiplied by average net earnings. A lower (higher) number of EP gives proportional lower (higher) pension benefit.[42] The 1992 reform linked the growth rate of ARW (pension adjustment rate) to the growth rate of average net earnings.[43] Therefore, as already mentioned, the ratio of (individual) pension to net average earnings remains constant over time for all pensioners.

The former (Christian Democratic/Liberal) government had already decided to introduce an additional factor into the pension formula, based on the development of life expectancy. In the case of an increase in life expectancy, this factor should reduce the growth rate of ARW.[44] The former government decided the target pension level for the 'standard pensioner' (45 EP) would become 64 per cent in the year 2030 (instead of 70 per cent according to the '1992 pension reform').

The Social Democratic Party, being in opposition, was strictly against this reduction of the benefit level and made it a much-debated topic in their election campaign. But the new (Social Democratic/Green) government coming into power finally decided on a target pension level for the standard pension also of 64 per cent, and with the reduction of the benefit level to take place even more quickly.

In contrast, for example, to the latest Swedish pension reform, the '2001 pension reform' was decided relatively quickly. No consensus was realized between government and opposition in parliament. Trade unions finally agreed. One reason may be that several incentives for occupational pensions were finally included in the reform package, but it can be assumed that there was also some compensation given by the government outside the pension field.

The new government finally abolished the linking of *ARW* to net average earnings. The main reason was the effects of a change in the strategy of tax policy on the financing of social pension insurance by reducing income tax and shifting the tax burden more towards more indirect taxes (VAT and ecological tax). The growth rate of net earnings compared to gross earnings increases. Because of the net adjustment formula, this increases the pension adjustment rate, pension expenditure and the need for additional revenue. The new pension adjustment formula is no longer based on the development of average net earnings but only on average gross earnings (as in the 1957 pension reform, in principle) and the contribution rate of only social pension insurance. In addition, the government decided to introduce another factor.

The first two elements of the pension formula had already been proposed by the author for about 20 years. The main idea of this proposal was that the pension formula should only take into account such factors which are direct elements of the social insurance pension scheme, gross earnings and the contribution rate to social pension insurance. If pensions become more costly (for example, because of demographic aging) this will burden not only employees (and employers) with a higher contribution rate but pensioners as well with a reduction in the pension adjustment rate. In 1999, this formula was again introduced into the public debate by the Social Advisory Council of the German government on pension policy.[45]

The government finally adopted this proposal, but added an additional element, a fictitious contribution rate for saving in private pensions.[46] The transparency of the formula in its original version became diluted by this additional element and will be open to manipulation. One reason is that the additional factor is independent of the empirical saving rate of contributors for private pensions. The factor is determined by the government as a certain percentage. This percentage can be changed, independent of the saving for private pensions of the employees. An increase in the percentage will reduce the pension adjustment rate.

It is important to realize that there is now a direct link between the 'determined' contribution rate for private pensions and the benefit level of public pensions. The new factor will be introduced in four steps, from one percentage point (starting in 2002) to four percentage points (in 2008). Over the period of increasing this contribution rate, the development of *ARW* – and by this the adjustment rate for public pensions – will be reduced in eight steps of about 0.5 percentage points each. By this instrument the benefit level will be reduced for all present and future pensioners. This clearly underlines the character of the new (subsidized) private pensions as a partial substitute for public pensions.

It should be borne in mind that, for present pensioners as well as for those employees near retirement age, it is not possible to compensate for the loss in public pensions by additional private saving for old age.

A brief remark seems of interest regarding the original version of the paradigm shift the government had in mind. I refer here to proposals published in May 2000. They show more clearly what the government had in mind. For future pensioners the PAYGO-financed public pension should be reduced by half of the amount of the private pension which employees in principle could realize if they were saving 4 per cent of their earnings. The younger the employee is, the more time he has to save for old age. Therefore the reduction of the public pension is greater the younger the employee is.[47] The reduction of the public pension takes place irrespective of whether and how much the employee was saving in addition for a private pension. This approach would have changed the social pension insurance into a system of partial income testing based on the assumed possible amount of a private pension.[48] The factor burdening future cohorts was eliminated during the reform debate and replaced by an additional factor integrated into the pension formula now affecting all pensioners.

General reduction of the public pension level resulting from the new pension adjustment formula and its effects on the pension scheme

It is intended by the government to reduce the level of public pensions, the development of contribution rates and federal grant. This, however, may have remarkable distributional effects on the concept and future development of the public pension system. Without going into detail, one can say that it is intended to reduce the 'standard pension level' (pension based on 45 earnings points) from 70 per cent to 64 per cent compared to average net earnings.[49] The government finally decided that the standard pension will not fall below this percentage.[50]

My hypothesis is that such a reduction of the public pension level may result in a conflict with the design of the pension scheme and its underlying concept: on one hand, there will be a close contribution–benefit link in social pension insurance. The new government also underlines this. But, on the other hand, the general reduction of the pension level may have the effect that, even after long periods of paying contributions, the individual pension benefit is no higher than a full (means-tested) social assistance benefit. This may undermine the willingness to contribute and the acceptance of this mandatory scheme that is based on earnings-related contributions.

This possible development will be illustrated by some figures. The public debate was focused on the 'standard pension' only. Regarding the reduction in the standard pension level one has to take into account, first, that the standard pension is always based on 45 earnings points, independent of any changes in pension law which may affect the individual number of Earnings Points a contributor is able to accumulate; and, secondly, that about 50 per cent of all male pensioners and even about 90 per cent of female pensioners have fewer than 45 earnings points (hence a pension below the standard pension). The distribution of pension benefits therefore matters a lot.

A further aspect that is relevant in judging the meaning of figures for pension levels is the following. The full pension without deduction will only be paid when claiming the pension at reference retirement age, that is (in the near future) age 65. Starting in 2012, the earliest retirement age will be 62, for both men and women. Early retirement reduces the pension and the pension level by 3.6 per cent per year. Retiring at age 62 therefore reduces the pension benefit by 10.8 per cent. Disability pensions as well are calculated as if the pension is claimed three years before the reference retirement age.

An additional piece of information is relevant: a full social assistance benefit is about 40 per cent of net average earnings today. If we assume that this social assistance level will remain also in the future, we can calculate, for example, how many earnings points are necessary to receive a pension just as high as social assistance in the case where the standard pension level is (a) 70 per cent of average net earnings or (b) 64 per cent.

It is obvious that, if the pension level is reduced, a higher number of earnings points is needed to receive a pension just as high as social assistance. If the standard pension level is 70 per cent, a pensioner needs about 25 earnings points if he retires at age 65. In the case of a standard pension level of 64 per cent, about 28 earnings points are necessary. If retirement is at age 62, almost 32 earnings points are needed.

One should bear in mind that a certain number of earnings points can be the result of quite different combinations of numbers of years of insurance and the relative level of earnings a contributor gained on average during his working life (that is, the earnings position).

Figure 6.4 shows that, even in the case of a standard pension level of 64 per cent, an employee with an earnings position of 70 per cent on average over the lifetime (that is, 30 per cent below the average earner) already needs 40 years of insurance for a pension as high as social assistance, if retirement is at age 65. An earnings position of 70 per cent is most often realized by women.

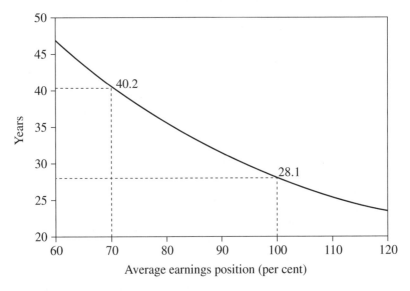

Note: 'Standard pension level' of 64 per cent, own earnings-related contributions
          assumed.

*Figure 6.4   Possible combinations of lengths of service with relative
             earnings positions leading to a pension at social assistance level
             in Germany*

To clarify: even if the social insurance pension is below social assistance, this does not necessarily mean that the pensioner is eligible for social assistance, because this depends on the total income of the pensioner and his spouse. But the result of such a development in public pension benefits might be a conflict with the realization of a strong contribution–benefit link of the public pension scheme. Such a close link will reduce negative effects on labour supply, reduce the 'tax wedge',[51] reduce attempts to avoid the contribution payment and give public support to such a pension scheme. If, however, fewer and fewer pensioners receive a pension that is clearly higher than social assistance, this will erode the basis for supporting such a mandatory scheme and will undermine its legitimacy and the willingness to contribute to such a scheme.

Additional reductions of social insurance pension benefits

The above discussion referred to a general reduction of social insurance pensions in cases of old age as well as of disability. Three areas should be mentioned, where benefits will be reduced further.

Regarding disability pensions, additional changes were already implemented at the beginning of 2001.[52] Up to the year 2000, there existed two types of disability pensions: occupational disability (*Berufsunfähigkeit*) and 'incapacity to work' (*Erwerbsunfähigkeit*). The first was designed to compensate for a partial loss of working capacity in one's occupation. Therefore the pension is lower than the second one and it is assumed that one can take up a part-time employment in a job that was considered 'reasonable', account being taken of the qualification of the employee. If there was no such possibility, the occupational disabled person became eligible for the (higher) pension as if there existed incapacity to work.

Since the beginning of 2001, there are now two degrees of a new disability concept related to the number of hours an employee is still able to work per day. If not able to work more than three hours, he/she is 'fully disabled', and if able to work between three and six hours, 'partially disabled', with a pension half that in the case of being fully disabled. In contrast to the former rules, now all types of available jobs are considered as being 'reasonable', irrespective of the former job or qualification of the insured person. This means that the 'risk' of becoming occupationally disabled is no longer covered by social pension insurance.[53] Disability pensions are now calculated as if the pension is claimed three years before the retirement age for a full pension. Therefore, as already mentioned, a reduction of 10.8 per cent takes place. This became necessary because of the introduction of reductions from the full pension in the case of retirement. Otherwise incentives for claiming disability pensions were expected. This reduction is compensated (but only partly) by higher credits for insurance periods after disability occurred.[54]

Widows' and widowers' pensions are linked to the insurance pension of the former spouse. Therefore the reduction in the benefit level of insurance pensions affects widows/widowers, too. But the benefit level of widow(er)s' pensions is reduced even more because of two effects. First, widow(er)s' pensions are a certain percentage of the insurance pensions of the former spouse. This percentage will be reduced from 60 to 55 per cent.[55] This reduces the pension in addition to the general reduction of the benefit level. While pensions for the insured persons will be reduced by 8.5 per cent because of the new adjustment formula, the reduction for widow(er)s' pensions amounts to 16.2 per cent because of the two effects.

Second, if the survivor's pension is above an allowance, an income test has already existed since 1985 which takes into account earnings and pension benefits of the surviving spouse. This income test will be extended to all kinds of income (except the new subsidized private pension). The allowance remains dynamic, that is, linked to the development of average gross earnings. But the original plans of the government were to freeze the absolute amount of the allowance in nominal terms, which would have reduced the payments considerably over time.

The reduction of the widow's pension is based on the normative approach that women should have sufficient pension claims of their own from earnings and additional credits for child care (at present three earnings points per child are credited for the pension of the insured person) and that therefore widows' pensions should be phased out in the future. Whether this is a realistic assumption for the next decades in the light of female labour force participation (often on a part-time basis) is questionable.[56] And whether the new percentage of 55 will be reduced further or the parameters of the allowance will be changed remains an open question.

Because the calculation of the widow(er)s' pensions is based on an income test, the present way of financing these benefits (mainly) by earnings-related social insurance contributions can hardly be justified from a distributional point of view. Financing from general tax revenue would be adequate. Widow(er)s' pensions are about 20 per cent of total pension expenditure. Because of this volume at present no political force is interested in touching this topic. If widow(er)s' pensions were financed in an adequate way from general tax revenue, this would make it possible to reduce the contribution rate to social pension insurance by more than three percentage points: that is, more than the reduction in contribution rates resulting from the total 2001 reform package up to the year 2030 (see below).

There is a third example: the unemployment insurance pays a contribution to social pension insurance in the case of unemployment for those beneficiaries receiving unemployment benefits or, after longer periods of unemployment, (means-tested) unemployment assistance. Now the contribution payment of unemployment insurance to pension insurance for those who receive unemployment assistance is reduced, too. Therefore, long-term unemployed especially will get lower pensions in the future. This reduces the burden of the federal budget, because these contribution payments are refunded by the federal budget.

These three measures are affecting certain groups of the population in addition to the general reduction of the benefit level realized by the new pension formula. Up to now, there has been no differentiated analysis available showing the distributional effects of all these measures (also in a life cycle context). But all three measures are aiming at the same goal, reducing public pension expenditure, and by this also the contribution rate necessary to balance the budget as well as the payments from the federal budget (federal grant).

EFFECT OF THE '2001 REFORM' ON THE DEVELOPMENT OF CONTRIBUTION RATES

The new rules in the social insurance pension scheme have only a modest effect on the development of the contribution rate in social insurance up to the year 2030 (see Table 6.5). According to official projections, the necessary contribution rate in 2010 or 2020 is only one percentage point and in 2030 1.6 percentage points below the contribution rate necessary for financing pension benefits according to the 'old' rules and the higher benefit level.

Because the general federal grant,[57] besides being linked to the development of average gross earnings is also linked to the development of the contribution rate of social pension insurance, reducing the increase in this contribution rate also reduces the development of federal grant.[58]

Regarding the payment of contributions by employers compared to those of employees, there will be a shift from dividing equally because employees have to pay not only the employee's part of the contribution to social pension insurance[59] but, in addition, the full contribution rate for private pensions. The government expects this contribution rate to be paid by employees if they want to fill the gap in the benefit level that results from the reduction in public pensions. It is obvious from the beginning that the sum of the two contribution rates is higher compared to the 'old law'. For example, in 2010 and 2030, the contribution rate in old age insurance will be three percentage points above the rate under the former conditions (that is, without these reform measures).[60]

Prior to the reform, a contribution rate of about 24 per cent was declared by the government to be too high (and an indicator of a 'demographic crisis'). After the reform, a total of 26 per cent becomes politically acceptable. The reason for this cannot be discussed here. The reduction of employers' contributions,[61] however, is very moderate: 11 per cent instead of 12 per cent in 2030. This means that the effect on non-wage labour costs is marginal. Although the burden for employees will be reduced by subsidies (see below), the partial replacement of public by private pensions will impose an additional burden on private households for a long time. These are part of the well-known transition costs when shifting from PAYGO to capital funding.

MAIN ELEMENTS OF THE PARADIGM SHIFT REGARDING THE SOCIAL PENSION INSURANCE: A SHORT SUMMARY

Before dealing with the new possibilities for private pensions introduced by the '2001 pension reform', the main elements of the paradigm shift which

Table 6.5 Contribution rates for old-age pensions

Year	Contribution rates social pension insurance (per cent)		Additional contribution rate for private pension (per cent)	Contribution rate (per cent)		
	without Pension Reform Act 2001	Pension Reform Act 2001		Total	Share	
					Employer	Employee
2001	19.1	19.1	–	19.1	9.55	9.55
2002	19.2	19.1	1	20.1	9.55	10.55
2003	19.1	18.8	1	19.8	9.40	10.40
2004	19.2	18.9	2	20.9	9.45	11.45
2005	19.1	18.7	2	20.7	9.35	11.35
2010	19.5	18.5	4	22.5	9.25	13.25
2020	20.6	19.6	4	23.6	9.80	13.80
2030	23.6	22.0	4	26.0	11.00	15.00

Source: Bundestags-Drucksache, 14/5146.

affect the statutory (social) pension insurance are summarized. First, a fixed pension level and financing (by contribution revenue and federal grant) being the dependent variable in social insurance were the explicit objectives decided in 1989 (implemented in West Germany from 1992 and in East Germany as early as 1990). Since the 2001 reform package, the development of the contribution rate has become the principal objective and the benefit level the dependent variable. This is a shift from an 'expenditure-oriented revenue policy' towards a 'revenue-oriented expenditure policy'. It can be expected that, if the 'contribution objective' of the present government[62] cannot be realized, the benefit level will be further reduced. The new design of the pension adjustment formula opens up an easy way to reduce the benefit level in social pension insurance without attracting much public attention.

Second, subsidized private pensions are no longer only a supplement, but become a substitute for a part of the public pensions. This is obvious from the direct link of contributions for subsidized private pension and the level of public pensions in the pension formula of statutory pension insurance.[63] This partial replacement of public by private pensions also has the result that funding will in part replace PAYGO financing.

In general, there are no very convincing economic arguments in favour of the reform measures, if we look at the officially mentioned objectives, for example the effects of contribution rates. They were mainly a political reaction to expectations created in the public debate by a number of actors. Therefore this seems to be above all a political project. But the reform will have a number of economic effects, for example on personal income distribution. This results not only from changes in public pensions but also from changes in private and occupational pensions. These measures will be discussed next.

NEW RULES FOR PRIVATE AND OCCUPATIONAL PENSIONS: A SHIFT TOWARDS INDIVIDUAL ACCOUNTS FINANCED BY EMPLOYEES

It is the declared objective of the government to compensate for the reduction in public pensions with additional private pensions.[64] To realize this, some new fiscal incentives are introduced.

The original plan of the minister of labour (Walter Riester) was to introduce a mandated private pension. The plan to mandate private pensions was attacked in particular by a large and influential newspaper, *Bild-Zeitung*. This changed the political decision process remarkably: the government decided to subsidize voluntary private pensions with incentives which are particularly attractive for those with low earnings and with children. These incentives are only provided if the old age provision meets several restrictive criteria (see below).

Originally, there were no plans by the government for new incentives regarding occupational pensions. Reacting to pressure, particularly from trade unions, saving in some types of occupational arrangements is now subsidized as well. In addition, a number of measures regarding occupational arrangements were decided upon. There now exists a right of the employee to the conversion of 4 per cent of earnings up to the ceiling for social insurance contributions (that ceiling was, for a long time, about 180–90 per cent of average gross earnings and it increased in 2003 to 200 per cent). While products for private pensions need a certificate, occupational pension arrangements do not need this in order to become eligible for subsidies.

In the following, the basic features of first, the private pensions and then the occupational arrangements will be outlined. It has to be underlined that even now (in July 2002) there are a lot of open questions regarding important aspects of new rules. And there are still new decisions regarding changes in the design of measures. Above all, there are no empirical data on the way the new rules will affect behaviour of the people who are eligible to use some new instruments for saving in old age. And, of course, there is no information on the effects of the new measures on income in old age.

When talking about private pensions and their role in compensating for a loss in public pensions, it has to be taken into account that private pensions are taken out only for the purpose of financing one's living in old age, while the statutory pension insurance also has the task of providing transfer payments in the case of disability and death of the insured person for the surviving spouse and children. This has to be taken into consideration, too, when comparing, for example, rates of return of different schemes.

Private Subsidized Pensions: Saving in Individual Retirement Accounts

The loss in public pension benefits will be compensated by voluntarily saving for old age. Fiscal incentives will stimulate these savings. The precondition for becoming eligible for subsidies is that saving products have to fulfil several (restrictive) criteria. These criteria – together with incentives – will prevent some negative distributional effects. The following are most important.

1. It is necessary to save regularly, but payments can be interrupted, for example, in the event of unemployment or long periods of illness. With

such interruptions no private pension claims are accumulated, in complete contrast to the social insurance pension scheme, where health or unemployment insurance then transfers contribution payments in favour of the ill or unemployed person to the social pension insurance.

2. There has to be a guarantee of the nominal value of savings, which means there is a nominal rate of return of zero. Therefore no protection against inflation is guaranteed.

3. The accumulated assets can be used at retirement or when claiming a disability pension. In principle, the assets must be paid out as a lifelong pension or as planned withdrawal up to the age of 85, and thereafter as a lifelong pension. With one exception, no lump-sum payments are allowed.[65] Otherwise, the subsidy has to be paid back.[66] The criterion that saving must in principle be for a pension is the consequence of the aim that the private pension will be a substitute for a public pension.

4. There are special requirements for distributing the fees over a longer period in order not to deduct costs from contributions at the beginning of the contract. There are also requirements aiming at cost transparency.

There was and remains much criticism concerning the regulation of the certified products, that is, products that meet in total 11 criteria. Especially negative effects on rates of return are often mentioned by suppliers of products.

The supervisory authority for insurance companies issues the certificate for products. This only means that the product meets the criteria. It does not say anything about the quality of the product or the costs. Since the beginning of 2002, products with certificates have been offered by insurance companies, banks and investment funds. The decision on granting the subsidy is made by a new public office (which will have about 1000 employees).

Regarding the incentives in using certified products, there is a transfer payment (subsidy) or a tax exemption (a deduction from taxable income). The tax office will check which instrument is more favourable for the private household. Both elements are aimed at exempting the contributions for saving in these products from income tax (but not from social insurance contributions[67]). Interest on investments will be exempted from tax, while pensions will be fully taxed. This differs from present rules of taxation for many types of pensions. At present, pensions from social insurance, from private life insurance and direct insurance are only partially taxed according to a real or fictitious return on former saving (for example, at age 65 only 27 per cent of the social insurance pensions is taxable income).[68]

The fact that the subsidized private pensions will be fully taxed in old age seems not to be recognized today, because nobody can make realistic assumptions on how income will be taxed 20 or 30 years from now. The dominating idea of this rule for taxation is that, in principle, saving for old age (using this new instrument) will burden the private household less than other forms of saving which are not privileged (if saving is from net income after tax).

The subsidy is especially attractive for people with low incomes and for families with children, because there is an additional transfer payment for children which is higher than the basic payment for (each) husband and spouse (see Table 6.6). The tax exemption is attractive for those with higher incomes because income tax is progressive. The incentives will be phased in over time, with the full incentives being given from 2008 onwards when 4 per cent of earnings are saved (if saving is less than the required percentage, the subsidy is cut proportionally).

The transfer payment or tax exemption is counted as 'own' saving. However, the full sum of saving plus subsidy cannot be invested because costs have to be deducted. Although transparency of costs is required, the recent experience with savings products shows that there is much 'creative' work done in defining and hiding cost elements. In most cases it is impossible for the client to see in advance what the total costs will be. This can have remarkable effects on the rate of return.

Table 6.6   Subsidy in case of a private certified pension contract

Year	Required contribution rate as percentage of earnings	Transfer payment		Exemption from income tax base (maximum)
		Basic payment for adult persons	Additional payment per child	
		Euros per year		
2002 and 2003	1	38	46	525
2004 and 2005	2	76	92	1050
2006 and 2007	3	114	138	1575
2008 and later	4	154	185	2100

Table 6.6 also shows that, after 2008, there will be no increase in the nominal level of subsidies. This means that the value of the subsidy relative to own savings in the case of increasing earnings over time is decreasing as well as the real value of the subsidy in the case of a rising price level. In occupational arrangements (discussed below), the ceiling for subsidies is dynamic.

There already exists intense competition between suppliers of different certified products. It will be interesting to see how much will be saved in the future via private pensions and how much via occupational arrangements which can also be industry-wide arrangements. Costs of employer (firm)-based arrangements can be expected to be lower than those of individual contracts.

New Possibilities in Occupational and Firm-based Pension Arrangements

One of the decisions of the 2001 reform package was to reduce the vesting period for pension claims based on payments of the employer, from ten to five years. Compared to other countries, the German vesting period was relatively long and, for a long time, there had been a demand – also at the European level – for a reduction, especially regarding the effects for women who more often than men left their job before the pension claim became vested. (This could be a reason for indirect discrimination which is forbidden under European law.)

As mentioned there already existed four types of occupational pensions and a great variety in the design of pension plans. In addition, some new possibilities for occupational arrangements were created by the '2001 reform'.[69] A new right to earnings conversion of the employee and the introduction of a fifth type of occupational pension arrangements – 'pension funds' – are of special importance. These measures will stimulate the sluggish development of occupational pensions that has taken place in Germany for a number of years and will, in particular, extend coverage in the private sector which is very unequal according to branch and size of the firm.

While for subsidized private pensions a contribution rate of (at the beginning) only 1 per cent and only from 2008 on a contribution rate of 4 per cent of individual earnings is possible, the earnings conversion starts in 2002 with a full 4 per cent. And while for private pensions the subsidy is only for a percentage of individual earnings, in the case of earnings conversion subsidized saving is possible up to the amount of the contribution ceiling in social pension insurance.[70] While for private pensions the subsidy will not increase after 2008 in nominal terms, the contribution ceiling in the case of earnings conversion is linked to earnings development and therefore is dynamic.

In the case of earnings conversion there also exists the possibility of parts of earnings being exempted not only from income tax (as in fact for private pensions) but also from social insurance contributions. However, according to present law, this is only possible up to the year 2008. This possibility has several effects on the financing of social insurance and on the accumulation of individual earnings points in social pension insurance. Earnings conversion without contributions being paid on this amount will reduce the individual public pension in addition to the general benefit reduction. Up to now, this effect has hardly been recognized in the German debate.[71] And, of course, contribution revenue is reduced. This depends on how much earnings will be converted. This development can increase the contribution rate necessary to balance the budget. If, for example, an average 2 per cent of the wages are converted, then the contribution rate in social pension insurance would increase by 0.4 per cent. This may be an element over time explaining why the declared contribution objective (2020 not above 20 per cent for example) may not be realized. In such a case additional measures to reduce public pension benefits can be expected.

As already mentioned, collective agreements on occupational pension arrangements in the private sector were rare. This is changing now. In a number of important industry branches (such as the chemical and metal industries) social partners have already negotiated collective agreements based on the possibilities of earnings conversion and also establishing industry-wide pension funds. Because of the attractive conditions of arrangements via the firm or even a branch of industry compared to individual contracts (lower costs and information provided for investment) it is to be expected that many employees will choose this way instead of a private pension. First data will be available at the end of 2002 (the first year after introduction) at the earliest.

The existing different types of incentives can be used in addition if people can afford to save higher amounts. This already points to some distributional effects that will be discussed below. Employees are faced now with a great number of alternatives for subsidized saving for old age (see Table 6.7). Saving can be

- private saving – up to 1 per cent of earnings (2002), increasing to 4 per cent in 2008 – from net earnings in certified products and being eligible for subsidy or tax exemption (in Germany called 'Riester pension' after the minister of labour who was politically responsible for the '2001 reform') or
- saving via conversion of earnings up to 4 per cent of the contribution ceiling in specific occupational schemes and becoming eligible for the subsidy or tax exemption (as in the case above) or
- saving from gross earnings (exempted from income tax and social insurance contributions up to 2008) also in specific types of occupational schemes or
- saving in direct insurance with a flat-rate tax of 20 per cent (instead of individual tax) and without paying social insurance contributions (up to 2008 and only in the event that earnings conversion is not by regular elements of earnings, but, for example, a holiday or Christmas allowance).[72]

Table 6.7 *Alternatives in subsidized saving for old age*

Private saving	Earnings conversion	
1% (2002) up to 4% (2008) of earnings	Up to 4 % of earnings at the ceiling for social insurance contributions	Up to 3.25% of earnings at the ceiling for social insurance contributions
Saving is in principle from net earnings (after tax and contributions), but eligible for (a) subsidy or (b) tax exemption	Only until 2008 Saving from gross earnings (exempted from tax and contributions)	Saving only from lump-sum payments (single payments) instead of individual income tax rate of 20% No social insurance contributions (only until 2008)
if saving is in certified products	if saving is in direct insurance pension insurance funds support funds pension funds / if saving is in direct insurance pension insurance funds pension funds	if saving is in direct insurance pension insurance funds (only if tax- and contribution-free saving in pension insurance funds or pension funds is already exhausted)
new alternatives		already existing alternative

The decision process necessary for employers and employees is complex and difficult, which means that it is an interesting and attractive field for consultants. No empirical results are available yet, because the new rules became effective only in 2002.[73]

It is not clear to what extent employers will also contribute to pensions of their employees, which in the past was usual in most occupational pension schemes. Now there seems to be a clear tendency towards private saving by employees themselves for old age (private pensions) via the firm. The focus of the 2001 reform was on those possibilities where the employee is saving directly, while those types of occupational pension schemes where only the employer pays for the pension (that is, direct pension commitment and support funds) were outside the focus of the government (Heubeck, 2002, p.347).

Regarding the different organizational types of occupational pension arrangements besides the already existing four types,[74] a fifth type has been established: pension funds. In contrast to already existing types, these new funds have no cap on investing money in different types of assets. They can, for example, invest 100 per cent in equities, while a pension insurance fund can only invest up to 35 per cent in equities. The establishment of such new pension funds was delayed because of late publication of specific rules.

Companies with direct pension commitments based on book reserves have the possibility of outsourcing the pension liabilities without negative effects regarding taxation. This underlines the already mentioned aspect of bringing money, not only from private households, but also from self-financing within the firm to the capital market.

Meanwhile, the collective agreement in the public sector was fundamentally changed. Instead of the PAYGO-financed integrated defined benefit scheme providing the employee with a certain percentage of final earnings as pension income from social insurance, together with the occupational pension, in the future employees will only have the right to a defined contribution type of pension, which means that no benefit level is guaranteed any more.

SOME FIRST LESSONS, IMPLICATIONS AND EFFECTS OF THE '2001 PENSION REFORM' IN GERMANY AND TOPICS THAT WILL REMAIN ON THE POLITICAL AGENDA

The decisions and instruments used in the context of the recent German pension reform are aiming at a partial shift from (mandatory) public to (voluntary) private pension provision; in the social pension scheme from expenditure-oriented revenue policy to revenue-oriented expenditure policy; from defined benefit to defined contribution schemes in general and in the occupational arrangements; and from PAYGO financing to capital funding.

This is done by reducing the benefit level in public schemes (social insurance and civil servants) and improving possibilities for private saving for old age on individual private accounts and via the firm. The state strengthens its role as regulator in private arrangements and channels some additional tax money (transfers or tax expenditure) into the private market to stimulate saving for old age.

The new rules in pension policy in Germany have been enacted from the beginning of the year 2002, with some measures being phased in over the years. It is much too early to make a comprehensive evaluation of the reform measures. In the political process especially, effects regarding income distribution are more or less not noticeable to the ordinary public. However, some effects seem to be obvious and others plausible.

The obvious present tendency is to reduce the benefit level in public schemes. Taking into consideration the development in many other countries, it is not at all surprising that minimum elements become an integrated element in pension policy (the means-tested tax-financed pension). Although private pensions as a substitute for public pensions are voluntary at present, the topic of mandating private (or occupational) pensions will be on the political agenda at least in the event of a low participation rate of employees in the new possibilities for saving (in certified pension products or in using the possibilities via collective agreements) and/or if the benefit level in public pensions is reduced even more than officially declared today. Such mandating may be based on industry-wide collective agreements (quasi-mandating as in the Netherlands) or mandating by law (as in Switzerland). A combination of low mandatory public PAYGO-financed pensions and mandatory private funded elements already exists in many countries.[75] This is in line with a strategy the World Bank is proposing worldwide (World Bank, 1994), with some modifications depending on country-specific circumstances.

A further push towards reducing public PAYGO pensions can be expected at the European level. Influencing factors include the Maastricht stability criteria and the demand for reducing public debt as well as the need to balance the public budgets. Arguments in support are the sustainability of fiscal policy in general and of pension policy in particular and the goal of intergenerational equity. These seem to be important political arguments. The main instrument to realize this is seen to be reduction of PAYGO financing (Schmähl, 2002b).

Another influencing factor coming from the European level and also linked to the above-mentioned aspects may result from the current process of implementing an 'open method of coordination' in pension policy for EU member states by deciding on common goals in pension policy and on a set of indicators being the basis for benchmarking pension policy of the member states. This benchmarking will depend on which indicators will be chosen as relevant. Taking into account the important role of the ministers of finance in the EU, it may happen that, for example, indicators like the ratio of public pension of GDP will become decisive in the process of evaluating different pension arrangements in the member countries. It is obvious that the ministers of finance are looking particularly at the 'burden' for public households, and less at the 'burden' for private households if there is a shift from PAYGO to capital funding in private forms. The decision on the set of indicators will determine how the pension arrangements in the member countries will be evaluated. This process has not finished yet, but it may become a highly important factor in the national pension debate and may influence the mix of pension schemes at the national level.[76]

Regarding the public pension scheme in Germany it does not seem unrealistic to assume that in the near future there will be a further demand to reduce the benefit level, especially if the politically decided target contribution rate in social insurance is in danger of not being realized. Such a further reduction of the benefit level would make the conflict between pension level and desired structure of the scheme even more obvious. Will it be possible to realize politically a close contribution–benefit link in a mandatory scheme, if the benefit level is so low that a great number of employees, even after a long period of contributing, can only expect to receive a pension below or scarcely above the social assistance level? The trend towards basic pensions with strong redistributive elements will then be a realistic assumption.[77]

While Germany today is still a country with an earnings-related public pension scheme as first tier (aiming at much more than simply avoiding poverty in old age by income smoothing over the life cycle) and with voluntary funded pensions (for example as a second tier of supplementary occupational pensions), it may not be fully unrealistic to say that a shift in the first tier towards primarily avoiding poverty and in the second tier towards mandating may take place – a pattern to be seen in other countries, such as the Netherlands or Switzerland. The development in these countries is often mentioned in Germany as an attractive model for pension policy, especially by those actors aiming at an extended capital-funded part of pensions.[78] It should be remembered that the present minister of labour originally favoured mandated private pensions and that this is proposed by, among others, people from the banking industry, consultants and advisors to the present federal German government.

If a development takes place as mentioned just as a possibility, the development process in Germany would move in quite the opposite direction from that in many other countries where a low and insufficient first tier is supplemented by a mandatory second tier. Germany would then reduce its first tier, which would become insufficient. To realize a sufficient replacement level in old age, a mandatory second tier would be added.

Regarding occupational pension arrangements, they have already become an important element in collective bargaining following the 2001 reform Acts.[79] For a long time, trade unions were hardly interested in occupational pensions. Now they have discovered this as a new field for activity in a period of diminishing influence of trade unions. This new interest of trade unions in collectively agreed occupational pension arrangements may also be based on expectations regarding the influence on investment decisions of new industry-wide pension funds.

It is to be expected that financing of occupational pensions in the future will mainly be by employees instead of employers as was mostly the case in the past. Only if labour market conditions improve considerably, may occupational pension schemes as an instrument of personnel policy become interesting for employees again. The trend towards defined contribution schemes will shift risks from employers to employees.

The new strategy in pension policy in Germany will have many important effects regarding social policy and income distribution. Whether the shift towards funded private pensions of the defined contribution type will result in adequate pensions in old age remains an open question and is dependent on many influencing factors. The effects on personal income distribution depend on (among other things) who is able to save and to take up subsidies and what investment decisions will be made. Those who can afford to save can profit from fiscal incentives. The possibility of using different types of incentive requires, however, that income be high enough to make use of a number of possibilities.

Those with low income may not have enough money to save in these subsidized types of saving. There is a remarkable percentage of German households (at present about 9 per cent) that cannot even meet their financial liabilities (their obligations to pay back accumulated debt although they have already reduced their living standards). If they have some money left, it will be preferable for them to reduce the debt instead of saving in subsidized forms for old age.

It has been overlooked in the present public discussion that these fiscal incentives are not only given but have to be financed, too. If tax expenditure for incentives to save are financed mainly by indirect taxes (such as VAT or tax on petrol and so on), all households, including households with low incomes, have to finance the incentives, while not all households are able to profit from the subsidies. And also households with many children are burdened relatively highly by indirect taxation. This in fact reduces part of the bonus they can get from the family-oriented design of the subsidies.

First results of a simulation study illustrate the fact that the reform, at least in part, withdraws effects within the German pension system, for example, in favour of families with children because of the shift towards more private pensions (Himmelreicher and Viebrok, 2003).

Concerning the development of saving, it is an open question whether and how much additional saving can be expected. Judging by the experience of former attempts to stimulate saving,[80] there are severe doubts that the new financial incentives will increase total saving. It is to be expected that there will be a high percentage of substitution within different types of saving from non-subsidized to subsidized types or towards higher subsidies.[81]

Financial market actors recommend a shift towards saving based on equities. It is expected that saving for private funded pensions will fuel the stock market. This does not necessarily mean that there will also be an increase in real capital. Often the difference between financial capital (or liquidity) and real capital is not fully recognized.

As already mentioned, there was great pressure from actors in financial markets towards a reduction of PAYGO financing as well as to reduce occupational pensions based on book reserves, in favour of a shift towards capital funding in Germany. These attempts, supported by many politicians as well as academics and by the mass media, were obviously successful. But even after the new pension reform Acts there are still demands for more activities in the same direction, to replace public with private pensions and even to mandate private pensions. Whether the pension reform would have been realized in the political process if the stock market in 2000 had been as in 2002 remains an open question.

There also remain many open questions regarding the effects of the new strategy in Germany's pension policy in the future. Germany's pension arrangements are in the process of transition. It will be decisive whether in the future a further trend towards substituting private for public pensions will be realized. In this chapter it has been argued that this would fundamentally change the character of the German pension scheme. And there are many open questions regarding, for example, the income of pensioners in the future.

The appropriate level of income in old age cannot be discussed without taking into account the development of other areas besides formal pension schemes. Health insurance and long-term care insurance in particular are decisive. In Germany, a tendency exists to outsource expenditure from the social insurance schemes and to finance care from the individual household budget of those who are ill or need long-term care.[82] A debate on the adequacy of retirement income is lacking.

It is to be expected that the distribution of income in old age will become more diversified and income inequality in old age will increase. This may be the effect of different participation in private pension funds as well as in different amounts of saving, but also in different net rates of return. For Chile, where mandated private funds have been operating since 1980, it is reported that the coverage is less than expected and that pension benefits can differ remarkably even for workers of the same age and with the same number of years of services and the same monthly income. This illustrates the assumption that more private voluntary pension arrangements replacing mandatory public schemes will result in an increasing income inequality in old age. This may be evaluated differently according to different value judgments, but should be recognized.

The move towards substituting private pensions for public pensions, together with interruptions in the working life, will result in a greater inequality of income in old age in the future. This will be more obvious if private pensions are voluntary (even when there are tax incentives), but will also occur in the case of collective agreements (especially if there is no obligation for the employee to save for old age) and even in the case of mandating private pensions by law. While today in Germany, in the event of illness, unemployment or caring for children or frail elderly, the responsible institution makes a contribution to pension insurance for financing a pension claim, it is questionable whether this will also be done in the case of private old age security, because this would be against the political will to reduce contribution rates in social insurance. The present dominant strategy in pension policy in Germany will make old age security more costly for a long time and the costs will be shifted more directly towards private households. The distribution of costs within households will change, too.

In recent years a biased political debate regarding the effects of different pension arrangements has taken place in Germany.[83] This influenced political decisions or was used to gain popularity for the new approach in pension policy by focusing the public attention on the subsidized private pensions. It will take a long time for the population fully to become aware of the effects of the new pension policy on the living conditions of the elderly.

After the '2001 pension reform' there will be no standstill in pension policy in Germany. Several important topics remain on the political agenda. One is the taxation of provision for old age and of pensions. Here the Constitutional Court is demanding a change by the end of 2004. Another topic is the retirement age in public pension schemes. This was explicitly excluded from the latest reform package.

One powerful measure to cope with challenges of population aging in the financing of public pensions could be to change the rules for the retirement age in the case of increasing life expectancy, aiming at an increase in labour force participation of older workers, and to retire later, or to reduce pensions if early retirement is still chosen by employees.

Changing the rules for retirement can be done in several ways. For example, the rate of deduction (3.6 per cent) could be made more actuarially fair. But at present this is not a topic of discussion in Germany. Another proposal of the author was to decide now on linking the reference retirement age (for the full or even earliest retirement pension) to a life expectancy indicator.[84] By this, for example, the ratio of years of receiving pensions to years of paying contributions can remain constant even in the case of increasing life expectancy. This new rule may become effective in about ten years when demographically induced structural changes in the labour market (and a fundamental change in labour market conditions) are expected to occur. The 'retirement age' topic was not integrated in the present reform package. However, soon after the reform in Germany, as well as at the European level, an increase in the labour force participation rate of older workers has been demanded – after a long period of promoting early retirement. Trying to extend the phase of employment would, however, require, among other things, much more training for older workers.[85] Demographic changes, labour market development and the financing of social security will stimulate a discussion about postponing retirement age in the public schemes for claiming the full pension in the near future.[86]

Finally, how families with children will receive an additional bonus in the public pension scheme besides the already realized crediting of three earnings points in the case of child care is also on the agenda following another decision by the Constitutional Court. Up to now, not much attention has been given in Germany to the fact that investment in human capital is an important instrument for coping with the challenges of an aging population in social security and in other areas. The focus today is still primarily on financial capital, proposed by many powerful actors and arising as an outflow of the present *Zeitgeist*.

What is still needed in Germany is a comprehensive approach, linking pension policy not only to public finance and capital market development but also to labour market and educational policy. This is especially necessary in the light of an aging workforce aiming at an increase in productivity. Human capital investment – and not only financial capital, as at the centre of current discussion – is an important factor for productivity development and for coping in a fair manner with the challenges of structural changes in economy and demography for different groups of the population.

NOTES

1. Among these elements is the organizational structure, the division of contribution payments between employers and employees and the financing also from the general public budget. See Ritter (1983) for the founding period of social insurance in Germany.
2. Schmähl (1993a) gives an overview of proposals for introducing flat-rate pensions in the German debate.
3. These decisions affect social insurance pensions at first, but there are also decisions affecting (tax-financed) civil servants' pensions.
4. As can be seen from Figure 6.1, some groups of self-employed are also integrated into the statutory pension insurance.
5. This refers to *formal* arrangements of old age security. But there are also informal arrangements based on intra-family transfers. Besides income from pension schemes, there are other sources of income that may be relevant for people in old age, such as income from labour (as in the case of claiming a partial pension), means-tested social assistance or other public transfer payments and income from assets.
6. The social insurance system for miners is a combination of basic (first-tier) and supplementary schemes. Most of the pension expenditure is financed from the federal public budget.
7. For 1997, it was estimated that funds in occupational schemes to cover pension claims were about 531 000 million German Marks (DM). Regarding the different types of occupational schemes 56.5 per cent of the funds are in book reserves, 22.4 per cent in Pension Insurance Funds, 13 per cent in Direct Insurance and 8.1 per cent in Support Funds. The total volume of funds compared to GDP is 14.5 per cent, including book reserves (without book reserves, 6.3 per cent). Compared to the macroeconomic weight of occupational schemes in the Netherlands, the UK or the USA, Germany looks underdeveloped. However, this also reflects the quantitative importance of the social insurance pension scheme and the benefit level provided compared to the basic first-tier arrangements in the Netherlands, the UK or the USA. For a detailed analysis of occupational schemes in Germany, and also their links to the first-tier pension schemes, see Schmähl (1997) with further references.
8. These have existed in the building industry and for employed journalists.
9. Both schemes were relevant for the development of the supplementary pensions: from the civil servants' scheme the development of the target replacement rates, and from the statutory pension scheme the development of the benefit amount, were decisive.
10. This is measured on the basis of expenditure, not financing. In recent years there has been an increase, for example, in life insurance premiums which may in the future change the weight between the different tiers. That this also is an explicit political objective will be discussed later.
11. Not including intra-family transfers in cash and in kind, not including subsidized goods: transport, entrance fees in museums, and so on.
12. For details, see Schmähl and Fachinger (1999), Altenbericht (2001, pp.185–211).
13. It can be expected that a high percentage of those people not claiming social assistance in old age would only receive a small additional social assistance payment. There is, however, the assumption that not claiming social assistance in old age mainly occurs because of the fear that children will have to pay back these transfers to the social assistance organization.
14. It has to be mentioned, however, that there already exist tax-privileged types of private saving and incentives for occupational pensions. Official statements read as if the '2001 reform' introduced such incentives for the first time.
15. This was before political unification, which took place in October 1990.
16. For details, as well as the integration of East and West German pension schemes, see Schmähl (1992). This could only be realized in a PAYGO scheme.
17. Sozialbericht (1958), Beiheft zum Bundesarbeitsblatt (1958, pp.154–5).
18. There was the requirement of a reserve after a ten-year period covering benefits for one year.

19.   Particularly because of economic circumstances, in reality there was often more PAYGO financing than capital funding.

20.   This was in fact relevant primarily for men, because it was already possible for women to claim an old age pension at age 60. There also existed the possibility of retiring at age 60 after a period of unemployment – still without deductions from the full pension.

21.   As well as the average age of exit from the labour force.

22.   For a detailed discussion, see Schmähl (1993b).

23.   This should be phased in, beginning in 2001 over a period of more than ten years. The full amount of the deduction is 3.6 per cent per year of retiring before the reference retirement age (this will be age 65). In the future, age 62 will be the earliest retirement age (for old age pensions), equal for men and women. The 3.6 per cent reduction per year was and is too low to eliminate the incentive for early retirement. In 1996, it was decided (among other measures) to start the phasing in of these deductions as early as 1997 (and not in 2001) and to do this, not over a period of ten years, but of only five years. See, for details, Schmähl (1999b).

24.   Korpi and Palme (1997).

25.   The Swiss pension scheme is discussed by Bonoli, Chapter 4 of this book.

26.   For more information, see Schmähl (1991).

27.   This is not without empirical problems. For example, GDP in West Germany may be too high because of accounting principles for companies with headquarters in West Germany and firms in East Germany, and vice versa.

28.   The contribution ceiling in social pension and unemployment insurance is about 180 per cent of average gross earnings. The contribution ceiling in health and long-term care insurance is lower, namely 75 per cent of the contribution ceiling in pension insurance.

29.   This, however, is not the correct reference variable for information regarding the development of the financing base of social insurance contributions, because the base for contribution payments is the sum of contributory gross wages. This variable does not, in contrast to figures of National Accounts, include employers' contribution payments, voluntary social expenditure by firms, labour income of civil servants and labour income from wage and salary earners below the lower limit for contribution payments and above the contribution ceiling. The share of gross earnings subject to contributions in total labour income remained stable from the mid-1970s and therefore developed parallel to the labour income share. There seems to be no additional erosion of the financial base by structural changes within the labour income share.

30.   Often this development in factor income shares is extrapolated into the future. The development in countries like the United States or Holland show, however, that, if labour market performance gets better, labour income share increases. This can also be expected in the future in Germany in the process of demographic change.

31.   An analysis of economic consequences is given in Atkinson (1999).

32.   For example, see Neumann (1998), also Siebert (1998). For a detailed description of the coming crisis because of the population aging, see Wissenschaftlicher Beirat (1998), which is an Advisory Group of Scientists for the Federal Ministry of Economics. For a discussion of these findings, see Schmähl (1998a).

33.   Advocates of a remarkable shift towards funding do not focus so much – as in former times – on the argument of higher saving rates, increased investment and positive effects for economic growth, arguments which are intensely debated and often questionable. The debate is instead now primarily focused on rate of return.

34.   Regarding the biased discussion concerning financing methods, see Schmähl (2000b).

35.   For more information regarding the framing of the public debate, especially focusing on intergenerational aspects, see Schmähl (2001c).

36.   This approach towards a closer contribution–benefit link was continued after the successful election campaign and the change in government in autumn 1998 (from Christian Democratic and Liberal Party to Social Democratic and Green Party).

37.   Described in Schmähl (1999b).

38.   The political process that took place after the change of government in autumn 1998 regarding pension policy cannot be outlined here. The approach of the new government

is in complete contrast to former Social Democratic pension policy and to arguments used in the last election campaign.

39. Although the government officially always labels it 'supplementary' or 'additional'.
40. The last-mentioned two types of pensions are based on the insurance pensions of the late insured person.
41. Here other institutions are paying the contribution.
42. It has to be mentioned that this pension level is not the replacement rate, because the pension is based on the average of relative earnings over the whole earnings span and not linked to last earnings. Only in the case of an identity of last earnings of the employee and the average relative earnings position over the insurance period does this also give information about the replacement rate.
43. This, however, is a simplified version. Since pensioners themselves pay contributions to health and long-term care insurance, the effect of these contribution payments had to be eliminated in the pension adjustment formula. For a detailed discussion of the net adjustment formula, see Schmähl (2001b).
44. The definition of the factor, however, was arbitrary (change of life expectancy of persons aged 65 in year t-8 compared to t-9; from this 50 per cent is taken into account) and open to manipulation; see Schmähl (1999b).
45. The author was chairing the Social Advisory Council (from 1986 to 2000). For a detailed analysis of the net adjustment formula and the proposed changes, as well as its 'history', see Schmähl (1999a).
46. It has already been decided that this formula will change in its parameter values after ten years.
47. This means that the contributors receive different pensions in the case of an identical sum of earnings points, depending on the age of the pensioner.
48. According to the proposals in May 2000, the result would have been a standard pension level for new retirees (at age 65) in the year 2030 (for persons born in 1965) of about 58 per cent; in 2040, 54 per cent (born 1975) and in 2050, 50 per cent (born in 1985). The official figures as percentages of average net earnings were about four percentage points higher, because the government deducted the voluntary contributions to private pensions by 4 per cent from average net earnings, independent of whether such saving took place or not. This redefinition of average net earnings gives higher pension levels. Such a reduction of the pension level would also change the ratio of PAYGO financing and capital funding. There were proposals that the present ratio of PAYGO to capital funding of 80:20 should be changed to 60:40 in the long run. If we start with a standard pension level of 70 per cent and replace PAYGO with capital funding, the standard pension level, *ceteris paribus*, would be 52.5 per cent = (70:80) × 60. Therefore the above-mentioned original proposal would realize this.
49. Officially, the government redefined net earnings by considering the voluntary private contribution as a mandatory levy which reduces net earnings.
50. This was a compromise especially with trade unions. Originally, the government planned to reduce the pension level much more, as already mentioned.
51. Compared to direct levies without benefits based on the idea of reciprocity (some equivalence); see Schmähl (1998c).
52. For a detailed analysis of the old as well the new rules, see Viebrok (2002).
53. The new rule will be phased in. Transition rules exist; see Achenbach *et al.* (2002).
54. Now the period up to age 60 is credited as years of insurance, while the years between age 55 and 60 were only credited by one-third before.
55. For those who raised children, a bonus is introduced as an element of family policy; however, this is not financed from the federal budget but from revenue of the pension insurance. The bonus is two earnings points for the first child and one earnings point for all other children. Whether this differentiation, which originally was not intended, will get approval at the Constitutional Court of Justice is an open question.
56. For a discussion of pensions for women, see the contributions in Schmähl and Michaelis (2000). In addition, it might be possible, in the meantime, for widow(er)s' pensions to be extended to people in a now legally regulated 'homosexual partnership'. According to

the German constitution, marriage and family especially should be protected. But this does not seem to be a hindrance as more and more rules originally aimed at married couples will become relevant for people living in a homosexual partnership. This might additionally increase expenditure over time.

57. This is by far the most important part of all transfers from the federal budget to statutory pension insurance of blue- and white-collar workers. In addition, there exists an additional federal grant linked to the development of VAT as well as to ecological tax revenue. These two elements were introduced to cover part of the pension expenditure aiming at interpersonal redistribution; for details see Schmähl (2001a).

58. It could be argued that, if the government considers the contribution rate for private pensions as necessary and implements it in the pension formula, it could be a consistent approach to link federal grant as well to the development of this (fictitious) contribution rate. As this would increase federal grant, no such idea arises.

59. That is, half of the contribution rate.

60. Taking into account the subsidies or tax incentives in the case of saving of specific types for old age, the direct burden is lower compared to the rates mentioned, especially for low-income households. But these subsidies have to be financed, too, and can also burden (above all if financed by indirect taxation) these households. This will be discussed later in the chapter.

61. The question of shifting employers' contributions backwards to employees or forward into prices is not discussed here, nor is the question whether trade unions will try to compensate for increases in the private pension contributions in the process of wage negotiations.

62. Not more than 20 per cent in 2020 and 22 per cent in 2030.

63. And it was even more obvious in the original plans published in May 2000, when there was the idea of reducing the 'standard pension' officially to 54 per cent in 2050 (in fact to about 50 per cent).

64. Nevertheless, the government rejects the idea that private pensions in part replace public pensions. The official announcement calls this a supplement to the public pension; see, for example, Riester (2002, p.29).

65. The exception is a maximum 20 per cent of assets at retirement age.

66. This is also the case if the pensioner lives outside Germany. It may be expected that this will be brought to the European Court of Justice if the pensioner lives in a country of the European Union.

67. There exists, however, a specific possibility in the case of earnings conversion. These earnings are also exempted from social insurance contributions, but only up to the year 2008. This will be explained below.

68. On 6 March 2002, the Constitutional Court decided that the present rules for taxing social insurance pensions are in conflict with the constitution. There has to be a change until the end of 2004. It is to be expected that reforming social insurance taxation will affect all types of provision for old age.

69. See also Deutsche Bundesbank (2001).

70. The contribution ceiling is about 180–90 per cent of average gross earnings. Therefore saving of 4 per cent of earnings at the ceiling is, for example, 7.2–7.4 per cent of average earnings.

71. Only for those employees with earnings above the ceiling does this exemption of private saving from contribution payment not affect the earnings points in the year because they get only the maximum earnings points (1.8–1.9) in one year. For the part of earnings above the ceiling no social insurance contributions have to be paid, but also no earnings points can be accumulated.

72. This possibility also exists for saving in a pension insurance fund, but only if exemption from tax and contributions payment is already exhausted by saving in a pension fund or a pension insurance fund.

73. Newspapers reported that about 3500 products were certified in February 2002 and that 1.5 million saving contracts existed, as well as 300 collective agreements covering in principle more than 15 million employees who are eligible to use the existing possibilities

(*Süddeutsche Zeitung*, 13 February 2002). But there is no information on how many employees used the possibility.

74. Direct pension commitment (based on book reserves); pension insurance funds; support funds; direct insurance.
75. For examples, see Schmähl (1991). Some former socialist countries have also established such a combination of schemes or are in the process of doing so.
76. For more aspects concerning this process, see Schmähl (2002b).
77. For a detailed discussion of these conceptual aspects, see Schmähl (2001b).
78. For example, the basic tier (AHV) in Switzerland is often mentioned because it covers the whole population and is highly redistributive because of earnings-related financing, but with only a little difference between lowest and highest (100 per cent) pension. What is overlooked is that the aim of avoiding poverty is realized much less by the AHV compared to the earnings-related social insurance pension in Germany. And it is often overlooked, too, that occupational pensions are mandatory. For details, see Bonoli (Chapter 4).
79. This is discussed in Steinmeyer (2002).
80. See Börsch-Supan and Essig (2002, p.93).
81. Deutsche Bundesbank (2002) offers some reflections on this topic.
82. If income is not sufficient, social assistance payments are needed. For example, in the German long-term care insurance the benefits are still fixed in absolute terms, while on the other hand expenditure for long-term, especially residential, care is increasing.
83. This is discussed in Schmähl (1998a; 1998d; 2000).
84. See Schmähl and Viebrok (2000) with further references.
85. A discussion of this topic is to be found in Enquête-Kommission (2002) with detailed information, for example, on the expected demographic development and effects on the labour market.
86. Different proposals on how to react in PAYGO pension schemes to increasing life expectancy are discussed in Schmähl and Viebrok (2000).

REFERENCES

Achenbach, V. *et al.* (2002), 'Die Erwerbsminderungsrente – Grundsätze der gesetzlichen Rentenversicherung', *Deutsche Rentenversicherung*, 81–213.

Altenbericht (2001), 'Dritter Bericht zur Lage der älteren Generation', Bundestags-Drucksache 14/5130.

Atkinson, Anthony B. (1999), *The Economic Consequences of Rolling Back the Welfare State*, Cambridge, MA: MIT Press.

Börsch-Supan, Axel and Lothar Essig (2002), *Sparen in Deutschland*, Cologne: Deutsches Institut für Altersvorsorge.

Bundesministerium für Arbeit und Sozialordnung (1999), 'Sozialbudget 1999 – Tabellenauszug', Berlin.

Deutsche Bundesbank (2001), 'Die betriebliche Altersversorgung in Deutschland', *Monatsbericht März 2001*, 45–61.

Deutsche Bundesbank (2002), 'Kapitalgedeckte Altersvorsorge und Finanzmärkte', *Monatsbericht Juli 2002*, 25–39.

Enquête-Kommission Demographischer Wandel (2002), 'Schlussbericht, Bundestags-Drucksache', 24/8800, 28 March.

Fachinger, Uwe and Angelika Oelschläger (2000), 'Selbständige und ihre Altersvorsorge: Sozialpolitischer Handlungsbedarf', in Dieter Bögenhold (ed.), *Kleine und mittlere Unternehmen im Strukturwandel – Arbeitsmarkt und Strukturpolitik*, Frankfurt (Main): Peter Lang.

Heubeck, K. (2002), 'Nach der Reform ist vor der Reform – weitergehender Handlungsbedarf im Bereich der betrieblichen Altersversorgung', *Betriebliche Altersversorgung*, 57, 345–51.

Himmelreicher, Ralf K. and Holger Viebrok (2003), 'Die "Riester-Rente" und einige Folgen für Alterseinkünfte', Zentrum für Sozialpolitik, working paper 4/2003, Universität Bremen.

Korpi, Walter and Joakim Palme (1997), 'The Paradox of Redistribution and Strategies of Equality: Welfare State Institutions, Inequality and Poverty in the Western Countries, Institutet for Social Forskning, working paper 3/1997, Universitet Stockholm.

Neumann, Manfred J.M. (1998), 'Ein Einstieg in die Kapitaldeckung der gesetzlichen Rente ist das Gebot der Stunde', *Wirtschaftsdienst*, 78, 259–64.

Riester, Walter (2002), 'The German Pension Reform in the European Context', in Verband Deutscher Rentenversicherungsträger (ed.), *Open Coordination of Old-Age Security in the European Union*, DRV-Schriften vol. 35, Frankfurt (Main): Wirtschaftsdienst, pp.26–30.

Ritter, Gerhard A. (1983), *Sozialversicherung in Deutschland und England*, Munich: Beck.

Sachverständigenrat zur Begutachtung der gesamtwirtschaftlichen Entwicklung (SVR) (2001), 'Für Stetigkeit – Gegen Aktionismus, Jahresgutachten 2001/2002', Wiesbaden.

Schmähl, Winfried (1991), 'On the Future Development of Retirement in Europe, Especially of Supplementary Pension Schemes – An Introductory Overview', in Winfried Schmähl (ed.), *The Future of Basic and Supplementary Pension Schemes in the European Community – 1992 and beyond*, Baden-Baden: Nomos, pp.31–70.

Schmähl, Winfried (1992), 'Transformation and Integration of Public Pension Schemes – Lessons from the Process of the German Unification', *Public Finance*, 47, Supplement: Pierre Pestieau (ed.), 'Public Finance in a World of Transition, Proceedings of the 47th Congress of the International Institute of Public Finance', Foundation Journal of Public Finance, pp.34–56.

Schmähl, Winfried (1993a), 'Proposals for flat-rate public pensions in the German debate', in Jos Berghman and Bea Cantillon (eds), *The European Face of Social Security*, Aldershot: Avebury, pp.261–80.

Schmähl, Winfried (1993b), 'The 1992 Reform of Public Pensions in Germany: Main Elements and some Effects', *Journal of European Social Policy*, 3 (1), 39–51.

Schmähl, Winfried (1997), 'The Public–private Mix in Pension Provision in Germany: The Role of Employer-based Pension Arrangements and the Influence of Public Activities', in Martin Rein and Eskil Wadensjö (eds), *Enterprise and the Welfare State*, Cheltenham, UK and Lyme, USA: Edward Elgar, pp.99–148.

Schmähl, Winfried (1998a), 'Kapitalmarktorientierte Reform der gesetzlichen Rentenversicherung – der Stein der Weisen? – Anmerkungen zum jüngsten Gutachten des wissenschaftlichen Beirats beim Bundeswirtschaftsministerium', *Wirtschaftsdienst*, 78, 264–7.

Schmähl, Winfried (1998b), 'Insights from Social Security Reform Abroad', in R. Douglas Arnold, Michael J. Graetz and Alicia H. Munnell (eds), *Framing the Social Security Debate: Values, Politics, and Economics*, Washington, DC: Brookings Institution Press, pp.248–71, 280–86.

Schmähl, Winfried (1998c), 'Financing Social Security in Germany: Proposals for Changing its Structure and Some Possible Effects', in Stanley W. Black (ed.),

Globalization, Technological Change and Labor Markets, Boston/Dordrecht/London: Kluwer Academic Publishers, pp.179–208.

Schmähl, Winfried (1998d), 'Comment on the Papers by Axel Börsch-Supan, Edward M. Gramlich and Mats Persson', in Horst Siebert (ed.), *Redesigning Social Security*, Tübingen: Mohr, pp.186–96.

Schmähl, Winfried (1999a), 'Die Nettoanpassung der Renten "auf dem Prüfstand"': Für eine Modifizierung der Nettoanpassung und für einen Übergang zu einer "lohn – und beitragsbezogenen" Anpassungsformel – Gründe und Wirkungen', *Deutsche Rentenversicherung*, 8–9, 494–507.

Schmähl, Winfried (1999b), 'Pension Reforms in Germany: Major Topics, Decisions and Developments', in Katharina Müller, Andreas Ryll and Hans-Jürgen Wagener (eds), *Transformation of Social Security: Pensions in Central-Eastern Europe*, Heidelberg: Physica Verlag, pp.91–120.

Schmähl, Winfried (2000), 'Pay-As-You-Go Versus Capital Funding: Towards a More Balanced View in Pension Policy – Some Concluding Remarks', in Gerard Hughes and Jim Stewart (eds), *Pensions in the European Union: Adapting to Economic and Social Change*, Boston/Dordrecht/London: Kluwer Academic Publishers, pp.195–208.

Schmähl, Winfried (2001a), 'Finanzverflechtung der gesetzlichen Rentenversicherung', in Klaus-Dirk Henke and Winfried Schmähl (eds), *Finanzierungsverflechtung in der Sozialen Sicherung*, Baden-Baden: Nomos, pp.9–37.

Schmähl, Winfried (2001b), 'Umlagefinanzierte Rentenversicherung in Deutschland, Optionen und Konzepte sowie politische Entscheidungen als Einstieg in einen grundlegenden Transformationsprozeß, in Winfried Schmähl and Volker Ulrich (eds), *Soziale Sicherungssysteme und demographische Herausforderungen*, Tübingen: Mohr, pp.123–204.

Schmähl, Winfried (2001c), 'Generationenkonflikte und "Alterslast" – Einige Anmerkungen zu Einseitigkeiten und verengten Perspektiven in der wissenschaftlichen und politischen Diskussion', in Irene Becker, Notburga Ott and Gabriele Rolf (eds), *Soziale Sicherung in einer dynamischen Gesellschaft*, Frankfurt/New York: Campus Verlag, pp.176–203.

Schmähl, Winfried (2002a), 'Introduction', in Winfried Schmähl and Sabine Horstmann (eds), *Transformation of Pension Systems in Central and Eastern Europe*, Cheltenham, UK and Northampton, MA, USA: Edward Elgar, pp.3–24.

Schmähl, Winfried (2002b) '"Open Coordination" in the Area of Old-Age Security – from the Point of View of Economics', in Verband Deutscher Rentenversicherungsträger (ed.), *Open Coordination of Old-Age Security in the European Union*, DRV-Schriften vol. 35, Frankfurt (Main), pp.101–12.

Schmähl, Winfried and Uwe Fachinger (1999), 'Armut und Reichtum – Einkommen und Konsumverhalten älterer Menschen', in Annette Niederfranke, Gerhard Naegele and Eckart Frahm (eds), *Funkkolleg Alter*, 2, Opladen and Wiesbaden: Westdeutscher Verlag, pp.159–208.

Schmähl, Winfried and Klaus Michaelis (eds) (2000), *Alterssicherung von Frauen*, Wiesbaden: Westdeutscher Verlag.

Schmähl, Winfried and Holger Viebrok (2000), 'Adjusting Pay-as-you-go Financed Pension Schemes to Increasing Life Expectancy', *Schmollers Jahrbuch, Zeitschrift für Wirtschafts- und Sozialwissenschaften*, 120, pp.41–61.

Siebert, Horst (1998), 'Pay-as-You-Go versus Capital-Funded Pension Systems: The Issues', in Horst Siebert (ed.), *Redesigning Social Security*, Tübingen: Mohr, pp.3–33.

Steinmeyer, Heinz-Dietrich (2002), 'Die Rolle der Kollektivverträge nach dem neuen Altersvermögensgesetz', in Uwe Fachinger, Heinz Rothgang and Holger Viebrok (eds), *Die Konzeption sozialer Sicherung*, Baden-Baden: Nomos, pp.245–59.

Verband Deutscher Rentenversicherungsträger (ed.) (2001), *Rentenversicherung in Zeitreihen*, in DRV-Schriften, 22, Frankfurt (Main): Wirtschaftsdienst.

Viebrok, Holger (2002), 'Disability Pensions in Germany (Country Report for the OECD study "Participative Disability Policies for the Working Age Population: Towards a Coherent Policy Mix"', OECD Directorate for Education, Employment, Labour and Social Affairs, Paris.

Wissenschaftlicher Beirat beim Bundeswirtschaftsministerium (ed.) (1998), 'Grundlegende Reform der gesetzlichen Rentenversicherung', mimeo.

World Bank (ed.) (1994), *Averting the Old Age Crisis*, Washington, DC.

7. Individual accounts and the continuing debate over social security reform in the United States

Barry L. Friedman

The United States has taken another step in the debate over social security reform. The president's Commission to Strengthen Social Security submitted its final report in December 2001. This commission clearly favours individual accounts: all three of its alternative plans include them. In the debate over reform advocates of the current system have argued that 'minor tinkering' would be sufficient to solve its problems without individual accounts. In contrast, the commission believes that the current system has structural problems and that these need structural reforms. The commission probably made a better effort at addressing the criticisms of individual accounts in its design plans than all the numerous previous proposals. It sought to create individual accounts that would have a good chance of making retirees better off. There is potential pain in its recommendations, but it is mostly not from the individual accounts. On the other hand, the timing of the commission was unlucky. Its report came out in the midst of a prolonged downturn in financial markets. Moreover, the report was written in a style that did not clearly set out the accomplishments of its recommendations. Since the report came out, it has received barely any attention, while critics have been vocal in criticizing 'privatization', the somewhat inaccurate term that has come to be used for individual accounts.

While the debate over social security reform has gone unresolved for years, the private sector pension system in the USA has been moving ahead with its own changes that have involved the greatly expanded use of individual accounts. So many individuals now participate in employer-provided individual accounts and individual retirement accounts that the concept is now familiar. These accounts seemed attractive during the 1990s, when investment returns were so favourable, but in 2001 and 2002 the returns were poor and in some notable cases even disastrous. Individual accounts have similar risk characteristics whether offered privately or as part of social security. Developments in the private sector will no doubt retard any movement towards individual accounts in social security for quite some time.

Although the political environment is not favourable for reform, the underlying problems have not gone away. It may one day be necessary to act and it would be best to be prepared. This chapter will use the commission report as a focus in reviewing the issues involved in social security reform in the USA. The commission's proposals show that it is possible to deal with issues like risk, redistribution and the transition to individual accounts in a framework that combines individual accounts and the traditional defined benefit programme. On the other hand, the commission has not eliminated all problems with individual accounts and has probably not produced a product that will prevail politically.

The chapter begins with the financial problems in the current system and projections of revenues and costs if reform is not carried out. However, the financial problems are related to other structural problems. The next section reviews structural problems in the system and the controversies over how to address these problems, if at all. Then the chapter turns to the commission proposals, considering the design of the individual accounts, the proposals to slow the growth in benefit payments and hence costs and ideas to smooth the transition to individual accounts. The chapter relates these proposals to the general debate. Finally, the chapter considers trends and problems in the private pension system, which has gradually but substantially expanded the use of individual accounts. While individual accounts may meet different needs for social security and employers, all individual accounts have certain common features, particularly related to risk. The section considers the risk that remains a problem for both public and private individual accounts.

THE FINANCIAL VIABILITY OF THE US SOCIAL SECURITY SYSTEM

The biggest issue in the social security debate in the USA, one that concerns all sides, is that of cost in relation to revenue. Currently, there is no problem. Social security takes in more revenue than it pays out as benefits, and this situation is likely to continue for a number of years. However, as population aging proceeds, it is expected that eventually the surpluses will end and some time later the accumulated reserves will be depleted. At that time the system will face the difficult choice of cutting benefits or raising taxes. The time horizon for this problem is far longer than those usually facing policy makers. The current situation is not urgent, and it is easy to postpone action in such a case. On the other hand, advocates of reform argue that delay is not costless, that acting now could avoid more difficult problems later. Sound decisions require information. In this case information must come from long-run projections of revenues and costs.

In view of the long-run nature of the problem, the Office of the Actuary of the Social Security Administration is required to prepare projections of revenue and cost each year looking ahead over a 75-year horizon. Given the gradual nature of population aging, potential social security problems could be missed with a short horizon. But the long horizon strains the ability of actuaries to develop reliable projections. Nevertheless, projection models are a way to bring together relationships concerning what is known about demography and the economy in a consistent way. Of course, many assumptions are needed. Recognizing the importance of assumptions, the actuarial report develops three projections based on different sets of assumptions, low cost, high cost and intermediate. It also does extensive tests of sensitivity to many of the assumptions. Other researchers have also explored the reliability of the estimates. For example, Lee and Tuljapurkar (1998) have developed stochastic forecasting models for social security to produce not only estimates but also confidence limits for those estimates. These show not only the limits in our understanding, but also the risks policy makers face, since the estimates involve some margin of error. While researchers do work on this issue, in practice users tend to rely heavily on the intermediate projections of the Actuary. In view of its widespread use, this is the projection that is most influential in policy discussions.

The driving force behind the projected cost increases in social security is population aging. But population aging will also drive up the costs of other social expenditures such as health care and long-term care. Aging is a problem to the extent that it increases the total cost of all the programmes it affects. Table 7.1 shows cost and financial projections for the programmes for the aged financed by payroll taxes. These include Old Age, Survivor and Disability Insurance (OASDI) under social security and the hospital insurance benefits covered by Medicare (the health insurance programme covering those over 65 and some younger disabled people).[1] Medicare is included because it is part of the problem, although solutions are likely to come one programme at a time. Thus a reform that constrained cost growth in the pension system would not only help it, but would also hold down the cumulative cost of all aging-driven programmes.

Table 7.1A shows projected cost rates, that is, costs relative to taxable payroll, assuming current benefit schedules remain unchanged over time. Thus cost rates can be compared to contribution rates, which are also expressed relative to taxable payroll. The table shows the combined employer and employee contribution rates (they share equally) for each

*Table 7.1   Projections for contributory programmes: old age, survivor,
          disability (OASDI) and Medicare (hospital insurance part)*

A. Projected cost rates, as percentage of covered payroll

	Contribution rate (current) 2002	Cost rate (projections) 2002	2025	2050	2075	Per cent increase, 2002–75
Intermediate						
OASDI	12.4	10.84	16.02	17.92	19.76	82
Medicare	2.9	2.75	4.19	7.16	10.61	286
Low-cost						
OASDI	12.4	10.71	14.09	14.21	14.23	33
Medicare	2.9	2.66	2.63	3.43	5.08	91
High Cost						
OASDI	12.4	11.02	18.23	22.88	28.30	157
Medicare	2.9	2.85	6.66	14.89	22.06	674

B. Seventy-five year actuarial balance rate (addition to contribution rate restoring actuarial balance over 75-year horizon)

	Actuarial balance rate	75-year constant contribution rate	Per cent change from current rate
Intermediate			
OASDI	1.87	14.27	15
Medicare	2.02	4.92	70
Low-cost			
OASDI	−0.44	11.96	−4
Medicare	−0.20	2.70	−7
High-cost			
OASDI	5.00	17.40	40
Medicare	6.47	9.37	223

Sources: US Social Security Administration, *2002 Annual Report*, Tables IV.B5, p.60, VI.E2, pp.158–9; US Health Care Financing Agency[2], *2002 Annual Report*, Table II.B.11, p.62.

programme. The current contribution rates exceed the cost rates, indicating that both OASDI and Medicare are currently running surpluses. But the cost rates then rise over time, eventually exceeding the current contribution rate under all sets of assumptions. In other words, both programmes will eventually run deficits. Under the intermediate assumptions, OASDI deficits will begin in 2017 and Medicare deficits in 2016. Of course a deficit alone will not bring a crisis. Both programmes can draw on their trust funds that are accumulated from past surpluses plus the interest on these funds. Under the intermediate assumptions, these funds will be exhausted in 2041 for OASDI and in 2030 for Medicare. Exhaustion will occur somewhat earlier under the high-cost assumptions, but under the low-cost assumptions the trust fund will not run out over the next 75 years and will be more than enough to cover the small projected deficit. After exhaustion, if it occurs, there are only a few choices: benefits can be cut, or the contribution rate can be raised, or another revenue source can be found. To illustrate the option of raising the contribution rate to preserve benefits, it will have to increase to the cost rate in order to restore financial balance. Under the intermediate assumptions the OASDI contribution rate will have to be around 20 per cent in 2075 and the Medicare rate around 10 per cent for a total of around 30 per cent compared to the current 15.3 per cent, roughly a doubling.[3] While a 30 per cent rate might not seem bad in some other countries, in the USA it would be considered high, certainly a sizable change. But this projection is based on preserving current benefits with no preparations in advance.

In contrast, Table 7.1B shows the results of reform begun immediately and maintained throughout the 75-year period. The actuarial balance rate can be interpreted either as the reduction in the cost rate for each of the next 75 years or, alternatively, as the increase in the contribution rate over the same period that will restore financial balance.[4] Table 7.1B also shows the increase in the contribution rate if this is the option selected for bringing actuarial balance. The higher contribution rate of 14.27 per cent for OASDI could be maintained as a constant over the 75 years under intermediate assumptions. This is only a 15 per cent increase, as opposed to the 82 per cent increase that would eventually be needed without early intervention. Assuming the same reform in Medicare, the combined contribution rate could be kept near 19 per cent, substantially less than the 30 per cent predicted eventually with no corrective action. There is, however, a limitation to this approach. The immediate increase in the contribution rate or cut in cost rate will maintain actuarial balance for 75 years but not beyond. In year 76, there will be a gap again. Realistically, contribution rates and/or benefits will have to be reviewed periodically and revised based on the next 75 years. Thus, with complete inaction, the combined OASDI and Medicare contribution rates will approach 30 per cent. With immediate adjustments to maintain benefits, we might begin around 19 per cent with the possibility of gradual subsequent increases. There are countries where a combined contribution rate for social security and a part of medical care of 20 or even 30 per cent would seem reasonable, but in the USA the increase on the current level appears large. These results suggest that the looming social security deficits will be a problem politically and perhaps economically, but they do not show a solution.

STRUCTURAL PROBLEMS IN SOCIAL SECURITY: DO THEY REQUIRE STRUCTURAL REFORMS?

In addition to the prospective deficits, there are structural problems in the US social security system. Indeed, the deficits themselves will result not only from population aging but also from a structural problem. In principle, the structural problems could be solved under a system of individual accounts. There are, however, counterarguments against this form of structural reform. Actually, there are counterarguments against virtually every theoretical argument made about social security and so these arguments have not been decisive in the political debate. Nevertheless they have helped to frame the issues. In this section we review briefly some of these arguments before moving on to consider concrete reform proposals.

Social security in the USA began as a pay-as-you-go (PAYGO) system in which the payments to current retirees were financed by contributions from current workers. This met the urgent need of the depression period to start paying pensions to old people immediately. The PAYGO approach also seemed affordable since there were relatively few retirees drawing pensions relative to the number of workers paying contributions. But a PAYGO system has well known structural problems. First, as the ratio of retirees to workers increases with population aging, the contribution per worker must rise to cover the payments to the rising number of retirees. This is a consequence not only of the aging but also of the PAYGO structure. It does not happen in a system of individual accounts where each retiree draws her pension only from her own accumulated contributions made during working years. Since there is no redistribution across workers, the individual's contribution rate does not depend on the number of other retirees. A second structural problem relates to the rate of return to individuals from participating in social security. Considering social security contributions as an investment and pension payments as the return, the rate of return to early generations in a PAYGO system may be high, but it is well known that it will eventually diminish, approaching the rate of growth of the wage bill as the system matures. In contrast, in a system organized from inception as individual accounts, the rate of return to an individual account holder is simply the rate of return on the investments in the account. Market rates of return tend to be more volatile than the rate of wage growth, but the average market rate of return has been higher than the rate of wage growth historically. Third, the social security system may discourage saving. By its PAYGO nature the current system transfers resources from workers to retirees without generating saving. And, by guaranteeing a retirement income, it might even discourage individuals from saving. In contrast, individual account contributions could be a source of saving to finance investment during the individual's working years.

The relevance of these structural problems for reform has been challenged in several ways. Their empirical importance has been questioned. There are other social concerns related to distribution and politics that may outweigh the structural issues in deciding on reform. And the structural advantages of an individual account system are clearest when the system begins with individual accounts. The transition from a PAYGO system to individual accounts raises difficulties that could outweigh the benefits.

Considering the empirical problems, the PAYGO contribution rate will tend to rise. The empirical question is the magnitude of the increase, an issue already discussed. Similarly, there is no question that the rate of return to participants will tend to fall in the current system. Empirically, would people earn a higher rate of return under an individual account system? This depends on whether the rate of return from investments exceeds the rate of wage growth. Historically it has. Will this pattern continue? More particularly, might some cohorts receive lower returns under individual accounts compared to the current system? One other complication is that the costs of transition to individual accounts could deduct from the returns under that system, depending on how they are covered. The impact of social security on saving has long been an area of empirical controversy. In the reform context the issue is the comparative effects of the current system and individual accounts on saving. The existing system is not strictly PAYGO. Currently, there is prefunding, all of which is used to purchase US government bonds. The comparative issues involve the extent and timing of prefunding under the two alternatives and the best way to invest the funds. We return to these issues in relation to specific plans.

Although the current system has structural problems, advocates point also to its strengths. It performs a number of redistributive functions. It lifts many poor people above the poverty line, in part because the benefit formula is tilted in favour of those with lower lifetime earnings. It provides support to spouses who did not have substantial earnings. It provides death and survivor benefits. And these benefits are provided without a means test. It also provides protection against some risks, including inflation. In contrast, a simple individual account system does not redistribute across individuals, nor does it provide protection against inflation. On the other hand, the current system also has distributional shortcomings. Within generations, the rate of return to those with lower earnings is not raised in spite of the tilt in the benefit formula, mainly because such individuals have lower life expectancies and many do not live long enough to draw benefits. Across generations, the rising contribution rate tends to favour early over later generations. In view of the distributional issues most individual account proposals call for two tiers, one an individual account and the other a scaled-back version of the current system. Such proposals even attempt to improve on distributional shortcomings in the current system. But opponents of individual accounts are also seeking to deal with distributional problems in the current system.

Another argument of opponents of structural change is that the current system commands political support. Rich and poor alike are willing to support the redistributive provisions in the current system. On the other hand, a system with individual accounts might shift the focus to individual gain and might lead to an erosion of support for the redistributive component, which is also the part that will be growing in cost. In this view, individual accounts might endanger the social solidarity of the current programme. A counterargument is that the political support for the current programme has always been based on self-interest as much as on social solidarity. The programme was popular because it provided secure benefits and a high rate of return. But as the rate of return falls and the future deficits raise concerns, public support is likely to diminish even without reform. Proponents of reform expect their reforms to overcome the weaknesses in the current system that are likely to undermine support for it.

Finally, even if the idea of individual accounts were accepted in principle, the transition from PAYGO to individual accounts creates problems. Those already at or near retirement would not have individual accounts. Contributions would be needed to continue PAYGO benefits to them even while beginning contributions to the individual accounts. The PAYGO benefits would diminish eventually, but very slowly. Thus, in the early stages of transition, there could be double costs. A two-tier system with relatively small individual accounts reduces but does not eliminate this problem. As we shall see, current reform plans try to ease the transition.

CSSS AND STRUCTURAL REFORM

The President's Commission to Strengthen Social Security (CSSS) is concerned about the structural problems in social security. In contrast to those who think minor tinkering will suffice, it sees a need for structural reforms. Individual accounts are a basic part of the reforms. In all three models individuals would continue to contribute to and draw a defined benefit (DB) pension and they might choose also to participate in an individual account. One goal for the individual accounts is to help close the financial gap in the system. In one model the only reform is the addition of the individual account component. However, this is not enough on its own to establish financial balance over a 75-year horizon. The other models thus add other reforms to slow the growth in the cost of benefits. This section will review the three plans while highlighting issues that have played a role in the broader debate in the USA over social security reform. We consider the design of the individual accounts; benefit growth reduction strategies along with redistribution issues; and the transition to individual accounts together with prefunding.

The Design of the Individual Accounts

In all three CSSS models, individual accounts are voluntary. For those who opt out, their full contribution will go into the current programme and they will receive the full defined benefit. For those who participate, a limited portion of their total OASDI contribution of 10.4 per cent will go into their individual account and the rest into the DB programme. Table 7.2 summarizes key features of each model. The contribution rates differ by model, but Models 2 and 3 also set a dollar limit of $1000 for contributions into the accounts.[5]

On the benefit side, the pension will include returns from both programmes, but the DB will be offset, based on the contributions to the individual accounts. Each model sets a DB offset rate (shown in Table 7.2) that is treated like an interest rate for computation. As contributions are made to the individual account, interest is credited each year at the real DB offset rate, producing a notional total at retirement. This total is then converted to a notional lifetime monthly annuity. This annuity is then subtracted from the person's DB benefit. The total social security benefit is thus the individual account benefit plus the DB benefit after the offset. This leads to a simple interpretation of the DB offset rate. It is a hurdle rate for the actual real rate of return on an individual account. If the actual rate exceeds the DB offset rate, the individual with the individual account will receive a higher benefit than the like individual without. For example, the real DB offset rate of 3.5 per cent in Model 1 means that a person must earn a rate of return 3.5 per cent above the inflation rate if she is to do better with an individual account. In contrast, the rate in Model 2 is only 2 per cent, a much smaller hurdle. One purpose of the DB offset is to reduce the cost of the DB part of the system, which is the part with the rising long-run costs. The higher the rate, the greater DB savings will be achieved. But the DB rate is also set at a level below the expected rate of investment return. It is hoped that individual benefits will be raised by individual accounts even as the system reduces its costs. Of course investment returns are risky. The higher the DB offset rate, the greater is the risk that the individual account holder will not come out ahead. There is a trade-off, and each model makes it in a different way.

Several features of the individual accounts are intended to deal with potential risks. To protect people from the risk of making bad investments

Table 7.2 Features of CSSS social security reform models

	Model 1	Model 2	Model 3
Individual accounts			
Contributions out of regular contribution rate	2%	4% up to $1000 annually (indexed to wages)	2.5% up to $1000 annually (indexed to wages)
Additional contributions			1% of wages required to participate (subsidized through income tax)
DB offset rate	3.5%	2.0%	2.5%
DB cost-saving adjustments			
Indexation of starting pensions		Indexed to inflation instead of wages, beginning in 2009	Indexed to gains in average life expectancy (expected average annual growth of 0.5% over inflation)
Early retirement penalty			Reduce benefit for early retirement and increase it for late retirement
Benefit formula			Reduce bend point factor for highest income bracket from 15% to 10%, beginning in 2009
Distributional adjustments			
Minimum benefit		120% of poverty line for 30 year minimum wage worker	100% of poverty line for 30-year minimum wage worker (111% for 40-year worker)
Widow/widower benefits		Increased to 75% of couple benefits (currently 50% to 67%) for lower wage couples	Increased to 75% of couple benefits (currently 50% to 67%) for lower-wage couples
Splitting of contributions and account earnings in case of divorce	yes	yes	yes

and from some financial risks, investment choices will be limited. All three models propose an arrangement similar to the Thrift Savings Plan (TSP) set up in 1986 as part of a pension reform for federal civil servants. Civil servants used to have their own pension system that was more generous than social security. It was decided to bring them into social security. To compensate for the difference in benefits, TSP was established to manage an individual account system for them. Individuals can choose their own investments, but from very limited choices, originally three funds and now five, all index funds. TSP is managed by a board having fiduciary responsibilities and insulated from political influence by having long terms. The funds are actually managed by private firms selected competitively. For individual account holders, choices are limited, but administrative overhead has been low, about 0.1 per cent of the value of the assets managed (Thompson, 1999, p.15).

CSSS proposes a similar structure for the individual accounts in its models. The same five index funds would be offered, plus three balanced index funds, plus an inflation-protected bond fund. In addition, a fairly conservative standard fund would be established for individuals who do not choose investments on their own. CSSS also proposes that a threshold accumulation level be established. Once a person's account reached the threshold, she would be allowed to invest in a broader range of private sector funds. The funds would have to satisfy stringent rules to be set by the governing board for the individual accounts. Earlier individual account proposals would have imposed far fewer investment restrictions. CSSS apparently is responding to the arguments that systems with wide choices may have high administrative costs and that individuals may make investment choices that are too risky.

There is some convergence in management approaches between the CSSS proposal for individual accounts and other proposals for managing the OASDI Trust Fund under the current system. Those who want to maintain the current DB system have become concerned about the present system where the whole fund must be invested in special government bonds. They see a need to invest in market securities while protecting the investment choices from political influence. Aaron (1999), an advocate of maintaining the current system, has urged that up to 40 per cent of assets be invested in private securities under the direction of an independent board. The Railroad Retirement System is a separate government programme and, in 2001, it did decide to allow private investments. It pays a benefit that is larger than social security. It is paid in two parts, a social security equivalent benefit and a supplementary benefit. The social security equivalent benefit is maintained on a PAYGO basis with surpluses being transferred to social security. But the supplementary benefit has a trust fund, which had been invested in US government bonds. The reform sets up a new independent board to manage the fund. Investments in private securities will be allowed (US Railroad Retirement Board, 2002, p.2). On the other side, the CSSS models would limit choices substantially for individual accounts. The CSSS models, the Railroad Retirement system and the Aaron social security proposal would all set up an independent board to oversee the system, contract actual investment to private management companies and allow investment in private securities.

Another kind of risk arises at retirement. Under the DB plan, each individual gets a lifetime inflation adjusted pension. There have been proposals for lump sum withdrawals from individual accounts, but, with growing life expectancy, CSSS proposes that at least a portion must be withdrawn only gradually. The governing board should make available several types of annuities, including some that are inflation-adjusted and some that offer the option of leaving a bequest. A threshold will be established for the combined DB and individual account distributions that is sufficient to keep the individual or couple safely above the poverty line. Lump sum withdrawals will be permitted from individual accounts as long as that threshold is maintained.

One other kind of risk relates to death. When a person dies before retirement, he does not get back his contributions, although his survivors may qualify for benefits under OASDI. The family of an individual account holder would get back all contributions plus interest. However, death would be the only condition allowing a withdrawal before retirement. After retirement, any portion of the account not converted to an annuity would be paid out at death. And a payment at death may be made with an annuity if the annuity includes a provision for a bequest.

The risks in individual accounts have been a major issue in the social security debate. There were previous individual account proposals that would have permitted investment choices and lump sum withdrawals with few restrictions. The CSSS proposals have clearly sought to reduce these risks, although some risks are inherent in the nature of individual accounts.

Benefit Growth Reduction Strategies and Redistribution

The CSSS individual accounts are expected to reduce the costs of the DB benefits, but not by enough to restore financial balance to the system. Thus Models 2 and 3 propose additional measures to slow the growth of benefits. These models also address distributional issues, partly to protect the most needy from the benefit adjustments and partly because there are currently distributional issues in social security.

Social security benefits are indexed in various ways. Modifications in the indexation could slow benefit growth. For example, after retirement, benefits are indexed to prices. But it has been argued that the consumer price index (CPI) overstates the true extent of inflation, and corrections have been urged. This is one reform that would take place without explicit action by the social security system. The CPI is calculated by another agency. As the index is revised, social security increases will automatically be scaled back.

Wages are indexed to average wage growth before retirement in calculating average indexed monthly earnings, which help determine a person's benefit. But the CSSS models focused on the indexation of the starting benefit for retirees. Each year the starting benefit for new retirees is indexed up by the rate of wage growth.[6] Models 2 and 3 propose reducing the rate of this indexation, but in different ways. Model 2 would switch to price indexation. This means that the starting pensions for new cohorts of retirees will always keep up with inflation. However, the general standard of living tends to rise over time and usually faster than inflation. As individual wages rise from cohort to cohort faster than prices, starting pensions will also rise faster than inflation, but not as fast as the wages themselves. Currently, the starting pensions rise as fast as the wages, that is, they keep pace with the rising standard of living. While the change initially will be small, over time pensions will not keep up with the rising standard of living, even though they will not go down in real terms. The intermediate social security projections assume an average inflation rate of 3.0 per cent and a rate of wage growth of 4.1 per cent. With price indexation and assuming individual wages grow at the average rate, the starting pension will increase by 178 per cent in 30 years and by over 12 times in 75 years. But with wage indexation the increases would be 234 per cent in 30 years and by a multiple of 19 in 75 years. The differences give an idea of how new retirees will be falling behind relative to the standard of living. But they also show how powerfully price rather than wage indexation can slow the growth of costs.

In view of the large effect on future generations of retirees, Model 3 uses a different indexation procedure intended to lie between price and wage indexation. It would adjust starting pensions below the rate of wage growth on the basis of increases in life expectancy. Starting pensions will grow faster than in Model 2, but cost savings will be smaller. To achieve financial balance, Model 2 needs additional benefit modifications. While keeping the normal retirement age the same, it would increase the penalty for early retirement while increasing the benefit for delayed retirement. It would also change the benefit formula to reduce pensions for individuals with higher lifetime earnings.

In view of the modifications, both models try to help those with low lifetime earnings. A person who worked 30 years at the minimum wage would be guaranteed a benefit equal to 120 per cent of the poverty line in Model

2 and 100 per cent in Model 3. In the individual accounts the $1000 maximum means that lower income individuals can contribute at a higher rate. The ownership rights in the individual account give the family an extra death benefit should a person die before retirement, and lower income individuals tend to have shorter life expectancies. Widows and widowers tend to have lower incomes. Both models increase the benefits to lower income widows and widowers to 75 per cent of the benefits to the couple. Currently, the benefit ranges between 50 and 67 per cent. Others have proposed similar adjustments also. CSSS has tried to stay in line with general thinking relating to distributional issues.

Transition and Prefunding Mechanisms

A problem with the US DB system is that costs and contribution rates will have to rise over time, putting future generations of workers at a disadvantage. On the other hand, shifting from DB to individual accounts creates the problem of double costs during the transition. It is necessary to pay for the unfunded liabilities under the old DB plan while making contributions into the individual accounts. Eventually, the DB costs go down, but only slowly. Thus transition can put the current generation of workers at a disadvantage if it must pay the double costs. Even if individual accounts have desirable properties, it may not be desirable to change systems if the transition will put a disproportionate burden on one generation. The CSSS proposals are interesting because they try to avoid the heavy burden on the first generation of the transition. And the DB benefit adjustments are intended to avoid the future increases in cost.

DB contributions go to pay for current benefits plus some prefunding. Individual account contributions are all for prefunding. Individual accounts by their nature are fully funded. The CSSS strategy for the initial transition is to change the prefunding to avoid the double costs. Contributions will go into the individual accounts, but contributions for the prefunding of DB benefits will stop. Since the proposed individual accounts are small, they can be funded without a need for an increase in the contribution rate for a number of years. Of course, prefunding for the DB benefits has been considered a necessary preparation for rising future DB costs, but in the CSSS plan it is not necessary because other reforms would hold down the future cost growth in the DB system. First, as people with individual accounts begin to retire, the DB offsets will begin to reduce the cost of DB benefits. It will be several decades before this effect becomes large and will also depend on the number of people who choose to participate in the individual accounts. Second, Models 2 and 3 include additional benefit modifications intended to slow the growth of the DB costs. Thus the

CSSS models are designed to control costs in the early years and the later years of the transition process. But all three models will incur transition costs in the middle years.

To give an idea of the timing and cost, Model 2 has the largest reduction in the growth of benefits and has the smallest transition costs. However, the combination of contributions and the Trust Fund will not cover costs between 2025 and 2054. But the need for outside funds will be temporary. After 2054, the system is expected to have surpluses again because of growing cost savings resulting from the benefit reforms. Indeed, the present value of the surpluses after 2054 (but within the usual 75-year social security time horizon) is expected to equal the present value of the extra funds that will be needed. Since the need for funds is temporary and the funds can be repaid, Model 2 proposes to draw on general revenue. If the infusions from general revenue were viewed as a loan, the system would have the ability to repay it within 75 years from now.

Model 2 is the only one that can fully repay its transition costs. In Model 3, extra revenue will be needed between 2034 and 2063. Beyond then surpluses are expected to resume, but they will not be sufficient to pay for the transition loan in present value terms over the standard 75-year horizon. Cost savings will continue beyond 75 years and may eventually be sufficient. However based on a 75-year period, this model proposes permanent extra financing in addition to the transitional infusion of general revenue. CSSS seems to feel that general revenue is not a suitable source of permanent financing.[7] The permanent financing would probably be an increase in the contribution rate. An increase by 0.63 per cent is expected to restore actuarial balance. This is only about a third of the increase that would be required to restore balance under the current system. The Model 1 reform is individual accounts only. It would not reach actuarial balance in the 75-year period.

PENSION CHANGES IN THE PRIVATE SECTOR

While individual accounts have been debated for the public social security system, their use has grown rapidly in the private sector. Employers are major providers of pensions. Forty-seven per cent of the employed labour force was covered by a private pension in 1998 and 43 per cent of the people who were 65 or older received pension income.[8] While employers still offer DB pensions, there has been a rapid growth of employer-sponsored 401k plans, which are tax-sheltered individual accounts set up by the employer under a provision of the US Internal Revenue Code. In addition to employer plans, individuals may set up individual retirement accounts (IRAs) on their own, also sheltered under the income tax laws. Private pensions reflect the independent decisions by employers and employees. However, the government in seeking to stimulate saving has also been a player, since it created the incentives through the tax system and regulation for employers and individuals to set up individual accounts. Advocates in the public debate hope individual accounts will solve structural problems in social security. Employers have their own structural issues in deciding between DB, individual account or no pension that relate to cost and worker incentives. But there are common issues that arise in all forms of individual accounts and these tend to relate to risk.

Among employers, there has been rapid growth in defined contribution (DC) plans like 401ks, but the trends in DB plans have been less pronounced and have tended to vary by firm size. The number of large firms offering DB plans has been relatively stable over a long period, while the number offering DC plans has grown substantially. In large firms, DC plans tend to be added as supplements to already existing DB plans. On the other hand, small firms did increase participation in DB plans in the 1970s before the clarification of 401k rules in 1981. Since then, however, the number of DC plans has increased dramatically while DB offerings have diminished. For small firms, the DC plan is often the only kind offered (Mitchell and Schieber, 1998, pp. 1–2).

Considering the employer plans there are risks, but the risks differ between DB and DC plans. DC plans by their nature are fully funded. Employers are also required to fund DB plans fully, but this takes deliberate action. An employer is allowed time to restore full funding when its DB plan is underfunded. Thus both types face financial risk from fluctuations in returns on the investments in the pension fund, but there is a difference in who bears the risk, just as in the public debate. In a DB plan, the employer bears the risk while paying a fixed benefit to retirees, while in a DC plan the individual bears the risk. There are, however, other kinds of risk in DB plans.

The most serious risk in a DB plan is that the employer will go bankrupt at a time when its plan is not fully funded. An employer approaching bankruptcy is likely to fall short in its obligation to keep the plan funded. To protect workers, the government has established the Pension Benefit Guarantee Corporation (PBGC), which insures DB pensions and requires that all employers offering DB plans pay a premium for the insurance. However, the coverage is not complete and there have been cases of workers from bankrupt companies not getting their full promised DB benefit. A second risk is more subtle and can happen if an employer changes pension plans. Since accrued benefits are supposed to be fully funded, workers will not lose these if a plan is terminated. Moreover, terminated plans are generally replaced by new plans. The problem for some workers is that their benefits under the new plan may be less than they expected under the old plan.

An example comes from cash balance plans, which many large employers have used as replacements for traditional DB plans. A cash balance plan is often described as a hybrid that is DB but has characteristics of a DC plan. Each individual has an individual account, but it is notional and may not contain real assets. Interest is credited each year, but the company specifies the rate, which may not be the market rate. Contributions may not be at a fixed rate as they would be in a DC system because the employer can reduce its contribution in years when the plan is overfunded (EBRI, 1997, ch. 10). High investment returns go to workers in a DC plan but to the employer in a cash purchase plan. Companies switching to cash purchase plans tend to switch from DB plans. In a common type of DB plan the benefit is based on final wages. In such a plan pension credits are small for young workers but get large as the worker nears retirement. In contrast, the notional accounts of young workers build up more rapidly in cash purchase plans. But older workers who got small credits under the old plan are at a disadvantage after a switch to cash balances where their later contributions will be relatively small. A company can continue to cover older workers under the old rules during a switch in systems. Many, however, did not. Moreover, the notional rules have not always been transparent to older workers who could not assess the effects on them of the switch.

The risks in employer DB plans parallel in some ways those in the social security DB benefit. While the social security system will not have an outright bankruptcy, if future deficits become large, there may be adjustments in benefits or contributions. There will be a new generation of people in the electorate, and it is hard to predict the outcome. There is a political risk that benefits promised might not actually materialize. There is also one difference. At least in recent discussions of deliberate reform, there has been a clear intention to keep older workers covered under the old rules. Younger workers have time to adjust to a change in rules, but older workers do not. On the other hand, if reform is forced by a crisis, it may be difficult to predict the outcome.

The kind of risk currently receiving the most attention in US discussions is the financial risk in DC plans. During the 1990s, when investment returns soared, people were generally happy with their IRAs and 401k plans. But the fluctuations that are inevitable in financial markets have now gone the other way. The broadly based Standard and Poor Index of 500 large stocks was down by roughly 40 per cent in July 2002 from its peak in early 2000. People have watched their retirement savings tumble in value. In addition to the fluctuations in the overall market, employees with 401k plans in certain troubled companies have had special problems. These were successful companies that induced employees to invest much of their 401k in company stock. For a time, these 401k investments did very well and the employees seemed to face the prospect of comfortable retirements. But when the companies got in trouble, 401k values were nearly eliminated. Market fluctuations are unavoidable. However, the 401k problems at troubled companies result from insufficient diversification. This problem can be avoided, but current regulations do not impose strong requirements for diversification.

The risk problems in private DC plans parallel those that would arise in individual accounts in social security. The CSSS models propose that investment choices be limited and that only highly diversified funds be allowed. This should afford protection against the problems faced by Enron or WorldCom employees, whose 401k plans collapsed in value. But there is no protection from market-wide fluctuations that cannot be diversified away. Of course, in any one year the market may have large fluctuations. But individual accounts are accumulated over an entire career. The ups and downs in market returns should average out over time. On average they do. It turns out, however, that lifetime average returns are sensitive to beginning and end points of an individual's career. Burtless (2000) found that, if people had invested in individual accounts using the actual securities in the USA from 1911 to 1999, on average returns would have been good. But there would also have been large fluctuations across cohorts in the pensions that would have been earned by workers with similar lifetime earnings.

For both public and private DC accounts there are risks. There are policies that can reduce the risks, but the risks cannot be eliminated. DB accounts also have risks of different types. It has been argued that combining DB and DC is better than relying on either type alone, since the different kinds of risks would be diversified. This argument does not satisfy everyone. Risk remains an issue for the private pension system. There are calls for reform in the private system to protect people from risk. And risk is one of the unresolved policy issues in the debate over social security reform in the USA.

CONCLUSION

Individual accounts have become a major part of the private pension system in the USA. They have also become an important issue in the debate over public social security reform. The recent presidential Commission to Strengthen Social Security made them a centrepiece in their reform proposals. Currently, fluctuations in financial markets have raised concerns over the risks in all forms of individual accounts. The commission's recommendations have been largely ignored. However, long-run problems remain. Although the US social security system is currently running comfortable surpluses, projections show that these surpluses will end and accumulations will be depleted over the coming decades. The commission sees individual accounts as a way to deal with long-run problems in the system. Although its recommendations have not moved the political debate, they have provided insights on opportunities and limitations in an individual accounts system.

In the commission proposals a defined benefit based on the current system would be a substantial part, combined with a voluntary individual account. The individual account is designed to raise the total expected pension of an individual who opts for it, although there is a chance that it will not, because of market fluctuations. The individual accounts are also expected to reduce the growth in the defined benefit part of the system, which is the driver of the increasing costs. But it turns out that the individual accounts alone are not sufficient to solve the financial problems of the system. The commission tried one model with individual accounts only, but it could not close the financial gap. The DB side of the system must be modified to slow its growth in order to restore financial balance. The commission DB reforms would not reduce real benefits, but they would eventually make new retirees considerably worse off than they would be under current benefit formulas. Critics have focused on the individual accounts, which offer some hope of making retirees better off. But the pain is more likely to result from the proposed reforms in the DB benefits.

The proposals explore ways to address problems in individual accounts, which are often criticized for not dealing with redistributional issues. The proposals do address some of these through the combination of the DB benefit and the individual account. The transition to individual accounts can impose a heavy burden on the early generations of workers during the transition. The proposals find a way to avoid this early cost. The commission is willing to regulate investment choices and withdrawal options at retirement in order to reduce some of the risks inherent in individual accounts. Its proposals could not eliminate risk or completely smooth out the transition costs. The precise commission proposals will probably not be the ultimate social security reform policy, but they show that a system including individual accounts can be flexible enough to deal with a number of important problems.

Perhaps the biggest concern with individual accounts relates to risk. Given the current problems in financial markets in the USA, there is little interest in adopting new reforms that will expose people to more financial risk. On the other hand, we have come to understand that virtually every kind of pension, public or private, has some form of risk. Even the DB social security benefit may face a future risk of political change when financial pressures grow. The ultimate challenge for social security reform is to find a suitable balance between the various kinds of risk, recognizing that no system is likely to eliminate risk totally.

NOTES

1. There are other programmes affected by aging, but they are financed out of general revenue rather than the payroll tax. These include the rest of Medicare, which is financed by a combination of general revenue and contributions by the elderly, and Medicaid, the health care programme for the poor, which pays for long-term care for those with limited assets and income. The programmes financed by payroll taxes are set up as trust funds. They have separate accounting systems so it is easy to keep track of the balance between revenues and expenditures. The programmes financed from general revenue may also involve a rising burden, but one that is more difficult to predict under current accounting and financing procedures.
2. The US Health Care Financing Agency is now known as Centers for Medicare and Medicaid Services.
3. Strictly speaking, the OASDI and Medicare cost rates cannot be added. They have different denominators since the taxable payroll differs between the two programmes. Medicare taxes all earnings while OASDI taxes only to an upper limit ($84 900 in 2002). If the OASDI payroll base were used for both programmes, the total would be higher than the simple sum of rates in Table 7.1A.
4. The actuarial balance rate is actually the difference between the 75-year cost and income rates, which are calculated as the present value of cost and income, respectively, as a percentage of taxable payroll. Income equals contributions plus other income of the system such as taxes paid by retirees on their benefits. There are other technical adjustments in both cost and income rates. Assuming that the reforms do not change the revenue from taxes on benefits or the other adjustments, the actuarial balance rate gives the increase in the contribution rate, if that is the reform selected. Under this alternative, it provides the extra prefunding needed to support current benefits.
5. One result of the $1000 limit in Model 2 is that individuals earning up to $25 000 could contribute the full 4 per cent it allows. For Model 3, the limit is $40 000 to be able to contribute the full 2.5 per cent it allows. Model 3 also requires an extra 1 per cent contribution in order to qualify to make the basic 2.5 per cent individual account contribution. The 1 per cent is not included in the $1000 limit.
6. Technically, it is the bend points in the benefit formula that are indexed to average wage growth. But the effect is that the starting benefit is also indexed.
7. A portion of Medicare and all of Medicaid are funded permanently out of general revenue. Medicaid is the health care programme for the poor, but it has become the main government programme for long-term care. Apparently, there is a desire to limit the burden on general revenue from aging-related programmes.
8. The figure for retirement income includes all pensions outside of social security, including some government pensions and individual retirement saving plans. It comes from US Social Security Administration (2000, p. 16). The figure for employee coverage is only for employer-provided pensions. It comes from US General Accounting Office (2000, pp.7–9).

REFERENCES

Aaron, Henry J. (1999), 'Social Security: Tune It Up, Don't Trade It In', in Henry J. Aaron and John B. Shoven, *Should the United States Privatize Social Security?*, Cambridge, MA and London, England: The MIT Press.

Burtless, Gary (2000), 'Social Security Privatization and Financial Market Risk', Center on Social and Economic Dynamics, The Brookings Institution, working paper no. 10.

Employee Benefit Research Institute (EBRI) (1997), *Fundamentals of Employee Benefit Programs*, 5th edn, Washington, DC: EBRI Publications.

Lee, Ronald D. and Shripad Tuljapurkar (1998), 'Stochastic Forecasts for Social Security', in David Wise (ed.), *Frontiers in the Economics of Aging*, Chicago: University of Chicago Press.

Mitchell, Olivia S. and Sylvester J. Schieber (1998), 'Defined Contribution Pensions: New Opportunities, New Risks', in O.S. Mitchell and S.J. Schieber (eds), *Living with Defined Contribution Pensions*, Philadelphia: University of Pennsylvania Press.

Thompson, Lawrence H. (1999), 'Administering Individual Accounts in Social Security', The Retirement Project, The Urban Institute, Washington, DC, occasional paper no. 1.

US General Accounting Office (2000), *Pension Plans: Characteristics of Persons in the Labor Force Without Pension Coverage*, GAO/HEHS-00-131, Washington, DC: US Government Printing Office.

US Health Care Financing Administration (2002), *The 2002 Annual Report of the Board of Trustees of the Federal Hospital Insurance and Federal Supplementary Insurance Trust Funds*, Washington, DC: US Government Printing Office.

US Railroad Retirement Board (2002), *Railroad Retirement System Annual Report.*

US Social Security Administration (2000), *Income of the Aged Chartbook, 1998*, Washington, DC: US Government Printing Office.

US Social Security Administration (2002), *The 2002 Annual Report of the Board of Trustees of the Federal Old-Age and Survivors Insurance and Disability Insurance Trust Funds*, Washington, DC: US Government Printing Office.

8. Public pension reform and contractual agreements in Sweden: from defined benefit to defined contribution

Edward Palmer and Eskil Wadensjö

INTRODUCTION

Beginning with reform of the public pension system in 1994, Sweden's mandatory public and contractual, quasi-mandatory old age pension schemes underwent radical change from defined benefit to defined contribution. The new framework can help eliminate the moral hazard involved in traditional defined benefit schemes, does away with impediments to mobility of especially older workers, and, generally, is neutral in terms of incentives to work and retire. This paper analyses the transformation of the mandatory and quasi-mandatory schemes from defined benefit to defined contribution, discusses how the public and contractual benefit schemes interact and the implications of the new Swedish pension regime for the future.

Beginning with the publication of the new concept for the public pension system in 1992 and the passage of the principles of reform legislation in 1994, Sweden began conversion of its mandatory and quasi-mandatory pension schemes from defined benefit (DB) to defined contribution (DC) schemes.[1] The public system was converted into two mandatory defined-contribution pillars, notional defined contribution (NDC) and financial defined contribution (FDC). Both are based on contributions from lifetime earnings, a rate of return (economic in the NDC scheme and financial in the FDC scheme) and with annuities based on life expectancy at retirement.[2]

From 1960 to 2001, benefits provided by the public system were the flat-rate *folkpension*, which all Swedes residing in Sweden were entitled to, and the earnings-related *allmän tilläggspension* (ATP) benefit. The *folkpension* provided a universal income guarantee for persons 65 and older. ATP provided universal old age insurance for everyone working in Sweden. With the reform, the *folkpension* was replaced by a guarantee pension that supplements the new NDC and FDC schemes at the lower end up to a maximum guarantee level. The NDC and FDC schemes will be the main sources of earnings replacement in old age for people working in Sweden.

From the mid-1970s, up to 90 per cent of the Swedish workforce have been covered by contractual benefit schemes. In the 1990s, coverage fell to around 80 per cent, but it was never lower than this in the last quarter of the century. The contractual schemes provide a supplement to the public scheme up to a ceiling on covered earnings for the public scheme. They provide the sole source of earnings replacement for the share of earnings above the ceiling, up to a higher ceiling. For individual earnings replacement, and also for the total effects of the mandatory and quasi-mandatory schemes on individual decisions to work and save, it is important to view the mandatory and contractual schemes together.

The disposition of the chapter is as follows. The next section presents and analyses the pension system prior to the reforms of the public and contractual schemes during the 1990s. The following two sections deal with the reforms of the public and contractual schemes and, in the final section, conclusions are drawn.

THE PENSION SYSTEM IN SWEDEN PRIOR TO THE REFORMS OF THE 1990s

The pre-1990 Setting

Contractual benefits in Sweden date back to 1770 when the *Riksdag* granted civil servants the right to retire at age 70 with the salary they had prior to retirement. However, the first important milestone for the development of modern contractual insurance was the passage in 1904 of legislation for creating regulations and the national supervisory board for private insurance. With this infrastructure in place many of the larger companies started schemes for white-collar employees – but generally not blue-collar ones.

In 1917, a group of major companies established an administrative organization for their pension plans, *Svenska Personalpensionskassan* (SPP), which later became important for administering most company plans in Sweden, and for ensuring portability of acquired rights. Initially, it was only possible to purchase one type of plan from SPP. From 1925, however, the insurance could be adapted to the needs of the client company. By the 1950s, a contribution rate of 24 per cent of the salary, with two-thirds paid by the employer, was common for private sector contractual plans, and this provided a substantial benefit with contributions up to a normal retirement age by the 1950s of 65 for men and 60 for women. These company plans typically concerned only white-collar workers. In fact, there were no contractual plans for blue-collar workers until the mid-1970s.

Pension plans for local government (county and municipality) employees were modelled on the scheme for civil servants. For some groups who were employed by the local government, for example teachers and policemen, benefits were regulated by the state, but financed by the local governments. By the mid-1940s almost all counties, larger municipalities (250) and towns had pension plans for their employees. Initially, for county employees the retirement age was 65 for men and 60 for women, and in the municipalities 65–7 for men and 60–62 for women. From 1976, the retirement age distinction between men and women in this area and also among white-collar workers in the private sector gradually disappeared, as all schemes moved towards age 65 as the norm.

The first milestone for public pensions in Sweden was the passage of legislation in 1913, which created a universal public benefit from age 67 from 1914. The next milestone for public pensions was 1960, the year in which the universal public earnings-related scheme, ATP, was introduced. From its implementation in 1914, the *folkpension* provided a substitute for the poorhouse and relief for the elderly poor. Preceding the introduction of ATP, a reform of the *folkpension* in 1946 was aimed at creating a benefit that would free the elderly from poor relief or assistance from relatives. Thus, originally, from 1914, the public old age pension was designed to provide relief from extreme deprivation, and, then, from 1946 a minimum, albeit low, universal income standard from age 67.

Because the flat rate was not sufficient to live on, the universal earnings-related scheme, ATP, was introduced by the Social Democratic Party explicitly for blue-collar workers, although the approximate half of the private sector's white-collar workers not covered by contractual arrangements in 1960 also benefited. ATP provided earnings-related coverage above the flat rate. The alternative, a Beveridge model, with a flat rate supplemented with private (or contractual) pensions for all employees, proposed and supported by the liberal and conservative parties in the 1950s, was rejected in the political process.[3] This event, together with the implementation of the ATP scheme in 1960, set the scene for the development of the Swedish pension system in its present form.

Sweden's integrated model of public and contractual benefits consists of a large public segment up to a ceiling on earnings, with a smaller contractual supplement. Above the ceiling on earnings for the public system, the contractual benefit is the only component. The ceiling has performed important insurance and political functions in the past decades. The ceiling on covered earnings was high in 1960, when ATP was introduced. It has been indexed to the rate of inflation indirectly since it is expressed as 7.5 times the basic amount (see the note to Table 8.1), which has been indexed to inflation. No account was taken of the rate of growth of the average real wage, however, and so by the end of the century, the ceiling was only about one and a half times the average wage of a full-time worker. This process has gradually shifted a greater share of the financial responsibility for Swedish pensions back to contractual benefits.

As is discussed in Palmer (2001), leaving the ceiling fixed as long as possible was to the advantage of both the blue-collar union and the employer confederation, albeit for entirely different reasons. Since the earnings of blue-collar workers were generally not above the ceiling, and since contributions were paid on all wages from 1983, this arrangement meant that, *ceteris paribus*, money was being shifted from white- to blue-collar workers within the ATP scheme. The employer confederation favoured a fixed ceiling as a matter of principle, since they were against any measures that might increase the contribution rate paid by employers. The non-socialist parties could also consider a fixed ceiling as a means of privatizing old age insurance, while the Social Democrats were interested in catering to the interests of LO (*Landsorganisationen*).

In accepting the reform proposal in 1992, all of these opposing interests lined up to support a continuation of a universal, public earnings scheme as the main pillar of the system.[4] However, by the time this occurred, there was much more room on the top left for contractual and other private arrangements. In the new public system, the ceiling is indexed to wage growth, so the relative importance of the public system should be largely maintained in the future.

In sum, Sweden considered Beveridge in the 1950s, and chose an alternative path. In the absence of a universal public pension plan, had the low level of the flat-rate benefit been retained, it would nevertheless have been necessary to mandate employer coverage to achieve universal coverage of all private sector workers, and it would have taken much longer for an employer-mandated scheme to provide adequate coverage. Had this course been pursued, it would have been difficult, if not impossible, not to share high economic growth after the Second World War with retiring workers who had struggled through the depression and ensuing war. Sweden returned to the discussion of the 1950s in the reform years of the 1990s, and once again chose in favour of a universal public earnings-related system topped up by contractual arrangements, and supplemented by an income guarantee.

Public Pensions from 1960 to the Reform of the 1990s

The ATP reform of 1960 represented a paradigm shift for Sweden, by introducing a universal earnings-related benefit, on top of the guarantee provided by the *folkpension*. Poverty relief, although always the main goal of public pensions, was no longer the sole goal. By providing a universal, earnings-related social insurance pension scheme for old age a country can prevent poverty, at the same time aspiring to provide an adequate income standard in old age for all career workers. From 1960, with the introduction of ATP, Sweden had chosen to provide universal, public old age pension insurance for everyone working in Sweden. This decision would be reinforced in the reform work of the 1990s, although the framework for the public scheme would be rebuilt.

The earnings-related supplement to the flat rate introduced in 1960 was meant to give the average worker a decent standard of living in old age. ATP required 30 years of coverage (contributions) to acquire the right to a full benefit from age 67 (age 65 from July 1976), with the benefit calculated as 60 per cent of the average of the 15 best years of earnings. However, there were two transition rules. The first applied to individuals who were older than 46 in 1960 and required 20 years of participation for a full benefit, and the benefit was reduced by one-twentieth for each year less than 20. The second enabled those who were 36 to 46 years old in 1960 to receive a full benefit provided they worked and contributed to the scheme continuously until they retired. The transition rules made it possible for workers to begin to obtain substantial earnings-related benefits by the end of the 1960s. Note, however, that the retirement age in the public system was 67 until 1976.

From 1960, all resident Swedes[5] had an income guarantee in old age provided by the *folkpension* and, if they had earnings from work, a supplement from the ATP scheme. The 1994 reform maintained these two essential characteristics: an earnings-related benefit supplement with a guarantee, but, as we shall discuss, geared to give better intragenerational equity and financial stability over generations. In addition, in the new system designed in the 1990s, the guarantee is designed as a supplement that brings the total amount up to a guarantee level when the earnings-related scheme fails to do this.

Contractual Benefits from 1960 to the Reform of the 1990s[6]

In 1992, at the time when the new pension system was being discussed and formulated, there were four main occupational pension schemes that together had covered 80 to 90 per cent of the labour force since the mid-1970s.[7] These were (1) ITP for white-collar workers in the private sector, (2) one scheme for blue-collar workers in the private sector (STP), (3) *kommunal tjänstepension* (KTP) for employees of counties, municipalities and parishes, and (4) *statlig tjänstepension* for those employed as civil servants and other employees of the state government. There are many similarities but also important differences between the four systems. The schemes as they existed immediately prior to the reforms of the 1990s are presented in Table 8.1. Each of the four schemes is discussed briefly below.[8]

Table 8.1   A comparison of the four main occupational pension schemes prior to the reform

	White-collar workers (ITP)	Blue-collar (STP)	Central government	Local government
Principle for calculation of benefits	Defined benefit	Defined benefit	Defined benefit	Defined benefit
Employment requirements for full pension	30 years (after age 28)	30 years (after age 28)	30 years (after age 28)	30 years (after age 28)
Base for calculation	Salary year before retirement (plus defined contribution part)	Average of 3 of the 5 years between age 55 and 59	Average of the 5 years before retirement (plus defined contribution part)	Average of the best five of the last seven years before retirement
Rate of compensation	10%–7.5 ba 65% 7.5–20 ba 32.5% 20–30 ba	10% up to 7.5 base amounts	10%–7.5 ba 65% 7.5–20 ba 32.5% 20–30 ba	96%–1 ba 78.5% 1–2.5 ba 60% 2.5–3.5 ba 64% 3.5–7.5 ba 65% 7.5–20 ba 32.5% 20–30 ba
Financing principle	Premium reserve	Funds for those pensioned	Pay-as-you-go	Pay-as-you-go
Financing rules	Payroll fee	Payroll fee	Payroll fee	Pension costs paid from the municipality and the county to KPA for their own pensioners
Partial pension supplement	Yes	No	Yes	Yes

Notes: ba = base amount (*basbelopp*); with an exchange rate of 9 SEK per USD a base amount was about 4000 USD in the year 2002.

Civil servants

With the introduction of ATP in 1960, benefits for central government employees were coordinated with ATP. The total pension level was set for state employees through collective agreement (see Table 8.1) and the difference between this and the ATP benefit was covered by the separate scheme for state employees. In 1960, the majority of the state government employees had a lower pension age (65 or lower) than that set for the national scheme (67), and the state scheme covered total costs from that lower retirement age up to the age of 67.

When the pension age in the ATP scheme was lowered to 65, in 1976, it was no longer necessary for the contractual scheme to cover the benefit of early retirement between 65 and 67. The lowest retirement age is now 65 for almost all jobs in central government, and jobs with a lower pension age than 65 are covered by the contractual scheme to age 65. In 1992, the benefits for state employees were made the same as for private white-collar workers. Table 8.1 describes this benefit as it was prior to the reform.

Local government employees

As for civil servants with the introduction of the ATP scheme, the pensions for those employed by the local government (counties and municipalities) were coordinated with the public scheme. As for the civil servants, a defined benefit level was set and the difference between this benefit and the level provided by ATP was paid by the contractual scheme. In 1960, the majority of the local government employees had a lower pension age (65 or lower) than that for the national scheme (67), and the difference was financed by the contractual schemes. Of those employed in the local government sector, 65 per cent have the opportunity to claim a benefit at a lower age than 65. This means the lifetime benefit is reduced, however, and, for this reason, most continue to work up to the age of 65.

Private sector white-collar employees

Also with the introduction of ATP in 1960, a new pension scheme – *Industrins och handelns tilläggspension* (ITP) – was established for white-collar workers in the private sector, with the aim of providing the same scheme for all affiliated employees. Prior to 1960, around half of all private white-collar workers were covered by a contractual benefit plan. The ITP pension was constructed to supplement the public scheme, and the administration went to the SPP. An alternative, book reserve option was also introduced in 1960, secured through a special insurance company set up to protect against insolvency. This is called the FPG-PRI scheme.

In 1974, a new agreement was concluded between the employers' confederation, *Svenska arbetsgivarföreningen* (SAF) and the unions representing the private sector, white-collar employees in industry and commerce. This agreement was implemented in 1977, and with it just about all white-collar employees in the private sector (about 22 per cent of the total workforce in 1977) were covered by ITP.

The retirement age for white-collar workers in the private sector was 65 for men and 60 for women when ATP was introduced in 1960. The retirement age for women was raised to 62 in the 1960s and to 65 from 1971. For the period from age 65 to 67 for men and from the lower age to 67 for women, the pension was 65 per cent of the salary for the part of earnings up to the ceiling for coverage in the public system and 32.5 per cent for the part of earnings exceeding this. From the age of 67 this scheme provided an additional replacement rate of 10 per cent below the ATP ceiling and 32.5 per cent above it. Later the rules were revised, as shown in Table 8.1. The ITP plans were the only advance funded contractual plans in Sweden until the 1990s. To date, returns have been sufficient to enable price indexation of benefits. Any surplus in the ITP scheme is distributed to the employers by adjusting the contribution rate.

Private sector blue-collar workers
Blue-collar workers still had less generous benefits than white-collar employees in the private sector and public sector employees after the ATP reform in 1960. They had a lower overall benefit, since they lacked the contractual supplement enjoyed by other groups; also they had no separate arrangement for ages 65 and 66 that enabled them to leave the labour force at age 65 without having to claim an actuarially reduced *folkpension* and ATP benefit. This took a little more than a decade to change.

In 1973, an agreement was reached between the central confederation of blue-collar workers, *Landsorganisationen* (LO) and the employers' confederation, *Svenska arbetsgivareföreningen* (SAF), to provide a supplement to the public system for blue-collar workers. From 1 July,1973 'STP 1' was paid between the ages of 65 and 67, followed by 'STP 2' at age 67 as a supplement to ATP. 'STP 2' replaced 10 per cent of earnings up to the ceiling in the ATP scheme and was price-indexed. When the pension age in the public system was reduced to 65 on 1 July 1976, 'STP 2' became the sole old age benefit that was provided to blue-collar workers by STP.

In 1974, blue-collar workers covered by STP consisted of about 33 per cent of the workforce and, in fact, this is also about the same percentage of the workforce covered by this agreement today.

The relative importance of the occupational pension schemes
As mentioned, most employees are covered by occupational pension agreements. The main groups who are not covered, besides those outside the

labour market, are the self-employed and those working short part-time. As relatively few are outside the labour market, work short part-time or are self-employed all their working lives, the great majority receive at least some occupational pension when retiring. In 1996, 83.4 per cent of men and 75.1 of women aged 65–9 received income from one or several occupational pension plans.

The occupational pensions are most important for those with high incomes. This is shown in Table 8.2. For men in the tenth decile, the average occupational pension is higher than the average ATP pension. The reason for this is that three of the four occupational pensions plans cover earnings above the 7.5 ceiling in the public scheme. This also indicates that the problems with mobility incentives (and for the employer to recruit) are especially pronounced among those with high incomes.

Table 8.2 *Pensions from the public and occupational pension schemes in 1996 according to income deciles for those aged 65–9 (in thousands of SEK)*

	Men			Women		
Decile	Folkpension	ATP	Occupational pension	Folkpension	ATP	Occupational pension
1	30.5	27.2	1.8	36.8	4.1	0.5
2	29.2	69.0	10.3	34.0	14.3	4.0
3	28.8	81.1	15.0	30.9	24.6	7.3
4	28.5	87.8	17.6	31.0	33.0	9.1
5	28.1	93.9	19.8	30.1	44.4	11.6
6	27.6	100.2	22.7	29.7	55.6	14.5
7	27.1	107.5	27.1	29.5	64.7	17.8
8	26.6	110.9	34.1	28.6	72.3	21.2
9	26.1	112.5	49.1	27.7	82.1	26.4
10	25.7	116.6	126.3	26.6	87.6	41.0
All	27.8	90.7	32.4	30.5	48.3	15.3

Source: Computations made for this study by Statistics Sweden.

Problems with the defined benefit construction of contractual schemes

By the mid-1970s, practically all public and private sector employees had a supplementary benefit in old age covered by one of the four major schemes for these groups, and this is still the situation. In principle, this meant that rights were vested, since workers could move freely within and between contractual categories. These benefits became an integral part of the pension people could expect at retirement. As a rule of thumb, they provided about an extra 10 per cent earnings replacement on top of the public benefit, for earnings under the ceiling in the public ATP scheme.

From 1960, three of the four major schemes provided replacement from age 65, thus skirting the pension age of 67 in the public system, and from 1973 even the blue-collar workers were able to leave the labour force at age 65 with the help of a contractual benefit. It seemed logical then to lower the full-benefit retirement age in the public scheme to 65, which was done in July 1976. In retrospect, 1976 was the last year of around two decades of high postwar economic growth, and a time at which growth optimism was at its highest level in Sweden. The decrease in the pension age in the public scheme to age 65 shifted substantial, unfunded pension debt from the private sector and local governments to the public pension system, which was not recognized as such at the time. In fact, in 1976, pension costs as a percentage of GDP were low, and on a current budget basis this shift presented no problem.[9]

The alliance of unions, management and government in the mid-1970s behind the decrease in the maximum pension age from 67 to 65 in 1976 offered short-run advantages for all the institutional players. Age 65 became a maximum because employees were required to retire by contractual agreement. The Social Democratic government could point to a major reform creating a longer period of paid leisure at the end of the working life. Unions could enjoy popularity for the same reason. County and local governments and private employers could breathe a sigh of relief as they had pushed a large debt over to the national ATP scheme, although this would have to be paid for in the long run regardless of who was to pay the benefits. Finally, the employers' confederation in the private sector, SAF (Svenska arbeitsgivareföreningen), was opposed to increases in the contribution rate, as a matter of principle. It was probably their hope that cost increases could be shifted over to the general budget and financed by general revenues. In fact, this was an inevitable result of the fixed ceiling on covered earnings in the ATP scheme.

In principle, people changing contractual groups retained their acquired rights from the first system and accumulated rights in the contractual scheme covering their new occupation. Common to all four schemes is that the employee had to work up to the age of retirement to be entitled to a pension determined by the rules described in Table 8.1. If a person left the labour force earlier, an annuity was granted from age 65, but this meant that accumulated rights were not indexed in the interim.[10] With high inflation, as in the 1970s and 1980s, leaving the labour market early generally resulted in a lower occupational pension. This was not generally well understood by participants, however, and it is probable that some chose this option – which was cheaper for the employer – with less than full information.

In addition, the fact that benefits were based on final salary years may have tended to lock older workers into occupations and consequently, places of employment. For example, a teacher who left teaching (a local government scheme) at age 50 to become a business accountant (a private white-collar worker scheme) would have acquired rights to age 50 as a teacher, but these would not grow in line with normal wage increases (since the teacher had left his/her occupation as a teacher). Since the 'final' years that would be used for computing the benefit would occur much later on in a normal career pursued to the 'end', a career switch would lead to a reduction in pension wealth compared with remaining in the same occupation and obtaining normal salary increases until retirement. For the teacher who has tired of his or her job and risks being 'burned-out', a job change well in advance of being 'burned-out' is a logical option, but a job choice outside the individual's occupational group could lead to a relative decline in lifetime pension wealth. Instead, a disability pension was the best option. For this reason, this sort of rule system leads to unnecessary cost dumping on the public sector's disability system, and it reduces the overall supply of labour and potential economic growth.

Finally, the contractual defined benefit schemes also contained a lower limit for the minimum number of working hours that qualify for coverage. Part-time workers risked not acquiring rights, without always being aware of this effect, while employers could utilize this feature of the system to save on overall costs. Younger employees and mothers with children who often seek part-time jobs are especially at risk of being taken advantage of with regard to minimum hour requirements for insurance coverage.

REFORM OF THE PUBLIC SYSTEM AND REPERCUSSIONS FOR CONTRACTUAL BENEFITS

The Background of Reform

The ATP scheme did not begin to provide full benefits until 1980, and it took a couple more decades before the majority of pensioners were ATP pensioners. Hence, in the first half of the 1970s, when the new contractual schemes for blue- and white-collar workers were being conceived and the pension age was reduced from 67 to 65, the new public pension introduced in 1960 was still a long way from maturity.[11] Well into the 1970s there was still good reason for blue-collar and many white-collar workers to continue to work until the age of 67 or more, as over a third of male workers did at that time. This would get them a better benefit. Hence the impact on costs of lowering the pension age to 65 was still not dramatic.

From the mid-1970s to the end of the century, male workforce participation declined by about four years (Palmer, 1999), mainly because of lower participation of older workers. In aggregate, this was counterbalanced by an increase in female participation. By the end of the century, there was a difference of only a couple of years in the average number of years in the labour force of men and women, based on cross-section data provided by labour force surveys. Nevertheless, the overall trend was towards earlier exit for older workers, helped largely by a fourfold increase in disability grants from 1960 to 2000, but with around the same number of hours worked during most of the period. In spite of this, Sweden looks better than most other OECD countries in terms of keeping older workers in the workforce, according to a study by Gruber and Wise (1998), which is attributed to a tax benefit structure for older workers that does not promote exit to the same extent as in many other countries in the study.

Longevity of men and women together continued to increase at the pace of about one additional year for every ten years that passed. Compared to 1975, full benefits were attainable two years earlier at age 65, but had to be paid out on average two and a half years longer. Every new demographic outcome and accompanying new projection brought additional costs for the pension system. In addition, the development of costs was highly unresponsive to changes in the economy. When Sweden was hit by a deep recession in 1991–4, during which the wage base declined by roughly 10 per cent, the consequence of this inflexibility of commitments became emphatic.

Other than in the very long run, acquired rights and benefits did not respond to changes in the economic environment, whereas the contribution base needed to finance them did. For financial stability, acquired rights and benefits need to grow at the rate of growth of the contribution base, which is determined by growth of the real wage (productivity) and the labour force. In the ATP scheme, acquired rights and benefits followed the development of the basic amount, which was price-indexed. With strong economic growth, for example growth of 3–4 per cent typical of the period 1955–75 around the time of the introduction of ATP, the contribution base grew faster than commitments. With slow growth, this was not necessarily true, especially since commitments were growing too, with the rate of increase in longevity, since the benefit calculation did not take increasing life expectancy into account. It is not surprising, then, that actuarial projections showed that, because of the sluggish response to changes in growth, costs would become unaffordable with poor long-term growth, for example around 1 per cent, and, by the 1980s, a growth rate of 2 per cent or lower had become a fact of life.[12] In fact, in the deep recession of the first years of the 1990s, the wage base declined by about 10 per cent, providing a resounding illustration of the problem.

The trend towards increasing financial costs for the public pension system was one of two major reasons for reform, although, without the feeling of financial urgency, there would probably not have been a reform. The other reason was the 15–30 rule for a full benefit in the ATP scheme (the ATP pension was based on the person's best 15 years and for a full pension, 30 years of employment were required). This was generally agreed to be to the advantage of workers with shorter careers and/or steeper lifetime earnings profiles, and to the disadvantage of those with long careers and/or relatively flat career earnings profiles.[13]

Sweden's reform of the public system in the 1990s was therefore motivated by a desire to create both a fairer and a financially more stable system. The first would improve intragenerational fairness, the second intergenerational fairness. In addition, national saving was low, mainly because household saving was low at the end of the 1980s. Hence a third goal of reform was to redesign the system so as to create more national saving than would be expected to occur by maintaining the old system, which was destined to use up its otherwise large reserves[14] by, at the latest, 2020, depending on the rate of economic growth and the need to utilize funded reserves.[15] This was part of the motivation behind the creation of a financial account component within the mandatory public system.

These were the goals of both the Social Democratic government that left power in 1991 and the new non-socialist coalition government that took over the government in the autumn of 1991. Nevertheless, although their goals were similar, political visions of the means to achieve them differed. For this reason, the political consensus reached among five major parties representing over 80 per cent of the vote in the parliament was remarkable.[16]

The Reforms of the Public System

In 1992, with the results of the Pension Commission's investigations and the ensuing discussion in hand, the multi-party Working Group on Pensions, created by the government to present a proposal for pension reform, published its concept in the autumn of 1992. This provided a basis for public discussion, and a more detailed proposal was submitted to and approved by parliament in 1994. The reform itself was legislated and implemented in stages, beginning with the setting off of funds for the mandatory financial account system from 1995, and ending with full implementation in 2003, when the first birth cohort covered by the new scheme, those born 1938, turned 65 (although this cohort could retire already in 2001 under the new rules). Although retirement is flexible, the fact that the age cohort is covered by the rules and practices of the old contractual schemes means that 65 will be the 'normal' age of retirement for them.[17] This may – and is hoped to – change, however, as younger birth cohorts enter their sixties and are increasingly covered by the new rules.

The new public system's two earnings-related components are both based on contributions from lifetime earnings. The NDC pay-as-you-go component is based on a contribution rate of 16 per cent and the FDC component on a contribution rate of 2.5 per cent. In the NDC scheme, contributions are noted on an account and the past year's balance is given a rate of interest based on the rate of growth of the average contributions per contributor – more or less the per capita wage (or long-term productivity growth). In the financial account scheme, individuals choose from a large number of registered funds during the saving phase.

The annuity in the NDC scheme is based on unisexual life expectancy at retirement and a real rate of return of 1.6 per cent.[18] In NDC schemes, the present value of a pension is always what is seen on the account of the participant. This also presumes aggregate equality between liabilities and assets in the scheme. Aggregate equality holds if the rate of return used to index accounts values and benefits is the rate of growth of the contribution base, and if the estimate of life expectancy used in computing the annuity is – on average – correct when the outcomes are known. In addition, funded reserves need to earn at least the rate of return used to index acquired rights and benefits. Finally, changes in the age distribution of earnings and outlays can affect the liquidity of the scheme.

The Swedish NDC scheme uses per capita wage growth for indexation and an estimate of life expectancy based on the current outcome (not a projection). For this reason, in scenarios with a declining labour force and increasing longevity after the age at which life expectancy is computed for the calculation of benefits, the system will tend towards instability. On the other hand, the system began with a large reserve fund, which with a substantial financial rate of return creates a surplus. In addition, with labour force growth, the chosen form of indexation creates an undistributed surplus that, for example, can cover the remaining (uncovered) change in longevity. As long as there is financial balance, there is no problem.

An integral part of the Swedish NDC scheme is, thus, the development of the financial balance of the aggregate scheme. Balance means that estimated assets equal estimated liabilities. Both the capital of workers and the annuities of pensioners will be adjusted downward if the ratio of assets to liabilities in the system falls below unity. That is if liabilities exceed assets. Imbalance between assets and liabilities can occur, basically, for four reasons: (1) overall contribution growth is less than the per capita index actually used in indexing notional capital and benefits because of negative labour force growth, (2) life expectancy increases faster than the estimate used to calculate the annuity, (3) the rate of return on the reserve fund is less than the rate used to index notional capital and benefits, and (4) the liquidity of the system changes owing to a change in the time during which money is retained in the system (so-called 'turnover time'). Sweden has set up an account system measuring assets and liabilities that makes it possible to perform the calculations on the basis of known data rather than projections (Settergren, 2001).

The financial accounts in the FDC scheme are administered by a government agency, *Premiepensionsmyndigheten* (PPM) that is a part of the social insurance administration. The PPM buys and sells fund shares on behalf of the participants, and is the sole supplier of annuities. The annuity in the FDC scheme is based on life expectancy at retirement. The annuity can be single or joint with a spouse, and can be a variable or fixed annuity. A fixed annuity entails turning over an account to the PPM upon claiming an annuity and, thus, contracting for the PPM annuity. A variable annuity is obtained by leaving capital in market funds and allowing it to adjust annually with the change in the market value of a participant's fund(s).

Annuities in the public NDC and FDC schemes can be claimed any time from age 61. There is no upper age limit for claiming an annuity. They can be claimed at the same time or separately, partially or in full, and with or without leaving the workforce. If the individual continues to work while claiming a partial or full annuity, it will be recalculated given additional contributions from work during this period. In this way, every krona paid always leads to a higher benefit, regardless of the participant's work status. The tax system was also restructured for pensioners in the reform. In order to give pension income the same status as income from work, the extra deduction for pensioners in the old system was abolished, equalizing the tax status of earned income and public pensions.

The minimum guarantee in the new system applies from age 65. It is also taxable. A guarantee benefit level is not by itself enough to meet the minimum subsistence level set by the National Welfare Board. If one actually ends up in the situation where the guarantee is the sole source of income, a rent and means-tested housing allowance tops up the benefit. If this is not sufficient, which it normally is, means-tested social assistance is available. The reform is actually neutral in this respect, as the level of the guarantee after tax was set so as to provide the same benefit level as the *folk-pension*, after tax, in the old system. In this way, the basic goal of poverty alleviation is maintained, while the earnings-related scheme has been transformed into a financially stable self-contained scheme.[19]

The new public scheme envisages people gradually leaving the workforce even past the age of 65 – and with no upper limit. Both central unions and representatives of management were reluctant to change the 65-year limit in their national contracts, however. This forced the government to legislate the right of workers to remain in the workforce at least until the age of 67 from 2002. When they reach the age of 67, people can still work, accumulate more capital on their accounts and get a higher pension, although the employer will have the right to conclude their employment, still by contractual agreement. In order to continue under these circumstances, the individual will have to change employers or become self-employed.

THE NEW CONTRACTUAL PENSION SCHEMES

The financial environment in Sweden changed radically from the late 1980s. The first step, accomplished by the end of the 1980s, was the deregulation of the domestic financial market and the opening of the country to the free flow of financial capital. Important in the chain of events affecting the development of financial funds and insurance was the legislation permitting unit-linked funds from 1993.[20] Both the financial account component of the mandatory public scheme and the contractual schemes for private blue-collar and municipal employees make use of the idea that the saving (accumulation) phase in insurance can be separated from the annuity phase. That is, during years until retirement, money is saved and then the savings on a capital account can be converted into an annuity at retirement. With unit link, people could buy and sell units in funds during the accumulation phase, moving savings from one fund to another, until it was time to claim the annuity. The annuity is then based on life expectancy at retirement and whatever rate of return funds held during the retirement phase may earn.

In unit-linked insurance in Sweden, from 1993 it became possible to choose among many funds, including funds with foreign portfolios, during the saving phase prior to contracting for an annuity at retirement. In the public FDC scheme there are practically no restrictions on the funds that can be chosen by the participant. Participating funds must be registered with the PPM to operate in Sweden and subject to the rules and supervision of financial institutions operating in the country.

When these ideas were first announced by the Working Group on Pensions, the central blue-collar organization, LO, in particular, was sceptical. On the other hand, it was time to change the blue-collar arrangements by the mid-1990s in order to bring them into line with the reform of the public scheme. It was necessary to create additional coverage in line with the new system, if previous standards were to be maintained. LO in negotiations with the representatives of management chose to do this by creating a supplement with advance funding. In practice, the new contractual scheme resembled the new mandatory FDC scheme, but contracts were limited to insurance companies. In practice, since most of the participating insurance companies could offer a choice of funds and the freedom to move between them, there was close similarity to the public scheme from the point of view of the participant. The blue-collar scheme began in 1998 with a 2 per cent contribution rate that was increased to 3 per cent from the year 2000.

The local government sector followed the lead of the blue-collar workers and in 2000 local government also converted to a partial FDC, with a contribution rate of 3.4–4.5 per cent, depending on the employment category. The agreement for local government employees stipulates that the employee must be given the opportunity to choose how to invest at least one percentage point, but the employer can opt to let the employees decide over the whole sum. If the employer keeps his portion of the contribution for investment, then the lowest return allowed is a government bond rate. For those with earnings over the ceiling of 7.5 base amounts there is a complementary old age pension of 62.5 per cent for earnings between 7.5 and 20 base amounts and 31.25 per cent for earnings between 20 and 30 base amounts if there has been at least 30 years of employment (in other cases a proportional reduction will be made). Those are the amounts if the person retires at the age of 65. At early retirement, the pension is reduced by 0.4 percentage units for each month of early retirement (and enhanced in the same way as postponed retirement). The system is financed by fees from 1998.

In 2002, an agreement was also reached that converts the contractual scheme for state government employees (civil servants) into an FDC scheme. State employees are to be covered up to the earnings ceiling in the public scheme by two FDC schemes, with a total contribution rate of 4.3 per cent above that in the public scheme. The first, with a contribution rate of 2.3 per cent of salary, is allocated to funds that the participant chooses from 2003. The remaining 2 per cent is invested collectively by a state insurance company designated for this purpose. Earnings above the ceiling in the public scheme are still covered by a defined benefit equal to 60 per cent of earnings up to a higher ceiling (20 base amounts) and 30 per cent in an interval above this (20 to 30 base amounts). A special feature in the new agreement is an option of the part-time pension from the age of 61 with no actuarial reduction in the future old age pension. Such pensions are to be financed from the budget of the state authority at which the person is employed.

At the time of this writing, the private sector white-collar workers have not changed their contractual scheme in line with the reform of the public mandatory scheme, although a change has been considered and may come eventually. Table 8.3 gives information on the present occupational pension schemes. Note that the scheme for the private sector white-collar workers is the same as in Table 8.1.

Table 8.3 A comparison of the four main occupational pension schemes after the reform

	White-collar workers (ITP)	Blue-collar (STP)	Central government	Local government
Principle for calculation of benefits	Defined benefit	Defined contribution	Defined contribution and defined benefit	Defined contribution and defined benefit
Employment requirements for full pension	30 years (after age 28)		30 years (after age 28) for the defined benefit part	30 years (after age 28) for the defined benefit part
Base for calculation	Salary year before retirement (plus defined contribution part)		Average of the 5 years before retirement (plus defined contribution part)	Average of the best five of the last seven years before retirement
Rate of compensation	10%–7.5 ba 65% 7.5–20 ba 32.5% 20–30 ba		Defined benefit part: 60% 7.5–20 ba 30% 20–30 ba	Defined benefit part: 62.5% 7.5–20 ba 31.25% 20–30 ba
Financing principle	Premium reserve	Funded	Funded for the defined contribution part Pay-as-you-go for the defined benefit part	Funded for the defined contribution part Pay-as-you-go for the defined benefit part
Financing rules	Payroll fee	Payroll fee (3%)	Payroll fee (4.3%) for the defined contribution part)	Payroll fee (3.4–4.5% for the defined contribution part)
Partial pension supplement	No	No	Yes	No

Notes: ba = base amount (*basbelopp*); with an exchange rate of 9 SEK per USD a base amount was about 4000 USD in the year 2002.

243

The conversion to defined contribution has largely eliminated the problems outlined above with the older DB schemes. In principle, rights can easily be granted on all earnings and there is no excuse to exclude part-time earnings. In addition, capital account values can be transported between systems, yielding more returns in the next system after a transfer. In sum, this framework enables complete mobility, thereby eliminating disincentives to move between jobs in the old DB schemes. However, there are still disincentives for those with earnings over the ceiling in the public pension scheme.

Table 8.4 illustrates the situation for a person born in 1975, based on present estimates of life expectancy for this birth cohort. With a 2 per cent real rate of return in the FDC schemes, the public and contractual schemes give a replacement rate of about 60 per cent at age 67 but about 80 per cent with a real rate of return of about 5 per cent. The latter is interesting because this is the average rate for a fund split 50–50 between equities and bonds over the past half-decade (based on Frennberg and Hansson, 1992).

Table 8.4   Replacement rates: annuity as a percentage of last earnings

Age	PAYGO Contribution rate of 16%	Public second pillar (2.5%) + group occupational (3.5%) Return of:			Total: public PAYGO and second pillar + group occupational Return of:		
		2%	5%	8%	2%	5%	8%
61	0.32	0.12	0.23	0.47	0.44	0.55	0.79
62	0.33	0.13	0.25	0.52	0.46	0.58	0.85
63	0.35	0.14	0.27	0.57	0.49	0.62	0.92
64	0.37	0.15	0.29	0.63	0.52	0.66	1.00
65	0.39	0.15	0.31	0.69	0.54	0.70	1.11
66	0.42	0.16	0.33	0.76	0.58	0.75	1.18
67	0.44	0.17	0.36	0.83	0.61	0.80	1.27
68	0.47	0.18	0.39	0.92	0.65	0.86	1.39
69	0.50	0.19	0.42	1.01	0.69	0.92	1.51
70	0.53	0.20	0.45	1.12	0.73	0.98	1.65

Note: The individual's earnings are assumed to grow at a real rate of 2 per cent per year throughout the earnings career. The rate of growth used for indexation of capital in the PAYGO system is 2 per cent. The pay-as-you-go, second pillar and occupational annuities are all based on unisex life expectancy and a real rate of return on capital from retirement of 1.6 per cent. The Swedish system also includes inheritance gains from deceased workers in the benefits of the survivors. This raises the replacement rate by around 8 per cent compared with the figures in the table. On the other hand, administration costs have not been deducted from calculations in the table.

Source: Based on Palmer (2000; 2001).

The replacement rates for these schemes together at age 65 may seem low, with the low rate of return of 2 per cent. What should be pointed out in all discussions is that the de facto rate of replacement in the old public system was never really 65 per cent, although this was the official picture given. Why is this? First of all, the ATP benefit was based on an average of the best 15 years, that is an individual's earnings level eight years prior to retirement if they occurred at the end of the career. Hence a replacement rate of 65 per cent with no growth (as it is usually presented in examples) becomes a replacement rate of around 56 per cent with individual earnings growth of 2 per cent per annum.

Finally, recall that the individual in the example was born in 1975 and is expected to retire after 2040, with life expectancy that is four years longer than a person who was born in 1935 and has just retired. It is probably not unreasonable to assume that the normal working career will be longer in 2040 than today, bolstered by even better health and work environments then.

In sum, together the public and contractual schemes will provide an acceptable rate of replacement in the future. In fact, if the financial rate of return were to be as high as 8 per cent, it would be easy to claim that people are overinsured. On the other hand, on an historical basis, this sort of return would imply that everyone earned the average real rate for the equity market, which seems an unlikely assumption.

CONCLUSIONS

The development of contractual benefits in Sweden has closely followed the development of the public system. In 1960, and then again in 1994, Sweden opted in favour of a universal earnings-related framework. What the 1994 reform did was to change the paradigm in order to create redistributional neutrality and financial stability in the public insurance scheme. The new system is supplemented by a guarantee that will protect the low-income elderly, and supplementary contractual benefits that provide an even higher benefit up to the ceiling in the public system, and provide all the benefits in a range above the ceiling in the public system. This is in keeping with the framework developed already by the 1970s. Now, however, the supplementary benefit provided by contractual schemes is an advance-funded DC benefit. This has the long-term advantage of dealing with the previously unfunded commitments within the three schemes that have converted.

Perhaps the major advantage of the combination of NDC and FDC schemes is that, in principle, it will be possible to move accounts between different contractual sectors, which will eliminate the barriers to labour mobility in Sweden. This is why it is important for all the major schemes to adopt the DC framework. Not only will this make it possible for workers to combine work and benefits at any rates (zero, partial or full), including going up and down in benefit take-up, but, in addition, older workers will be free to move between sectors and employers in old age. This opens opportunities for both blue- and white-collar workers (and public and private employees) to seek new occupations and suitable jobs in any sector without being penalized through their contractual benefit schemes. The contractual schemes still retain an element of defined benefit, however. Earnings above the ceiling in the social insurance system are defined benefits. Full removal of impediments to mobility would require converting even these into defined contribution.

NOTES

1. Implementation occurred in steps. In 1995, contributions to the new financial component of the public system were placed in a blocked, interest-bearing account at the National Debt Office. Most new legislation was passed in 1998 and account statements were sent to all participants in early 1999. NDC accounts were finished in 1999 and FDC accounts in 2000. Individual fund choices in the new financial account system were made in 2000. The first NDC and FDC benefits were paid out to claimants from the first birth cohort covered by the new rules (people born in 1938) in 2001, and the first guarantee, which is only granted at age 65, can be claimed in 2003 by persons born in 1938.
2. Góra and Palmer (2001) discuss the similarities and differences between notional defined contribution (NDC) and financial defined contribution (FDC) schemes in depth.
3. The political sentiment of the time was about 50 per cent for and 50 per cent against. See Eriksen and Palmer (2003) for an account of the political process preceding the introduction of ATP.
4. See Palmer (2001) for a more detailed discussion of the various political positions and political economics of the reform.
5. Residents of other countries could also be covered by the *folkpension* depending on the treaty status between Sweden and the country of citizenship of the resident. When Sweden joined the European Union, residents from all member states enjoyed the same rights as Swedish citizens.
6. Wadensjö (1997) provides references to Swedish language publications on contractual schemes.
7. The percentage covered by these schemes fell to around 80 per cent by the end of the 1990s as many new groups, especially in IT-related occupations, chose to remain outside these schemes.
8. There are a few other schemes, for example for people employed in the insurance, banking and consumer cooperative sectors. The construction of the schemes closely follows that of the ITP scheme.
9. At the time, there was little interest in actuarial projections (see Eriksen and Palmer, 2002). At the Ministry of Finance, thought was focused on the short-term problems of evening out unemployment (business) cycles.
10. In the ITP scheme, decisions to adjust for inflation have been made annually since 1985.
11. Although 30 years were required for a full benefit when the system was at maturity, people born between 1896 and 1913 could only receive a partial benefit based on 20 years of acquired rights from 1960, with the first benefit being three-twentieths of a full benefit and granted to a 67-year-old in 1963. Thereafter, coming age cohorts were required to have 21, 22 . . . years of acquired rights for a full benefit until 30 was reached.

12. Palmer (2000; 2001) discusses the economic background of the reform in greater depth.
13. Ståhlberg (1990), in work performed for the pension commission in the 1980s, showed that the ATP scheme redistributed resources from those with low earnings to those with high earnings.
14. At the time of the reform in the mid-1990s, pension fund reserves were comparable in size to over 40 per cent of GDP. On the other hand, the national debt had swollen enormously during the deep recession of 1991–4, and the pension funds were simply helping to finance current consumption rather than to create real reserves for the future.
15. For details about the financial status of the old system, the reader is recommended to turn to Palmer (2000) and the references provided there.
16. The reform process and how the political process led to the particular construction of the reform are discussed in detail in Palmer (2001).
17. Also this is the age at which disability benefits are converted into old age benefits, and the age at which the low-income guarantee benefit in the new system can be obtained.
18. Divergence of the actual rate from the calculation rate gives rise to adjustments in the rate of indexation. For example, if the actual rate of growth is 2 per cent, then the difference between this value and the norm of 1.6 per cent is accredited accounts, and used to index benefits. In this sense, the method used is a form of real wage indexation, taking real growth of 1.6 per cent out in advance. Benefits are price-indexed.
19. Note that non-contributory rights (such as for childcare) exist, but are financed by general revenues. Periods of sickness and unemployment covered by national social insurance for these are also covered, and financed with general revenues. (See, for example, Palmer, 2000, for a discussion, and *www.pension.nu* for more details.)
20. The mandatory FDC scheme in the public system has also contributed to the development of the Swedish financial market. See Palmer (2001) for an account of how the reform of the public scheme and the development of the private market reinforced each other in the 1990s.

REFERENCES

Eriksen, Tor and Edward Palmer (2003), 'Early exit from the labour market and other aspects of the Swedish pension reform', in E. Overbye and P.A. Kemp (eds), *Pensions: Challenges and Reforms*, Aldershot: Ashgate (forthcoming).

Frennberg, Per and Björn Hansson (1992), 'Swedish Stocks, Bonds, Bills and Inflation', *Applied Financial Economics*, 2.

Góra, Marek and Edward Palmer (2001), 'A New Paradigm in Pension Economics', working paper, Center for Economic and Social Research (CASE), Warsaw.

Gruber, Jonathan and David Wise (1998), *Social Security and Retirement Around the World*, National Bureau of Economic Research Conference Report, Chicago and London: University of Chicago Press.

Palmer, Edward (1999), 'Exit from the Labor Force of Older Workers: Can the NDC Pension System Help?', *The Geneva Papers on Risk and Insurance*, 24, October, 461–72.

Palmer, Edward (2000), 'The Swedish Pension Reform Model: Framework and Issues', Social Protection Discussion Paper no. 0012, The Pension Reform Primer, World Bank, Washington, DC.

Palmer, Edward (2001), 'Swedish Pension Reform – How Did It Evolve and What Does It Mean for the Future?', in Martin Feldstein and Horst Siebert (eds), *Social Security Pension Reform in Europe*, Chicago: University of Chicago Press.

Settergren, Ole (2001), 'The Automatic Balancing Mechanism of the Swedish Pension System – a non-technical introduction', *Wirtschaftspolitische Blätter*, 4/2001.

Ståhlberg, Ann-Charlotte (1990), 'ATP-systemet från fördelningspolitisk synpunkt', Expertrapport till pensionsberedningen, Sweden's Official Publications SOU, 78.
Wadensjö, Eskil (1997), 'The Welfare Mix in Pension Provisions in Sweden', in Martin Rein and Eskil Wadensjö (eds), *Enterprise and the Welfare State*, Cheltenham, UK and Lyme, USA: Edward Elgar.

D

Pathways towards a mixed public–private pension system

9. How societies mix public and private spheres in their pension systems

Martin Rein and John Turner

Most countries with occupational pension systems have developed policies designed to increase the percentage of workers taking part in the systems. Countries with well-developed pension systems have a considerable variety of pension policies to do this. While some countries rely on voluntary provision by employers with tax incentives for motivation, other countries have mandated that employers provide occupational pensions, and still other countries have widespread pension coverage through collective bargaining because of the pervasive role of labour unions in their economies. In some countries, pensions are provided in addition to social security, while in a few countries pensions can be an alternative to social security. In some countries, pensions are primarily provided by employers, while in others pensions are primarily offered in the form of individual accounts provided through financial institutions, with the employer only providing payroll withholding.

In this chapter, we categorize and analyse the pension policies around the world in countries with well-developed pension systems. We consider both employer-provided pension plans and individual account plans.

PATHWAYS AND PLANS

We categorize the wide variety of policies around the world as four pathways to increase pension coverage. Those pathways are voluntary provision with tax incentives, contracted out, widespread labour contracts, and mandatory (see Table 9.1). These pathways range from unrestrained choice, to a choice between a government provided pension and a private sector pension, to mandatory provision determined by collective bargaining between employers and trade unions, to a government-imposed mandate. The latter could mean that employers are mandated to provide pensions or that workers are mandated to have individual accounts.

A different framework classifies pension plans according to their relationship to social security and to whether they are mandatory or voluntary. This framework yields a two-by-two matrix of add-ons to or carve-outs from social security and mandatory versus voluntary provision of plans. Plans that are add-ons are provided in addition to social security, while carve-outs are plans that are financed by a reduction in social security contributions and benefits. Combining these two analytic frameworks yields the following combinations of pathways and plans shown in Table 9.1. Within this framework, plans can be employer-provided defined benefit plans, defined benefit plans sponsored by unions, or individual account defined contribution plans provided either by employers or by individuals through financial institutions.

Table 9.1   Pathways, plans and sponsors

Pathways	Plans	Sponsors
1. voluntary with tax incentives	voluntary add-on	ER, I, U
2. contracting out	voluntary carve-outs	ER, I
3. labour contracting	quasi-mandatory add-ons	ER, U
4. mandatory	mandatory add-ons, mandatory carve outs	ER, I

Notes: ER = employers, I = individuals, U = unions.

While countries can be classified according to whether they follow one of the four pathways to increase pension coverage, they often follow mixed strategies that combine a dominant pathway with one or more other pathways. Thus, for example, tax incentives, mandatory elements and labour unions play a role in most systems. In addition, they often follow a sequence of pathways, starting with the voluntary approach but moving to another pathway as the dominant approach in an effort to further expand coverage. Within each pathway and each sequence of pathways, different patterns can be seen that are particular to the particular country. By examining the pathways and sequences of pathways in different countries, lessons can be drawn for countries that wish to expand their pension coverage.

This hierarchy of institutional arrangements with differing degrees of incentives and compulsion to increase pension coverage is one dimension of mandating. A second dimension is the percentage of pre-retirement income that is replaced by retirement income; that is, the replacement rate. A third dimension that connects the first two is the split between public and private sources in providing mandatory sources of retirement income. While a complete analysis would integrate all three dimensions, we focus on the first dimension because it has received little attention up to now.

We examine the development of pension coverage following each of the four pathways, and consider them in the order given above: from unconstrained choice, to greater degrees of constraint, to mandate. For each pathway, we consider the distinctive elements of the pathway and then examine its historical development in particular countries. We consider factors determining why a country chose a particular pathway as the dominant approach to increasing pension coverage.

We examine at least two countries using each pathway in order to provide a comparison of countries taking each approach. Every country has a mix of pathways, and the comparison indicates the variety among countries choosing the same dominant pathway. We also see that each country uses the dominant pathway it chooses in different ways. In some cases, however, we also see that, in particular between the mandatory pathway and the contractual pathway, the distinctions become blurred.

In this approach, we focus on two issues: the degree of compulsion in the pension system, and the relationship of the pension system to the social security system. Other analyses (World Bank, 1994) take as the main issues the degree of funding and the sponsorship of the plan (government versus private). We focus on compulsion and relationship to social security because those are key issues in the degree of coverage of the private system.

A VOLUNTARY PATHWAY TO EXPAND EMPLOYER-PROVIDED PENSION COVERAGE IN THE PRIVATE SECTOR

A plausible way to enter into the discussion is to clarify the meaning of the voluntary pathway. The most obvious meaning of the term 'voluntary' is that initiating the pension is totally at the discretion of the employer, and the design of the pension plan is exclusively the prerogative of the employer. The ideal type of voluntary institutional plan is dictated by the unrestrained preferences of the employer. It is therefore independent of the input of organized employees and is not mandated or conditioned by law. In this situation, employers would take into consideration the competitive conditions in the labour market, which determine the compensation offer they must make to attract employees, but not be constrained with respect to the provision of a pension by legal requirements or contractual requirements of collectively bargained labour contracts.

The meaning of 'voluntary' and its opposite, 'mandatory', can also be viewed from the employee's perspective. A voluntary system is one where the employee is not required to participate in a pension, meaning that the employee is free to choose a job that does not provide a pension. For some jobs and in some occupations, however, a pension may be a mandatory aspect of compensation. This is particularly the case in occupations that are covered by a union.

Within a voluntary framework, the government may choose to encourage the provision of pension coverage through tax incentives. The more governments tax corporations and workers, the greater the value of these tax concessions to the firm and to workers.

United States

Within a voluntary system, the primary policy tool governments use to encourage pension coverage is tax incentives. In general, tax expenditure should serve a public purpose, otherwise it simply amounts to tax evasion. In 2003, the revenue lost from these tax concessions was an astonishing $116 billion, which makes this the largest indirect form of government spending.

The greater the regulative restrictions placed on a firm concerning the minimum requirements and maximum limitations for a pension plan, the less value a pension has for that firm. From the firm's perspective, the erosion of unrestrained voluntarism has to be balanced against the cost of maintaining the pension plan and the value of the tax advantage. Together, these factors shape the arithmetic of the incentive structures that influence a firm's decisions, but this arithmetic is further balanced by more subliminal calculations related to an implicit understanding of the interplay between the public and private spheres. This understanding provides scope for evasion and collusion with an ambivalent government, which may lack the resources or the incentive for enforcement.

Since a Supreme Court decision in 1949, pension benefits have been a mandatory subject of collective bargaining. Thus, if unions want to bargain for pensions, employers are required to bargain in good faith. Employers are not mandated to provide pensions when there is a union, but they are mandated to include pensions in collective bargaining if the union wants to do so. Employers are not required to negotiate over the enhancement of benefits that are already being paid to retirees, for example cost of living adjustments to benefits in payment. Employers are only required to negotiate benefits that are accruing to current workers.

The historical evolution of voluntarism in the United States can be briefly summarized as occurring in six different phases: welfare capitalism; the failure of the private pension movement; the creation of a public pension system as a stimulant for the rapid growth of private pensions; the golden age of public pensions; the transformation of private pensions, under the influence of government; and, from private personal accounts, the possible reform of the public pension system (Hacker, 2000).

Phase 1: the Era of Welfare Capitalism

Voluntary pensions typify the welfare capitalism that emerged around the 1920s. These pensions were neither add-ons to social security nor carve-outs from social security because at that time there was no social security programme. The system was voluntary because it was initiated solely at the discretion of the corporation as a managerial strategy to recruit, maintain and motivate its workforce to higher levels of productivity. In an emblematic form, these pensions signalled Corporate America's belief that private pensions, inspired by the benevolence of large firms, could provide a viable substitute for public intervention and thus inhibit the movement that argued for the expansion of comprehensive public provisions. In that sense, they were intended to be a substitute for a social security programme.

Welfare capitalism failed on two counts. First, the coverage rates for private pensions barely reached 5 per cent during the 1920s and only 10 per cent of the 5 per cent of the workforce who were covered actually received a private pension (Hacker, 2000, p.139). This was because the weak rules covering portability when employees changed jobs and vesting (that is, the years of continuous employment required before entitlement to a pension is assured) created large holes in the bucket that contained the corporate pension fund promises. The story is not uniformly bleak, however, since by 1935 some 9 per cent of the employed non-agricultural workforce was covered by private pensions (ibid., p.153).

Second, many firms during the Depression years went bankrupt. In the case of the largest private pension fund, that of the railway industry, organized political pressure forced the federal government to intervene and take over the financial obligations of the bankrupt system. The anomalous Rail Road Retirement Act remains as part of the Social Security Act, bearing witness to the failed idea that private pensions could flourish independent of government intervention. But this example also shows that, in the case of a large-scale collapse of a private pension industry, the government could not simply stand by and do nothing to relieve the situation.

Phase 2: the Creation of a National Public Social Security System

The public social security programme was established, in part, as a reaction to the failure of the voluntary pension movement in the era of welfare capitalism. But, even though the public programme was established in the absence of a viable private pension system, there was always an implicit understanding that the private sector would contribute significantly to the American retirement system, acting as an add-on or supplement to the public system. This understanding restricted the social security programme for middle- and upper-income workers so that it could focus on providing relatively high replacement rates at the lower end of the earnings spectrum. Therefore it seemed important to design a public system that would both avoid the pitfalls of the private pension plans and leave room for a future emergent private system. The public system had to be universal, contributory, self-financing and distributional, favouring low-wage workers.

That the public system of old age pensions was in place before the expansion of private employer-provided pension systems makes an important difference for the evolution of both spheres in the USA, ensuring that the public social security system would provide the basic pension and the private would act to supplement the basic scheme.

Phase 3: the Rise of Pension Fund Capitalism in the 1940s

Between 1935 and 1950, coverage under private pensions increased in the non-agricultural workforce from 6 per cent to 20 per cent (Hacker, 2000, p.168). During the 1940s, the stagnation of public social security set the stage for the rapid growth and entrenchment of private occupational pensions.

First, the public social security system provided broad social protection on which to build a private supplementary system. Social security became attractive to employers because they could use it as a base on which to reward better paid workers through a mechanism known as 'integration' which harmonizes the public and private pension systems. Hacker explains,

> Paradoxically, then, a program that aimed to redistribute income down the wage ladder (Social Security) pushed private pension plans up several rungs. Employers who started plans after the enactment of Social Security covered a much smaller portion of their workforce than was previously the norm, and most 'actually excluded wage workers altogether' . . . by factoring Social Security benefits into their pension formula. . . . Private pensions could be combined with Social Security in ways that allowed them to use corporate plans to influence the career patterns of their employees, especially the better paid among them. (Ibid., pp.156–7)

Thus the social security system was not a burden to employers, but an opportunity to create integrated plans that had the state pay for the low-wage workers while the private pension covered the higher-paid workers at much lower costs to the firms.

Second, the unions also recognized the stagnation of public social security benefits in the 1940s, and they provided an additional political force for the expansion of private pensions with new labour-oriented plans mush-rooming alongside and in combination with company-provided plans. Thus the labour movement was tied to the expansion of private pension plans. This tie became even further strengthened when unions accepted the value of negotiating pensions benefits along with wages in their labour contracts. Then the federal government itself required collective bargaining over fringe benefits.

> The first breakthrough was the Truman Administration's agreement with the UMW (United Mine Workers) in 1946 mandating an employer-funded plan managed by unions and the mine industry. . . . By 1960, labor negotiated plans covered . . . about half of the total covered workforce. Pension coverage rose from 19% of private workers in 1945 to 40% in 1960. (Ibid., pp.196–7).

Third, the federal tax system, which had been in place since 1914, offered deductions from corporate income taxes for firms that created private pension schemes. These tax concessions gradually expanded over time, with the view that pensions were a form of postponed wages and should not be taxed both as personal and corporate income. Thus the deferral of taxation became a well-established principle of tax policy. These tax advantages only became important to the corporation when taxes on corporations increased dramatically in the 1940s and tax deferral became an important fiscal issue for firms eager to postpone or evade taxes. Thus the availability of tax concessions was the third important factor stimulating the expansion of private pensions during this era. This expansion was a by-product of increased tax rates and not the result of a federal commitment to encourage the development of the private sector pension system.

Phase 4: the Golden Age of the Expansion of Public Pensions

After the 1950s, we entered the golden age of the public pension system which paralleled and built on the period of private sector expansion in three different ways: coverage, benefits and regulation. In the period of stagnation, the public social security system covered only a little more than half of the workforce. Agricultural workers, domestic workers and blacks who were concentrated in these sectors were excluded, as were the self-employed and non-profit organizations. Civil servants were covered by their own pension plans at the federal and state level. Slowly, social security broadened its base and began to cover all the groups. Eventually, Congress decided to include civil servants in the public social security system, and gradually coverage expanded from around 50 per cent to over 95 per cent of the civilian work-force, not mandatorily covering only clergy (on grounds of separation of church and state) and employees of state and local governments. This meant that the American basic social security pension became a virtually universal system of coverage.

A notable feature of this period was a government commission, started in the Carter years, that recommended the establishment of MUPS (Mandatory Universal Pensions). These were mandatory individual retirement savings plans. This commission released its report in 1981, at the start of the Reagan era, and its recommendation was completely ignored.

Phase 5: the Transformation of the Private Pension System into Individual Retirement Savings Plans

It is now increasingly accepted that it is important to consider public and private plans jointly. Above we discussed the changes in the public system of benefits and regulation that focused on three dimensions: the extension of coverage to a near universal system, the expansion of benefits and replacement rates up to the 1980s, and the creation of an extensive system of regulation. But the basic structure of the public social security system has remained surprisingly stable over the past 60 years. In sharp contrast to the period of stability in the public sphere, the private sector has undergone dramatic changes. These changes have occurred not only in the increase in the private share of total pension spending but also in the conversion of employer-provided defined benefit plans to an elaborate system of individual retirement accounts in which individuals can decide how much to contribute and how to invest.

In 1980, 92 per cent of pension fund contributions were employer-provided and two thirds of these were for defined benefit plans. In contrast, 20 years later, 60 per cent of private contributions were to personal retirement accounts and three-quarters of these plans were based on individual choice of pension portfolio (Gruber and Wise, 2000, § E).

What are the driving forces generating this radical transformation of the private sector? Some analysts point to growth in the regulatory system introduced by the passage of the Employee Retirement Income Security Act of 1974 (ERISA).

> The architects of ERISA hoped to make pension promises more secure, more portable from job to job, and more equitable in their distribution. . . . ERISA thus represented the culmination of a century long redefinition of pensions from an employer gratuity in which government had little interest or influence to an earned right supported and ultimately guaranteed by the State. (Hacker, 2000, pp.21, 216)

The story does not end here, but continues as the efforts of the state reshape the actions of the private sector. These regulatory efforts to make the private system more similar to the public programme also may have been interpreted as an increased burden on the private sector. Moreover, the favourable tax treatment of private pensions was less attractive as income taxes declined sharply in the 1980s (Reagan and Turner, 2000). But at the same time the federal tax system introduced new forms of tax deductions, first available to individuals in the form of IRAs (Individual Retirement Accounts), that bypassed firms altogether.

Later employers set up individual account 401(k) pension plans that meant that employees could pay tax-deductible contributions into defined contribution plans without imposing fiscal burdens on corporations. These plans, introduced by Congress in 1978, were authorized by a change in the tax code. These would come to dominate the provision of private retirement pension systems. Thus firms reacted to regulatory efforts of the state through pension legislation enabling 401(k) plans and to the tax policy of the state, which had an indirect driving effect on pension policy. It would appear that we have a classic example of public–private transactions, where changes in state policy led to changes in private practice and this in turn could lead to changes in the way that the public social security is organized.

Phase 6: the Transformation of Private Personal Accounts into the Reform of the Public Pension System.

'It is perhaps not an exaggeration to say that the personal control of retirement savings is progressing more quickly than any resolution of the debate about social security personal accounts. Universal 401(k) coverage would indeed look much like a social security system with personal accounts' (Gruber and Wise, 2000, § E). There are many proposals for reform, such as the plan proposed by the Social Security Advisory Council in 1997. To fund an individual social security account, they proposed that the payroll be reduced by 5 per cent and a mandatory 5 per cent contribution be deposited into a newly formed personal account, thus leading to a gradual introduction of personal accounts. Many other variations are currently on the pension reform agenda.

In 2002, a new conservative president (George W. Bush) is committed to some reform of the public system. But it is clear that the experience with defined contribution plans and personal accounts in the private sector is an important factor in the growing political interest in incorporating a defined contribution plan for public social security. The President's Commission to Strengthen Social Security in 2001 proposed three alternative variations for voluntary carve-out individual accounts. The unifying element with these three alternatives is that with each, if workers choose to do so, the current contributions to social security could be reduced in exchange for a reduced benefit and a contribution to an individual account. If this concept moves beyond debate to actual reform, we will have a clear example of how the evolution of private pension systems, stimulated by innovations in the federal tax exemption system, can feed back to a reform of the public system. The process is unfolding and predictions of the outcome are premature.

Canada

In Canada, as well as the United States, employer-provided pensions predated government-provided social security benefits. A study found that, by 1929, at least 48 large firms headquartered in Canada were providing pensions (Latimer, 1932, cited in Williamson, 1992).

While labour unions later played a positive role in the development of pension coverage in Canada and the United States, in the early part of the century some union leaders complained that pensions were part of company anti-union tactics and were designed to tie the worker to the firm. These leaders felt it was preferable to bargain for a better wage so that workers could save for retirement on their own. By 1928, however, 13 unions in Canada and the United States were providing pensions directly to their members. Generally, the unions with pensions were in industries with few or no employer-provided pensions (Williamson, 1992).

In Canada, government-provided means tested benefits were instituted 40 years before an earnings-related benefit was provided through social security. In 1927, the Old Age Security Act introduced a means-tested old age pension that provided very low uniform benefits for poor Canadians over age 70. The Canadian constitution was amended in 1951 with provincial agreement to allow the Government of Canada under the Old Age Security Act to provide uniform pensions for all Canadians over age 70. An earnings-related benefit was not added then because the French-speaking province of Quebec opposed the expansion of federal power in the predominantly English-speaking national government that providing such a benefit would represent (Myles and Quadagno, 1994).

While the USA had been providing earnings-related old age benefits for its citizens since 1940, Canada did not begin doing so until 1966. During the debates over the introduction of the Canada/Quebec Pension Plans in the early 1960s, the main defenders of the existing flat benefit OAS programme were insurance companies and other service providers for pensions who viewed the Canada/Quebec Pension Plans as partial nationalization of their industry (ibid., 1994). In 1964, Canada amended its constitution to authorize the inclusion of an earnings-related benefit in the Canada Pension Plan, which became effective on 1 January 1966. Quebec, however, exercised its constitutional right at that time to establish and operate a separate plan (the Quebec Pension Plan) for workers in that province, although the terms of the plan are very similar to those of the Canada Pension Plan that applies to the other nine provinces. These two plans provided full benefits in 1977, following a ten-year transition period that was used to build up an initial fund for the plans. In 1971, the Old Age Security Act was amended to provide uniform benefits to all Canadians over age 65.

The development of earnings-related social security benefits in Canada was influenced by the split between English- and French-speaking Canadians, and that split has also influenced the development of pensions. Because of the desire for autonomy by the French Canadians, the Canadian provinces have much more power relative to the national government than do the states in the USA. Under Canada's constitution, the ten provinces have been given authority over nearly all aspects of the relationship between employers and employees, which has been interpreted as including the authority to regulate pensions.

Thus, for constitutional reasons, the regulation of occupational pension plans is divided among the ten provinces plus the national government, which regulates pensions in some industries of national significance, such as the banking industry. All ten provinces plus the federal government have enacted legislation, generally known as Pension Benefits Acts, regulating pension plans. The first of these Acts became effective in 1965. Pension regulation varies across the 11 jurisdictions. Approximately 40 per cent of Canadian employees work in the province of Ontario, however, and that province has a major effect on the pension legislation enacted in other provinces. Ontario has taken the lead in pension reform, and most provinces copy its reforms, though not in all respects (Conklin, 1990). By contrast, in the USA, federal pension law pre-empts pension law at the state and local level.

The Canadian federal government also regulates all pension plans through requirements they must meet to qualify for favourable treatment under the income tax. In addition, all pension plans must comply with actuarial rules set out by the Canadian Institute of Actuaries and with accounting rules set out by the Canadian Institute of Chartered Accountants.

In spite of there being 11 different jurisdictions regulating pensions in Canada, all jurisdictions have chosen the voluntary pathway with incentives as the way to encourage pension coverage. The uniformity of basic approach chosen by the 11 jurisdictions doubtless reflects the fact that the tax incentives for pensions are uniform across all jurisdictions, the actuarial and accounting rules are uniform, and the social security system is basically uniform across all jurisdictions.

In both Canada and the USA, the public sector has important effects on the private sector through the structure of social security benefits and through the incentives provided by the tax system. Both Canada and the

USA provide relatively modest social security benefits in comparison to other high-income countries, leaving room for the development of a private pension system. Both countries have fairly widespread integration of pension benefits with social security, where social security benefits reduce the benefits provided for low-wage workers through private pension plans. They also provide similar tax preferences for the private pension system. The USA requires that mandatory premiums be paid by defined benefit plans for pension benefit insurance. Similar payments are required of pensions in the province of Ontario.

Empirical comparisons of pension coverage of private sector workers in Canada and the USA are difficult because the distinction between the private sector and public sector is not as clear in Canada as in the USA. It appears that some public sector Canadian workers who work for public institutions such as universities, hospitals and public corporations (such as Air Canada), rather than traditional government bureaucracies, indicate in household surveys that they are private sector workers. Owing to this error in reporting on surveys, Canadian data on pension coverage for the entire workforce are more reliable than data that attempt to separate private sector workers. Because the public sector is relatively larger in Canada, however, and because pension coverage rates are considerably higher in the public than the private sector, empirical comparisons across the two countries are difficult. The coverage rate for the entire workforce has the advantage that it indicates the percentage of the workforce in the two countries that has an employer-provided pension that supplements social security. It has the disadvantage that it is influenced by government policy concerning the relative size of the public sector.

One study has attempted to measure private pension coverage on a comparable basis for Canada and the USA (Dailey and Turner, 1992). That study found that, for many years, the private pension coverage rate has been about 50 per cent higher in the USA than in Canada. Since 1975, the pension coverage rate for full-time private sector workers has varied between 28 and 30 per cent in Canada, while it has varied between 44 and 46 per cent in the USA.

Several problems cause these figures to overstate the difference in private sector coverage rates between the two countries. In comparison to Canada, the US figures are overstated because the Canadian figures are for the labour force, including the unemployed, while the US figures are for wage and salary workers, excluding the unemployed. Adjusting for these problems on the basis of a subjective assessment of the magnitude of their effects, it appears that the private sector pension coverage rate was at least five percentage points higher in the USA than in Canada.

While the private sector pension coverage rate is higher in the USA than in Canada, because of high coverage rates in the public sector, coverage rates for all workers, public and private sector, are higher in Canada than in the USA. This is true for all income levels except the lowest, where the rate is marginally lower in Canada. The coverage rates are 10 to 20 percentage points higher in the middle-income categories. In the highest income category, which starts at US$45000, the difference is only four percentage points (Pesando and Turner, 2001).

A primary objective of the Canadian tax treatment of pensions is to provide equitable tax assistance for retirement, regardless of whether a worker participates in a company-sponsored pension plan or in an individual account pension plan. In Canada, workers who set up an individual account Registered Retirement Savings Plan can enjoy approximately the same amount of tax assistance as workers who participate in an employer-provided plan. In the USA, no attempt has been made to equalize the treatment between employer-sponsored plans and individual account plans. US employers have a near-monopoly in the provision of tax-favoured pension benefits.

A major factor discouraging establishment of new plans in Canada is the complexity of pension laws. The Pension Benefits Acts are detailed and differ among the 11 jurisdictions. Laws designed to reduce risks to workers have become so expensive for employers to comply with that the laws may be counterproductive. Some employers have switched their defined benefit pension plans to money purchase (defined contribution) plans or have terminated them in favour of group Registered Retirement Savings Plans.

When a pension plan covers members in more than one province, the laws of each province apply to the members in that province. Likewise, if benefits have accrued to an employee for work in more than one province, the laws of each province may apply to the benefits accrued within that province, even for work within a single plan. Although US pension law is complex, and is thought to be a factor discouraging small firms from establishing defined benefit plans, the variation across provinces in Canada is an added aspect of complexity not faced by employers in the USA. Canadian federal and provincial regulators have made little progress towards uniform legislation.

Canada and the USA differ in terms of the mandatory elements within their essentially voluntary systems. In the USA, workers can often cash in their pension benefits when they change jobs. In Canada, however, generally when pension benefits are vested as stipulated by the requirements of the relevant Pension Benefits Act, they are locked in until retirement. This requirement has two opposing effects on pension coverage. Pension benefit receipt by workers at retirement is raised because there is no leakage from the system as occurs in the USA. It is lowered to the extent that workers choose not to participate because of the forced illiquidity of their money in their pension accounts. Which effect dominates is an empirical question, with there being currently no empirical evidence on which to base an answer.

For several reasons, Canada, like the USA, has chosen the voluntary pathway with incentives. The choice of that pathway is made clear by examining the reasons why the alternatives were not taken. An important similarity between Canada and the USA in social policy is the relative failure of organized labour to play a major role (Myles and Quadagno, 1994). For this reason, while pension coverage rates are higher in sectors of the economy that are unionized, organized labour has played a limited role in the extension of pension coverage in both countries.

Similarly, several reasons dictate why mandating has not been chosen. Mandating has not been chosen in Canada largely because of the opposition of Quebec to a strong national government. In the USA, it has not been chosen because of strong philosophical opposition by conservatives to mandates as opposed to free choice. In Canada, the role of conservative political philosophy is much weaker. The contracting out approach was explicitly considered by the US Congress and rejected. Canada also considered and rejected contracting out as an option.

CONTRACTING OUT

Japan

Contracting out occurs when an individual or an employer can be exempted from making part or all of the mandatory contribution to social security. In exchange, they are required to provide a pension meeting minimum standards. For an employer who would otherwise provide such a plan, the reduction in mandatory social security contributions is a subsidy. For other employers, the reduction in mandatory benefits provides an incentive to provide a pension plan.

Japan has a well established public and private pension system but is in the midst of a turbulent period of transition with regard to accommodating itself to economic downturn, a changing labour force, rapid population aging and new ideas about how the public–private mix should be reorganized to deal with these challenges. In 1985, major changes in the social security system took place when a common flat rate basic pension was introduced. There is also an earnings-related contributory programme organized along five different public systems and three different private pension systems providing, in principle, supplementation to the basic pension. All countries that have followed this logic of group rather than national solidarity have found it to be unstable and the process of pension reform continues unabated.

A major difficulty with both the basic and private occupational systems is erosion of the contribution base. The evasion of contributions in the basic pension is a central issue, with most estimates affirming that about one-third of those required to contribute to the basic national pension fail to do so.

The private occupational pensions established in 1966 permitted employers to opt out of a portion of the earnings-related public pension known as Employees' Pension Insurance. The National Life Insurance Institute prefers to call this partial contracting out 'substitution', because the employer-managed pension plan acts to substitute for only a portion of the public pension.

Why were Employees' Pension Funds (EPF) introduced in 1966? One interpretation was that employers had argued that the public pensions were too generous (100000 yen) and the contributions of 5.5 per cent were too high. The generosity of the public pension thus threatened to replace the two types of private pension then in place. These plans are known as the corporate lump sum payment system which was tax-subsidized under legislation known as Tax Qualified Plans, and the Employees' Pension Funds, which provided an income stream for a limited period of 15 years. To meet the concerns of the employers, it was decided to introduce a plan that replaced part of the public earnings-related social insurance with the corporation private pension funds. The government would provide a rebate for the replaced portion contributed by the employers.

This privatized component of the public sector's earnings-related tier is also experiencing erosion, but for different reasons than the basic pension. One of the main reasons is probably a shift in the financing of corporate private pensions. Before the 1960s, most companies followed the German system of company book reserves. But then several large companies shifted to pre-funded schemes as a way to smooth out cash pay-outs of benefits after age 55. In recent years, however, with the economic downturn, these funded pension schemes have yielded zero interest instead of the projected 5.5 per cent. Not surprisingly, under these conditions, the total number of plans in the Pension Funds has declined and so too has the total number of persons covered by these plans. It reached a peak in 1997, when the Funds covered 12.3 million employees in a total of 1883 employer provided plans. By March 2000, coverage had fallen to 11.7 million members and the number of plans declined to 1835. Erosion took other forms as well. In 1999, 1300 plans were in deficit, many went bankrupt and were terminated, and many failed to honour their defined benefit promises (Liu, 1999, p.7). Having a regulatory framework in place is not enough to rescue insolvent plans or to deal with employers' disinclination to preserve the existing system of 'contracting out' or substitution.

Although the private pension system of opting out, known as Employees' Pension Funds, is in transition, it has been an important mechanism in expanding pension coverage since it was first introduced in 1966, when coverage was limited to only half a million employees. These plans were organized either by single employers, such as large corporations, or by groups of employers, that is, aggregates of smaller firms. These plans were required to be defined benefit plans, with the requirement that the benefit levels should pay out at least 30 per cent more than the public earnings-related programme (EPI) that they replaced.

The public pension is reviewed by the government every five years. In the four intervening years, benefits are adjusted for prices and in the fifth they are further adjusted for wage changes. This system of indexing is a Japanese version of the Swiss method of indexing, which is the average of both the wage and price index. When the public system contributions could not cover the benefits there was a decision to drop wage indexing in the fifth year.

The norm in wage agreements in the large firms in Japan is to provide lump sum bonus payments twice during the year. In the past, social security contributions were based only on earnings, but the 1999 reform introduced the requirement that 1 per cent of the bonuses should be taxed as social security contributions. Employer-provided substitute payments only replace past earnings, however, and take no account of any wage or price indexing. In addition, Employees' Pension Funds provide supplementary private pensions, which augment the component of the public earnings-related pension without adjustments. Taken together, this is the amount that the funds pay out as a corporate pension. Note, however, that the supplementary funds can be paid out as either a lump sum or an annuity. In 1997, 40 per cent of pensioners chose to collect the supplementary pensions payment as a lump sum. In return the funds receive part of the insurance premium payable to the public scheme to meet the costs. This is an important feature of the principle of substitution for only a portion of the public earnings-related benefits plus a private supplement. These rules are not hidden, but are characteristic of the complex structure in the design of the substitution rule. This has made private pensions less than transparent, but at the same time provides room for retrenchment that is not noticeable.

In the 1950s, the traditional form of paying out private pensions was a lump sum payment on retirement. This form of payment, however, was also used for other purposes as well, such as bonuses for achievement, and severance pay if the employee left the firm before the age of retirement. Information on the age distribution of recipients of severance payments needs to be known if we are to understand how many of these payments in fact amounted to pension benefits equivalent to an age pension. Employers clearly needed some tax incentives to introduce these lump sum benefits and, on their initiative, Tax Qualified plans were introduced in 1962.

Over time, the relative importance of these different forms of private pensions changed. Lump sum retirement payments as the participant's only form of payment declined from 62 per cent of the total of private arrangement in 1978 to 48 per cent in 1997, while lump sum payments to participants combined with their receiving corporate pensions increased in the same period from 22 per cent to over a third (Wakabayashi, 2001). Another way to present the data on the relative importance of private pensions is to recognize that the total labour force consists of 65 million workers, of which 11 million are self-employed, 5 million are civil servants and 48 million are employed in the private sector. Contracting out is available only to the 48 million employees in the private sector. (This is different from the UK case, where most of the civil servants are contracted out through private and personal pensions.) We can further differentiate private sector workers in that there are 11 million part-time workers of which only 1 million receive corporate pensions, and 37 million full-time workers of which 4 million are not covered by a private pension. If we focus only on the 33 million employees with private retirement pension, 18 million are members of corporate pension funds, 9 million receive only lump sum payments and the rest receive both (National Life Insurance Research Institute, 2000).

The public Employees' Pension Insurance is the earnings-related component of the Japanese multi-pillar social security system. It covers all private sector workplaces with more than five employees and is mandatory for both employers and employees, with contributions of 8.7 per cent of their monthly salary and 1 per cent of their bonus. This premium also includes the contributions for the basic National Pension. One recent estimate for 1997 showed that it paid out average monthly benefits amounting to 48 per cent of the average monthly salary of employees and covered most of the population. For the same year, corporate pensions covered about half of the population and nearly 90 per cent of the benefits paid out were in the form of a lump sum payments (National Institute of Population and Social Security Research, 2000, p.11). Converting these payments to an income stream is a difficult exercise that is sensitive to several questionable assumptions. For purposes of this chapter, we focus on only one component of the private pension system, the Employees' Pension Fund, which covers 17 million people, with half the Fund's financial obligations being to finance the substituted or opting out part of the public earnings-related insurance.

A reform of the contracting out system occurred in 2001. It resembles the US individual account 401(k) plan, but Japanese style. It is widely hoped that the introduction of a variant of such a plan will boost the stock market, as it was believed in the 1990s happened in the United States. But the pressure for reform is intense, because the two main corporate pensions in Japan have defined benefit obligations that they are unable to meet since they cannot reduce the benefit payments or the assumed interest rate of 5.5 per cent in calculating the liability for benefits. With the economic recession of recent years, interest rates have declined to virtually zero per cent and firms have had to make up the shortfall from profits. This problem is most acute for the pension funds that were contracted out from part of the public system's responsibility to provide earnings-related social insurance. The original justification of this unique feature of Japan's pension system was to provide 'corporate pension plans to manage so they can enjoy better returns through diversification' (National Life Insurance Research Institute, 2000, p.32). This justification made sense when the real rate of return on investments was higher than the fixed return in law. Under these conditions the firms could use the excess to improve the pensions system of its employees. Not surprisingly, the 1999 pension reform liberalized the reserve fund rules to 4 per cent in order to stop the shortfall rising. But this was only meant to avoid a deficit; contributions would have to rise as well. At present, uncovered pension liabilities are not recorded in the public balance sheets of firms, but new pressure for increased transparency in the rules of accounting will make this more difficult, thus damaging the credit-worthiness of these firms. All these different developments, taken together, increase pressure for reform of the contracting system.

Some companies see a solution in retreating from the contracting out system altogether and are asking that the government resume full responsibility for the privately substituted obligations of the pension funds. Other companies have managed to use the new rules to reduce the temporary shortfall in funds. These responses are interesting because they suggest that the original pressure for opting out did not fully arise from the interests of the corporations alone, but from the interplay between public and private interests.

The United Kingdom

Comparing the UK and Japan in terms of contracting out highlights the different rationales behind the idea. In the UK, the government tried to promote contracting out by providing it on favourable terms: everyone could contract out, whereas in Japan the terms were more neutral and limited. But the difference in the rationales behind contracting out in the two countries is most distinctive. In the UK, the government's overriding agenda was an attempt to reduce the direct cost to the state of public pension provision, and the state was willing to do this by increasing the indirect cost to the state in the form of subsidies and tax forgiveness. The new Labour government shares the same objective of transferring the burden of provision to the private sector with the introduction of the Stakeholder Pension Schemes. Both the Conservative and the Labour governments encouraged the greater and more effective use of private pensions as a strategy for reducing the cost of public pensions and both political parties used contracting out as the vehicle to realize this objective. However, they pursued this goal in somewhat different ways. It is possible to trace both governments' experiences but there is more evidence about the outcome of the Conservative practice. We consider each in turn before returning to a comparison of Japan and the UK.

In the United Kingdom, there was a rather large private system in place prior to the introduction of public pensions, and this pattern of the private preceding the public is part of the long history of the interplay between the public and the private. First, in the early part of the twentieth century, there was a well-established system of Friendly Societies in the civil society to provide contributing members with protection and offering income when wages were disrupted in old age, and also to pay for funerals. Thus the government could only offer non-contributory old age pensions, because a contributory system would compete with the Friendly Societies' benefit scheme and would entail double contributions in the public and private spheres.

But the more recent history of occupational pensions offers an even more telling story. From its early history, before the Beveridge Plan after the Second World War, public pensions had to make concessions to the already established private pension system. The most important of these concessions was to permit opting out of the public system if the private system could provide at least equal benefits. A similar effort to permit private pensions was proposed in the United States with the introduction of the Clark Amendment, but the effort failed to pass both houses of Congress. This was not a politically viable alternative in the British case, since the private pension was already well established when public pension reforms were initiated.

The basic pension in the UK consists of two public tiers: a basic flat rate public pension and a public supplementary pension, which provides a state earnings-related pension (SERPS) within a band of earnings between a lower and an upper limit. The band covers 16 per cent below the average weekly earnings and 29 per cent above it. Contracting out in the UK means opting out of the SERPS public programme into a private occupational or personal pension (Blake, 2000; Hanna, 1986; Thane, 2000; Liu, 1999).

An understanding of contracting out requires first an appreciation of the fate of SERPS over the nearly 25 years since it was introduced in 1978. At its inception, the programme was to replace 25 per cent of the best 20 years of employment, revalued to take account of changes in national average earning. The programme was abandoned altogether by the Labour government when it came to power in 1997. When the programme was still in place, the basic pension replaced about 16 per cent and SERPS about 15 per cent of average earnings (Blake, 2000). Thus the public pension by itself could not provide the foundation for an adequate income in retirement without supplementation from either means-tested public programmes for low-wage earners or contracted out occupational and personal pensions for average, medium and high earners.

Contracting out is not a new idea in the history of pension policy in the UK. It is a natural outgrowth of the reality of the introduction of a public pension on top of a pre-existing and well-established private system. The public system politically needed to accommodate and to make concessions to the reality of a private system that would not let itself be ousted by a strong public system. Contracting out was a design invention that permitted such a compromise. It was politically naïve to proceed to build a public edifice without accepting this reality. This is very different from the American experience after the Depression years when there was no established competitive private sector. It was only in the 1940s, after the passage of the Social Security Act and the failed bid to revise the legislation to permit opting out, that the private sector accepted that there could be advantages to building and expanding private pension on the foundation of a well established and secure public pension system.

In the USA a parallel to contracting out can be found in that the major programmes that existed before the Social Security Act of 1935 were not required to participate in the social security system when it began. But, gradually, over time all new civil servant workers in the federal government and most in state and local governments were required to join the public social security programme.

Employees in the UK with earnings above the lower earnings limit are automatically enrolled in the state earnings-related SERPS programme unless they opt to contract out of the public system into an employer-provided or personal accounts pension. In the case of contracting out, if the employer provides such a scheme, both the employer and the employee receive a rebate from their national insurance contributions, with the employer and the employee getting a 3 per cent and a 1.6 per cent rebate, respectively. The national insurance programme is much broader than just a pension, offering individuals entitlement to health, sickness, disability and other benefits.

The rules in Japan are not very different from the rules permitting rebates in the UK, but there are some important differences. In Japan, contracting out is only available to private sector workers, whereas in UK it is open to all employees. Rebates have increased over time in Japan, while they have declined in the UK: since 1993, in the UK, they have remained the same for employers and declined slightly for employees. This seems rather odd, since the original rationale for the rebate was based on the estimated cost of providing the guaranteed minimum pension, which has since been eliminated. The stability of employer rebates is also puzzling because the earnings-related pension, which is protected by the contracting provision, has declined sharply over time. The rebate is intended to at least provide the worker with the same level of benefit as would have been provided through the public social security programme alone. But the value of this benefit has declined and, as a result, the stability of rebate for employers since 1993 is not altogether clear. When compared, however, to the 4.5 per cent level of rebates in 1978, in the UK a decline is clearly evident (Turner and Watanabe, 1995, p.40).

Contracting out into the private sector is available in two different forms for employees in the UK: an employer-provided pension and an Appropriate Personal Pension. The personal pension, however, is the only vehicle available for the 3.2 million self-employed. About half of the self-employed are enrolled in such a plan (45.4 per cent) and half are without a personal pension and only have coverage in the basic public pension. But the system is more complicated since there are four different types of employer-provided pensions: salary-related defined benefits, money purchase defined contributions, mixed benefits schemes and hybrid schemes. Some of these distinctions apply to a time when there was a guaranteed minimum pension. There are at least two different types of personal accounts, depending on whether additional contributions can be provided. Data from 1996 show that 30 per cent of employees remained contracted in the SERPS public programme and an additional 5 per cent were contracted in with a supplementary occupational pension. However, 37 per cent were in contracted out occupational schemes. About 85 per cent of new schemes that were started after 1998 were money purchase or hybrids, whereas 85 per cent of the older schemes were salary-based. In summary, 76 per cent of all the schemes were either in SERPS or in a contracted out occupational scheme and with respect to the type of scheme, 28 per cent were in personal pension schemes (Blake, 2000, p.2).

This is the story in brief. After the Second World War, Britain entered the era of the growth of newly nationalized industry, so by 1950 about a quarter of the labour force was in the public sector. During the Second World War, the standard rate of income tax rose to 50 per cent and taxes on companies typically could be even higher. After the war, the standard income tax for employees never fell below 30 per cent. So most workers, except those with the lowest pay, were expected to pay income tax as well as national insurance tax. With the spread of tax coverage and higher tax rates, every tax consultant could easily show 'that all parties could benefit from an extension of private pensions at the expense of the Treasury . . . In 1956 the cost to the Treasury of relief . . . had reached 120 million pounds'. The tax deductions for pensions that had been on the books since 1921 now became very attractive (Hanna, 1986, p.45) and, politically, there was little government interest in creating a strong earnings-related public pension system.

These factors, nationalized industries and high taxation combined with high tax exemptions, and government indifference to a strong public pension, taken together, set the stage for the rapid expansion of occupational pensions in the public and in the private sectors. This happened in the public sector because the largest and strongest unions concentrated their effort in organizing the public sector. Given the political vacuum for a strong public earnings-related programme, unions instead negotiated for earnings-related occupational pensions. By 1979, coverage in occupational pensions was almost complete in the civil service, the armed forces and the nationalized industries (Thane, 2000, p.381).

A similar phenomenon of growth occurred in the private sector as well: 'In 1956 it was rare for large companies to have a pension scheme, just less than half of male employees (and only about one quarter of female employees) were likely to be admitted to the scheme' (Hannah, 1986, p.42). Labour's National Superannuation proposals of 1957 were designed to halt and reverse the increasing power and importance of occupational pension funds and to replace them with a state earnings-related scheme. Hannah interpreted this action by the Labour government as 'the last practical moment at which a state earnings-related pension scheme could have wiped out the built up demand for private pension in Britain' (ibid., pp.50–51). When the scheme was announced, shares in insurance companies dropped and private employers and insurance companies were advising conservative ministers to introduce legislation 'to compel all employees to join occupational pension schemes' as the only viable approach to overcome the major weakness of private pensions, low portability of schemes across firms (Thane, 2000, p.382).

But in practice the 'last moment' was not seized, and the option of mandatory private pensions was not considered. A potentially reversible history of path dependency was not charted. Instead, British public policy followed the path of contracting out of the public earnings-related programme into first employer-provided occupational pensions and then, after 1986, to individual account Appropriate Personal pension programmes.

During the Conservative era of Thatcher and Major, between 1979 and 1997, the government changed its mind about the preferred form of private sector contracting out. This shift in preference occurred gradually, but with many errors in judgment and at considerable cost. Through a series of steps, the government shifted its preferences toward personal accounts. It removed any obligation from employers to create their own employer-provided pension and then removed the obligation of the employee to join such a scheme, even if it were offered. Fewer than 50 per cent of workers accepted the firm's pension offer voluntarily. Further legislative changes enabled members of occupational pensions to join personal pensions if they chose to do so.

But then the government sweetened the offer to switch to personal accounts by providing a special bonus in the form of an additional 2 per cent rebate between 1988 and 1993. During this period, about half a million members of occupational pensions switched to personal accounts, but 90 per cent of those who transferred were given bad advice by an over-aggressive salesforce eager to encourage switching. There was a huge public outcry about this failure to protect individuals from market forces and, eventually, the personal pension industry was legally forced to compensate individuals who had been made worse off by the transfer. The amount of compensation came to over £11 billion (Blake, 2000, p.4).

In an effort to reverse the tide from the private into the public, the government was forced in 1993 to offer an age-related 1 per cent national insurance rebate for those over the age of 30. But this attempt to discourage contracting back into the public sector proved to be very expensive. 'The net cost . . . during the first 10 years was estimated by the National Audit Office to be about 10 billion pounds' (ibid.). But, as late as 1997, the UK simplified the occupational pension scheme, making it a more attractive option to some employers. It did this by abolishing the requirement that these schemes must provide a Guaranteed Minimum Pension (GMP). The same legislation required that pensions only be indexed up to a maximum of 5 per cent and tried to improve the security of assets by creating a Compensation Fund, specifying minimum funding requirements and investment principles.

The Blair government continued the practice of transferring public provision to the private sector, but it created a new vehicle in the form of Stakeholder Pension Schemes, which were designed so that middle-income workers with no existing supplementary pension scheme could contract out of the public system. At the same time, a new public programme that became effective in 2002, called a new State Second Pension (S2P) was set up to replace SERPS. This new programme started as an earnings-related programme and after five years will become a flat rate pension that will only be indexed to prices, and not wages. This signals that, over time, the value of the benefits will decline, thus reinforcing the need for a private contracted out programme to provide adequate replacement income during retirement. Membership in the second private pillar remains voluntary. Thus the new Welfare Reform and Pension Act introduced by the Blair government ensures that contracting out will remain a dominant feature of the Labour government.

CONTRACTUAL AGREEMENTS

We start with a simple working definition of labour contracting as a pathway. Essentially, these are schemes agreed upon by the labour market parties through labour negotiations. These agreements can be organized by industry, by occupation, or at a corporation level, particularly in large companies and firms. In all countries, there is a regulatory framework within which these agreements are set, although the extensiveness of these regulations varies by country. Civil servant retirement schemes typically differ from these labour market pensions for those employed on a contractual agreement basis. In most countries, civil servant agreements are legislated for and are therefore different from private or public sector agreements, which are voluntary agreements between employers and employees. The state is both an employer and a general provider. These civil servant pensions, moreover, tend to be financed from general taxation, whereas contractual agreements are typically fully or partially funded.

In Germany, contractual agreements in the private sector are quite modest. Non-civil servant public employees organized collective agreements to improve their pensions so that they would be more in line with civil servants who pay no contributions but are entitled to excellent benefits. There are many women among this type of employee, so contractual arrangements have turned out to be important in improving the position of women. The issue is even more complicated because some public employees are not civil servants, but do enjoy the same status of entitlement as all individuals who contribute to the state's public social insurance programmes. The Germans distinguish between Beamte and Angestellte, with the former having agreements based on a special law for this particular category of workers, whereas the latter can have contractual agreements that supplement their public pension programmes. The contractual plans for public employees are based on collective agreements that are closely integrated with social security benefits. The pensions for employees in the public sector are governed by civil service law and based on collective agreements. The laws governing pensions for civil servants have been affected by political demand for more equal treatment of civil servants and other employees with the increasing burden of old-age protection.

France, the Netherlands and the Nordic countries have the most extensive system of contractual agreements for private sector workers and for those employed by the government but without civil servant status. In other countries, like Germany, contractual agreements within the public sector are perhaps more important than such agreements in the private sector. This distinction is important because of the tendency to think of contractual agreements as being private and driven by the market.

Denmark

The history of these contractual agreements differs by country. In order to highlight this variety, we start with a brief account of some differences between Denmark and Sweden. Labour market-related pensions for active workers did not come to Denmark until the build-up of labour market pensions in the public sector, which occurred around the end of the 1980s. This was a time when only one-third of active workers were covered by a labour market pension. Until this time the basic public old age pension was the main pension and was independent of any previous relation to the labour market. It was a citizen or resident-based pension to cover virtually all 67-year-olds. But the basic pension did depend on the family income and the pensioner's own earned income. (Danish Ministry of Foreign Affairs, 2000, p.25). In 1998, the value of this basic means-tested public pension amounted to 4.7 per cent of GDP, and the government pension for civil servants amounted to 1.1 per cent of GDP.

Denmark was later than Sweden in accepting the need to augment the basic pension with a variety of supplementary schemes. These included the following: a Labour Market Supplementary Pension (ATP), a Special Pension Savings Scheme (SP), and a Capital Pension Fund (LD), which is now being slowly phased out, and, in addition, the contractual Labour Market Pension and Company Pensions. These schemes will be focused on in this chapter. Pensions paid from the second pillar amounted to 2.8 per cent of GDP (Seendergaard, 2001). But this mix of public supplementary programmes and contractual pensions will change rapidly in the next 40 years.

Denmark has a pension system that has transformed the model of a resident-based, universal pension system that is means-tested, flat rate and contributory with no earnings ceiling. But different means are tested in two main components of the programme, conventionally referred to as the first pillar. This differentiated test of need is central to the evolution of the scheme. The basic component is based on an earning test, meaning that the more an individual works the less he/she receives in benefits and, since the supplement to the basic programme is based on a transfer test of need, the more public and private transfer payments received, the lower is the value of the supplement. In both programmes the taper rate or the rate of decline of the benefits is 30 per cent, without a free zone permitting the accumulation of both sources of income. The distinction is crucial, since the model will be increasingly a residual component of an evolving hybrid institutional mix that takes as its central component a decentralized, contractual pension that is fully funded in both the public and private spheres and is based on the principle of a defined contribution plan. This labour market or second pillar now reaches 80–90 per cent of wage and salary workers, and as the programme matures the value of the benefits it can offer will grow and thus the transfer-tested, public supplement to the basic scheme will decline in importance, if the present rules of tight coupling are not changed.

The second pillar is now the mainstay of the evolving new pension arrangements. But it took a long time for this labour market component to become the settled foundation of decentralized contractual agreements. The story of its development is interesting. The first stage of the creation in the public employment sector of occupational branches was based on contractual agreements and thus wage and salary workers were separated from civil servants whose pensions were financed from general taxation and whose benefits were set by legislation. But the private sector unions could not reach agreement with employers' associations on how pensions should be organized. There was considerable interest in a central fund to be managed by the unions, which employers viewed as a threat to the market system. Eventually, the metalworkers' union in the LO abandoned this plan and agreed on a contractual agreement with employees only for their workers. Other unions followed their lead, as was customary in wage agreements. Once the practice of creating such branch funds on a decentralized basis was accepted, legislation in 1991 followed the practice that had evolved. The legislation did not mandate that firms provide occupational pensions, but facilitated the practice through tax exemptions. Contributions to these schemes is now 9–14 per cent of total earnings to be invested in fully funded pensions.

Contractual agreement will become the dominant structure on which the Danish system evolves rather than the universal resident-based uniform and means-tested scheme. This is a remarkable evolution from the dominance of universalism to the dominance of collective contractual agreements.

As it was recognized that the resident-based scheme paid only modest benefits, it was decided to create an earnings-related supplement called ATP. The Danish system was inspired by the Swedish programme with the same name that was designed to create benefits tied to increasing income but the Danish programme was reluctant to reproduce pension benefits that corresponded in retirement to the distribution of earnings during the working life. So it evolved into a modest supplement to the resident-based programme and was regarded as part of the first pillar. But the two means-tested programmes continued to spawn other programmes that had their origin in the commingling of economic and tax policies, given the political commitment not to raise the already high tax rate, but confronted by a period of inflation that threatened economic growth. It is estimated that one-third of the increase in wages costs were put into forced savings programmes that decreased consumption as social policy was the handmaiden to economic policies.

Consider, for example, the new legislation passed in 1999 to create a Special Pension Savings programme, known simply as SP. In this programme, 1 per cent of total earnings combined with taxable benefits was set aside in a special funded scheme administered by the ATP programme which in turn is managed by a non-profits private company. Now this mandatory savings programme, SP, could be seen as part of the first public pillar or as part of the third pillar of personal savings, and different reports place it conceptually in one or other of these places.

What we have, then, is a hybrid coordination, continuously evolving but subordinating the basic scheme to new models of contractual agreement combined with individual savings accounts. We think this is an evolving model that is not easy to classify because it merges resident-based universal pensions with contractual agreements as dominant, followed by individual accounts which are a product of forced saving and individual choice.

Sweden

The Swedish contractual agreements followed a different path. In 1959 Sweden decided to introduce its ATP system of earnings-related public social insurance that was to gradually make the basic public pension residual, since benefits were to be transfer-tested, rather than means-tested. In other words, the higher the ATP transfers level, the lower the basic pension. Before ATP was introduced, white-collar workers had developed an elaborate system of contractual agreements. Blue-collar workers put their faith in the political creation of a public earnings-related system, which they succeeded in doing with the creation of ATP. But even after the public system was in place, white-collar workers continued to receive contractually agreed supplements. Slowly, blue-collar workers opted for the same arrangements. Contractual agreements now cover about 90 per cent of all workers including not only blue- and white-collar private sector workers, but also public employees at the level of local government and at the federal level. Thus, in Sweden, contractual agreements are now a well-established part of the pension system, augmenting the income of pensioners by about 10 per cent.

In 1995, Sweden reformed its public pension system once again and introduced the idea of notional accounts. This is basically the conversion of the defined benefit programme of ATP into a defined contribution individual account plan without actually investing the contributions, hence the idea of a notional system. In addition, Sweden introduced the idea of a mandatory funded individual account pension, with 2.5 per cent of earnings being contributed for investment into individual accounts of the individual worker's personal choice. This new programme, called the Premium Pension, had a ripple effect on the contractual system.

Contractual agreements, since the introduction of the Premium Pension, are in a state of transition. They are designed to reinforce personal accounts. It is still too early at this time to give an account of these developments.

The Dutch Model

A peculiar characteristic of the Dutch General Old-Age Act (AOW) is that private pension companies have an informal, unwritten implicit understanding that nevertheless imposes a strong normative obligation to set up a pension scheme in such a way that it takes account of the size of the pension payment of the public pension scheme. Employer-provided pension schemes are fully funded and designed to guarantee a pension benefit related to the income earned during a lifetime of work. The combined public and occupational pension provides at least 70 per cent of the worker's earnings at the time of retirement in some schemes and average lifetime earnings in other schemes. These pension plans are decided by pension funds that are managed by a board that is equally divided between representatives of the employer and of the employee.

In the Dutch context, a private pension is viewed as a pension programme that is not state-operated and therefore operates within the regulatory framework set by the state for all private plans. In 1995, the civil servant pension system was privatized, and the privatized public sector pension fund (ABP) is therefore now considered as one of the four main types of private supplementary pensions. It is private because it is subject to the same rules as the other private sector funds. The civil servant and the health occupations pension funds (PGGM) are the largest private sector funds.

The main types of pension plans are industry-wide or organized by industrial sectors. In all, there are 70 such plans, including the two largest plans, which are for the civil servants and the health sector, as well as plans in industrial and other sectors. This way of deciding pension plans ensures maximum diversity in design of plans, which leads to a high degree of inequality. Some plans are very generous, in terms of benefits levels, replacement rates and supplementary fringe benefits. One of the most important variations in practice is how the integration with the public sector AOW takes place (discussed below).

In addition to the industry-wide plans, there are also 850 corporate pension funds, the largest of which are global in nature, with firms like Royal Dutch Shell, KLM and Philips, and 11 professional association funds. Also there is an association of small pension plans, which because of their size are inefficient to manage by the firms. While there are thousands of funds, the 100 largest account for almost 69 per cent of the total pension coverage (Clark, 2000, p.7).

The basic public old age pension system (AOW) was implemented in 1957 and guarantees a flat rate pension designed to cover all residents, and treats wives as individuals with a pension in their own right. Fifty years' residence is required for maximum benefits, and 2 per cent of the value of the benefit is accumulated each year. Immigrants and those living outside the country are penalized through the accumulating entitlement. In practice, this seems to be a problem for about 30 per cent of all current pensioners. The benefit level of this public pension rose sharply during the 1960s and 1970s, having been linked in 1964 to the minimum wage, which is linked in turn to the growth of average wages in the economy. The value of the minimum wage is about 65000 guilders. In 1970, the basic pension was linked to the net minimum wage, which takes account of the tax burden falling on the general population and comes to 40000 guilders, about two-thirds of the average wage. With this change, the public pension was equal to about 45 per cent of the net minimum wage.

One interpretation of the complementary relationship between the public and private pension schemes was the expectation that 'the public pension scheme would become superfluous as soon as every member of the Dutch society would have joined a private pension scheme' (Verbon, 1988, p.2). But this depended on how the franchise was computed in the determination of the private pension. The higher the value of the franchise, the lower the obligation of the private pensions to fill the gap between these benefits and the target of a 70 per cent replacement rate. But if the value is much lower, the private pensions will try to offset the increased cost by switching from replacing 70 per cent of the final wage to 70 per cent of the average wage, which is much cheaper. So this is an important political issue that the pension covenant must resolve. The covenant is the regular meeting held every few years (usually three) between the social partners and the government.

But the benefit levels of the public system must be understood in relation to the premiums or contributions that are levied on residents to pay for the benefits. Only employees contribute to the basic pension. A further examination of the 'who pays' question reveals an anomaly in the Dutch system since the burden falls on the low end of the income distribution system, even though there is a provision that those without taxable income are not required to contribute. But who pays for this group, which constitutes about 20 per cent of the potentially eligible population?

There are four tax brackets: on the first tier are those who pay no taxes, because their income is too low to be taxed. The second and third tax brackets pay 17.9 per cent of their income up to a ceiling of about 40000 guilders. The third and fourth tax tiers are for medium and high-income groups. In 1992, the first tier of no taxes was created and it was decided that the second tier would have to pay the increased contributions needed to cover the added cost; this meant that the premium was raised from about 14 per cent to its present level. There is a general recognition of some of these anomalies, and tax reform is high on the political agenda.

One possible justification for this arrangement is that the tax rates are very progressive: after the tax reform, the highest level pays 56 per cent, the middle level pays 42.5 per cent and the bottom tax level pays 37 per cent. If all levels contributed to social security contributions, some argue, there would be too steep a reduction in inequality. Hence only the lowest tier contributes directly to social security, while the other tax tiers pay for the other obligations citizens have for paying for all the other functions of government. Another possible justification is that the private pension system will offset the contribution burden, but this is not altogether convincing since the private and supplementary pensions are financed by both employers and employees. These systems are fully funded, however, and their return from their invested assets is substantially higher than the amount they need to pay in benefits. In 1998, the average aggregate income of the funds was 996 billion guilders and the average outlay in benefits was 730 billion guilders. These amounts are more than 100 per cent greater than the GDP of the country. This makes it possible to have contribution holidays or the paying back of contributions. But who benefits from these arrangements varies according to the type of plan that one is enrolled in. When the plan has more resources than it needs to cover its present and future obligations, a politically unresolved issue has emerged: to whom do these assets belong? Can the employer simply claim these resources, or do they also belong to the employees?

'For the participants in occupational funds, the AOW retrenchment did not matter in financial terms, as the defined benefit target of 70% (AOW plus occupational pensions) did not change. Relative losses in basic pensions were compensated by the occupation tier, which increased in importance' (Haverland, 2000, p.15). So privatization, mandating and funding, the hallmarks of a market-oriented system of provision, worked in the

Dutch system to offset fluctuations in the generosity of the public provision. One can get a better sense of the relative size of the private and public tiers in Holland by examining their relative share of GDP. In 1998, the first pillar was 5.0 per cent of GDP, the second pillar was 4.7 per cent of GDP and the third pillar was 0.4 per cent of GDP. Thus the public and private pillars are about equal in size.

It works this way because the system of private sector obligations is based on the principle of solidarity. A 1996 survey showed that private pensions covered 91 per cent of the working population, compared to 85 per cent in the 1985 survey. It is not possible to achieve such high coverage rates without some element of compulsion. Compulsory membership prevents the firms from defecting from the contractually agreed upon plan. Joint representation in contractual bargaining is designed to dampen inter-firm rivalry and preserve the value of pension funds' replacement rates. The system of regulation preserves the principle of oversight (for example of pension portability) and the autonomy of pension funds to follow the rule of the prudent investor with minimum interference. Still there are what the Dutch call 'white spots', a reference to the 9 per cent of the population who are not covered by a private pension. About half of these 'white spots' refer to people who are excluded from pensions because they have low wages, or part-time or seasonal work: usually the kind of jobs women are more likely to have. The firms are trying to eliminate these 'white spots' on their own initiative because they want to avoid the government's introducing a mandatory system, like that in effect in Australia and Switzerland.

MANDATING AS A PATHWAY TO EXPAND PENSION COVERAGE IN THE PRIVATE SECTOR

Mandating plays a role in the retirement income system in nearly every country in the world. Because social security policy makers believe that many workers would not save enough for their own retirement in a purely voluntary system, government typically mandates a portion of the provision of retirement income through social security. In countries where the mandate refers to employer-provided occupational pensions in the second tier, with government social security benefits providing the first tier, mandated pensions generally play a different role than in countries where second tier pensions are voluntary. Mandated second tier pensions more clearly substitute for a portion, or all, of the earnings-related part of social security that is commonly found in other countries.

As well as mandating of employer-provided pensions, mandating can also take the form of mandating individual accounts. This approach has been used in Sweden, which has mandated funded individual accounts as well as a notional account system. The approach has also been used by a number of countries in Latin America, starting with Chile in 1981. Both Australia and Switzerland are commonly considered to mandate private pension coverage.

In analysing the mandating of pension coverage, we first consider what the term 'mandating' means. The simplest form of mandating would be that all employers are required to provide at least a minimum level of pension coverage for all their employees. An expanded form of mandating, which would provide more complete coverage, would require that all self-employed workers provide and contribute to a pension for themselves. An even further expanded form would mean that all non-workers, including the unemployed and people out of the labour force, within a certain age range would be required to contribute to a pension for themselves.

While mandating with full compliance would raise coverage of the population to which the mandate applies to 100 per cent, in reality compliance is never complete. The actual level of coverage depends on the extent of compliance with the mandate. This, in turn, depends on the views of the population concerning the fairness of the mandate; the incentives, such as tax preferences, for employers and employees complying with the mandate; and the enforcement effort of the government, including the penalties on employers and employees for non-compliance. Another limiting effect on the mandate, is that, typically, it does not apply to all workers as it excludes the self-employed and non-workers as well as employees with low wages or low hours.

Mandating earnings-related pensions through private sector provision or through government provision with a social security programme are alternative or substitute approaches. It is interesting to consider why a country would choose to mandate private pensions rather than mandating earnings-related pensions through social security. The reasons may be that a country mistrusts the power of government, it feels that the government is inefficient in providing pensions and the citizens of the country have a philosophical bias towards private sector provision of pensions. These reasons are balanced in the minds of the citizens against the costs and risks of providing pensions through private sector employers.

Australia

Occupational pensions in Australia were started in the 1800s, but did not provide much coverage until after the Second World War. Even by the 1970s, coverage was concentrated among larger employers. Uneven coverage was a factor in nationwide bargaining for pensions by the labour unions during the 1980s, which resulted in greatly increased coverage by the early 1990s. The establishment of industry-wide pensions facilitated the expansion of coverage, since small employers could provide a pension on a cost-efficient basis by participating in an industry-wide pension. The development of industry-wide pensions was largely the result of a powerful union movement that encouraged their development (Schulz, 2000). This pattern of development of industry-wide pensions negotiated by labour unions, leading to mandating of pensions, also occurred in France. A similar pattern leading to less than complete mandating also occurred in the Netherlands, as discussed earlier in this chapter.

The role of labour unions received legal backing in the *National Wage Case* decision of June 1986. In that decision, the Conciliation and Arbitration Commission made legally binding the agreements between employers and unions concerning employer contributions to pension funds. This decision strengthened the bargaining position of unions concerning pensions. Thus, in Australia, mandating was favoured by powerful labour unions, namely the Australian Council of Trade Unions, with the legal backing of the government in their negotiations.

The majority, but not all, of employees were covered by collective bargaining at the beginning of the 1990s. Because of political pressure from the Australian Council of Trade Unions to extend mandatory pension coverage to all employees, in 1992, the Australian government introduced the Superannuation Guarantee Charge that set a minimum rate of employer support for pensions for employees. The Australian Council of Trade Unions made the expansion of pension coverage a condition in their negotiations on wage restraint. Support also came from the insurance industry, which stood to benefit because it would manage the funds. The minimum level of contributions by employers began at 3–4 per cent of workers' earnings, depending on the size of the employer, and gradually rose over time, reaching 9 per cent in 2002.

Employees who earn less than 13 per cent of the earnings received by the average wage-earner are not required to contribute. This rule applies to about 10 per cent of the total workforce and this group consists mainly of women (ibid.). Also excluded are employees under 18 or over 70 years of age and the self-employed.

The Australian government does not have the constitutional authority to compel employers to contribute to a pension plan. It does, however, have the authority to tax. A penalty tax equal to the required contribution is levied on employers who do not contribute the minimum amount. This tax is not tax-deductible, whereas contributions to pensions are, providing a substantial incentive to most employers to contribute. Thus, in a semantic sense, it could be argued that Australia does not mandate pension funds but merely strongly encourages them through the tax system. In a practical sense, however, the encouragement is so strong that most observers considered it a mandate.

The plans resulting from the mandate in Australia are primarily defined contribution plans that are sponsored by employers. While Australian law does not require that defined contribution plans be the type provided, it is simpler for employers to comply with the law if they provide that type of plan.

Switzerland

Rather than resulting from pressure on the government by the unions, mandatory pensions in Switzerland were decided upon directly by Swiss voters in 1972 through a national referendum. At that time, the Swiss had a retirement income system where the social security system provided a low level of benefits for middle- and upper-income workers, while a voluntary private pension system was well developed, with a fairly high level of coverage of the workforce.

One explanation for the popular support for mandating among Swiss voters is that they favoured it as a way to prevent the government expanding the social security programme (Helbling, 1991). Also they may have favoured it as a means of preserving the role of private sector pension plans. The Labour Party of Switzerland favoured the government's nationalizing all employer-provided pension plans, but Swiss voters rejected that approach. Earlier, in 1968, Swiss voters had rejected the idea of compulsory pensions in a referendum that resulted from organizing by the Confederation of Christian Trade Unions. So the idea of mandating had been seriously discussed for several years before it was accepted. The referendum of 1972 was not implemented until 1985, however, because of delays due in part to disagreements as to the form of the mandated pensions.

The mandatory pension system is fully funded by employers and is privately managed. It aims, in combination with social security, to provide a replacement rate for middle-income workers of 60 per cent of earnings for single persons and 80 per cent for married couples.

Pension funds can be established as single employer plans or as various types of multi-employer plans. The multi-employer plans include plans through insurance companies, professional associations and plans set up by groups of employers. Roughly 90 per cent of all participants are in multi-employer plans (Queisser and Vittas, 2000). Small employers usually affiliate with insurance companies for the provision of pension benefits. Multi-employer plans play a major role in the mandated pension systems in Australia, Switzerland and France, as well as in the system of labour contracting in the Netherlands.

The mandatory pension system in Switzerland excludes a number of groups: the self-employed, the unemployed, those aged under 24, those working less than three months and those outside the labour force. Also workers earning below 40 per cent of the average wage are excluded from compulsory participation. Researchers have estimated that only three-quarters of workers are subject to compulsory participation (ibid.). Thus pensions are mandated for most, but not all, workers. The mandatory pension system does not provide universal coverage.

The mandated pensions are required to provide a minimum guaranteed rate of return of 4 per cent. Because of this, most employers maintain cash balance plans, providing a 4 per cent rate of return regardless of the underlying rate of return received by the pension fund.

The French model

In France, the contractual programmes are complementary schemes that are built on the basic first pillar of government social security. In the private sector, which contains about 68 per cent of the labour force, the complementary pillar is composed of contractual plans called ARRCO and AGIRC. ARRCO is a mandatory plan for private sector employees. Private sector managerial and professional employees are also covered by ARRCO. Up to 1999, ARRCO was a federation of plans with different features. Since 1999, it has been a single plan. This plan covers most private sector employees. ARRCO grew out of a labour agreement in 1962. This plan has been mandatory by law since 1972. It is co-managed by the social partners (trade unions and representatives of firms). So, in the French context, contractual arrangements need to be broadened to include co-management. The AGIRC plan was created in 1947 by an organization of managerial employees and their employers. It implemented a single system for all managers in the private sector. Both ARRCO and AGIRC are financed on a pay-as-you-go basis. In addition to these plans mandated by legislation, in France there are optional plans that are not mandated by legislation but are mandated by labour agreements (Auclair, 1999).

FURTHER ISSUES

While the pathways approach is useful for understanding pension policy, this approach requires further elaboration to more completely describe the complexity of pension systems. For example, some plans can have features of both add-ons and carve-outs: one of the three proposals of the President's Commission to Strengthen Social Security in the United States was for a plan that would have an add-on of 1 per cent of pay contributed to an individual account, combined with a carve-out of 2.5 per cent of pay contributed to the account, with that portion causing a reduction in contributions to social security.

A further complexity is that it can be difficult to distinguish between a mandatory add-on and a mandatory carve-out from social security, with the perspective depending on what is considered to be the starting point. For example, in Sweden the old social security system was ended and a new system was started. The new system contained a mandatory individual account. In the context of the new system, that account could be viewed as an add-on. However, the system to which it is added on receives a lower payroll tax rate contribution than does the old system, so, from the perspective of the old system, it could be considered to be a carve-out.

A further issue relates to mandates. It has been implicitly assumed that a mandate meant that employers were required to provide a plan, and/or that employees were required to participate in one, whether employer-provided or provided through a financial institution. A different approach to mandates is that employers would be required to provide a plan if the workers chose to contribute to it, but workers would not be required to contribute to the plan. Thus the mandate can be split as to whether it applies to the employer or the employee.

CONCLUSION

What factors affect which approach countries adopt? And, closely related to this question, why are employer-based pension programmes so popular in such different economic and political settings? Do these pathways, especially when they are funded, provide a framework for understanding the meaning of the idea that the welfare state is in transition?

The following stylized analysis goes some way to answering these questions. Three alternative assumptions about the role of the public system and the interplay between the public and private spheres provide the starting point for understanding how a country considers one or another of these pathways. The starting point is how the public pension system is conceived and designed. The design of the public system, including the level of benefits it provides, is a major influence on the pathway used to increase coverage by the private system. When the public system does not provide a substantial earnings-related benefit, a mandatory private system is more likely to develop, but other factors, such as the political views concerning free choice, also enter into the political process determining the pathway chosen. One perspective is that the public pension should provide the foundation for a pension system that should provide adequate income in retirement. The guiding principle is solidarity as expressed in a flat-rate benefit.

A second view is that the state should only provide a minimum foundation on which the private sector builds its edifice of employer-provided benefits. The third approach starts with the assumption that an integrated public and private system is the only viable foundation to design pensions. But exogenous factors, such as political regime shifts, economic recessions, unintended and unwanted side-effects, new ideas about the role of the state and partisan protest can interfere with this process of deliberation and introduce its own dynamics of policy change. As a result, during the last two decades we have witnessed the growing importance of employer-provided pensions. What follows from this observation is that a useful interpretation must somehow also take account of the meaning of the terms 'public' and 'private' and should focus, not only on historical events, but also on the dynamics of change.

A system based on solidarity derives its energy from a view that all residents should have universal access to public benefits, equal protection and equal burden. In the post-Second World War period, the UK and many continental countries designed legislation that would embody these governing principles in programmes conceived as folk pensions, or flat-rate contributions and flat-rate benefits. Of course, in practice these principles of solidarity were played out in a variety of different designs, and they changed over time as questions of cost and efficiency came to play larger roles. Within the last 40–50 years, however, these systems based on solidarity, and their many variations, were transformed, producing paradoxical results. The system of solidarity evolved towards its own negation, that is, towards both principles of equivalence between contributions and benefits and towards employer-provided pensions in the private sector and among public employees. For a variety of financial and other reasons, the struggle to achieve the elusive goal of adequate benefits proved difficult to sustain in the long run (van Gunsteren and Rein, 1985, p.132).

The Dutch experience is instructive because not only was the public flat-rate benefit raised, it was also transformed so that benefit should be pegged in relation to the minimum wage and, then, again when the minimum wage was conditionally indexed to economic growth. If the appropriate economic conditions prevailed, the minimum wage could grow and would provide a strong foundation, in combination with the private second tier pension, to ensure adequate and viable income in retirement. The government contributed financially to the basic pension so that benefits could be raised without a corresponding sharp increase in contributions. Public benefits in this era increased from a third of total public and private benefits to over half, but, in the 1980s, the pattern was reversed, as public benefits declined and the private occupational pension became increasingly central. Of course, the experience in the UK was even more dramatic, since it was never really able to go through an initial period of growth. Eligibility for benefits depended on continuous periods of contributions and was access- ible only to those above a minimum earnings level. As a result, the univer- sal ideal only covered 84 per cent of the population and benefit levels were lower than the means-tested welfare programme. A third of the aged found themselves dependent on means-tested welfare.

Not all countries turned to employer-provided private pensions to sup- plement the basic pension. The first wave of reforms was a turn to the public sector to provide a model of equivalence based on a variation of the insurance principle that called for broad equivalence between contributions and benefits. As early as 1959, Sweden created a public earnings-related social insurance programme that would eventually make the solidarity folk pension residual. But, over time, the earnings-related pay-as-you-go prin- ciple resulted in a new pension reform, in 1994–9, based on the principle of notional defined contributions and funded defined contribution pensions fashioned after a public programme of personal accounts which permitted individuals to invest in the private market, based on their own choice. In the meantime, Sweden had also created an extensive programme of employer- provided pensions based on contractual agreements. So solidarity evolved to public equivalence and to employer-provided pensions and, currently, to personal accounts. What we see is a system that has been continuously under change over the past 50 years.

In the second view, the starting assumption was based, not on solidarity as the principle of equal protection, equal burden and universal access, but the principle of minimum needs to be satisfied by a national means-tested programme that was both income and asset-tested. Australia is the proto- type of this second approach. In some ways, health care insurance makes this model clearer than it is in the area of pensions. This approach applied to health insurance says that the government should provide minimum care which individuals can supplement as they choose if they prefer different forms of elective surgery or better hotel services in hospitals. Access to sup- plementary services does not lead to a loss of basic care. In other words, self-reliance does not threaten access to the minimum benefit. Australia tried to resolve this tension between self-reliance and basic needs by cre- ating a very high asset test that still gave scope for self-reliance and a flow of income as the basis for the income test. By converting income to assets, the means-tested system is able to cover about 80 per cent of its aged pop- ulation on a minimum flat rate means test. The other way to avoid tension between self-reliance and need is to make the receipt of the public pension non-conditional. In other words, higher incomes and private pensions will not reduce the value of the public programme. A compromise can be made by setting a non-conditional free zone and then a zone above that where people lose half their benefit if they receive supplementary benefits.

These issues then lead us to our third hybrid model, which from the outset tries to integrate the public and private schemes. This can be done as the Dutch did it by agreeing on a replacement rate of, say, 70 per cent of past earnings. The public sector contributed a large share, in the 1960s and 1970s, but when the public budget came under stress the private sector contributed more. Such a system can become very complicated, depending on how public franchise and earnings are calculated. In the United States, the principle of integrated public and private pensions created a world where low-wage workers only received the public social security programme and higher-wage workers received both public and private pensions. But these different arrangements had the effect of stimulating the growth of private pensions, with the public providing the foundation on which to make the private system attractive. The hybrid system, however, can also create contracting out, as in the case of Britain, or contractual agreements, as is the case in the Netherlands and the Nordic countries.

We have tried to describe the process by which a country starts with a debate about what kind of public system it has while, in the meantime, a private system is already in place for historical reasons. In most situations in developed countries, a small private system and a well-developed civil servants programme exist before the public system is established. Then a country tries to work out the public pathway it has chosen in its political debate about pension reform. This debate may lead to one of three different approaches: solidarity, minimum means-tested needs, or a hybrid system based on integrating the public and private system. But the concrete ways that the public system is worked out, in practice over time, can make it attractive for the private system to expand and to enter as a player in a new public–private mix. It can do so, as it did in Britain, because the size of the private sector means it can insist politically on a share of the spoils and get its way by insisting that individuals can contract out of the public system into private pensions and then personal pensions. It can do so, as it did in the United States, where a national public pension system stimulated the growth of private pensions. It can do so for reasons that are independent of the situation in either sphere. For example, in Australia, in an inflationary period, contractual agreements led the unions to bargain for pension rights instead of wage increases. When the unions tried to further expand the system, the Arbitration Board complained that there was too much non-compliance. To get firms to expand their coverage, the state decided to ensure compliance by making the agreements mandatory. So unintended effects and exogenous events lead to changes

Table 9.2   Pathways to private pension coverage as percentage of the private sector labour force in selected OECD countries, and beneficiaries and benefit levels for those who have benefits from a supplementary pension

Type of programme	Country	Coverage rate	Beneficiaries	Benefit levels	Poverty rate age 65–9 (1994–5)
Voluntary with incentives	United States	46	46.7	32.1	16.8
	Canada	29	56.5	32.6	4.3
Opting out	Japan	39			—
	United Kingdom	29	77.2	31.9	6.5 (1991, 13.0)
Contractual agreements	Denmark	80	36.2	36.3	3.0
	Sweden	90	87.3	16.7	0.8
	Germany	40	29.3	32.5	6.4
	Finland	90	98.7	65.3	3.0
	Norway	—	63.3	21.6	5.1 (1986, 11.0)
Mandatory	Australia	85	18.4	51.7	12.5 (1985, 19.2)
	Switzerland	92	59.8	32.8	3.6 (1982, 14.6)
	Netherlands	66	75.4	34.7	6.6 (1991, 2.3)

Sources: Coverage: Dailey and Turner (1992); Schulz (2000); Stanton and Whiteford (2002); poverty rates, beneficiaries and benefit level computed from LIS data, for 1994–5, computed by Christina Behrendt, March, 2000.

that shape the pathways chosen and redefine the initial images of the public and private mix.

The second issue we want briefly to discuss is the consequences of choosing one of the different pathways for reducing a country's poverty rate. Tables 9.2 and 9.3 set out information about OECD countries that can help to answer this question. The data in Table 9.2 do not imply a causal relation between pathway selection and poverty rates, but are a preliminary exploration of a complicated and important question. The countries shown are those with 40 per cent or more coverage in an employer-related pension system. The remaining OECD countries with low occupational pension coverage are not included. The data in Table 9.3 provide indication of the generosity of pension systems. The most striking conclusion that emerges from an examination of the data is the variations in poverty rates within a pathway. Consider the difference in the poverty rates within the voluntary and mandatory pathways. The USA has a poverty rate of almost 17 per

Table 9.3   Ratio of gross income from public pensions and supplementary pensions of couples 65–9 to the gross earnings of prime age couples

Country	Ratio of public pension gross income age 65–9 to gross earnings, age 15–54	Ratio of supplementary pension gross income age 65–9 to gross earnings, age 15–54	Gross income ratio of couples 65–9/15–54
Australia	34.2	24.8	0.50
Canada	37.6	27.4	0.70
Denmark	44.0	29.4	0.72
Finland	19.1	73.5	0.83
Germany	44.1	18.7	0.55
Holland	37.5	25.8	0.63
Norway	44.3	21.9	0.82
Sweden	57.3	17.3	0.83
Switzerland	43.3	32.7	0.85
UK	23.9	20.5	0.58
USA	37.7	24.1	0.44

cent, a figure much lower than the rates in 1979, but still the highest rate of any of the countries. By contrast, Canada, with a very similar profile of coverage, beneficiaries and benefit levels, has a poverty level of only 4.3 per cent, substantially lower than the 17 per cent level in 1981. So countries with a similar private sector profile can reduce their poverty levels and end up being very different. It seems clear that it is not the voluntary pathway by itself that determines a country's poverty level.

But if we turn to the mandatory pathway in Switzerland, the sharp decline in Swiss poverty rates is attributable to the pathway chosen. In the Netherlands this is even more striking, where the poverty rates are comparatively low, but have still shown modest increases in recent years. Australia is especially striking with declining poverty rates since the introduction of mandatory pension coverage in 1992. The British pathway of opting out is full of surprises, because public sector pension coverage and levels are in decline and yet there is evidence that the poverty rate has halved in a very short period of time. The decline is so sharp that one is more likely to conclude that there must have been a change in the measurement parameters. Almost uniformly, countries with strong contractual agreements also have the lowest poverty rates.

One general conclusion, suggested by the data in Table 9.2, is that countries with the highest coverage and benefit level also have the lowest poverty rates. Of course, the private sector pensions are concentrated in the top 60 per cent of the income distribution, but in some countries, such as Holland and Switzerland, private pensions play a surprisingly big part in the bottom 40 per cent of the distribution, suggesting that in some situations the private sector can play an active role in poverty reduction.

In conclusion, we feel that the four pathways approach is a useful analytical approach for understanding the policy options for extending pension coverage. It provides a framework for organizing thinking about the many different approaches to providing supplementary retirement income. It is a useful framework for analysing the lessons concerning pension coverage policy from other countries. The approach recognizes the diversity in policies across countries. It recognizes the different types of relationship of supplementary plans to social security, it recognizes the role of government mandates and it recognizes the role of labour unions in some countries.

NOTE

The opinions expressed here do not represent those of AARP.

REFERENCES

Auclair, André (1999), 'France', in David Callund and Melvin Nightingale (eds), *International Benefits Yearbook 1999*, London: Sweet & Maxwell, pp.110–29.
Blake, David (2000), 'The United Kingdom: Examining the Switch from Low Public Pensions to High-Cost Private Pensions', paper presented at the NBER conference, March, revised May.
Clark, Gordon L. (2000), 'The Dutch Model of Sector-wide Supplementary Pension Fund Governance, Finance, and European Competition Policy', University of Oxford, 3 March.
Conklin, David W. (1990), 'Pension Policy Reforms in Canada', in John Turner and Lorna Dailey (eds), *Pension Policy: An International Perspective*, Washington, DC: USGPO.
Dailey, Lorna M. and Turner, John A. (1992), 'U.S. Private Pensions in World Perspective, 1970–89', in John A. Turner and Daniel J. Beller (eds), *Trends in Pensions 1992*, Washington, DC: US Government Printing Office, pp.11–34.
The Danish Ministry of Foreign Affairs (2000), *A Sustainable Pension System*, June.
Gruber, Jonathon and Wise, David (2000), 'Different Approaches to Pension Reform from an Economic Point of View', paper prepared for an NBER–Kiel conference in March, Berlin.
van Gunsteren, Herman and Rein, Martin (1985), 'The Dialectic of Public and Private Pensions', *Journal of Social Policy*, 14 (2).
Hacker, Jacob (2000), 'Boundary Wars: The Political Struggle over Public and Private Social Benefits in the United States', unpublished dissertation, Yale University, October.
Hanna, Leslie (1986), *Inventing Retirement: The Development of Occupational Pensions in Britain*, Cambridge: Cambridge University Press.

Haverland, Michale (2000), 'Another Dutch Miracle? Dutch and German Pension Trajectories Compared', paper presented at the Annual Meeting of the Dutch Political Association.

Helbling, Carl (1991), *Les Institutions de Prévoyance et la LPP*, Berne: Haupt.

Latimer, Murray W. (1932), *Industrial Pension Systems in the United States and Canada*, New York: Industrial Relations Counselors, Inc.

Liu, Lillian (1999), 'Public Pension Reform in Japan', *Social Security Bulletin*, 62 (1).

Myles, John and Quadagno, Jill (1994), 'The Politics of Income Security for the Elderly in North America: Founding Cleavages and Unresolved Conflicts', in Theodore R. Marmor, Timothy M. Smeeding and Vernon L. Greene (eds), *Economic Security and Intergenerational Justice: A Look at North America*, Washington, DC: The Urban Institute Press.

National Institute of Population and Social Security Research (2000), 'Social Security in Japan', March.

National Life Insurance Research Institute (2000), 'An Overview of Japan's Pension System', March.

Pesando, James and Turner, John (2001), 'Risk in Pension Plans', in John Turner (ed.), *Pay at Risk: Compensation Risk for Canadian and U.S. Workers*, Kalamazoo, MI: Upjohn Institute.

Queisser, Monika and Vittas, Dimitri (2000), 'The Swiss Multi-Pillar Pension System: Triumph of Common Sense?', Development Research Group, The World Bank, January.

Reagan, Patricia and Turner, John (2000), 'Did the Decline in Marginal Tax Rates During the 1980s Reduce Pension Coverage?', in Steven Woodbury and William Alpert (eds), *Employee Benefits, Labor Costs, and Labor Markets in Canada and the United States*, Kalamazoo, MI: Upjohn Institute.

Schulz, James H. (2000), 'Older Women and Private Pensions in Australia', The National Center on Women and Aging, Heller School, Brandeis University, Waltham, Massachusetts.

Seendergaard, Jorgen (2001), Personal correspondence, Director General of the Danish National Institute of Social Research, 17 January.

Thane, Pat (2000), *Old Age: In English History Past Experience and Present Issues*, Oxford: Oxford University Press.

Turner, John and Watanabe, Noriyasu (1995), *Pension Policy in Industrialized Countries*, Kalamazoo, MI: Upjohn Institute.

Verbon, Harie (1988), *The Evolution of Public Pension Schemes*, Berlin: Springer-Verlag.

Wakabayashi, Midori (2001), 'Retirement Saving in Japan', *Journal of Japanese and International Economics*, January.

Whiteford, Peter and Stanton, David (2002), 'Targeting, Adequacy and Incentives: Assessing the Australian System of Retirement Incomes', presented at the 9th International Research Seminar on Issues in Social Security, seminar on Pension Reform, Sigtuna, Sweden.

Williamson, Samuel H. (1992), 'U.S. and Canadian Pensions before 1930: A Historical Perspective', in John A. Turner and Daniel J. Beller (eds), *Trends in Pensions 1992*, Washington, DC: US Government Printing Office.

World Bank (1994), *Averting the Old Age Crisis: Policies to Protect the Old and Promote Growth*, Oxford: Oxford University Press.

10. Whose money is it anyhow? Governance and social investment in collective investment funds

R. Kent Weaver

Over the past two decades, an aging population and budgetary stress have led to substantial changes in public pension systems throughout the world.[1] Many countries initially responded to pension funding crises with incremental reforms, including retrenchment of existing pension commitments (for example, lowering replacement rates and increasing retirement ages in defined benefit systems) and by raising payroll taxes or increasing commitment of general tax revenues to pay pensions.

A number of countries have also engaged in a more fundamental restructuring of their pension systems, both to deal with current problems in their public pension systems and to prepare for the coming demographic shock of the baby boom retirement. The reform that has received the most attention is a shift in some countries towards a pension system (or one tier in a multi-tier pension system) of compulsory, universal advanced funded 'defined contribution' individual accounts in which eventual retirement benefits are linked to an individual's contributions over his/her working life and the accrued earnings on those contributions.

A number of countries have also made changes in their defined benefit pensions, moving away from traditional pay-as-you-go financing practices towards building up collective investment 'reserve' or 'buffer' funds (Iglesias and Palacios, 2000; Palacios, 2000; Jacobs, 2002). Some of those countries, including Canada, New Zealand and Sweden, have also moved towards investing those surpluses in a broader array of instruments rather than the traditional low-return, low-risk lending to governments and (in some countries) housing authorities. Collective investment of social security trust funds in a broader range of securities was also proposed in the United States by President Clinton, but it has been strongly opposed by President George W. Bush and Federal Reserve Board Chairman Alan Greenspan, and seems unlikely to move forward while a Republican administration is in office.

Finally, some countries have changed the governance of tax-privileged pension savings to provide increased incentives for private retirement savings, despite very mixed evidence about whether such incentives are effective in increasing overall savings rates.

These seemingly disparate responses to the pension funding crisis in fact raise a common set of issues about the public/private divide in governance of such funds. Should their purpose be solely to maximize returns for their (individual or collective) beneficiaries, or should they serve 'public' ends as well? Should they, for example, stress domestic investment that may increase jobs within their home country, or should they spread investment risks across a range of global investments? Should they consider social and environmental criteria in investments – for example, by forgoing investments in companies that produce weapons or tobacco, or countries that have poor pollution or human rights records? And if they should pursue public objectives, what ends should they serve, and who should decide what those ends are? How should these investment funds be protected from the potential that groups within their societies will in fact use ostensibly 'public' mandates to pursue their own political objectives or economic interests?

These questions have been posed in particular for collective investment funds in partially-funded defined benefit pension systems. Critics of proposals to increase use, and broaden the investment range, of collective investment 'buffer' funds argue that decisions will inevitably become politicized (see Tamagno, 2001); rather than maximization of fund value being sought, funds will be used to bail out failing industries, squandering workers' contributions. Governments may also force 'buffer' funds to loan to government at below market rates, lowering returns available for lower pension payouts. Rather than spreading risks across all investment opportunities, funds will be forced to invest domestically, which may expose them to excessive country-specific risks of poor economic performance, especially in very small economies. And funds are likely to become a battleground between forces on the left, who may favour requirements for social and environmental investment criteria and shareholder activism in corporate governance issues, while political conservatives posit conflicting priorities. Collectively, these 'political risks' of suboptimal returns are used by critics of collective 'buffer' funds to argue for pre-funding of future pension liabilities through individual accounts rather than collective funds.

A recent World Bank study by Iglesias and Palacios (2000) suggests that publicly managed pension funds are likely to produce below-market returns on investment, and that these political risks are likely to be especially severe in countries with overall governance problems. But individual accounts have potential shortcomings of their own, such as potentially very high administrative costs, and uneven financial market and annuitization returns across cohorts, that raise concerns about them as well. And the costs of financing a transition to a fully-funded system of individual accounts are seen by politicians in most democratic countries as ranging between daunting and impossible. Broadening the range of investments and increasing the returns of collective buffer funds (especially where they are already in place), on the other hand, is seen by many politicians as the political equivalent of a free lunch – a way to meet existing expectations about future pension commitments without resorting to benefit and eligibility cuts or contribution increases.

Iglesias and Palacios note (ibid., p.7), moreover, that public management of pension funds should be regarded as a continuum rather than as an 'all or nothing' proposition. Countries vary in the investment criteria they use for investments, in the degree to which they are involved in the management of public funds, and in the degree to which management functions are contracted out to private managers. Palacios (2002) has identified a number of practices that can improve the returns on assets in collective pension reserve funds by reducing political risks. These practices include governance procedures that limit the role of politicians; an independent board with expertise in finance; outsourcing of many functions; clear, written investment policies that 'make explicit the Board's position on shareholder activism, social investment and economically targeted investments' (ibid., p.10) and focus on returns to plan members as their overriding objective; effective financial reporting with regular comparison against 'objective benchmarks' (such as stock index performance); and regular reporting to the public on investment returns, costs and compliance with governing regulations.

This chapter examines how some OECD countries have addressed the 'public/private divide' in collective investment 'buffer' funds, drawing on the experience of Canada, Sweden and New Zealand, as well as the Swedish experience with a 'default fund' (for those who do not make an active fund choice) in the individual account defined contribution tier of its public system. While most of these programmes are quite new, they nevertheless provide some interesting and useful lessons about the potentials and pitfalls of such funds.

CANADA AND QUEBEC

Canada operates a multi-tier public pension system, including a quasi-universal (clawed back for upper-income recipients) Old Age Security programme, and an income-tested tier made up of the Guaranteed Income Supplement and an allowance for their spouses and common law partners aged 60 and above. Both of these tiers are financed out of general revenues.

There is also a third, earnings-related tier financed through payroll taxes. But because this third tier is within provincial jurisdiction, provinces can opt out to operate their own programme. One province, Quebec, has done so since the inception of the programme in the 1960s. The result is an earnings-related Canada Pension Plan (CPP) operated outside Quebec and a parallel Quebec Pension Plan (QPP) that are integrated in almost all of their benefit and contribution provisions.

Both the CPP and QPP have had collective investment funds since their inception, but their investment practices have been very different. Until recently, CPP surpluses were loaned out to provincial governments at the federal government's borrowing rate, which was generally lower than their own. Thus, unlike what happens in many other countries, it was provincial governments rather than the federal government that benefited from their ability to borrow at below-market rates. The Quebec Pension Plan has always invested in a broader range of financial instruments, including equities and real estate.

In the 1990s, a funding crisis in the CPP and QPP led to a broad consensus on the need to raise revenues and returns in order to address anticipated long-term funding shortfalls. Payroll tax rates were raised dramatically, from a total of 5.6 per cent (employers and employees each paying half) in 1996 to 9.9 per cent by 2003. For the CPP, provinces were required to pay eventually higher rates on borrowings from the CPP. More importantly, current CPP surpluses generated by higher payroll taxes are being invested in a broader range of securities, including equities, with these investments managed by an independent board.

This change in investment practices moves the CPP closer to the practices of the QPP, which has long invested in a diverse set of assets through the Caisse de dépôt et placement du Québec (CDP), a unique Quebec institution that not only invests QPP funds, but also invests on behalf of Quebec public sector employee pension funds, public insurance funds, agricultural marketing boards and other Quebec financial institutions. Other public sector pension funds, including the huge Ontario Municipal Employees Retirement System (OMERS) and Ontario Teachers' Pension Plan are also major players on Canadian equities and real estate markets.

Although the Caisse served as a model for the new Canada Pension Plan Investment Board (CPPIB) in some ways, the two organizations are very different in their mandate, size and relationship to their sponsoring governments. Indeed, the CDP and the CPPIB represent strikingly different models for a pension plan investment fund. Perhaps the most obvious difference between the two entities is the greater size and broader range of clients served by the Caisse. While the CPPIB invests only for the CPP, the QPP is only the second largest depositor for the Caisse, behind Quebec's provincial employee pension fund. With a total of $133 billion (Cdn) in assets under management at the end of 2001, the Caisse has the largest portfolio of Canadian equities and the largest real estate portfolio in Canada. It is also the largest provider of private market and venture capital in Canada. The CPPIB, by contrast, managed only $17 billion (Cdn) in equity and real estate assets as of September 2002, with the federal Department of Finance holding another $38.4 billion in fixed-income securities.

The Caisse and CPPIB also differ greatly in their governmental links. The Caisse has, since its founding in 1966, been closely linked to the Quebec government. Indeed, it is the linchpin of what has been called 'Quebec, Inc.', a close alliance of the Quebec government and Quebec francophone business leaders (Arbour, 1993). These links are reflected in its governance procedures: all members of the Caisse's board of directors, including the chairman, who also serves as CEO, are appointed by the Quebec government. The head of the Régie des rentes du Québec, the agency that administers the QPP, serves as vice chair of the board. Of the nine additional members of the board, two slots are reserved for heads of Quebec government agencies or officers of the government, one from public employee unions, and one from the directors of cooperative associations. To protect the chairman of the Caisse from political interference, he or she is appointed for a term of ten years and removable only by a vote of the Quebec National Assembly, while other board members serve three-year terms. In practice, Caisse CEOs have generally had close ties to the provincial governing party (Authier, 1994; Dougherty, 2002). Indeed, the joint chair/CEO system was installed in 1995 by the new Parti Québécois government, replacing a system of a separate board chair and president both responsible to the National Assembly that was put in place by the previous Liberal government. The change coincided with the ouster of a Caisse chair and president with close ties to the Quebec Liberal Party.

In 2002, the Caisse's management proposed governance changes that would have given the Caisse's board a majority of independent directors, split the roles of chairman and CEO and given the Caisse's board rather than the Quebec government the lead role in appointing the Caisse's CEO. However, these recommendations were rejected by the Quebec government (Caisse de dépot, 2002; see also Gibbens, 2002). The CEO of the Caisse stepped down almost immediately, prompting speculation that the Parti Québécois provincial government, facing an uphill re-election battle in little more than a year, wanted to put in place a new chief executive for a new ten-year term who would be sympathetic to its views even after it had lost office (DeCloet, 2002).

Governance procedures for the CPPIB are very different. The legislation establishing the Board set up a complicated appointment procedure for CPPIB's board of directors that gives final responsibility to the federal Minister of Finance and the federal Cabinet, but utilizes a federal–provincial nominating committee in which the federal government nominates the chair and each participating province nominates one member. The CPP Investment Board Act requires that the composition of the board reflect 'the desirability of having directors who are representative of the various regions of Canada and having on the board of directors a sufficient number of directors with proven financial ability or relevant work experience such that the Board will be able to effectively achieve its objects' (*Revised Statutes of Canada*, 1997, c.40; see also Tamagno, 2001; Sarney and Preneta, 2001–2). Staggered terms of three years for the board give it some additional protection from government interference. In contrast to the Caisse, current members of the federal and provincial legislatures and employees of both levels of government are barred from membership on the board. Unlike Sweden and some other countries with collective investment funds, the CPPIB does not have reserved seats for 'social partners' (business and labour). In the short history of the CPPIB, appointees to the board have generally had financial sector experience rather than political or governmental experience, although one board member is a former member of Parliament who had responsibility for federal–provincial pension policy consultations in the period leading up to the 1997 CPP reform. The board chooses the CPPIB's president, who serves as CEO (government has no role in the selection). John McNaughton, the only person to hold the post so far, is the non-political, recently retired head of a major Canadian investment firm.

Staff size and outsourcing philosophy are two additional points of contrast between the Caisse and CPPIB. The Caisse performs most of its analysis and portfolio management functions in-house, and had a staff at the end of 2001 of more than 500, not including its huge real estate arm. The staff of CPPIB, on the other hand, is small – under 30 people – and is expected to remain so. The CPP board and senior management have decided that the organization should operate as a 'virtual corporation', relying heavily on outside managers and investment partners to handle most portfolio management.

Both the Caisse and the CPPIB are subject to limits on the percentage of non-Canadian assets that they can hold. These limits mirror those for Registered Retirement Savings Plans, a rough equivalent to American 401(k) plans, which until recently were set at 20 per cent of total assets. When the RRSP limit on foreign assets was raised to 25 per cent in 2000 and 30 per cent in 2001, the Caisse and CPPIB levels were raised as well. But the Caisse and the CPPIB differ strongly in their investment mandates and practices. From the outset, the Caisse has had a dual mandate: producing a strong return for investors and promoting the economic development of Quebec. Indeed, as one analyst put it, the Caisse was conceived in part as a mechanism to use 'the collective savings of Quebec citizens . . . to . . . reduce the political influence of the anglophone financial establishment in Quebec' (Brooks, 1987, p.320). Unlike the CPP, the QPP has through the Caisse invested in equities since its inception, sometimes quite aggressively. It has, for example, bought large stakes in companies such as the forest products company Domtar, which has large Quebec operations. In some cases, it has coordinated its purchases with a Quebec government economic development agency, the Société générale de financement du Québec (SGF). The Caisse's governing statute explicitly restricts its holding more than 30 per cent of the common shares of any enterprise except in situations such as start-ups, a need to ensure continuity of operations during market turnarounds, corporate reorganizations and lead-ups to a public issue. Normally, investments over the 30 per cent limit are limited to five years, but the Caisse's investment policy allows for exceptions (Caisse de dépôt et placement du Québec, no date).

In recent years, the Caisse has been involved in several takeovers that have sparked widespread criticism, and produced major losses. In the late 1980s, it bankrolled an effort to keep the Quebec grocery firm Steinberg's in Quebec hands – a bid that eventually ended up with the collapse of Steinberg's and major losses by the Caisse (Arbour, 1993, pp.46–55). In 2001, the Caisse teamed up with the Quebecor media group to block a merger between the Quebec-based Le Groupe Videotron Ltee. cable television company and the Ontario-based Rogers Communications cable firm. The deal kept Videotron in Quebec hands but left Quebecor with an unsustainable debt load and the Caisse with a 45 per cent stake in Quebecor's media subsidiary – and a write-off of almost a billion dollars. However, the Caisse has not had to endure substantial controversy over environmental or other social policy investment criteria.

Overall, the Caisse earned a 9.34 average return in the ten-year period ending in 2001, despite a −4.99 return in the final year of this period. This was far better than the CPP, which had invested exclusively in bonds for most of that period. But critics note that the Caisse's return was well below the best private plans – the Ontario Teachers' Pension Plan returned 11.6 annually over the same period – and attribute the difference to politically motivated investments and an overconcentration of investments in Quebec.

In setting up the Canada Pension Plan Investment Board, the Caisse's aggressive investment practices and economic development mandate served as both a positive and a negative example. The CPPIB is supposed to achieve a 'maximum rate of return, without undue risk of loss', but the

CPPIB's mandate does not include additional industrial policy or social policy objectives. Many features of the CPPIB governance structures were set precisely to prevent movement away from an exclusive focus on maximizing returns with reasonable risk.

To diversify the overall portfolio of the CPP (initially composed entirely of provincial bonds) the CPPIB from the outset decided that it would invest all of the funds transferred to it in equities. The CPPIB does have important limitations on its investment allocations, however. As noted above, it is subject to a 30 per cent limit on foreign assets. It is also prohibited from holding, directly or indirectly, more than 30 per cent of the voting shares of any company. Other restrictions on the board are intended to limit its exposure both to particular types of investments (such as real estate and natural resources) and in particular firms or projects. Section 11 of the board's investment regulations limit it to having no more than 10 per cent of its assets in the securities of any group of affiliated persons or organizations. In addition, CPPIB cannot have more than 5 per cent of its assets in any single 'real property or Canadian resource property', hold more than 15 per cent of its assets in all Canadian resource properties, or more than a total of 25 per cent of its assets in all real property and Canadian resource properties. The CPPIB's authorizing legislation also requires the consent of two-thirds of provinces participating in the CPP, with a population of at least two-thirds of the total population of participating provinces, to consent to any change in the board's investment regulations. Thus it is unlikely that any plausible combination of future governments would be able to shift CPPIB's focus towards industrial or social policy objectives.

The CPPIB has been given both more tasks and more freedom over its relatively short life-span. Initially, it was required to manage all of its Canadian equities portfolio passively by 'substantially replicating' the Toronto Stock Exchange (TSE) 300. The requirement for passive investing was later reduced to half of the Canadian equities portfolio and eliminated entirely in the autumn of 2001. In the summer of 2002, the government announced its intention to hand over management of CPP's bond portfolio to the Investment Board as well.

Saying that domestic investment standards have been relatively depoliticized does not mean that they have been problem-free, however. Implementing these standards in the relatively small Canadian equities market has created problems. The original mandate of the CPPIB to invest 80 per cent of its funds passively in Canadian equities quickly came into conflict with its mandate to limit exposure to one firm: at the height of the telecommunications boom at the turn of the new millennium, Northern Telecom was valued at more than one-third of the total value of the TSE 300 index. Late in 2000, the CPPIB utilized its newly granted authority to

invest more actively to begin using a 'TSE 299' to limit its financial exposure to Northern Telecom. This allowed it to reduce its exposure to
Northern Telecom to about 4 per cent of its equity portfolio at the end of
the 2000–2001 fiscal year – and reduce its equity losses by about $535
million in that year and $121 million in the following year over what would
have otherwise occurred if it had remained overconcentrated in Northern
Telecom. The CPPIB reverted to index investing in the third quarter of its
2001–2002 fiscal year when Nortel no longer dominated the index (CPPIB,
2001, p.5; 2002a, p.14). More generally, the CPPIB has expressed concern
that relatively large (by Canadian standards) inflows of $6 to $8 billion per
annum expected from CPP payroll taxes over the next few years could contribute to a bidding up of Canadian equity prices as well as inadequate
diversification of assets – betting too much on the performance of the
Canadian economy – under current investment rules (CPPIB, 2002a, p.7).

At the end of September 2002, just under 30 per cent of all CPP assets
were invested in public and private equity – primarily the former. The
CPPIB has recently begun to implement a policy to invest actively rather
than passively up to half of its Canadian equity assets, while keeping portfolio management costs low. Its most recent Investment Statement plans a
continued emphasis on public equities, with between 75 and 100 per cent of
total assets to be held in these assets, with between 45 per cent and 75 per
cent of the total portfolio in Canadian equities, 5 per cent and 25 per cent
in US equities and 5 per cent and 25 per cent in public equities from other
countries (CPPIB, 2002c, p.8)

The CPPIB has also begun working in partnership with merchant banks
and other pension funds to take advantage of venture capital opportunities
while spreading risks and minimizing its exposure to political flak by taking
minority stakes in funds managed by other parties. By the end of the 2002
fiscal year, 3.2 per cent of CPPIB's assets were invested in these vehicles,
and the board has declared its intention to invest up to 10 per cent of total
CPP assets in private equity, with another 5 per cent in real estate, natural
resource development projects and other private markets assets (CPPIB,
2002a, p.9; 2002c, p.8). While there are no legal or regulatory requirements
that CPPIB's private market investments be skewed towards Canada, the
firm's vice-president for private market investments has stated that CPPIB
is 'making a special effort to find the best opportunities at home before ven-
turing too far abroad'.[2]

The CPPIB has also taken a very cautious stand on social and environmental investment criteria. In March 2002, the board adopted a Social
Investing Policy statement that argued that (1) its 'statutory mandate and
fiduciary duty are based exclusively on investment considerations', (2)
responsible corporate behaviour in fact usually contributes positively to

investment returns in the long run, and (3) the religious, ethical, social and other views of Canadians are so diverse that they could not possibly be reflected in the board's investment decisions. Therefore, although the board would generally 'support corporate policies and practices that would result in the disclosure of information that could assist investors in assessing whether corporate behavior was contributing to or detracting from long-term investment returns', it would not use non-investment criteria to screen in or out any investments. Instead, it would consider for investments 'the securities of any issuer engaged in a business that is lawful in Canada' and 'the securities of issuers in any country with which Canada maintains normal financial trade and investment relations' (CPPIB, 2002d).

In the absence of screening in or out specific investments, CPPIB's other major mechanism for expressing social or environmental concerns relates to voting its shares. Once again, CPPIB has taken a largely passive approach, delegating its voting rights to external fund managers in most situations.

The CPPIB's investment performance has reflected the roller-coaster ride of equity prices in recent years. In the board's first few years of operation, CPPIB enjoyed very strong returns, followed by a disastrous 2000–2001 fiscal year, in which the fund lost $845 million on investments (−9.4 per cent return), and a modest gain in 2001–2002 (+3.4 per cent return). Overall, the CPPIB has lost money on its investments since its inception, because the inflow of funds as CPP payroll taxes rose meant that many more funds were at risk in the last few years of operations than in earlier years. Although CPPIB has beaten its domestic and foreign equity portfolio benchmarks in recent years, poor equity markets have caused it to fall short in both 2000 and 2001 of the actuarial target assumptions used by the Canadian government in projecting the long-term viability of the Canada Pension Plan (CPPIB, 2002a, p.15).

SWEDEN

Sweden has had collective investment funds as part of its contributory earnings-related pension system since that system was created in the late 1950s. The 'buffer funds' were intended in part to compensate for an anticipated decline in personal savings as Swedes came to expect a larger state pension. The buffer funds were relatively small, however, and most of the funds were loaned out to government and housing authorities (see Pontusson, 1994).

Sweden expanded the role played by the buffer funds as part of a comprehensive pension reform debated through most of the 1990s and enacted in stages from 1994 to 1998. The pension reform created a new 'premium

The experience of mature welfare states

pension tier' of individual accounts, and converted the defined benefit flat rate and supplemental earnings-related pensions into a dramatically restructured 'notional defined contribution' (NDC) earnings-related pension tier. The higher the return that the buffer funds offer, the more likely it is that the new NDC 'income pension' will be able to meet its planned funding commitments without triggering benefit cuts through a new 'automatic balancing mechanism.' (see Settergren, 2001; Palmer, 2002).

The current fund system was created by a complicated shuffling of assets held by the old buffer funds and the creation of four new bodies, collectively known as the First to Fourth Swedish National Pension Funds, or First to Fourth AP Funds for short. Another existing fund, the Sixth AP Fund, which was set up primarily to provide funding for unlisted companies, is much smaller. It was left largely untouched by the reforms and will not receive new funds on an annual basis like the others. There is no Fifth AP fund under the current system. The four main buffer funds received initial funding of more than 150 billion kronor, or 15 billion US dollars. An additional, Seventh AP Fund was created to serve as the repository for the funds of those who do not make an active choice under the individual accounts tier of the pension system.

The First to Fourth AP funds were given roughly equivalent portfolios at the outset that reflected the old ATP funds' heavy reliance on government securities. They were also given a complicated set of mandates and restrictions on investment practices. Overall they were that:

> The AP Funds should manage their assets to achieve the greatest possible benefit in safeguarding the income-related pension system. Their allocation of assets should be based on an analysis of the pension system's liabilities. The goal should be to maximize long-term return on capital in relation to investment risk. The funds should carry out their asset management with appropriate diversification of risk. The overall risk level in their asset management should be low. Industrial policy or other economic concerns must not be involved. The funds should take ethical and environmental considerations into account without relinquishing the overall goal of a high return on capital (Sweden, 2000).

While this mandate is relatively clear in some respects – a ban on industrial policy considerations in particular – it is contradictory on others. The fund was supposed to take a low-risk strategy, for example, but it was also supposed to keep in mind its pension liabilities, and a strategy that focused primarily on risk minimization would probably not be able to meet those liabilities. The wording on ethical and environmental investment criteria suggests that maximizing return 'should not be relinquished' as a goal but that it should be tempered to some undefined extent. The legislation also contained a complex array of investment restrictions, including the following requirements:

- at least 30 per cent of each fund's assets must be in low-risk interest-bearing securities;
- no more than 10 per cent of any funds assets 'may be exposed to a single issuer or group of issuers';
- no individual fund may hold more than 10 per cent of the voting shares of any listed company;
- at least 10 per cent of each fund's money must be managed externally by January 2002;
- no more than 5 per cent of assets of any fund can be held in unlisted securities, and any such investments should be made indirectly; and
- no fund may hold equity holdings in Swedish companies greater than 2 per cent of the capitalization of the Stockholm stock exchange.

There were no direct requirements that a minimum share of investments be in Swedish assets (which could have been highly problematic given Sweden's EU membership) but no more than 40 per cent of assets were supposed to be exposed to currency risk. This would allow the funds to use currency hedges to invest a greater share of their funds outside Sweden.

The governance arrangements for the funds added another layer of complexity to the system. Government is not allowed to issue directives to the firms, but employer and employee interests are represented directly on funds' boards, nominating two representatives apiece to each fund's nine-member board. Moreover, board members serve only one-year terms, so that government can presumably replace an uncooperative board in relatively short order if it chooses to do so.

The new buffer fund system is still very new – funds were transferred only at the beginning of 2001, with each of AP Funds 1 to 4 receiving identical portfolios of assets of about $134 billion kronor (roughly $US14 billion), split between 69 per cent in bonds and 31 per cent in equities. But some patterns are already emerging, and are evident in Table 10.1. First, each of AP Funds 1 to 4 has moved rapidly to change its asset mix to invest much more heavily in equities. By the end of 2001, all four funds had a majority of their funds in equities, ranging from 51.5 per cent for AP3 to 63.3 per cent for AP4. The four funds also differ in the degree to which they hold Swedish equities, with a range of between 12 and 24 per cent of total assets.

A second area of difference includes their attitudes towards internal versus external portfolio management and internal versus external management. The First AP Fund has set a goal of managing the bulk of its portfolio both actively and internally, for example, while the Second AP Fund has adopted a near-term strategy of relying almost entirely on external management. These differences reflect changes in the two organizations' histories – AP1 inherited much of the staff of the old buffer funds in

The experience of mature welfare states

Table 10.1   Characteristics of Swedish buffer funds

	First	Second	Third	Fourth	Sixth
Asset allocation as of 31/12/01					
Equities	59	58	51.5	63.3	NA
Swedish equities	12	21	17.9	24.3	NA
Global equities	47	38	33.6	39.0	NA
Fixed income	37	37	45.6	33.9	NA
Swedish fixed income	12	NA	17.5	NA	NA
Global fixed income	17	NA	20.9	NA	NA
Index-linked bonds	8	NA	9.2	0	NA
Real estate	3	3	2.9	2.9	NA
Cash	1	1	0		NA
Return on total assets, 2001	−5.6	−3.7	−4.4	−5	−8
Benchmark index return		−5.4	−4.6	−4.5	−14.2
Employment, average for 2001	64	NA	NA	39	NA
Employment, end of 2001	65	28	38	47	43
Operating expenses (SEK millions)					
Personnel costs	74	22	51	55	64
External asset management	78	47	5	18	124
Other administrative costs	24	118	54	102	84
Total	176	187	110	175	272

Notes:
NA = Not available.
Data for 1st AP fund are from pp.6, 46 of 2001 Annual Report (English version).
Data for 2nd AP fund are from pp.1, 18 of 2001 Annual Report (English version).
Data for 3rd AP fund are from pp.10, 11, 15, 20 of 2001 Annual Report (English version).
Data for 4th AP fund are from pp.19, 20, 33 of 2001 Annual Report (English version).
Data for 6th AP fund are from pp.2, 24, 25 of 2001 Annual Report (English version).

Stockholm, while AP2 was started from scratch in a new city, Gothenburg – and are in turn reflected in the two funds' employment at the end of 2001, with AP1 having more than twice as many employees (65) as AP2 (28).

It is too early to say whether competition between the AP funds has spurred improved performance, but this competition has to some extent been institutionalized. The First AP Fund, for example, has instituted an employee bonus system that is based in part on beating the performance of Funds AP2 to AP4 and in part on beating benchmark indexes established for each part of the fund's portfolio (First National Swedish Pension Fund, 2001, p.27).

The different funds are also taking somewhat different stances on social, environmental and corporate governance concerns. The Second AP Fund, for example, has been active in lobbying companies on environmental and business practices. It has disposed of stakes in two companies that did not provide adequate responses to their inquiries. The Third AP Fund, on the other hand, has focused on pressing Swedish companies to limit management bonuses, and has thus far paid limited attention to environmental issues.

Nor is there a complete consensus yet on the relatively non-restrictive investment practices carried out by managers of the state AP pension funds acting both as buffer funds for the income pension and a default for the premium pension. Leaders within the Social Democratic Party have criticized the funds' practices as undermining Swedish industry in their single-minded pursuit of high short-term returns. Even Prime Minister Göran Persson has lamented current investment rules, arguing that a pensioner depends not only on 'the yield in state pension funds, but also on Sweden having a functioning industry that pays taxes in Sweden. That is the crucial security for me as a pensioner' (Svensson, 2001). The head of the Seventh AP Fund, which administers the default fund for non-choosers, has vigorously defended current investment practices as necessary to protect the value of future pensions (Feldt and Norman, 2001).

The Swedish experience with the premium pension also suggests that moving to an individual account system will not necessarily eliminate debate over domestic, ethical and environmental investment practices. Indeed, the Seventh AP Fund, the default fund for those who do not make an active choice in the individual account tier, has taken an even more aggressive stand on these issues than the other state pension funds. It decided to disinvest in companies that had been found guilty by impartial tribunals of violating international conventions to which Sweden had adhered, including conventions on human rights, child labour, various ILO conventions, international environmental conventions and conventions against bribery and corruption. On the basis of these criteria, AP7 decided in 2001 to sell its shares in 27 companies, including such well-known multi-national companies as Coca-Cola, General Motors, ITT, Nestlé, Sears, Texaco and Wal-Mart, as well as one Swedish company, Esselte. Investment in these companies was to be barred for five years, although the fund's board could restore them earlier if there was evidence that they had come into compliance with the relevant conventions (Seventh Swedish National Pension Fund, no date, p.2; Svenska Dagbladet, 2002). But the fund continued to invest in companies with interests in tobacco, gambling, alcohol and weapons production – indeed, its general manager argued that, since the Swedish state had interests in those same sectors, following such a rule consistently would mean that it would have to get rid of Swedish government bonds.

Reflecting the poor performance of equities generally (and Swedish equities in particular) in 2001, all of the Swedish buffer funds lost money in that year, reporting returns near those of their benchmark indexes (Table 10.1). Overall, it remains to be seen just how meaningful and useful competitition between the funds will be. The head of one AP Fund gave a mixed evaluation in an interview, noting:

> I do feel the competition: noone wants at the end of the game to be last in performance when it comes to the highest costs or whatever. There are drawbacks and there are positives [to this]. The positives are that you are much more on your toes to perform better. The risk is that we don't differentiate ourselves enough, that we tend to look at one other and copy each other. Of course that's part of competition: you look at each other and copy the best ideas from competitors . . . But when it comes to pension fund management maybe it's a good idea if we tried to seek different solutions . . . The idea of having four separate funds was not only to have competition but to have separate solutions, and if you look at us, the separateness might be small. (Interview, May 2002)

NEW ZEALAND

New Zealand created a Superannuation Fund in 2001 to ease the future financing burden of its general revenue-financed, and flat-rate, superannuation programme. This debate over whether buffer funds should be created and, if so, under what terms, is part of a bitter debate over what is one of the world's most highly politicized pension systems. In 1997, a coalition National/New Zealand First government proposed moving to an individual account pension system, which was rejected by more than 90 per cent of voters who participated in a mail referendum. After coming to power in 1999, a minority Labour/Alliance coalition government proposed that a buffer fund be created as part of a 'tax smoothing' effort to partially prefund the baby boomers' retirement.

In the absence of a dedicated funding source such as a payroll tax, there was substantial conflict over how a collective investment should be financed and how much money should be put into it. Adoption of a collective investment fund was also complicated by the fact that the governing coalition lacked a majority in the Parliament, and would have to win the support of at least one additional party (with the Greens or New Zealand First as the most likely candidates) to win approval for the legislation. A dedicated fund was opposed by the junior coalition partner, the left-wing Alliance, which feared that it would limit government's capacity to manage the economy. If a fund was to be created, they preferred that it be drawn from budget surpluses rather than a share of tax take, to make sure that it did not eat into social spending during lean times. The Greens also preferred to finance the fund out of overall surpluses rather than the income tax, because they want to leave political room for substituting eco-taxes for personal income taxes.

But Winston Peters of New Zealand First argued that simply applying (highly uncertain) budget surpluses rather than a stable, dedicated revenue source to a superannuation fund was unacceptable.

Labour and its coalition partner Alliance also disagreed on whether any investment fund should be tilted towards investment in New Zealand: the Alliance (along with the Greens and the populist New Zealand First Party) were in favour, while Labour (and the conservative parties) were opposed. Many experts, including the Treasury, warned that investing predominantly in New Zealand's tiny and slow-growing economy was also a very high-risk strategy for a retirement savings fund (Macalister, 2000; Brockett, 2000; New Zealand Treasury, 2000a). The Greens, on the other hand, were concerned that a fund oriented towards maximizing returns would ignore environmental considerations in its investment decisions, a position rejected by the other parties.

The coalition finally pushed legislation through Parliament in October 2001 with the support of New Zealand First after efforts to win a broad multi-party consensus failed. Responding to the concerns of the Alliance that the government retain spending flexibility to respond to future economic downturns, government contributions to the fund are not set as a fixed share of tax revenues. Instead, after a phase-in period, government contributions are to be set as a percentage of GDP, such that contributing that level of GDP over the next 40 years would be sufficient to fund anticipated Superannuation expenditures over that period. (Treasury planners had initially planned on a 60-year funding time horizon, which would have required a higher contribution rate. See New Zealand Treasury, 2000b, ch.12.) When fully phased in (in 2004–5), these contributions will initially total 5.54 per cent of GDP, with 3.8 per cent paid out immediately in benefits and the remaining 1.75 per cent being invested. Total contribution rates are expected to rise over time as more 'high-cost' years were included in the 40-year planning horizon. The share of contributions being invested will begin to decline around 2010, as more funds are required to pay current benefits for retiring baby boomers. Fund assets are projected to reach their peak between 2023 and 2029, then gradually decline to around zero near the end of the century. At its peak, the fund is supposed to pay for about 10 per cent of the costs of superannuation benefits.

Governments can choose to contribute less than the GDP percentage required for level 40-year funding in any given year, although not less than the amount required to meet the net cost of superannuation in the coming year. (Nor can they make net withdrawals from the fund before 2020, although a future parliamentary majority could change that restriction or any other aspect of the legislation.) But if a government does choose to underfund for future obligations in a particular year, the legislation requires them to publish in the government's annual Fiscal Strategy Report the amount of the undercontribution, the reasons for it, and their intentions and strategy for making up underfunding in the future. In other words, transparency and fear of political retribution for poor stewardship of pensions are the main barriers against potential underfunding.

The legislation also makes detailed provisions for the management and operation of the fund that are intended to limit interference. An elaborate nomination process for the fund's governing board (grandly labelled the 'Guardians of New Zealand Superannuation') is imbedded in the law. The process is a curious mixture of group inclusiveness and provisions intended to shield the board – and the investment managers it hires – from political interference. The law requires the finance minister to call for board nominations from organizations who are likely to be interested in the fund (notably those representing the elderly, employees and savings institutions). A nominating committee, appointed by the prime minister, will consider all nominations (including those from the groups). Final appointments to the board are to be made by Cabinet on recommendation of the finance minister, but the minister is only allowed to appoint persons who (1) 'in the Minister's opinion, ha[ve] substantial experience, training, and expertise in the management of financial investments' and (2) have been approved by the nominating committee. The legislation also requires that the minister consult with other political parties before forwarding a nomination from the nominating committee for final approval. Appointment of the chief executive officer for the fund is the responsibility of the 'Guardians' rather than government. And the board is given complete discretion in contracting out management of the fund or parts of it to one or more entities.

With regard to the operation of the fund, the main provisions are that it be managed on a 'prudent commercial basis' following 'best-practice portfolio management' while 'maximising return without undue risk to the Fund as a whole'. Although the legislation does allow the New Zealand finance minister, after consultation with the Guardians of the fund, to give the Guardians directions with respect to 'the Fund's performance, including the Government's expectations as to risk and return', it also states that 'the minister must not give a direction that is inconsistent with the Guardians' duty to invest the Fund on a prudent, commercial basis'. Moreover, those directions must be presented publicly to New Zealand's Parliament, and the Guardians are only required to 'have regard to any direction given by the Minister' and state publicly how they are planning to respond, rather than being required to follow the minister's directions.

The Guardians are not precluded from pursuing an active rather than passive fund management strategy, but the fund is barred from having a controlling interest in any company. A very modest bow to the concerns of the Greens that the fund undertake ethical investment practices was included by requiring that the fund investments 'avoid . . . prejudice to New Zealand's reputation as a responsible member of the world community'. These provisions were, New Zealand's finance minister stated, intended to bar fund investments in 'government securities of particularly obnoxious Governments that were dictatorships, or particularly obnoxious forms of companies engaged in strange criminal behaviour', but not to require 'invest[ment] only in companies that fulfilled some very strict criteria'.[3] Moreover, the legislation avoided both more specific directives and mechanisms that would give that directive more teeth. Nor were the fund's investments to be limited to or skewed towards New Zealand.

Up to 70 per cent of the fund is expected to be invested abroad to spread the risks of poor economic performance in the New Zealand economy (Venter, 2001). Critics of the government's proposal questioned the wisdom of taking huge quantities of New Zealand capital abroad and pointed to falling global equities markets and foreign exchange losses suffered by the government employees' pension fund as evidence that the fund was too risky (Howie, 2001).

Even after its adoption, the new Superannuation Fund plan could be dismantled or heavily modified by a simple majority in a future Parliament. That does not seem likely in the short term: in the July 2002 general election, superannuation was not a prominent issue, nor was it a major concern for the electorate. Labour increased its number of seats slightly, while its Alliance coalition partner split and virtually collapsed. Labour and its coalition partner the Progressive Coalition (a break-off of the former Alliance) are now seven seats short of a majority rather than just the two seats short before the election. But two other parties generally supportive of the Superannuation Fund, New Zealand First (which would prefer an individual accounts system) and United Future New Zealand, together gained 16 seats, while National lost 12 seats (see Milne, 2002).

In the absence of a strong commitment from National as well as Labour, however, there is no guarantee that the New Zealand Superannuation Fund will remain in place for the long term. And even if it does, the lack of a guaranteed payroll tax funding mechanism increases the likelihood that a future government may underfinance the system.

CONCLUSIONS

This very brief and selective review of the experiences of three OECD countries shows that collective investment funds are perceived by a variety of governments to be a viable option for dealing with the funding crisis associated with the retirement of the baby boom – even by a country like New Zealand that does not have a dedicated funding source for pensions. But these funds pose a number of issues revolving around the 'publicness' of the funds, notably how much influence governments should have in their governance, and whether 'private' calculations of risk and return should be the only factors in their decision making.

As shown in Table 10.2, there clearly is substantial diversity in the choices that countries make in structuring those funds. Differences are evident even within a single country, Canada, between the Canada and Quebec Pension Plans, and in Sweden, between the main 'buffer' funds, AP1–AP4, the regional investment fund, AP6, and the default fund for the individual account system, AP7. All of the cases here, except the Caisse, show a clear focus on the 'private' objective of increasing returns for the benefit of future pension beneficiaries, however, and the mechanisms they have evolved demonstrate a number of ways to advance that objective, such as clear statutory mandates to focus on economic risks and returns, insulated boards and nomination procedures for those boards, weak or non-existent domestic and social investment criteria, heavy use of external managers, and participation as a minority partner with private investment funds in private market investments.

The politics of investing collective buffer funds tends to reflect the broader politics of their countries in both style and substance. Sweden, for example, combines some deep ideological divisions with a consensus-building policy process that usually produces fairly broad agreement on how to proceed. Governance of the new buffer funds reflects longstanding Swedish practices of consultation with business and labour 'social partners'. Substantive debates on collective fund investment policies have focused on a variety of issues, including domestic investment, corporate ethics and environmental and labour issues. How these different concerns will play out in practice remains to be seen. The development of the practices of the Swedish funds to deal with social and environmental investment criteria bear particular watching. New Zealand has difficulties in reaching broad agreements across partisan lines and in keeping important issues out of partisan politics, but its investment mandates thus far are weaker than those in Sweden. Canada, too, has taken a more hands-off approach to its buffer funds. On the other hand, Quebec, with a strong element of economic nationalism among its political elite, has been by far the most aggressive in using collective investment funds to promote regional economic development.

The evidence listed here also suggests that policy inheritances are important factors in explaining those differences. In particular, rules that are put in place in one part of a country's overall pension regime may simply be

Table 10.2 Governance and investment practices of four collective investment funds

	Quebec	Canada	Sweden	New Zealand
Number of funds	One	One	Four main funds (AP1–AP4) plus a regional development fund (AP6)	One
Substantial contracting out of portfolio management	No	Yes	Yes	Yes
Group representation on board	Yes	No	Yes	No
Corporate control policies	Caisse may not in most cases directly or indirectly own securities providing more than 30 per cent of voting rights to board of directors for more than five years	CPPIB may not directly or indirectly own securities providing more than 30 per cent of voting rights to board of directors	Individual funds may hold no more than 10 per cent of any listed company or 2 per cent of Stockholm stock exchange valuation	Fund may not control any company
Domestic investment criteria	No more than 30 per cent invested in foreign assets	No more than 30 per cent invested in foreign assets	No more than 40 per cent of assets exposed to exchange rate risk	No criteria
Industrial policy criteria	Mandate to promote economic development of Quebec	Implicitly prohibited	Explicitly prohibited	Implicitly prohibited
Social/ethical investment criteria for collective buffer funds	No provisions	No provisions, but will not invest in countries where Canada has restricted trade relations	'Take ethical and environmental considerations into account without relinquishing the overall goal of a high return on capital'	'Avoid prejudice to New Zealand's reputation as a responsible member of the world community'

adapted for another part, as for instance in the adoption of foreign invest-ment rules for the Quebec and Canada Pension Plans that originated with Registered Retirement Savings Plans. There also appears to be a strong element of both within country and cross-national learning, however, as most countries in recent years have moved away from an interventionist course towards a more 'private' set of objectives and governance proce-dures when they set up new collective investment funds (New Zealand) or revised established ones (Canada and Sweden). But the Quebec Pension Plan's Caisse de dépôt, a product of the 1960s, when *dirigisme* and indus-trial policy were much more in vogue, has remained close to its original model of governance and investment practices.

Another lesson from these international experiences is that debates over investment criteria are likely to be a recurring issue rather than one that is resolved definitively when the initial legislation establishing buffer funds is enacted. The stakes are too large for such issues to be completely depoliti-cized. Even a strong set of insulation mechanisms could be challenged. Early evidence also suggests, however, that these funds can operate with a high degree of autonomy within their legislative mandates and match or exceed the returns of benchmark indexes, with very low administrative costs – at least in countries where the overall public governance structure is relatively sound.

The cases also suggest, even in the first few years of experience, some of the potential risks associated with domestic investment requirements, es-pecially in countries with relatively small capital markets and few very large firms. Both the CPPIB and the Swedish buffer funds found themselves heavily exposed to a single firm (Northern Telecom in Canada, Ericsson in Sweden) as the telecoms boom reached its peak. Only deviation from passive index investment policies could limit this risk.

Finally, the Swedish experience also suggests that creation of multiple funds may be a useful way to sharpen the attention of fund managers on their fund's financial performance rather than other objectives. This approach is not without costs or problems of its own, however. First, cre-ating multiple funds increases the costs of management. This is likely to be a particular issue in small countries like New Zealand. Second, a focus on the annual or even quarterly bottom line, or at least avoiding being at the bottom of a country's 'league tables' for fund returns, could lead fund man-agers to take excessive risks and/or focus on short-term returns rather than on building assets for the long term. An equally strong risk, however, given the small number of funds and incentives not to be the worst performer, is that multiple buffer funds might lead more to imitation than to differenti-ation and innovation.

NOTES

1. The research reported herein was partially funded pursuant to a grant from the US Social Security Administration (SSA) funded as part of the Retirement Research Consortium at Boston College. The opinions and conclusions are solely those of the author and should not be construed as representing the opinions or policy of SSA or any agency of the federal government.
2. Mark Weisdorf, CPPIB vice president for private market investments, quoted in CPPIB (2002b).
3. The provisions are in New Zealand Superannuation Act 2001, Public Act 2001, no. 84, s.58. The quotations are from Finance Minister Michael Cullen's answers to Green Party co-leader Rod Donald in *Hansard*, 11 October 2000, Question 1. On government resistance to more specific directives, see the exchange between Finance Minister Cullen and Green Party co-leader Rod Donald in *Hansard*, 29 November 2000, Question 3, and Small (2000).

REFERENCES

Arbour, Pierre (1993), *Quebec Inc and the Temptation of State Capitalism*, Montreal: Robert Davies Publishing.

Authier, Phillip (1994), 'Parizeau Makes Changes at Caisse', *Montreal Gazette*, 3 November, p.D1.

Brockett, Matthew (2000), 'Invest Offshore Treasury Says', *The Press* (Christchurch), 22 November, p.6.

Brooks, Stephen (1987), 'The State As Financier: A Comparison of the Caisse de dépôt et placement du Québec and Alberta Heritage Savings Fund', *Canadian Public Policy*, 13 (3), 318–29.

Caisse de dépôt et placement du Québec (no date), 'Policy applicable to Private Investments sector investments, with respect to the holding of more than 30% of a company's common shares' (available at *http://www.cdp.ca/pdf/30pourcent-a.pdf*).

Caisse de dépôt et placement du Québec (2002), *Modernizing to Ensure a Stronger Future: Recommendations Respecting the Governance of the Caisse de dépôt et placement du Québec*, Quebec: The Caisse.

Canada Pension Plan Investment Board (2001), *2001 Annual Report*.

Canada Pension Plan Investment Board (2002a), *2002 Annual Report*.

Canada Pension Plan Investment Board (2002b), 'CPP Investment Board Commits Half-Billion Dollars to Canadian Venture Capital', news release, 19 June.

Canada Pension Plan Investment Board (2002c), *Investment Statement*, 11 September.

Canada Pension Plan Investment Board (2002d), Canada Pension Plan Investment Board, *Social Investing Policy*, 6 March.

DeCloet, Derek (2002), 'Caisse Boss Falls On the Big Bets', *National Post*, 18 May, p.FP1.

Dougherty, Kevin (2002), 'Rousseau's Sovereignty Stance Key', *Montreal Gazette*, 30 May, p.C1.

Feldt, Kjell-Olof and Peter Norman (2001), 'Försämra inte pensionerna, Persson' (Don't endanger pensions, Persson), *Dagens Nyheter*, 16 October.

First National Swedish Pension Fund (2001), *Annual Report, 2001*.

The experience of mature welfare states

Gibbens, Robert (2002), 'Landry Sparks Alarm Over Caisse', *National Post*, 23 May, p.FP1.
Howie, Craig (2001), 'Super Fund Gets Burnt in Currency Dealings', *The Dominion* (Wellington), 13 June, p.1.
Iglesias, Augusto and Robert J. Palacios (2000), *Managing Public Pension Reserves Part I: Evidence from the International Experience*, Washington, DC: World Bank.
Jacobs, Alan M. (2002), 'Making Tradeoffs Over Time: Retrenchment, Investment and the Reform of Pension Systems', paper presented at the 2002 annual meeting of the American Political Science Association, 29 August–1 September.
Macalister, Philip (2000), 'Super Myths Debunked', *New Zealand Herald*, 5 August.
Milne, Jonathan (2002), 'Coalition Talks to Focus on Superannuation Funds', *Southland Times*, 31 July, p.2.
New Zealand Treasury (2000a), *Macroeconomic Effects of the Proposal for Pre-Funding New Zealand Superannuation*, Treasury Report T2000/1939, 18 September.
New Zealand Treasury (2000b), *Pre-Funding New Zealand Superannuation: Working Document*, 15 June.
Palacios, Robert (2002), *Managing Public Pension Reserves Part II: Lessons from Five Recent OECD Initiatives*, Washington, DC: World Bank Social Protection Discussion Paper Series No. 0219.
Palmer, Edward (2002), 'Swedish Pension Reform: How Did It Evolve, And What Does It Mean for the Future?', in Martin Feldstein and Horst Siebert (eds), *Social Security Pension Reform in Europe*, Chicago and London: University of Chicago Press, pp.171–205.
Pontusson, Jonas (1994), *The Limits of Social Democracy: Investment Politics in Sweden*, Ithaca, NY: Cornell University Press.
Sarney, Mark and Amy N. Preneta (2001–2), 'The Canada Pension Plan's Experience with Investing Its Portfolio in Equities', *Social Security Bulletin*, 64(2), 46–56.
Settergren, Ole (2001), 'The Automatic Balancing Mechanism of the Swedish Pension System: A Non-Technical Introduction', National Social Insurance Board, Stockholm, 21 August.
Seventh Swedish National Pension Fund (no date), *Sjunde AP-fonden. År 2001* (Seventh AP Fund, Year 2001).
Small, Vernon (2000), 'Cullen Camp Tips Hands-Off Style on Pension Funds', *New Zealand Herald*, 23 October.
Svenska Dagbladet (2002), 'Coca-Cola och Nestlé åkte ut när AP-fond följde etik-regler' (Coca-Cola and Nestlé went out when AP fund followed ethics rules), 22 February.
Svensson, Karin (2001), 'Göran Persson vill ha blå-gula AP-fonder' (Göran Persson Wants to Have Blue and Yellow State Pension Funds), *Dagens Industri*, 19 September.
Sweden (2000), 'The AP Fund in the Reformed Pension System', Government Bill 1999/2000:46, 13 January.
Tamagno, Edward (2001), 'Investing Social Security Funds: Principles and Considerations', Caledon Institute of Public Policy, Ottawa, February.
Venter, Nick (2001), 'Cullen's Super: The Risk and the Opportunity', *The Dominion* (Wellington), 9 June, p.2.

PART II

Economies in transition and Latin America

11. Home-made pension reforms in Central and Eastern Europe and the evolution of the World Bank approach to modern pension systems

Michał Rutkowski

One of the most interesting elements of a wave of pension reforms in Central and Eastern Europe is that those reforms were home-made: very different from the Chilean prototype, and not really following what was then perceived as 'the World Bank view', that is, promoting a Chilean-type reform as a blueprint in all client countries.[1] The World Bank played a certain role in the reform process; however, the views espoused by the Bank were simply different from those commonly believed. The first section of this chapter describes the views of the Bank, especially the transition from the research report, 'Averting the Old-Age Crisis' (World Bank, 1994) to 'World Bank Position on Pension Reforms' (edited by Robert Holzmann, in preparation). The second section examines pension reform developments in Central and Eastern Europe (CEE), especially in Hungary and Poland, in the light of those changes in the prevailing approach to pension reforms.

EVOLUTION OF VIEWS ON PENSION REFORMS

The World Bank has always supported a strong funded pillar as part and parcel of a fully reformed scheme. However, the approach of the Bank in the late 1990s had more nuances and actual reform design and implementation were made dependent on country circumstances and preferences.

With its 1994 publication, the Bank developed arguments for a multipillar pension system. The proposed model system consisted of a mandated unfunded and publicly managed defined benefit scheme as a first pillar, a mandated but funded and privately managed defined contribution scheme as a second pillar, and voluntary retirement savings as top-ups according to individual preferences as a third pillar. The 1994 publication was highly influential in focusing the mind of policy makers worldwide struggling with the need to reform their pension schemes. But, while essentially all reforms are moving towards a multi-pillar structure (see Rutkowski, 1998), the scope and shape of the pillars differ substantially, as well as the sequencing and financing of their introduction. The differences are much larger than those envisaged by the World Bank. They reflect the different starting conditions and different preferences in countries as well as innovations in each pillar (such as the notional defined contribution schemes to reform the first pillar, and the clearing house to reduce administrative costs in the second pillar), further thinking about the conditions for introducing funded provisions, and reform experiences and learning about the political economy of pension reform. As a result, the multi-pillar reform model emerged only as a benchmark, not as a blueprint for World Bank support.

This had important practical consequences since it meant that a range of reforms that could be supported by the Bank is broader than thought before. The Bank started supporting reforms that retained a dominance of an unfunded public pay-as-you-go (PAYGO) pillar within a multi-pillar framework (in Hungary, Poland and all other countries in Central and Eastern Europe). The Bank started paying enormous attention to the structure of an unfunded public pillar, and supported reforms that did not introduce a mandatory privately funded pillar (Lithuania, Czech Republic, first wave of Latvia reforms, Moldova, the Kyrgyz Republic). The Bank got involved in work on voluntary private arrangements in recognition of the fact that in some countries there are no initial conditions in place to be able to think of a mandatory funded pillar (Turkey, Georgia). Finally, the Bank started supporting reforms in which the funded pillar was not really private, at least for a transition period (Russia).

Those important practical consequences do not mean that the Bank abandoned worrying about the quality of pension systems, and that it became too 'permissive' or tolerant with respect to types of reforms. The new view of the Bank emphasizes that pension reform can have a very different shape but a new pension system has to do better on each of the three main items the existing pension schemes are criticized for, that is, providing and delivering adequate, affordable, sustainable and diversified pensions; supporting and not hindering economic growth; and being better able to cope with population aging. In order to do this, the reform has to move outside and beyond the traditional thinking and approaches.

Two main elements of such a reformed scheme, discussed in more detail below, are (a) a stronger individualization, that is, a close contribution/benefit link in benefit design to reduce distortions, and (b) some diversification of retirement income resources. A new system, let us call it 'a diversified system of individual accounts' (DSIA) helps in delivering on the above three criteria, as described below.

Delivering Adequate, Affordable, Sustainable and Diversified Pensions

The main elements in DSIA are fourfold: (1) introducing minimum benefits for the needy elderly, either as a minimum pension or as a guarantee; (2) keeping things small and simple; the 'small' refers to the mandated replacement rate which should be kept low for reasons of financing and compliance, the 'simple' refers to benefit design and the need for a close link between contributions and benefits. Distributive elements for lower income groups or other considerations (such as periods of unemployment benefit receipt and so on) can still be introduced but need to be done in a transparent manner; (3) achieving sustainability is easier with mandated lower replacement but also needs an appropriate mechanism of transparency and governance of the schemes to deal with projected developments, such as aging; (4) diversifying requires more than one funding source for old age income which can be mandated or voluntary. Adequate instruments for the latter are particularly important for informal sector workers.

Contributing to Employment and Output Growth

With the DSIA system in place, the dangers of deficit-induced macroeconomic instability and crowding out are reduced. But a changed system design should have further positive effects on employment and output. First, in order to further reduce distortions on the labour market and enhance labour supply, the suggested close contribution/benefit link should make the scheme largely actuarially fair and hence reduce the tax element of contributions. Introducing a system design which provides actuarial increments/decrements of earlier/later retirement should make the retirement decision more flexible and adjusted to individual preferences. Last but not least, a reformed earnings-related system which applies to all sectors of the economy allows for cross-professional mobility, including that between public and private sectors – an important feature of a modern economy. Second, a diversified scheme relying in part on mandatory funded provisions should provide an important impetus for financial market development and this in turn on economic growth. The Chilean experience is fully consistent with the view of the positive effect of mandatory funded schemes on finance market development and this in turn on a higher economic growth path (Holzmann, 1997; Schmidt-Hebbel, 1998). Third, while the effects of a (partially) funded scheme on the overall saving rate are uncertain, lower transfers and in most cases lower fiscal deficits will increase the national saving rate. Such a public saving effect is strengthened by a reform which (partially) moves from unfunded to funded provisions and repays the implicit debt which becomes explicit over time.

Better Coping with an Aging Population

A DSIA scheme which links contributions to benefits and disallows the externalization of costs to others should also be better able to deal with population aging for at least four reasons. First, a constant retirement age and increase in the cohort life expectancy would be translated into a lower benefit level enhancing the incentives to stay in the labour market. Second, with actuarial design features of decrements and increments, the continued labour force participation would not be punished. Third, such a scheme would support the breaking up of the rigid division between learning, work and retirement leisure since job interruptions, job changes and return to the labour market at later ages would not be punished. Fourth, it would allow more flexibility in individual retirement decisions. That is, individuals with strong preferences for early retirement would be allowed to take it, but this would require an individual contribution/saving effort and could not rely on the financing through others.

A particularly important innovation of DSIA schemes is a notional defined contributions (NDC) approach. This reform changes by definition the benefit structure of the scheme but leaves the form of (un)funding unchanged, but in reality the move from an unfunded defined benefit (DB) scheme to a notional defined contribution (NDC) scheme amounts essentially to making the underlying financial relationship more explicit and transparent. Formally, an unfunded DB system can be adjusted parametrically to mimic fully an NDC system, and a fully fledged DB system (such as the German or French point system) may come close to that (Góra and Palmer, 2001). But full equivalence would require that the DB formula exhibit variable and actuarially adjusted decrements/increments for earlier/later retirement and the building of increasing (remaining) life expectancy into the benefit formula. The experience in Germany and France – compared to Ecuador and Brazil[2] – suggests that such proposed adjustments in the DB system are politically difficult to implement and hence an NDC reform is not simply a subset of a parametric reform.

In an NDC system, an individual account is established to which contributions by the individual (and his or her employer) are earmarked and on which a notional interest rate is paid. The latter is consistent with the interest rate an unfunded scheme can pay, that is, the natural growth rate (essentially, the growth rate of covered wages in a mature system). At retirement, the accumulated notional individual fund is divided by an annuitization factor which reflects the remaining life expectancy of the cohort at retirement and the notional interest rate. The benefits are typically price-indexed, or at least not fully wage-indexed, to allow for the build-up of an (economic or demographic) reserve.

The appeal of this NDC structure is its simplicity and transparency, its incentive effects on labour supply and retirement decisions, adjustment to changing professional and family structures (and divorce), and automatic adjustment to increasing life expectancy. Specifically, (a) as in funded individual schemes, workers have an interest in and can easily verify the amount of contribution paid on his or her behalf; (b) the tax element of contributions and hence the labour market distortions are reduced (but not eliminated as long as the notional interest rate remains below the market interest rate/personal discount rate), as well as distortions on retirement decisions. Increments/decrements for earlier/later retirement are part of the benefit design and do not need extra political decisions; (c) the approach allows for an easy and quick harmonization between different schemes (such as public and private sector workers) since higher benefits for the former are essentially conserved for those close to retirement (if accrued rights are transformed into the appropriate notional amounts) while new entrants are subject to the same rights; (d) distributive elements can still be introduced (such as matching contributions to low-income workers or periods of sickness and unemployment) but require an explicit and transparent transfer from other sources; (e) the individual account structure allows an easy build-up of individual rights for women and splitting for periods of marriage after divorce and death; and (f) when the estimated life expectancy of a cohort increases, individuals receive through a reduced annuitization factor a lower pension and can adjust through later retirement or higher individual savings.

Some of these arguments have convinced policy makers in Sweden and Italy, Latvia and Poland, Mongolia and the Kyrgyz Republic to reform typical DB systems towards NDC schemes.[3] These reforms also highlight alternative reform approaches (such as immediate change towards NDC versus phasing in, and different methods to transform accrued rights into notional amounts) as well as basic weaknesses. The experience in these countries indicates that the NDC concept can still be highjacked by politicians and lead to less than optimal system design or potential disasters: for example (a) the continued financial unsustainability when choosing the 'wrong' notional interest rate, such as the per capita GDP or wage growth instead of growth of the total wage base; (b) the need to project the remaining cohort life expectancy and to implement it politically, and not to use a fixed factor, as in Russia; (c) the need for a buffer fund to deal with demographic and economic shocks; (d) the granting of contributions to the individual account which

have not been paid, as in Italy; (e) The substantial administrative requirements to run such a scheme, which should not be underestimated (as in the
Kyrgyz Republic or in Moldova). Still, reforming along NDC lines is quite
likely the best way to restructure the typical unfunded DB scheme within a
multi-pillar structure, if it is done well.

DEVELOPMENTS IN CENTRAL AND EASTERN EUROPE

Hungary and Poland are often described as leaders in pension reforms in
Central and Eastern Europe. Indeed, even though Latvia introduced an
NDC reform as early as 1996, Hungary and Poland were the only countries
in Central and Eastern Europe that had multi-pillar schemes on the ground
in the late 1990s (Latvia's funded pillar started operating only in 2002).

It is interesting to realize that the pension reform preparation process in
CEE countries, including Hungary and Poland, and the process of changes
in World Bank thinking on pension reforms, were mutually reinforcing in
the period 1995–9. First, it was quite clear that the situation on the ground
in CEE countries was very different from the one in Latin America from
where the first batch of reformers came. The difference was primarily in the
size of the PAYGO pillar, the attachment to it, and the transition costs of
reform which would be very high if the first pillar was going to be reduced
to a minor role. Second, with high returns in the stock market, but also high
volatility, the 'security through diversity' principle started crowding out the
'second pillar rush', as it was becoming clearer and clearer that the advantages of the reform system are related to diversification more than they are
related to second pillar returns. Third, it became clearer that a lot could be
improved *within* the PAYGO pillar, in terms of incentives, transparency and
its overall ability to deliver on promises. Those three realizations came
about more or less at the same time in the World Bank and in its main client
countries in CEEC.

Looking in more detail at the motivation for reforms in Hungary, Poland
and elsewhere in the region, one would be quick to realize that restoring
financial sustainability while ensuring adequate retirement income have
been the primary objectives of multi-pillar reforms in Hungary, Poland and
elsewhere in CEEC. Other goals have also featured high on the reform strategy, especially improving microeconomic and labour market incentives,
which were much distorted by the high payroll taxes, compressed benefit
structure and early retirement criteria of the former pension schemes.

These goals were very close to those formulated by the World Bank.
Their realization led to a new multi-pillar paradigm, in which pension port-

folios have become more diversified. The monopoly PAYGO has been reduced and complemented by a new mandatory funded pillar (privately managed) and a voluntary pillar with fiscal incentives. Risks in the public pillar determined by growth in wages are diversified against risks in the funded pillar determined by the return on capital. The two types of risks are not perfectly correlated. Other positive externalities are also expected, for example a more efficient intermediation of national savings.[4] Table 11.1

Table 11.1   Basic characteristics of mandatory pension systems in CEE countries following transition periods

Country	Contribution rate public/private	Retirement age	Public pillar structure	Mandatory pillar	
				Switching strategy***	Effectiveness date
Bulgaria	27–24/2–5	63/60	DB	M<40	2002
Czech Republic	26	62/61–57*	DB**		
Estonia	16/6	63/63*	DB**	M<18, V for existing affiliates	2003
Hungary	24–22/6–8	62/62	DB	M for new entrants, V for existing affiliates	1998
Latvia	25.5–17.5/2–10	62/62	NDC	M<30, 30<V<50	2001
Lithuania	25	62.5/60	DB**		
Poland	25.2–7.3	65/60	NDC	M<30, 30<V<50	1999
Romania	33	65/60*	DB		
Slovakia	28	60/57–53*	DB**		
Slovenia	24.4	63–58/61–58*	DB		

Notes:
  * Early retirement is permitted on an almost actuarially fair basis, except in Slovakia, where penalties on early retirement are less restrictive.
 ** The system remains highly redistributive.
*** M and V refer to mandatory and voluntary switching, respectively.

summarizes the main features of the reformed and unreformed systems in CEE countries (for a comprehensive overview of developments in EU accession countries and the other transition economies, see Rutkowski, 2002; Lindeman et al., 2001).

Moreover, the reform of the public pillar – supported by the World Bank as much as the changes in the overall structure of the system – has not been limited to downsizing (and the critics of the Bank often assert that it supports just downsizing of public pillars) but, in most of these countries, new features have been introduced to strengthen overall microeconomic incentives. Two different approaches have been followed. In some, the defined benefit (DB) principle has been preserved but the structure of benefits has changed. The new benefit formula accounts for the entire contribution history of the worker and decompresses pensions in order to tighten links between contributions and benefits. Early retirement has been eliminated or is permitted on a restricted and actuarially fair basis. Occupational privileges have been abolished in most cases; in others, Poland and Bulgaria, an innovative approach has been implemented. Separate funded schemes, privately managed, will finance the pensions of workers with a right to early retirement until they attain the statutory retirement age in the PAYGO. This framework enhances the transparency of financing these costly provisions. A limited number of countries, especially those with a highly skewed dependency ratio (for example, Bulgaria, Romania and Hungary), have complemented changes in the incentive structure with an increase in the minimum retirement age.

In Latvia and Poland, the public pillar has been transformed into a notional defined contribution (NDC) scheme. For these countries, the NDC scheme retains the PAYGO financing structure, but the replacement rate will be determined by the internal rate of return of the PAYGO, that is, growth in the covered wage bill and longevity at the time of retirement. This construction, as explained in the first section of the present chapter, tightens links between contributions and benefits, encouraging individuals to remain longer in the labour force. In addition, the NDC enhances the financial resilience of the PAYGO to demographic and labour market factors that cannot be predicted with certainty.[5] By contrast, in the DB structure, unpredicted demographic or economic changes are more likely to demand legislative amendments requiring a long process of political consensus to amend provisions in the scheme and restore financial stability.

The reformed DB (as in Hungary) and NDC (as in Poland) pillars have been able to enhance microeconomic incentives while preserving some key social objectives. For example, these systems maintain a minimum pension guarantee aimed at low-income workers and credit for non-contributory periods related to specific social circumstances (such as care of young children). In some countries, these benefits are now covered by the state budget, bringing greater transparency to the financing of special social programmes.[6]

One of the critical features of the new system that is often missed in comments and reviews is the fact that public pillars heavily dominate new pension systems in Hungary and Poland and elsewhere in the CEEC. Reforms, therefore, have very little to do with social security privatization. In terms of payroll tax, only 20 per cent of it goes to the second pillar in Poland, and 21 per cent in Hungary, while 80 per cent (79 per cent) remains available for first pillar retirement pensions, and all disability and survivorship benefits. Therefore the reform could be described as a very partial privatization, or, better, as providing slight diversification of methods of ensuring old age security.

In Hungary and Poland, the funded pillars are not identical but common important features apply. Assets are privately managed and workers freely select the asset manager to prevent inappropriate political interference. The private sector not only manages the assets but also administers the accounts. And, to minimize private sector risks, there is a clear legal separation between the property rights of fund managers and those of affiliates, preventing a siphoning of resources from workers to the fund administrator. The funded pillar will follow a defined contribution structure that is easier to supervise.[7]

The second pillar is financed by diverting a share of contributions from the PAYGO, a share that will range from 5 to 10 per cent of wages but will start at lower levels in some countries (for example, 2 per cent in Latvia and Bulgaria) to ease transition costs, as the diversion of contributions will expose the existing stock of liabilities within the PAYGO. In Hungary, the share is 6 per cent (with a now renewed promise to be increased to 8 per cent), and in Poland 7.3 per cent. Payroll taxes are already burdensome in CEE countries, which has prevented further increases. Only Estonia finances a share of the second pillar by raising the contribution rate of switchers to the funded pillar. Transition costs have influenced not only the size of the second pillar but also the switching strategy, namely the share of workers allowed to enter the new system.

For reasons of fiscal stability and intergenerational equity, Hungary, Poland and other CEE countries implementing multi-pillar reforms have spread transition costs among different generations. Existing pensioners are the generation least affected by the introduction of the second pillar, as their entitlements have been largely protected, excluding changes in benefit indexation. In some countries, older workers will bear some of the adjustment through a reduction in replacement rates and an increase in the minimum retirement age. Other transition costs will be financed through a

*Table 11.2   Projected financial performance of the public pillar following
reforms approved up to end-2001 (percentage of GDP)*

	2000	2005	2010	2020	2025	2030	2040	2050
Bulgaria*	−1.4	−1.3	0.1	0.3	1.0	1.4	0.6	0.6
Czech Republic	−0.9	−0.9	−1.3	−3.0	−3.8	-4.7	−7.6	−8.7
Estonia	—	0.4	1.6	1.9	2.1	2.2	2.8	2.9
Hungary**	−0.4	0.6	0.0	−0.3	−0.2	0.0	−0.3	−0.4
Lithuania	−0.2	0.5	1.3	1.4	1.0	0.6	0.1	−0.9
Poland***	−2.3	−2.2	−1.2	−2.5	−2.5	−2.2	−1.8	−2.2
Romania	−0.8	−0.7	0.3	1.0	1.0	0.6	−0.1	−0.3
Slovakia	−0.2	−0.4	−0.6	−2.2	−2.6	—	—	—

Notes:
  * Preliminary figures being revised.
 ** Excludes under-age disability pensions of the Health Insurance Fund.
*** Excludes the cost of farmers' pension programme.

combination of privatization revenues, fiscal adjustment and borrowing, transferring some of existing pension debt to future generations.

The long-term financial sustainability of pension schemes in most CEE countries has much improved following the approval of multi-pillar reforms (see Tables 11.A1 and 11.2). The pension schemes in Bulgaria, Estonia, Hungary and Latvia are better prepared to confront the aging demographics, even though some additional reforms might still be necessary to attain a balanced position in the long term, for example in Hungary.[8] In Hungary, for example, the reform was able to narrow the long-term (2050) deficit in the public pillar from nearly 6 per cent of GDP to only 0.5 per cent of GDP. In the medium term, some of these countries will continue to register a deficit as contributions are diverted from the PAYGO to the funded pillar.[9] In Poland, the reforms have much diminished deficits in the public pillar, from 7.5 per cent to 2.2 per cent of GDP in 2050, yet disability remains a burden in the public system and the cause of remaining imbalances. Table 11.2 illustrates that Lithuania's public pillar is also on a sounder financial footing. Projections on Romania suggest that financial viability could be restored in the public pillar if a prudent replacement rate and indexation rule are followed. In practice, the law entails excessive discretion for the calculation of benefits, creating high uncertainties on the future viability of the public pillar.

Hungary and Poland, as well as other reformers in CEEC, still have to address three key issues: enhancing coverage and compliance, consolidating the reformed public pillar, and promoting the safe development of private pension plans. The coverage of pension schemes was greatly diminished during the transition decade in most CEE countries. These countries have now to rebuild much of the lost contribution bases. Expanding coverage and enhancing compliance will improve the finances of the public pension scheme in the short and medium term and might even permit a modest decline in the hefty contribution rate with a positive labour market impact. If coverage is not re-established, a second negative outcome will arise in the long term, as many workers could be left without adequate retirement income, facing the risk of poverty during their old age or imposing an additional cost on the public safety net.

The minimum retirement age, particularly that of women, remains low compared to levels prevalent in OECD countries which are closer to 65 years. Besides gender inequity, the prevailing low retirement age for women imposes a cost burden on the DB-PAYGO, especially since life expectancy of women is higher. In the NDC schemes, benefits will vary according to the retirement age, and women face the risk of receiving inadequately low pensions during their old age. For this reason, Latvia is already eliminating the gender gap and increasing the retirement age to 62 years for both genders. Similar concerns are emerging in Poland, where the retirement age of women is 60 years. Disability insurance remains a potential source of rising expenditures within the public schemes, particularly as older workers might claim this benefit in response to tighter eligibility requirements for old age benefits.[10] The matter is especially critical in Poland, which has inherited a large stock of disabled pensioners. Poland also faces the challenge of revising the Farmers' Pension Scheme, a largely non-contributory scheme costing 2 per cent of GDP.[11]

The safe development of private pension plans will be paramount for the multi-pillar reform to reach its ultimate goals of providing adequate retirement. The institutional capacity to supervise the newly established pension plans, which will quickly become the most important institutional investors, needs to be much strengthened in most CEE countries. Assets of pension plans in Hungary and Poland will surpass 20 per cent of GDP by 2020. In some cases, a guarantee has been built into the mandatory second pillar through a minimum pension or other mechanisms.[12] Even without an explicit guarantee, the state will still bear an implicit liability in cases of poor performance owing to the pension plans' mandatory nature.

Rigorous provisions have been imposed on the investment regime of these plans including quantitative restrictions on asset classes (for example, equity, private fixed income and foreign investment) to reduce portfolio risks, given the early development of capital markets in most CEE countries. By contrast, investment restrictions in EU countries are largely limited to ceilings on a single issuer or an affiliated party. These tight provisions will need to be relaxed progressively as the experience of pension funds increases and the supervisory capacity matures, allowing pension funds to benefit from full integration with EU capital markets. An excessively tight regime will constrain diversification and opportunities to attain a higher return.

All in all, the transition decade imposed a severe shock in the PAYGO schemes inherited from the centrally planned era. But most countries, including Hungary and Poland, have emerged from it with systems that are better placed to face the challenge of the aging demographics. Indeed, many of these systems are now on a stronger long-term financial footing than pension schemes in many EU countries that are still to find a sustainable reform path. As Table 11A.2 in illustrates, public pension expenditures will rise by more than four percentage points of GDP in at least nine of the EU15 countries over the next four decades and, in three of them, the rise will even surpass 6 per cent of GDP.

CONCLUSIONS

This chapter has looked at two parallel processes: pension reforms in Central and Eastern Europe (EU accession countries) and the evolution of World Bank thinking on modern pension system characteristics. It is clear that the two processes have been taking place in parallel, and influenced each other, but they remained fundamentally independent. Pension reforms in Central and Eastern Europe borrowed the idea of a mandatory funded pillar from Latin America and some OECD countries, and were clearly inspired by the 'Averting the Old-Age Crisis' World Bank publication of 1994. However, pension reforms in Central and Eastern Europe, starting with Poland and Hungary, went much further towards introducing a much clearer link between contributions and benefits throughout the whole pension system (especially in the cases of notional defined contributions first pillars), and they took on board the idea of diversification of sources of retirement provision much more than any of their predecessors. The public pillar dominates the pension landscape even after the reforms. At the same time, the World Bank view evolved in the same direction, by both emphasizing those two features more than in the past and acknowledging that individual country circumstances differ markedly and that the choice of the pension system in different countries may, therefore, differ quite significantly. In both process, the pathbreaking idea of a multi-pillar pension system has been used as a benchmark, but not a blueprint for pension reform.

NOTES

1. The explicit or implicit critique of the perceived Bank's approach to pension reform covers a wide spectrum, ranging from the rejection of a multi-pillar concept and accusations of a blueprint reform approach to a more sophisticated critique questioning the perceived underlying economic rationale and the neglect of the specific needs of developing countries. For the latter group see, for example, Thompson (1998) and Barr (2000).
2. The recent pension reform in Ecuador introduced an automatic adjustment of the retirement age in line with the change in life expectancy every five years with the objective of maintaining a 15-year retirement spell. The recent Brazilian reform introduced life expectancy at retirement into the DB benefit formula.
3. See the arguments for Poland in Chlon et al. (1999).
4. Holzmann (1997; 2000).
5. In contrast to the Latvian and Polish model, the Swedish scheme incorporates an additional short-term stabilizer.
6. Non-contributory periods have generally been much rationalized in CEE countries and non-priority programmes, such as credit for students, have been eliminated.
7. Over the last two decades, defined contribution (DC) plans have been growing at a faster pace than DB plans, mostly offered through occupational schemes, in OECD countries. There is also an increasing tendency for new occupational schemes to follow a DC construction.
8. Projections from the Latvian Ministry of Labour and Social Protection indicate that the public pillar will attain a balanced position by 2005 and maintain small surpluses up to 2050.
9. The initial transition costs will be as high as 1.5 per cent of GDP in countries with a larger pillar.
10. In Lithuania, for example, the number of old age pensioners stabilized following the rise in the retirement age. In turn, the number of disabled has been rising at a fast pace.
11. Various approaches have been considered in the past, including the splitting of the system in two. Higher-income farmers would be switched to the contributory scheme available to other workers, and lower-income farmers would remain in the non-contributory one. But current capacity to assess farmers' income is weak.
12. In some countries (such as Poland and Hungary), the second pillar also carries a relative rate of return guarantee, an attempt to protect workers against poorly performing funds; the guarantee is financed from a special reserve created by the pension fund manager from his assets. In the case of Hungary, this guarantee is more loosely constructed allowing for some discretion. In addition, there is a guarantee fund in Poland and Hungary if the asset manager fails to cover this reserve. In Hungary, the guarantee fund will also cover any shortfall in the second pillar benefit below 25 per cent of the value of the first pillar pension. These guarantee funds are financed by pension fund administrators. A shortfall of reserves in these funds could lead to a state liability.

REFERENCES

Barr, N. (2000), 'Reforming Pensions: Myths, Truths, and Policy Choices', *IMF Working Paper WP/00/139*, Washington, DC.

Chlon, A., M. Góra, and M. Rutkowski (1999), 'Shaping Pension Reform in Poland: Security through Diversity', Social Protection Discussion Paper, no. 9923, August, The World Bank.

Góra, M. and E. Palmer (2001), 'Shifting perspectives in pension reform', Warsaw and Stockholm (mimeo).

Holzmann, R. (1997), 'Pension Reform, Financial Market Development, and

Economic Growth: Preliminary Evidence from Chile', *IMF Staff Papers*, 44 (2), June, 149–78.

Holzmann, R. (2000), 'The World Bank Approach to Pension Reform', *International Social Security Review*, 53(1), 11–34.

Lindeman, D., M. Rutkowski and O. Sluchynskyy (2001), 'The Evolution of Pension Systems in Eastern Europe and Central Asia: Opportunities, Constraints, Dilemmas and Emerging Practices', *OECD Financial Market Trends*, 80, October, 79–130.

Rutkowski, M. (1998), 'A New Generation of Pension Reforms Conquers the East – A Taxonomy in Transition Economies', *Transition*, 9, August (4).

Rutkowski, M. (2002), 'Pensions in Europe: Paradigmatic and Parametric Reforms in EU Accession Countries in the Context of EU Pension System Changes', *Journal of Transforming Economies and Societies (EMERGO)*, 9, Winter (1), 2–26.

Schmidt-Hebbel, K. (1998), 'Does Pension Reform Really Spur Productivity, Saving, and Growth?', Working Paper Series Central Bank of Chile no. 33, Santiago de Chile, April.

Thompson, L. (1998), '*Older and Wiser – The Economics of Public Pensions*, Washington, DC: Urban Institute.

World Bank (1994), *Averting the Old-Age Crisis: Policies to Protect the Old and Promote Growth*, New York: Oxford University Press.

ANNEX

Table 11A.1   Projected expenditures of the public pillar, 2000–2050 (percentage of GDP)

	2000	2005	2010	2020	2025	2030	2040	2050
Czech Republic	9.5	9.6	9.9	11.6	12.4	13.3	16.1	17.1
Estonia	—	7.7	6.5	4.6	3.7	3.0	2.3	2.2
Hungary*	7.4	6.0	5.2	5.0	4.7	4.4	4.4	4.3
Poland**	10.9	10.1	9.7	9.9	9.9	9.6	9.2	9.7
Romania	7.1	8.2	7.9	7.9	8.1	8.4	9.2	9.1
Slovakia	7.7	8.2	8.8	9.9	10.1	—	—	—

Notes:
* Excludes under-age disability pensions of the Health Insurance Fund.
** Excludes the cost of farmers' pension programme.

Table 11A.2   Public pension expenditures including all replacement revenues to people over age 55 before taxes (as a percentage of GDP)

	2000	2010	2020	2030	2040	2050	Peak* change
Belgium	10.0	9.9	11.4	13.3	13.7	13.3	3.7
Denmark[1]	10.5	12.5	13.8	14.5	14.0	13.3	4.1
Germany[2]	11.8	11.2	12.6	15.5	16.6	16.9	5.0
Greece	12.6	12.6	15.4	19.6	23.8	24.8	12.2
Spain	9.4	8.9	9.9	12.6	16.0	17.3	7.9
France	12.1	13.1	15.0	16.0	15.8	—	4.0
Ireland[3]	4.6	5.0	6.7	7.6	8.3	9.0	4.4
Italy	13.8	13.9	14.8	15.7	15.7	14.1	2.1
Luxembourg	7.4	7.5	8.2	9.2	9.5	9.3	2.2
Netherlands	7.9	9.1	11.1	13.1	14.1	13.6	6.2
Austria	14.5	14.9	16.0	18.1	18.3	17.0	4.2
Portugal	9.8	11.8	13.1	13.6	13.8	13.2	4.1
Finland	11.3	11.6	12.9	14.9	16.0	15.9	4.7
Sweden	9.0	9.6	10.7	11.4	11.4	10.7	2.6
United Kingdom	5.5	5.1	4.9	5.2	5.0	4.4	−1.1
EU-15	10.4	10.4	11.5	13.0	13.6	13.3	3.2

Notes:
Calculated from 5-year interval data.
1. For Denmark, the results include the semi-funded labour market pension (ATP). If the ATP is excluded, the peak increase will be 2.7 per cent of GDP.
2. Germany's projections do not incorporate the impact of the 1991 reform.
3. Results for Ireland are expressed as a percentage of GNP.

Source: Economic Policy Committee Report, 'Budgetary challenges posed by ageing populations', October 2001.

12. Public and private mix in the Polish pension system

Agnieszka Chłoń-Domińczak

INTRODUCTION

Poland introduced its pension reform in 1999, following many months of discussion and negotiations. The new pension system in Poland is based on a multi-pillar principle, with two mandatory pillars – pay-as-you-go and funded – and a third, voluntary, one. This structure follows the model recommended by the World Bank in the 'Averting the Old-Age Crisis' report from 1994.[1]

Mandatory elements of a multi-pillar scheme are usually built around two dichotomies: a public pay-as-you-go system, usually based on the defined benefit principle, and a private funded system, based on the defined contribution principle. However, if we investigate the exact nature of the mandatory pension system, there is more scope for a mixture of private and public components, within both pay-as-you-go and funded parts.

The aim of this chapter is to present a mix of private and public elements in the reformed pension system in Poland. In the first section of the chapter, a description of the reformed pension system in Poland is presented. The second section describes the process of changes in the pension scheme, while the third presents an analysis of the forces at play that contribute to the continuing evolution of the mix. A fourth section concludes.

THE PENSION SYSTEM IN POLAND – AFTER REFORM

Experts – demographers and economists – from the very beginning of transition, stressed the need for the reform of the pension system. The aging process in the Polish population was accelerating and the share of older people (above 65) in the population is most likely to double by 2050. Additionally, the existing pension system was facing financial difficulties. Widespread early retirement privileges, granted generously in 1980s, combined with early retirement options for laid-off workers, worsened the situation of the pension system. In 1991 alone, almost a million new pensioners were granted pensions (compared to some 300000 in 1999).

In 1999, after several years of debate, the reform of the pension system was implemented. The reform plan drew experience from existing concepts of pension systems and reforms. However, most of the existing ideas were adjusted to the Polish environment. The first pillar is the PAYGO type, but based on the new paradigm in social insurance, a defined contribution scheme with notional accounts (NDC).[2] A contribution of 12.22 per cent of salary is paid into the first pillar notional account, which is managed by ZUS, the Social Insurance Institution. Those who worked before the introduction of reform will have the initial capital calculated, which recognizes their pension rights from the old to the reformed system.

The second pillar is based on the financial defined contribution system (FDC). Insured people are mandated to save in specially created institutions – open pension funds (OFE). OFE are privately managed by pension fund societies (PTEs), which are joint-stock companies that hold a licence granted by Pension Funds Supervision. Contributions are invested in financial market instruments. The law specifies limits on particular investments, forcing proper diversification of the investment portfolio. The contribution to the second pillar is equal to 7.3 per cent of the worker's wage.

Both first and second pillars operate on the defined contribution (DC) principle. Future benefits will depend on the amount on the individual notional account in the first pillar and money accumulated in the second pillar and on the life expectancy at the retirement age. The system is constructed in such a way as to give people more incentives to work longer. The estimated replacement rate from both pillars is lower than in the past for the pensions from the compulsory system, ranging from 40 to about 60 per cent of final wage (for new entrants to the labour market that have no initial capital). By way of comparison, it was about 70 per cent in the old system. The third pillar is designed to provide additional pensions for those who decide to save more for their retirement. Voluntary arrangements can be either employer-based or individual.

The retirement age has been set at the same level as in the old system (60/65 years), although the initial reform proposal was to make it equal for men and women (62 years). The proposal did not get political approval and the retirement age was not changed.

There is a ceiling of insurable earnings introduced to the system, equal to 250 per cent of average earnings. The social security contribution is set at 36.59 per cent, shared between 19.52 per cent for old age purposes and 17.07 per cent covering other social security risks (disability, survivor, sickness and work injury). The system also includes a minimum pension guarantee that is designed to top up pensions from first and second pillars for those who did not save enough to have a pension higher than the minimum. The guarantee will be financed from the state budget.

In this chapter the main focus is put on the functioning of the mandatory part of the pension system. After the pension reform, the existing system, based fully on public management, was converted into a system where public and private components mix in all areas of pension systems management and operations.

Góra and Palmer (2002) define four issues where different mixes of private and public appear. These are private versus public management, well-defined contract versus a political promise, direct versus indirect claims and public debt versus private equities. Following those lines of division, the main features of the reformed pension system in Poland are presented in Table 12.1, followed by discussion on the public–private mix in all issues.

Table 12.1   Public and private mix in the reformed pension system in Poland

	NDC	FDC
Management	Public, but forced to improve efficiency	Private
Contracts	Public	Mixed
Claims	Public	Private $\Rightarrow$ Public
Assets	Public	Public (ca.70%)
	In the future, partially private (reserve fund)	Private (ca. 30%)

Management of the pension system

Both FDC and NDC systems can be managed by public and private administrations. The main tasks of such administrators are (a) to keep accounts and provide information, (b) to manage pension assets, (c) to provide insurance products, and (d) to collect contributions (premiums). The choice of manager (private or public) in theory should be made on the basis of economic efficiency. However, as the public system in Poland was traditionally managed by the Social Insurance Institution (ZUS), it was decided that this would be continued. Specific provisions on ZUS operations were legislated in the law of 13 October 1998 on the social security system. As the reform fully redesigned the way the pension rights are accrued, it meant in practice significant changes in the way that ZUS was operating, forcing efficiency improvements. What is also important, in the area of institutional contacts (for example, agreement with the provider of IT systems), the management of NDC is based on private arrangements.

Contributions for the entire social security system are collected by ZUS. The funded part is transferred by ZUS to pension funds selected by insured people. Thus one can say that this part of system management is fully public. Other tasks performed by ZUS include keeping accounts for people in the new pension system, assessing the right to old age pensions as well as other pensions (disability, survivor) and benefit payments. ZUS also manages short-term risks: sickness and work injury.

The funded tier is managed privately. The law of 28 August 1997 on organization and functioning of pension funds sets rules for establishment of joint-stock companies: pension fund societies (PTEs). Currently, one PTE can manage one open pension fund (OFE). The law envisages that asset management has to be conducted within PTE. Keeping an individual accounts register can be contracted out to transfer agents (also private) or kept in-house. As far as benefit payments are concerned, the issue is still unresolved. According to the draft law on annuity companies, institutions paying benefits from the funded tier will also be fully private. There is public supervision over all activities of pension funds and, in the future, this will be extended to activities of annuity companies.

Contracts in the Pension System

Contracts between parties specify terms of the agreements. As Góra and Palmer (2002) claim, most of the contracts in traditional PAYGO schemes are public, and thus can be changed by politicians practically at any time. Contracts with private companies are subject to the civil or commercial code of law. Any breach of the contract can be adjudicated in the civil court of law.

Contracts between individuals (the insured) and system administrators are of a public character, in both the NDC and FDC schemes. The insured do not have an option not to participate in the contract. However, in the case of the FDC system, there is a choice of pension fund. An insured person can also change a pension fund, if he or she is dissatisfied with its operations. Individuals can also claim their rights in court, if contracts have been breached. Taking into account these issues, it can be concluded that contracts in the FDC part of the system have a mixed character.

Claims

In the NDC tier of the Polish pension scheme, claims are public. The law of 17 December 1998 specifies all the conditions required to receive a benefit. In the NDC system, size of pension promised is related to the sum of contributions, which is accounted in money terms. Thus it is very difficult to revise the promise. For example, an increase in contributions automatically means an increase in future pension size. Reduction of pensions would mean reduction of notional capital. The only parameter that can be relatively easily used is the indexation of pension benefits. However, in the long run, indexation closer to price inflation leads to increasing differences in pensions between different cohorts: specifically, the relative size of pensions granted to older cohorts reduces.

In the FDC system, according to the draft proposal, claims will be addressed to private institutions, which would calculate and pay old age pensions. However, the draft law proposal includes two conditions for benefit payments, which make the claim partially public. The first is the minimum retirement age, which is the same as in the public system. In the new scheme, the pension from two pillars will be taken at the same time. The second is the requirement of no discrimination in pension calculation, with the exception of gender differences. As the draft law was discussed in the Parliament, all political parties expressed the opinion that benefits should be calculated on the basis of 'unisex' life expectancies. If such a condition holds, the law would compel no discrimination at all, increasing public character of this claim.

Assets

Contribution for old age is divided between NDC and FDC tiers in the proportion 5:3. The size of contributions does not reflect actual division of private and public assets. In the NDC part, by definition, most of the assets are public. However, a demographic reserve (a so-called 'Demographic Reserve Fund') is built up. The reserves can (and should) be invested in financial market instruments, including equity and non-government bonds. Thus it may be said that the NDC system's assets are partially private.

As practice shows, in Poland the FDC part is not fully private. Firstly, there are limitations on investments of pension funds set by law. Thus asset managers are not allowed to invest freely, as they have to comply with the limitations. Secondly, the managers of pension funds manage the risk within funds, not within the pension system. Thus they have a tendency to invest a part of their assets in public bonds, which are perceived as risk-free. In the Polish case, approximately 70 per cent of assets of pension funds are invested in government bonds and treasury bills.[3]

THE PROCESS OF CHANGES IN THE PENSION SCHEME

In this section, an overview of the reform preparation process is presented, with the focus on the process of shaping the public–private mix, as described in the first section. In the early 1990s, during the transformation of the economy, a pension reform with partial privatization was not an item that could gain high priority on the political agenda. High inflation rates and an underdeveloped financial market were the most important obstacles to the creation of private funded pensions. Nevertheless, in 1991, the first idea of pension reform that included the creation of a funded tier was presented by Topinski (president of ZUS) and Wisnewski (a Warsaw University professor). However, the government did not follow this proposal. As expenditure for pensions increased, most of the governments focused on changes in the pension system that reduced expenditure by making changes in the pension formula or benefit indexation. Such a policy was not sustainable in the long run and in the mid-1990s the pension reform debate started within the government.

The SLD–PSL government, which assumed office in the autumn of 1993, had reform of the social insurance system as one of the goals to be achieved during its term. The initial idea was to improve the existing system rather than change it radically. Therefore the initial plan was geared more towards protecting accrued rights than limiting them.

The pension debate was most heated in 1995–6. At that time, at least four distinct proposals for pension reform emerged in Poland. All of them envisaged some kind of public–private mix in the pension system, ranging from the development of a voluntary private scheme to almost full privatization of the mandatory pension system, following the example of Chile and second-generation reforms in Latin American countries. Figure 12.1 presents the timing of the most important proposals, with the assessed role of public and private elements and the importance of the proposal in the political agenda.

Out of the four proposals that were discussed in 1995–6, the Ministry of Labour proposal followed a more conservative and traditional path, most frequently presented by countries having traditional PAYGO DB systems (like, for example, those of France or Germany). The proposed solutions included changes in the PAYGO system (creation of the nationwide flat rate pension, topped up with an individual component). Private funding was envisaged on a voluntary basis only. The Ministry of Finance proposal (prepared by an advisor to the Minister, Marek Mazur) followed the Latin American example and included creation of a mandatory funded pillar and limiting the PAYGO system to a flat rate benefit. The Institute for Labour and Social Policy and the trade union, 'Solidarity', also presented their ideas for reforming the

340   *Economies in transition and Latin America*

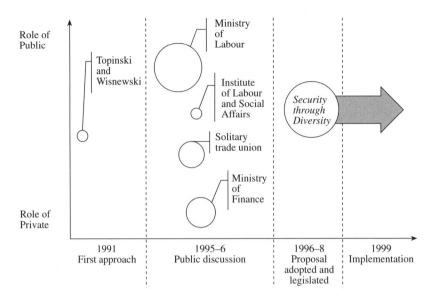

Note: The size of the circle represents relative importance of the presented proposal.

Figure 12.1   Pension reform proposals in the 1990s

pension system. Both proposals included strengthening linkage between wages (contributions) and benefits. The 'Solidarity' plan included creation of the mandatory funded pillar, while the Institute proposed the creation of voluntary funded pension savings, supported by preferential tax treatment. Basic elements of the four proposals are listed in Table 12.2.

Despite various proposals, there was still no comprehensive pension reform plan that could gain the acceptance of the government and Parliament. In April 1996, by which time a new prime minister (Cimoszewicz) and a new minister of labour and social policy (Baczkowski) were in office, the government decided to appoint a Plenipotentiary for Social Security Reform – a politician responsible for preparation of the pension reform. Baczkowski was appointed first plenipotentiary. He strongly supported fundamental pension reform, and said so in parliament. Baczkowski created an Office of the Government Plenipotentiary for the Social Security Reform (hereafter the Office for Pension Reform), a team of experts given the task of developing the reform proposal. Michał Rutkowski (a World Bank official, on leave from the Bank) was appointed head of the Office. He and Marek Góra (a professor from the Warsaw School of Economics) coordinated the work of the experts' team, comprising Polish and international experts in the field of pensions. The work on the pension reform was also supported financially by a World Bank grant.

The reform concept 'Security through Diversity' was prepared by the Office for Pension Reform after the sudden and unexpected death of Baczkowski. 'Security through Diversity' was wholeheartedly embraced by Baczkowski's successors, Jerzy Hausner (February–September 1997) and Ewa Lewicka (November 1997–October 2001). Their sincere conviction regarding pension reform and their professional and political efforts made it possible for reform to proceed. In April 1997, 'Security through Diversity' was presented by the Plenipotentiary and the reform team to the government and to the academic society. The programme formulated the framework for creation of a multi-pillar system in Poland, with a mandatory funded part.

The design of the new pension system in Poland draws experience from other countries. However, the ideas were not just copies of the international examples: they were tailored to the Polish environment. This could be observed best by monitoring the media and the opinions presented there. As far as the international aspects of the reform were concerned, some contradictory opinions were published: the reform proposal is based on the Chilean system; the reform proposal is not based on the Chilean system; the reform should be based on the Chilean system; the reform should not be based on the Chilean system; crucial elements are based on the experiences of Western Europe and Hungary; crucial elements are not based on the experiences of Western Europe and Hungary.

The differences were based on various approaches to the pension system, presented by commentators. For those that favoured pay-as-you-go solutions, the proposal was going too far because of the establishment of a relatively large funded pillar. On the other hand, those that earlier proposed complete privatization of the pension system viewed the proposal as rather conservative, with too big a pay-as-you-go component.

For instance, Minister of Labour and Social Policy, Tadeusz Zieliński commented on the proposal to the press: 'The new system can naturally give rise to doubts, as it was not checked on the Polish ground and differs from the traditional pattern of European law. It is closer to the Chilean solutions introduced by Pinochet' (*Prawo i Życie*, 26 April 1997).

The reform team members claimed that the proposal is rather balanced. For example, Jerzy Hausner, government plenipotentiary for the social security reform, stated in the discussion organized by *Gazeta Bankowa* (20 June 1997):

> Our proposals are not as radical as some people claim. We propose creation of a new system, with a mandatory funded component. For some it might seem radical. However, I think that the idea of rationalizing the existing pension system is not sufficient.

Krzysztof Pater (deputy director of the Office for Pension Reform) insisted: 'We analysed all solutions existing in the world, to avoid the mis-

Table 12.2   Basic elements of the pension reform discussion in Poland prior to formulating the final reform proposal

Main parts of the proposal	Reform proposals formulated between autumn 1995 and spring 1996			
	Ministry of Finance	'Solidarity' trade union	Institute of Labour and Social Policy	Ministry of Labour
Basic pension – first pillar	Flat pension at the level of 20% of average wage	Basic pension consisting of two elements, constant element financed from taxes and insurance element financed from contribution (individually determined)	Benefit dependent on the length of time contributing and size of contribution. Contribution is financed by employee and employer with cap on contributions and pensions (gradually going to the level of 100% of average wage)	Benefit based on the length of working career and individual's salary, financed from contributions and state subsidies with a cap of 250% of average wage (going down to 200% of average wage)
Additional pension – second pillar	Mandatory saving in pension funds	Mandatory saving in pension funds via shifting a part of social security contribution plus privatization bonds, given to all employees	Voluntary savings in pension funds by people earning more than average salary. Additional system integrated with basic one and combined with tax preferences	Voluntary savings in pension funds for people with highest income. Expected participation – marginal

Transition path	Mandatory participation for the new entrants, a choice between systems for employed, very high transition costs	Expected transition period for forming pension funds (app. 10 years), social security contribution divided between PAYGO and funded pillars, significant subsidies from the state budget	Change in the first pillar at the start of the process. Lower replacement rate in the pension system introduced when first pensioners buy pensions in the second pillar. Transition costs covered by lower expenditures from the first pillar	Beginning of the legislation process by the end of the 1990s, implementation in the first decade of the 21st century

Source: *Gospodarka i Przyszlosc*, special edition on social security after Orenstein (2000).

takes made elsewhere' (*Home & Market*, 9 April 1998). Marek Góra (pension reform team leader) said that the Polish system is similar to the Swedish and 'guarantees transparency, justice and stability' (Asekuracja & Re, June 1998).

The reform programme was also approved by international institutions. Basil Kavalsky (World Bank Representative in Warsaw) said to 'Rzeczpospolita' that the reform is a bold, but necessary, change of the logic of the pension system, based on other countries' experience, but adjusted to the specifics of Poland.

EVOLUTION OF THE MIX

The mix of public and private elements as described in the first section may, and should, evolve, adjusting to the requirements of the pension system. These may include changes in both directions – from the public to the private and from the private to the public. In this section, possible directions of changes in the Polish pension system are discussed.

The pension reform implementation of 1999–2001 initiated discussion on the shape of public and private parts of the pension system. Most importantly, it turned out that the public manager of social insurance (ZUS) was not prepared for the reform implementation. The most important tool facilitating management activities (contribution collections, individual accounts handling) – the Complex Informative System – was not completed. As a result, the process of registering contributions on individual accounts started only in August 2001. Before that date, information was processed only to the level that could allow for the transfer of contributions to private pension funds. As there were many errors in the documentation, which could not be corrected in the IT system as planned, only a part of contributions was transferred. Initially, this was estimated at 5 per cent of the amounts due (in May 1999). After a series of actions aimed at improvements in identification of payments, throughout 1999 the contribution transfer was estimated by ZUS at 70–80 per cent of amounts due. This caused a discussion on the possibility of privatizing a part of the management of the social security system. Proposals included privatization of contribution collection for pension funds. This could be done either by creating a single private collecting agency (as, for example, *Consar* in Mexico) or by decentralizing collection by shifting it to each of the pension funds. Other proposals included dividing ZUS into several smaller institutions and/or contracting out some of ZUS's activities (such as management of individual accounts, contribution collection or pension benefit calculation). These proposals, however, were not debated further. It was argued that the con-

tribution collection process has to be accompanied by enforcement procedures, which, under existing Polish law, could not be given to private institutions. As far as management of individual accounts or calculation of
benefit are concerned, it was argued that the situation should be assessed
when the IT system is fully functional. Only then should the decision
whether it is efficient or inefficient be made.

Other much-debated elements include part of the pension reform which is
not completed, which is annuitization of pension savings in the private tier.
The draft law currently envisages that annuities should be paid by specialized
annuity companies, licensed by private tier supervision (UNFE). However,
this solution was criticized as costly and difficult to manage, given constraints
on the annuity formula. During the parliamentary debate on the draft, all
political parties strongly supported using prescribed 'unisex' annuity tables
for calculation of benefits and keeping the costs as low as possible.

In the discussion two possible directions emerged: first, to entrust
annuity payments to insurance companies, hence reducing the costs by
mixing various types of risks; second, to create one institution paying benefits that would poll the survivor risk of the entire population. In this case,
management of assets could be contracted out to private asset managers.

A third element that should evolve over time is related to the assets of the
private tier. As described in the first section, currently around 70 per cent
of private pension funds' assets are invested in public instruments, mostly
government bonds. As the system matures, the share of investment in
equity should increase. As a result, the role of private financial instruments
in the funded part may be increased.

CONCLUSIONS

The evolution of the public and private components in the new pension
system in Poland came from a long process of consultations and compromise. As a result, the new pension system, though built around two dichotomies – first, a pay-as-you-go public tier and, second, a funded private tier
– cannot be classified along those lines. If we look at the specific components such as management, contract, claims and assets, a more complex
mix emerges. Some elements in the public pension system are private (for
example, investment of the reserves). In other elements, private clients force
increased efficiency on public management. In the funded tier, contracts
and claims are partially of a public character. This is caused by the defining of the terms of contract by separate laws. Also pension fund managers
diversify their portfolios and invest part of the private tier assets in public
instruments.

In the process of pension reform, international experiences have been used extensively, which helped to speed up the preparation of necessary legislative framework. The most important international influence in the design sphere was that of Sweden, in the case of the pay-as-you-go component, and Latin American reforms in the case of the second pillar. Experiences of those countries also influenced the specific design of private elements in the public tier and the public elements in the private tier.

The reform process was also a compromise. The compromise had to be reached within the government, with trade unions and within parliament. This resulted in many changes to the initial design of the system. The discussion on the pension system still continues and the shape of the public–private mix in the pension system may change. The mix should at all times be shaped in such a way that the advantages of both public and private elements are best used.

NOTES

1. Research was supported by a group grant from the Research Support Scheme of the Open Society Foundation (RSS No: 1209/1999, Project title 'Pension Reform in Transition Countries: A Comparative Analysis').
2. Góra and Palmer (2002) also define NDC as a non-financial defined contribution, contrary to FDC, a financial defined contribution system.
3. As observed in the period 1999–2001.

BIBLIOGRAPHY

Chłoń, Agnieszka (2000), 'Pension Reform and Public Information in Poland', Pension Reform Primer series, Social Protection Discussion Paper no. 0019 World Bank, Washington, DC.

Chłoń, Agnieszka, Marek Góra and Michał Rutkowski (1999), 'Shaping pension reform in Poland: Security through Diversity', Pension Reform Primer series, Social Protection Discussion Paper no. 9923, World Bank, Washington, DC.

Fultz, Elaine and Marcus Ruck (2000), 'Pension Reform in Central and Eastern Europe: An Update on the Restructuring of National Pension Schemes in Selected Countries', ILO-CEET.

Golinowska, Stanislawa (1995), 'Wybór reformy systemu emerytalno-rentowego dla Polski', *Polityka Spoleczna*, no. 5/6, pp.1–8.

Golinowska, Stanislawa (ed.) (1997a), 'Reforma systemu emerytalno-rentowego', CASE Reports no. 6, Warsaw.

Golinowska, Stanislawa (1997b), 'Eksperci Banku Swiatowego o reformach emerytalnych w Polsce i na swiecie: propozycje, wzory, kontrowersje', IPiSS, Warsaw.

Golinowska, Stanislawa and Jerzy Hausner (1998), 'Ekonomia polityczna reformy emerytalnej', CASE Reports no. 15, Warsaw.

Góra, Marek (1996), 'The Labour Market in Poland: 1990–1995. Empirical and Methodological Studies', Monografie i Opracowania, no. 421, SGH, Warsaw.

Góra, Marek (2001), 'The Polish way of Pension Reform', OECD.

Góra, Marek and Edward Palmer (2002), 'Shifting perspectives in pensions', e-paper, CASE, Warsaw.

Góra, Marek and Michał Rutkowski (1998), *The quest for pension reform: Poland's Security through Diversity*, Warsaw: Office of the Government Plenipotentiary for Social Security Reform.

Hausner, Jerzy (1998), 'Security through Diversity: Conditions for Successful Reform of the Pension System in Poland', Collegium Budapest working paper.

Kolodko, G.W. (1996), *Poland 2000: The New Economic Strategy*, Warsaw: Poltext.

Kurowski, Piotr (1998), 'Dylematy reformy systemu emerytalnego w Polsce', *Polityka Spoleczna*, no. 4, pp.1–5.

Ministry of Finance (1995), pension reform proposal (in Polish).

Ministry of Labour and Social Policy (1995), pension reform proposal (in Polish).

Office of the Government Plenipotentiary for Social Security Reform (1996), *Security through Diversity*, Warsaw.

Office of the Government Plenipotentiary for Social Security Reform (1997), *Polish Pension Reform Package: Part One*, Warsaw.

Orenstein, Mitchell A. (2000), 'How Politics and Institutions Affect Pension Reform in Three Postcommunist Countries', World Bank discussion paper, Washington, DC.

Palmer, Edward (2000), 'The Swedish Pension Reform Model: Framework and Issues', World Bank Pension Primer paper no. 0012, Washington, DC.

Perek-Białas, Jolanta, A. Chłoń-Domińczak and A. Ruzik (2001), *Country Report for Poland, Public Participation and the Pension Policy Process: The Citizen and Pension Reform project*, Warsaw: Pont-Info.

Valdes-Prieto, Salvador (2000), 'Financial Stability of Notional Accounts', *Scandinavian Journal of Economics*.

13. Conflicting interests in shaping Hungary's new private pension scheme

Júlia Szalai

INTRODUCTION

The wholesale movement over the three-year period between early 1998 and the spring of 2001* of almost two million Hungarians (that is, close to 90 per cent of those entitled to do so) to a private pension fund constitutes a major social upheaval. However, despite its enormous significance, both sociologically and politically, it has not yet been properly analysed. The shift reflects a strong desire for change and an implicit criticism of the prevailing social security system. The new legal framework put people – with the exception of those just entering the labour market[1] – into the position of having to choose: they had to weigh up whether they should continue to leave the formation of the main financial basis of their pensions (that is, of their livelihood during old age) to the state, or (at least within the limitations of the law) entrust it to some newly established, free-market private pension fund. We know for a fact that the overwhelming majority of those who, at least in principle, have a right to choose, did not choose the comfortable first option (remaining in the state system), but instead decided on the more risky, though at the same time more enticing, second variation.

This rather surprising development has yet to receive a thorough scholarly explanation. Moreover, the wave of people switching from one pension system to another, the size and intensity of which has surpassed all expectations, raises a whole range of important questions for analysis. Let me list just a few of them. Above all, what factors lie behind such a dramatic downgrading of the existing social security system? What can explain the failure of previous reform projects on the one hand and the popularity of this opening up to the private sector which no one had predicted on the other? How has the structure of interests which 'captured' the social security system in the 1980s changed in the 1990s? What kind of processes brought forth the judgment of policy-makers that, due to the decade-long crisis of state-run social security, internal reform of the old system would not be possible, and that the solution might be to open it up to competition with a new institutional network? Have initial experiences justified this hope? As far as the general functions of insurance schemes are concerned, a set of further questions arise concerning the extent to which the market and social solidarity came into conflict in the old system, and how far the new system will be capable of dealing with the tensions between them. Finally, who are the people behind the new institutions, what is their 'culture', what kind of expertise do they have, and what kind of vision of society does the new pension scheme embody?

In what follows, an attempt will be made to address these questions. In seeking answers to them, I have drawn on several sources. Above all, I have drawn extensively on interviews with representative figures involved in the provision and administration of private pensions who talked about their first experiences, longer-term plans and major difficulties in the course of the transformation of the pension system, as well as about the route they took to establishing or working in the new institutions. What follows builds on the institutional case studies which – partly with the use of the above-mentioned interviews, and partly with documents and statistics related to individual institutions – have been written about representative organizations embodying the main types of private pension system. The pension-related data set of TÁRKI's systematic 'Omnibusz' and 'Monitor' surveys have also been used, as well as the data on the basic characteristics, membership formation and business operations of private pension funds collected by the State Monetary Supervisory Agency.Last but not least, I have also relied a great deal upon a content analysis carried out on the basis of a selection of news reports, analyses and interviews published in the main national newspapers, and the leading economic dailies and weeklies in 1998, covering the rise and rapid expansion of the new private pension system.

THE ANTECEDENTS OF THE PRIVATE PENSION SYSTEM

If we are to understand the rapid development of the new private pension scheme, and the motives behind the choices of the surprisingly large number of people opting for it, we have to go back a little in time, and take a look at the tensions which have historically afflicted the Hungarian pension system, and also at the causes which eventually made the tensions in the traditional social security system unmanageable.

The story goes back to the years before the collapse of communism; more precisely, to the 1980s. The slowly creeping, seemingly unstoppable deepening of the social security crisis had its origins in two fundamental developments: on the one hand, there were latent, though significant, shifts within this important system of income redistribution and, on the other hand, the power struggles in respect of who would gain the upper hand in decision making over the enormous assets reached crisis point, especially when the transition to a market economy set the scene for reform-oriented changes.

Latent Functional Changes in the Social Security System

In a previous work,[2] I listed the socio-historical developments which, in the 1980s, led to social security becoming the principal financial channel of the social policy of the so-called Kádár-era[3] consolidation. As such, it obtained an increasingly significant role in the tacit compromise between the Hungarian people and the party–state leadership – silent assent to the existing regime in exchange for relative freedom – in its expanding and wide-ranging social interventions. More precisely, with the increase in the numbers of those entitled to social security benefits, and with the introduction of new forms of benefit, over the years large social groups came to be characterized by flexible entrance to and exit from the labour market, and – especially – policies were developed legalizing and legitimizing participation in the 'second economy'. The widespread use of the alternative paths offered by the social security system proved to be a particularly favourable outcome from a number of viewpoints. While in this way central control over incomes and consumption could be maintained, new, more indirect forms of exercising this control created a possibility for the development of 'small spheres' of personal freedom. Just as the more flexible labour market relied on the social security system – and wage policy – as a crutch, the ensuring of these small freedoms was the most important political pillar of the self-legitimation of the Kádár regime. It was above all its political advantages and those which accrued to the second economy which raised the social security system, beyond its original income-redistributing role, to its status as the main *social policy* instrument of the Kádár regime, and gave the principal players an interest in the maintenance of this role reinterpretation, and in its implementation in terms of continuous changes in the regulations.

My previous analysis, however, also showed that the coming to the fore of the above-mentioned social policy function entailed costs: that is, whatever headway may have been made, the traditional functions of social security were ranked ever lower down the list of priorities and became confused. On the one hand, in the 1980s, the role played by the social security system in the redistribution of incomes for the purpose of reducing inequalities became extremely questionable, while, on the other hand, at around this time, the 'equal sacrifice theory of taxation' element – which meant that the costs of particular 'life tasks' (above all the subsistence of the elderly and childrearing) could be partly or wholly met from social redistribution –

practically disappeared. The confusion of functions arising on the basis of the new interpretation of roles also appeared in several forms. On the one hand, over the years social security payments fell to ever more unsatisfactory levels, and so the system itself ever more markedly contributed to the sharpening of income inequalities between individual social groups, and to the appearance of distinct groups of the poor who were dependent on the state. On the other hand, social security benefits became ever more separated from their original foundations, that is, from wages and/or from types of need normatively determined on the basis of a set of principles.

This was more or less the state in which the social security system found itself on the threshold of the change of regime. Immediately before the passing of the party-state, however, the everyday functioning of the social security system underwent important changes (which largely determined later developments). On the one hand, in 1989, the social security system, which had hitherto been under direct state budget supervision, was turned into an independent institution, while on the other hand, in 1990, it was split into two independent parts: the Pension Insurance Fund which makes cash payments, and the Health Insurance Fund, which is responsible for the delivery of health care and related services. These two packages of measures were clearly of a totally administrative character (and with hindsight their introduction was by no means 'innocent') and had the effect of significantly deepening the existing functional confusions.

The setting up of the social security system as an independent institution took place without its being allocated any of the means required for the exercise of genuine independence. This sector was removed from the protective shield of the state budget and from the expert mechanisms of state budget planning but, in contrast to other sectors, it was left without a head: that is, no apparatus was put in place which could make decisions, or formulate and protect its own interests, and its relationship to the other institutional components of the state budget was not redefined. In reality, in the wake of its independence, the social security system became the government's 'personal cash-till', which, according to need, could cover a significant proportion of the budget deficit, which at that time represented the most disturbing 'motes' in the eyes of the international financial institutions (for example, price subsidies, cash payments made from tax and other contribution revenues, and so on). At other times it could be used for the flexible financing of certain items of central government expenditure (mainly the – at that time – fashionable housing bonds which it was mandated to buy up, in the form of direct credits to the state budget). In other words: in the absence of its own decision-making apparatus and internal decision-making mechanisms, and through its direct subordination to the government, an organizationally simple solution was created in terms of which the financial management and structure of expenditure of the social security system were determined primarily on the basis of its functioning as a stop-gap in the reduction of the dramatically increasing deficits which characterized the state budget at that time. With independence, the circle of players arguing over the system narrowed, while behind the closed doors of the agency, which had been made independent almost overnight, the reinterpretation of the actual functions of social security, which later acquired decisive significance, could be initiated.

Through the division of the two basic components of the social security system, the contribution-based redefinition of a fund for satisfying needs which had previously been understood to be a task of the state – delivery of health care – was legitimized, as was the sudden setting against one another of two equally important tasks: wellbeing in old age, and/or health maintenance for all. While at that time the expected advantages of the shifting of health care from the state budget to social security were at the forefront, with the transformation the long-term prospect of an explosive situation arose in respect of pension system reform: health care, which had been lagging behind for decades, and was replete with internal tensions, started to 'suck up' those funds which at that time did not have a 'proprietor' capable of looking after them. At the beginning of the 1990s, a situation arose in which the distribution of contributions between the two funds took place without the assessment of the necessary long-term cost–benefit calculations and of the structural changes expected in the pension system. The outcome was, however, foreseeable: the above-mentioned putting into competition of equally important tasks, with the effective cutting back of central funds for making cash payments in meeting welfare needs.

Tensions were only increased by the fact that, in the meantime, the number of those claiming cash benefits – above all, the diverse forms of early retirement – had increased by leaps and bounds. Whoever was able to retire early could thereby avert the threat of unemployment. The result was a continuous increase in the number of people on a disability pension and those claiming pensions by virtue of age exemption, through which process the number of those claiming pensions rose by around 600000 (almost a quarter) between 1990 and 1996.

The Struggle for Control over the Social Security System

Meanwhile, a heated power struggle for control over the social security system got under way. The becoming independent of the system in 1989 was not accompanied by an explicit assertion to that effect, but it was made absolutely clear that its secondary aim was the supplanting, through direct subordination to the Cabinet, of the role of the trade unions, which had traditionally regarded the social security system as almost their 'personal fiefdom'. Behind this ambition stood, on the one hand, the government and the (at that time) reform-oriented segment of the party-state, who made common cause with the traditional adversaries of reform in the trade unions and the main defenders of party-state social demagogy. On the other hand, there stood those economic groups, above all the financial managers of the health care system and the big pharmaceutical manufacturers and distributors, which hoped for a competitiveness boost under increased market competition or, in the given case, the obtaining of greater influence over social security funds and the modification of redistribution in a direction favourable to them. As a result of the modifications implemented in 1989 and 1990, the influence of different actors over these funds really did change, at least temporarily, which more than anything provides eloquent testimony of the much criticized and publicly discussed fact that expenditure on drug price subsidies and health care development was growing at an extraordinarily high rate at this time.[4]

Before the radical and permanent rearrangement of power relations in the social security system, however, a number of serious obstacles accumulated. Above all, the underperformance of the economy during these years constituted an objective barrier, in the face of which any significant tinkering with the social equalization function which the social security system had performed for decades demanded enormous care. The first democratically elected administration which came to power in 1990, the Antall government, was warned to take particular care by the shock which it experienced in the autumn of the same year: the taxi drivers' blockade. This taught the government that steps taken in pursuit of marketization – for example, withdrawal of price subsidies – could be made only with appropriate agreements and compromises, in the absence of which it could expect mass actions, strikes and boycotts. The taxi drivers' organization, and the solidarity which the general public displayed in their favour, drew attention once again to the 'sleeping lion', the trade unions: the taxi drivers' blockade made it clear that without them there would be no market transformation, especially not in respect of the social security system, which had been their domain not so long before.

But the social security system's own internal inertia also acted as a brake on radical transformation: besides satisfying the demands of the new players, the serious disruption of the principle of regular payment of contributions, as well as the above-mentioned increased social security claims, created a difficult situation. These factors had conjugate effects as a result of the drastic loss in value of each and every form of social security benefit. Particularly dramatic was the situation of pensions, which, between 1989 and 1992, barely three years, lost almost 20 per cent of their real value, a devaluation from which they have not recovered to this day. In this way, it became ever clearer that any kind of reorganization or marketization of the social security system would be nothing other than an exercise in political adventurism. In fact, the stabilization of the situation would require the restoration of the old power relations and their institutionalization in a new framework.

In these circumstances, the most important statutory development in respect of the social security system took place in the first half of the 1990s: the establishment of the social security self-governments. Overturning the schedule, in accordance with which social security payments and the regulation of the contributory basis of these payments would have to be put on the agenda first, and only after which the organizational system could be transformed accordingly, which had been the consensus among experts and legislators for years, in the autumn of 1991 the government unexpectedly submitted and then in spring 1992 passed the new self-government bill. However, as a result of this move, the substance of the system, the everyday operations of the social security system, remained unaffected in every detail: in fact, this temporarily immobilized the reform work on the raising of the pensionable age limit and on the revision of individual entitlements (for example, family allowance and maternity benefit) which commenced at that time.

Control over the two large funds in the reorganized system came into the hands of the representative organizations of three players – the employees, the employers and the government – which, practically speaking, became their all-powerful proprietors. Although the law retained unchanged parliamentary supervision of the social security system, in subsequent years in the formation of laws concerning the state budget and entitlement regulations the new self-governments acquired an unambiguously leading role. On closer inspection, the social security self-government law itself projected what in fact became reality: the new self-governments were destined to ensure the rehabilitation of the influence and, alongside that, the legitimation of the social role of the trade unions (and, among them, primarily the largest employees' organization, MSZOSZ). For this reason, MSZOSZ justifiably celebrated the first social security self-government elections as renewed recognition of its influence and institutionalized power and, in the wake of its electoral successes, rightly claimed for itself a leading role in the management of both self-governments, as well as the transfer of a substantial proportion of state assets under privatization so that it could perform its new market functions as a proprietor also in the short term.

(It is worth noting that, in the course of the debates which took place concerning the allocation of assets, the social security system itself was barely mentioned, let alone its ever-deepening financial crisis or what kind of use might be made of the allocated capital to alleviate the crisis, especially in the short term. The arguments adduced were, on the one hand, rather of a compensatory character: that is, they concerned restitution of the formerly state-owned assets of the insurance institutions nationalized in the late 1940s. On the other hand, the trade union leaders demanding assets, with a somewhat demagogic emphasis on social justice, came out in support of an equitable share in the general 'privatization' wave for those groups traditionally represented by the trade unions.)

With regard to the issue of control over the two social security funds, until the coming to power[5] of the new FIDESZ-led coalition government, the trade union dominance legitimized by the self-governments remained essentially unchanged.[6] Substantive reform of the social security system has been postponed indefinitely. Steps implemented in the course of the 1990s, as drastic as they were, were at best enough to put some sort of brake on the further erosion of the social security system, and to prevent the funds' sky-high deficit from burying the public finances as a whole. But alongside the continual tinkering, the unstoppable devaluation of benefits, the enforced increase in overall benefit expenditure – putting a brake on the economy – the (by now routine) avoidance of contribution payments, and the squandering (which from time to time leads to a public scandal) of the assets and property put into the hands of the social security system, have continued, as has the growth of the social security funds' deficit which can now be measured in many tens of billions of forints. The erosion of the system, so it seemed, and so it still seems, could scarcely be curtailed by means of internal reform.

The way out of this deepening crisis led elsewhere: first, by way of experiment towards voluntary pensions, then – after they had proved themselves – towards the establishment of statutory, institutionalized, compulsory and fully funded private pension funds.

THE PRIVATE PENSION FUNDS IN CLOSE-UP

If we had to briefly summarize what has been said so far, it could be stated that the bringing into being of the private pension funds was the logical and organic result of the coming together of processes which have different origins, but which over the course of time have become entwined and have amplified one another. Long-term macro-level changes generating ever-deeper conflicts at several points in the economy,[7] decades of resistance to social security reform, fundamental changes in everyday life, and mass 'embourgeoisement', have concurrently operated in the background, all of which worked towards the increase of tension between the delivery organization and its clients, and led, after all, to the extreme delegitimization of the social security system. All things considered, one can say that the processes characteristic of the gestation of the crisis of social security, and the alternative escape routes from it, were particularly many-sided and long-lasting. And it is precisely because of this that, looking at these processes from a historical viewpoint, we must contemplate with some surprise the fact that the new institutional system, like Pallas Athena from the head of Zeus, stepped fully armed, nevertheless almost without antecedents, onto the stage of the Hungarian market economy.

But in the wake of this long maturation anyone might with justification have supposed that the private pension fund network – and with it the whole new private pension system based on self-reliance – would soon be introduced, after protracted experimentation and ample discussions, and that the full range of expectations would be reflected in its final form. This was all the more justified because, besides many practical details, the new arrangements' basic functions were not unambiguously predictable even in the planning stage. That is to say, it was not written down and established in principle whether the new funds would be market agents or savings banks with the object of winning back the trust of the population, just as it was not established in principle whether they would be turned into privatized instruments of the state and kept on a short leash, or autonomous actors personifying the notions of market liberalism.

However, the actual establishment of the private pension funds was as rapid – almost like a coup d'état – as the process of latent maturation was long-drawn-out: from the parliamentary session which accepted the fundamental retailoring of the pension system no more than six months passed before the enacting of the bill on private pension funds and, after that, it took barely two more months to arrive at the firing of the regulatory starting pistol, which made it possible to set up the organizations of the funds, and then only another four months passed before the new funds opened their doors to hundreds of thousands of customers.

This great hurry requires an explanation. In all likelihood, the actual course of events was determined by fundamentally political processes. On the latter assumption, at least, all the different pieces of the puzzle fall into place. At that time the subject of social security was characterized by debates of a political nature and by one scandal after another, mud slinging and threats. Furthermore, the dominant party of the ruling coalition, the Hungarian Socialist Party (MSZP) had made up its mind regarding state budget reform, and among the main factions protecting the traditional power of the trade unions we may suspect that political deals were made, particularly given the imminent elections and daily rumours upon which no comment was made. Political agreements were probably also behind Hungarian diplomatic measures offering EU-conforming market institutions with a view to speeding up European integration. The winning back of the middle class, which had become estranged from the sitting government and was now considering whether to switch its allegiance to FIDESZ, was also a political question, and one which, moreover, greatly influenced the outcome of the imminent elections.

However, we can provisionally formulate all this as the set of symptoms immediately determining the creation of and exercising a decisive influence over the private pension funds only as a hypothesis: it will be for future historians to put together the history of this legislative haste, with suitable attention to detail and complete with all the relevant argumentation, with the processing and analysis of the documents related to social security which will some day become available, the minutes of inter-party and inter-state negotiations, and market contracts with relevance to interest groups. Contemporary interpretation of the facts must content itself, by combining the accessible (semi-public and public) documents, with trying to ascertain the relevant determining factors, as well as their extremely volatile formation, and the background of the very rapid and dramatic rearrangement in the sequence of leading motives.

For this purpose it is worth looking more closely at two outstandingly significant documents: the government's proposal of mid-December 1996 concerning the pension system, and particular details of Law 82 of July 1997 concerning private pensions and private pension funds. In order to lay down the fundamental arguments in favour of creating a new private pension system, the Government Programme stated the following:

> The Government supports the proposed new pension system for the following reasons:
>
> 4. The transformation of the pension system is in accord with international experience . . .
>
> 4.2. The new system guarantees the financial security of the elderly . . .
>
> 4.3. The new pension system improves the participation in the system of individual interests . . .
>
> 4.4. . . . the capital funded pension system . . . also increases the resources of the economy . . .
>
> 4.5. . . . Long-term savings which grow year-on-year have a beneficial effect upon economic activity . . .
>
> 4.6. . . . On our calculations, the introduction of a contributory element into pensions will, over the longer term, virtually double domestic credit opportunities for enterprises.[8]

In the introductory section of the law of July, 1997, entitled 'Basic operational principles and basic orders', we read the following:

5. § (1) In accordance with the principle of operation by a self-government the taking of fundamental decisions related to the fund shall be the exclusive right of fund members.

(2) The right to freely choose a pension fund may be exercised in terms of either signing up with a fund or of transferring from one to another . . . Discrimination against fund members on the grounds of religious faith, race, ethnicity, political beliefs, age, or gender shall be prohibited.

(3) Fund members jointly provide [financial] cover for the fund's operations and services on the basis of mutuality and the principle of self-reliance. . .

(4) The fund-member's balance – in accordance with the principle of ownership – is the property of the fund-member . . .

(6) The fund . . . is therefore obliged to increase its assets so that the meeting of its obligations is not jeopardised.

(7) In keeping with the principle of care exercised in relation to property with which one is entrusted, persons acting for the fund shall be obliged to proceed in the interests of fund-members with all due care.

(8) In accordance with openness and the principle of data protection, data related to the operations of the fund [shall be] publicly available.[9]

Comparison of these two texts gives rise to some instructive conclusions. Although it is clear that they were conceived with different aims and (at least partly) for different audiences, their striking differences in emphasis are nevertheless noteworthy. At centre-stage of the government document, which was intended to initiate a public debate lasting no more than a month, stand the economic (primarily macroeconomic) advantages promised by the new system and the features which it was hoped would promote the functioning of the rule of law: the coming together of individual and macroeconomic interests; the strengthening of contribution payment discipline; the expansion of funds available to the players in the economy; and so on. At the same time, the wording of the law tries to emphasize the marketization benefits of the new system. These paragraphs – which regulate the self-governing status of the new funds, the right to free consumer choice of pension fund, the individual ownership guarantee, public access to data and the basic conditions of fair competition – testify to many attractive individual rights and universally respected social values.

Moreover, closer examination of the text of the law makes it clear that the Parliament was able to curtail significantly the government's vehemently acquisitive intentions. The finally accepted law, that is, restricted the pension funds' lending and capital investment opportunities to an extremely narrow range and subjected them to close state supervision, while it also prescribed the creation of significant reserve funds and guaranteed coverage, and in addition, in contrast to what was outlined in the government programme, extended the range of individual rights (above all through the increased protection of pension contributions and the liberalization of the conditions governing the inheritance of pension fund contributions). That is, we can say with some justification that, in contrast to the strongly economy-oriented character of the government programme, the law which finally came into being is rather oriented towards the individual, and at its centre stands the emphasis upon a new relationship between state and citizen and the meticulous working out of the conditions underwriting the new relationship.

This significant displacement of points of emphasis appears to relate to two things. The first is the fact, already mentioned several times, that the pension question was a complex political issue over a long period, for which reason no one could say, right up to the last moment, which interest groups would determine the initial configuration of the pension funds. And although, according to the public opinion pollsters, the Parliament had become unpopular because it was out of touch with the electorate, the law on private pension funds was good news for those concerned about Hungary's political culture: after all, by focusing on basic 'bourgeois' values, and the relationship between state and citizen, the law satisfied one of the public's must fundamental wishes. To be more precise, it made it clear that standpoints and values which conflicted with public opinion, including those of the government, had to be put lower on the agenda.

The second consequence which may be derived from the above-mentioned strong shift in emphasis is less favourable. The strikingly large span of the two documents indicates that, at the end of the day, the pension funds were brought into being in the worst possible, unstable circumstances. The absence of firm consensus carried the seeds of subsequent events: although what we are considering is a law intended to apply for the very long term, its word is not sacred. If today the parliamentary majority which sustains the current government decides to change the timetable of the division of contributions envisaged from the beginning, then tomorrow there is nothing to stop it laying hands on any other component in this legislative package. But one scarcely needs to emphasize the fact that, in this way, a question mark would be put against the law's credibility, and directly in connection with the secret of its initial popularity as a set of rules establishing a new type of relationship between state and citizen.

In the summer of 1997, however, the latter danger could still be entertained at best only in theory. And, in any case, the balance now tipped temporarily in favour of the advantages. After the announcement of the bill, feverish activity got under way. With the agents of the large banks and insurance companies, whose training had been going on for months, the – finely calibrated – wages and fringe benefits system which would make possible the efficient acquisition of members, and the leading managers trained in the foreign mother-institutions all standing by, it was expected that establishment of the new funds would commence. The sector- and workplace-based apparatus, with its experience in the voluntary pension funds, deliberated over its ability to perform the new tasks. The public relations (PR) firms sharpened their expertise and mutual competition on reams of promotional materials. The relevant ministries worked on the production of masses of executive orders and record systems for the approaching deadline of introduction, 1 January 1998. The workplace personnel and wage administration directors made every effort to simplify rationally the enormous number of tasks falling to their lot as a result of the new transfer system. Finally, the general public (the citizens affected by it all) tried to find out what on earth was going on.

Information was not easy to come by, however. In the absence of long-term data it was difficult to assess the calculations on which the law was based – particularly in a fashion which could be understood in everyday terms – so that people could decide whether to make the switch or not. From our interviews, and from the TÁRKI surveys accompanying the reception of the private pension system, it turns out that most people soon gave up trying to obtain information of this kind, and relied instead on what others did: what their colleagues, bosses or close friends advised. But it was difficult not only to come to a conclusion concerning whether it was worth it or not, but also on which of the pension funds to choose. Needless to say, the pension funds were in keen competition to win the favour of potential customers. In the autumn of 1997, more than 50 organizations approached the State Monetary Supervisory Agency with requests to establish pension funds, and if, at the opening of business at the beginning of January 1998 fewer than this actually got off the ground, nevertheless they were more than enough, given the security (and revenue) indicators based on the expected number of customers which the experts had dared to estimate in advance.

In these circumstances, it is hardly a surprise that, while the law strongly emphasized every individual's right to choose the pension fund he or she liked the look of, in the event this right was quite restricted. Soon, a spontaneous social process emerged as the outcome of people's efforts to come to grips with the law: the workplace became the most important level of entry to the new pension system. This served the practical interests of many. On the one hand, there were the pension funds: in their ferocious battle for market share those able to take large bites from the cake at each stage of the rush would be at an advantage. What they classed as 'large bites' were the big companies employing several thousand workers. Understandably, there has been considerable competition to establish contacts with such companies. The banks and insurance companies with branch networks and a customer base going back decades at first built upon their own counter employees: by galvanizing their longstanding network of contacts, they tried to exert informal influence. With a little gentle persuasion their customers might facilitate a meeting with management and financial experts at their place of work. The banks and insurance companies would do the rest: agents in possession of fresh qualifications, and with a smile reflecting their familiarity with the new system on their faces, started out with a reasonable chance of success in winning the much-prized privilege of providing customers with information on the new pension funds ahead of the perhaps more professional, but 'alien' foreign companies. The foreigners, for their part, tried to obtain a solid customer base through their expertise, and the background of enormous capital and decades of international experience, as well as by dangling the prestige of contacts with a perhaps well-known foreign company before the eyes of the company directors. The new small companies, on the other hand, tied to the mast the attractions of transparency, a solidaristic way of doing business, and democratic decision-making procedures, and in the first instance tried to win over the big city intelligentsia classes who are susceptible to values of this kind. Finally, the sectoral and workplace funds pursued the trade union route: with the renegotiation and expansion of collective contracts, trade union members were directed to the new funds.

On the other side of the fence, the workplaces showed themselves open to mass recruitment. The persuasive agent took from their shoulders the burden of individual advice giving, and the 'production conference'-like nature of the presentation of information also, as it were, legitimized the access given to the workers. The employees involved scarcely protested. Usually, they took the view that they would not be able to reach a better decision than their superiors. In any case, what did it matter to them where their social security contributions went? They would suffer no personal loss if part of their contributions was henceforth paid elsewhere; compared with the operations of the social security system, which were certainly not open to their inspection, it was something of an improvement that in future they would personally receive the annual balance of their savings. In respect of choice between rival companies, however, they had nothing to go on at all.

As a result of this significant convergence of interests it emerged that, according to data from the TÁRKI Omnibusz and Monitor surveys, two-thirds of the new pension fund customers had made their choice on a workplace basis: they had done what their personnel departments, bosses or colleagues had recommended. In comparison with the informants' workplace, all other channels took second place: the activities of door-to-door agents, friends and family. And if we look at indicators characterizing the social positions of the enrolled, the picture, disregarding deviations of a few percentage points, is the same. There are at most very slight differences between individual social strata: more educated urban employees were reached by agents, while advice outside the workplace (from family members, friends, neighbours) was more prevalent in villages, and among the elderly and the less well educated.

Evidently, the fact that the number of customers rose with astonishing speed and that, in the space of only a few months, the theoretical maximum number of members was nearly reached, is certainly not independent of the fact that the recruitment process astonishingly resembled the well-known and sharply remembered methods of trade union foundation. After barely five months, the total membership of the private pension funds had reached around one million; by autumn 1998, it exceeded 1.2 million; and by the end of 1998 it was around 1.8 million. In the second year of the scheme, 1999 – the whole year up to August – there was very little growth (mainly young people entering the labour market for the first time), then a final injection of around 120 000 people who had been waiting for the concluding deadline laid down by the law of 31 August. Dynamic growth, so it appears, was unstoppable. The number of those returning to the social security system was insignificant and has remained so, and for the time being transfers between pension funds are sporadic. However, the ground beneath the new institutions themselves was shaken when five smaller funds folded after a few months, and some merged with larger ones, while the latter went through organizational transformations to a greater or lesser extent (mostly their voluntary and private pension fund businesses merged, but in many places and often, deposit and asset management institutions working together with pension funds converted.

Obviously, none of this shook the resolve of those who had already signed up or who were flirting with the idea: the unfavourable developments of 1998 on the stock exchange and in terms of legislation (as the law's initial 'generosity' was increasingly watered down) left them cold. The undiminished impetus behind the acquisition of new customers quite simply tells another story: mass abandonment above all expressed the expiration of the social security system, and for the time being only to a minor extent the fact that people wanted to live as self-conscious citizens with the subjective rights laid down so attractively in the law. Among these rights, it was clear to most that the freedom to select a pension fund had been tightly restricted from the very beginning. Furthermore, there had been very little time in which to exercise the other rights (self-governance, inheritability, public data access); everything was still very much at the formative stage.

As a result of all this, for the time being the main players in the private pension fund sector are less the members changing funds than the organizations which arrange things for them and in their interests. And although these organizations – the pension funds themselves just as much as the market and state institutions brought into being to supervise them – over the last two and a half years have rather busied themselves with moulding their image and their internal operations, some striking characteristics of the system's rapid internal articulation are already clear. Some of these characteristics are obvious, but there are also a number of somewhat surprising ones.

Size is an organic feature of any structuring process: accordingly, the approximately 38 funds which are still in existence are congregated around two poles. Around one of the poles are the five giants: the ÁB-Aegon, Nationale Nederlanden, OTP, Hungária Biztosító and Winterthur pension funds – all financial sector companies with great traditions. Over the last three years these five companies have attracted around 80 per cent of pension fund customers and an even higher proportion of pension contributions. Around the other pole are gathered the small companies: with one or two exceptions, the decisive majority of them are sectoral or workplace funds with several tens of thousands of members. Intensive analysis is not required in order to see that, in practical terms, size differences create (and express) functional differences. The big pension funds are the newest – above all from a finance policy and market standpoint – undertakings of the financial world's most illustrious institutions, while the small companies have grown on the basis of individual industrial sectors or workplaces: their primary role is not the winning of market share or profit growth, but rather the keeping alive of workplace traditions. In keeping with their origins, the big companies are led purely by profit: for them, the private pension sector is worth running to the extent that and while it produces profits, at least within a few years, and/or opens the door to other opportunities for market acquisition. The small companies look at their activities not only in terms of the return on their investment, whether in the wider or the narrower sense, but also in terms of considerations which cannot be measured in money: such emotionally coloured motives as their human resource policy, trade union members and tradition cultivation.

This close relationship between size and function is not entirely without consequences, however. The overlapping of these two sets of phenomena foreshadows possible substantial differences between the pensions of those served by the large companies and the pensions of those served by the small. Needless to say, the revenues determining the level of future pensions will be greater in respect of the well-capitalized big companies; it may be that over time a price will have to be paid for fidelity to a given company, measurable in thousands of forints per month. It is therefore worth calling attention to the fact that, as a result of the division along this dimension, a sense of frustration and of having been cheated will over time gain impetus, with good reason, which may easily turn into fervent anti-trade union feelings and, what is more, into feelings directed against the market and against foreigners. Radicalizing emotions of this kind are also nurtured by the fact that the membership composition of the large pension funds is markedly different from that of the small. Although the available data do not allow us to undertake a precise analysis of the social status of pension fund members, the somewhat aggregated indicators also indicate that the better educated, better situated social strata constitute the membership of the large funds, while less well educated, primarily manual workers constitute the membership of the smaller ones, generally organized around the workplace. If this is indeed the case, then, over the long term, we can depend upon it that attitudes directed against the large pension funds will be coloured by class-based feelings, and this would clearly bring with it an intensification of the conflict already alluded to.

Naturally, it is possible that over the next few years events will take a different turn: the trend towards consolidation will continue and as a result the small funds may simply disappear. Such convergence may be expected to come at a price, however: as a result, future pensions will in all likelihood be equalized, but the democratic elements built into the system will be eliminated from it: investment and market policy decisions will depend entirely upon negotiations between the state and the large pension funds. In consideration of the latter, all too likely, outcome, there is little hope that the benefits accruing to pension fund members from the existence of pension fund self-governments, the assertion of their ownership rights or the protection of their personal interests will constitute anything more than a high-sounding wish expressed in the law and will never be realized within the framework of the Hungarian pension system.

This is especially the case if we consider another aspect of the marked differences related to size and functions: the national affiliation of the founding institution. In fact, this element is perhaps the chief determinant of the differences which characterize the pension fund sector. In question here is not only the differences created between the foreign- and Hungarian-based pension funds by the (markedly different) amounts of capital available to the founders and by the costs related to the running in of the new private pension fund sector. In light of the general lack of capital in Hungary it is no surprise that in this regard the Hungarian and the foreign founders are simply not competing on a level playing field. This is the case with regard to practically all products and services, but perhaps especially in the area of pension services. A pension fund is an expensive undertaking, particularly at the beginning: during the period of getting the new activity off the ground, the funds simply spend money hand over fist, and covering one's costs is out of the question for a number of years. During this initial period, therefore, a great deal depends upon the ability of the founding companies to bear their costs. From the beginning, the capital-rich big banks and insurance companies have been in a better position than the industrial concerns flirting with establishing a pension fund, service-providing companies or individual departments in respect of which financial market investment could readily be described as a waste of money.

But besides these obvious, and almost unavoidable, differences, the nature of the respective pension fund founders influences the structuring process in other, less obvious ways. Their private pension fund 'philosophy' (and the whole culture behind it) draws an even sharper line between the foreign pension fund founders and their Hungarian counterparts than the technical one already considered. It was striking from our interviews and case studies how very different were the features which characterize the two different groups: from the formulation of their identity profiles and mission statements, through their recruitment policies, to their orientation in the Hungarian market; from the domestic politics standpoint to the taking into account of the wishes of important political actors or their skilful sidestepping. We found these differences even more surprising because the data on new members point to exactly the opposite: when making their choice, consumers, according to every indication, considered it a side issue whether or not a particular pension fund was in Hungarian or foreign hands. Nevertheless, as far as internal character is concerned, for the time being the two groups of pension funds might as well be on different planets.

From our interviews with pension fund bosses, department heads and agents, as well as from our case studies, it became clear that, although they are after the same consumers, and although everyone, naturally, counts on making a profit, the interests and concerns of the players entering the pension market are fairly complex. For the foreigners, a pension fund is in the first place a means of winning markets, a 'preparing of the ground' and a 'school of cultural study' conducted on new and ready-to-be-conquered territory for other companies with which they are directly connected. The Hungarian pension funds see themselves differently. For them, beyond immediate financial considerations, it is a matter of maintaining traditions, institutionalizing the defence of values which have been around for decades, and the possibility of having a say in Hungarian pension market policy, or, more generally, in the Hungarian economy, as well as the protection of market positions which had been established earlier on.

As a result of these differences, they set about both the acquisition/organization of their markets and the training of their experts very differently. The interviews eloquently reveal that the foreigners played for high stakes from the beginning: they systematically made large Hungarian companies their targets and regarded member recruitment through employers as their primary route. Their 'civilized' treatment of customers derives from their Western 'philosophy': they regard their efforts to ensure that East Europeans receive the same treatment as has been enjoyed by their Western counterparts for decades as an expressly modernizing and civilizing mission. Their attitude is also apparent from their choice of words. New fund members are 'clients', whom they 'advise' or 'notify', and with whom they establish a 'partnership'. In contrast, the Hungarian companies continue to employ the familiar paternalistic approach towards their customers, calling them 'members' or even 'old dears', and in the best case 'women', 'workers', and so on, while referring to their relations with clients in terms of 'teaching' and 'instruction'. Similarly, these companies purport to 'intervene in their [members'] interests' in business associations, at ministries, and so on.

At the same time, in the matter of business introductions, Hungarian companies put much more emphasis upon – and of course have more opportunity to do so – personal relations than their Western counterparts: either because each workplace or branch presents a ready-made set of customers (and ready-made and well-trodden trade union, departmental head or other relationships to set the ball rolling), or because, in the case of the banks, the counter staff in an established local branch network are able to draw in, within the framework of existing services, a customer base which is already familiar with them. Personal contact, then, and with it oral communication, remains an important element in relations between pension fund and customer in the case of Hungarian firms: this is also revealed, for example, by the fact that the employees of Hungarian pension funds without exception switched to particular customer service or 'maintenance' tasks as the member acquisition campaign wound to a close. At the same time, those conducting most of the member acquisition activities of the foreign-backed pension funds became insurance and credit consultants of the large employers with whom they had come into contact, or they were simply transferred to other spheres of banking or insurance activities, as the wave receded.

The differences, as already mentioned, were also clear in the pension funds' selection and training of specialized staff. In the course of setting up their pension funds, the foreign insurance companies and banks used methods tried and tested elsewhere. Mainly Hungarian headhunting companies were commissioned with assembling a workforce on the basis of guidelines well worked out in detail and precisely operationalized. Those selected were given technical training abroad and then indoctrinated in the culture of the firm. This indoctrination, as we have already seen, in fact amounted to nothing less than undergoing a solemn initiation rite, assigning a whole form of life and network of contacts to those whose future career was considered by their superiors as likely to see them being promoted through different levels in the company. And, as in the case of a mission in general, it is also true here that, after the completion of a particular range of tasks, one is likely to be moved on. When the higher management thinks it is appropriate, a tough rotation system moves local managers around so that they do not come to regard individual posts, services or positions as their personal fiefdom.

From our interviews it turned out that this kind of career is attractive only to some, primarily to a fairly well circumscribed group of ambitious, talented, young professionals. At one foreign-backed pension fund after another we found higher managers, now in their thirties, of this kind, most of whom had had a technical education, but who even from the beginning had not pursued an engineering career, instead studying foreign languages and trying to combine their technical knowledge with a knowledge of the modern world. They were excited by business, by administration, and by information technology; and, by combining these areas, they somehow got jobs in which they were not experts confined to a narrow sphere, but rather modern technocrats with wider horizons and a wider range of knowledge. From here the pension fund route was a true step forward: the technocrat's horizons, in business terms, were expanded considerably, and with a little humanistic culture into the bargain.

This 'expansion' also left its mark on their 'form of life': they were transformed into world citizens, in respect of which the reading of foreign newspapers and literature, regular foreign travel, wide-ranging political knowledge and, in the technical sense, an exhaustive knowledge of 'other worlds' play an important role. It is true that a good apartment, nice furniture and modern fixtures and fittings are important to them, but mainly from a functional standpoint: they crave not luxury but a rationally and properly arranged and varied life in the Western style. In their way of thinking and behaviour they are fairly autonomous, but they know the limits of their autonomy precisely: their foreign superiors and, to a much smaller extent, the Hungarian higher management.

The management and employees of Hungarian pension funds have different origins and see the course of their lives differently. They are usually administrators who had already provided evidence of their suitability and loyalty in one post or another in the enterprise founding the pension fund. Typically, they would have joined the former socialist institution with a background in economics, accounting or (sometimes) the law, and risen by order of seniority, becoming an administrator, then head of section and later head of department. Their technical knowledge would for the most part be linked to the company which employed them, although they would know it like the back of their hand. Not only their knowledge, but also their contacts would be linked to the company: they move with considerable confidence not only in the workplace in the narrow sense, but also among their superiors, and know everything which, in a changing world, it is appropriate or possible to know about everyone's past. This 'historical knowledge' is also the guarantee of their 'untouchability': they are an unavoidable 'old guard' on whom the new management coming after privatization can rely. After investing so much in one workplace they have no wish to change it, and even less to change their career.

Because they not only tend to be older, but also have a different attitude, those employed in the key positions in Hungarian pension funds are much less mobile than their colleagues at foreign-owned companies. Besides their more modest career aspirations, their life styles are more modest too, being at about the level of the Hungarian middle-class average, and they do not particularly wish to change that. Where they live, as at work, they above all want to feel at home; they would not exchange their neighbours' warm greeting for the world, let alone the rise in status which a move to a more elegant neighbourhood would bring. They love comfort, and want to dress and eat well; but with all this it is important to them not to stand out from the Hungarian middle class, in the form of their neighbours, friends and colleagues.

Accordingly, their aspirations are not particularly hedonistic: their ambitions are primarily connected to better performance in their new job. They want to learn clever business techniques and become acquainted with the workings of the stock exchange, but they are – and will continue to be – truly at home only in the public sector and its various bodies, and do their best to strengthen them. They press for good regulations, fairness and security, and promise in turn that in their hands the pension fund will become the wonder not only of Hungary but also of the wider world. They worry about competition, because they are not blind, and fear for their pension funds as for their own children; their barely disguisable concerns increase day by day in the face of the activities of ruthless and unfeeling foreign capital. We do not find equivalent feelings among the Hungarian management and employees of foreign companies, even occasionally. It is, of course, true that they have no reason to be jealous, and it would be distasteful to them to flaunt their superiority. As a result, their behaviour towards their small Hungarian counterparts is fairly indulgent, which only serves to emphasize their self-confidence, which is fully justified in light of their own and their company's successes, evidence of which is provided daily.

These different interests, and the different habits and aspirations which go with them, were soon institutionalized: shortly after the pension funds opened their doors, their diverging paths arranged the organizations and employees of the two distinct groups into separate associations. The big foreign pension funds backed by financial institutions created a cartel after a few months, within the framework of which they not only harmonized their capital market activities, and agreed on ways of acquiring new customers and how existing customers shall move from one pension fund to another, but also formed an association to protect their interests so that they could negotiate with the state and its representatives as a heavyweight partner. Similarly, the small Hungarian-founded pension funds, with their background in specific sectors and workplaces, founded their own chamber. As far as its functions and effectiveness are concerned, however, the latter is more reminiscent of a local trade association than a militant professional interest-protecting organization. The association of the sectoral/workplace-based pension funds is primarily a forum for technical discussion, where participants keep one another informed about the best ways of dealing with any technical problems which may arise. They also try to protect their own interests, but without the 'big guns' they are powerless, and state bodies do not really take the new association seriously. As a result, what remains for the members of this second association is the well-trodden path of individual lobbying: if the company bosses can arrange this or that at the ministry, at the State Monetary Supervisory Agency, or with the tax authorities, then there is a chance that they can stay in business; otherwise, and the pension fund directors know this very well, their days are numbered.

Looking at the above-described characteristics of the rapidly completed internal division of the private pension network, we are forced to draw an odd conclusion: this segmentation led very quickly to the formation of estate-like or even feudal positions. As I tried to point out, this took place, not simply along technical lines (size, capital), or in accordance with function (general customer base versus customers derived from particular employers), but also, on the one hand, with the almost total overlapping of these dimensions, and on the other hand – and perhaps most importantly – in accordance with whether the founders' capital originally came from the financial sector or not, or from Hungary or abroad. As we have seen, the latter considerations crushed everything beneath them, and in a short time organized the new institutions into segregated subdivisions (orders or estates) of the pension fund sector. The internal life, staff, behaviour and institutionalizing chambers of the two orders are markedly segregated from one another and there is little indication that any common ground will be found between them. Little of this is discernible from the outside for the time being because the two orders have only just set about defining their own self-representations, and it is not easy to see at the moment in which direction their investments, market roles and, later on, services will develop. In any case, this estate-like division into parts is only likely to be consolidated in the form of the establishment of a customer base made in its own image. Clearly, it can easily happen that the customers of the two subdivisions of the private pension funds come to form two groups, as a result of which the internal conflicts of the pension system, instead of moderating, will be intensified.

This danger is all the more real because, from the beginning, the differences which distinguish those who remained in the social security system from those who switched to the private pension system have been, as already mentioned, almost 'feudal' in nature. It is true that the mass character of the switch has so far had the effect of dimming this division. But with the hardening of the two subdivisions of the private pension funds the danger is that this separation will simply be transformed; it will not disappear. Apart from the fact that such a development would erode the still undoubted popularity and widespread societal support of the new system, further effects may be predicted. Among these effects we must include, as already mentioned, not only the conflicts between the social strata which feel themselves at home in the market and those which seek increased protection from the state, but also the antipathy, induced by frustration, felt by the latter towards the West and capital.

As far as political consequences are concerned, the strengthening of estate-like features may also easily lead to the discrediting of democracy, because it is clear that the latter is ridiculously weak in the face of the power of the market. Of course, all of this is, for the time being, only a possibility, which may be disregarded or even prevented from gaining ground. The taking of effective countermeasures, however, demands that the question of the operation of the pension system finally be opened up as a public issue in the classical sense of the term. That is, a public debate is required to clarify the question of the individual and collective responsibility for pensions, not to mention the pension market and the division of roles between the market and the state.

If a societal debate of this kind was finally able to clarify the key points, it would not be difficult to imagine what kind of balance would be struck between the ardently craved – but, as we have seen, conflicting – market and democratic values. Today, the primacy of market values is all too evident. But the main consequence of this unconditioned dominance is also clear: an increase in the extent of points of rupture in the still poorly integrated Hungarian market society. The successful history of the private pension funds so far could serve as a good platform for the experimental development of an alternative. The rapid consolidation of estate-like developments, however, serves to call our attention to the fact that no alternative will arise of its own accord: the pension funds will all too soon become prey to financial market movements (in the technical sense) and the object of mass societal disappointment.

NOTES

* Early 1998 indicates the actual start of Hungary's utterly new private pension system, while the spring of 2001 bears no such historical significance; it refers simply to the timing when I put the finishing touch on the current paper.

1. For them, the new private pension scheme is mandatory: their social security contributions are thus divided between the state scheme and the market-based private pension scheme.

2. Júlia Szalai, 'A társadalombiztosítás változó érdekviszonyai' (The changing patterns of interest in the social security system), in *Uram! A jogaimért jöttem!* (Sir, I have come for my rights!), Budapest: Új Mandátum Könyvkiadó, 1998, pp.280–305.

3. With special reference to Hungarian history, the notion of the 'Kádár-era' signals the 33 years of 'softened' totalitarian rule that followed the harsh defeat of the 1956 revolution. The period is named after János Kádár, who became First Secretary of the Communist Party (MS$_z$MP) by accepting the Soviets' claim for introducing extra oppressive measures to punish the revolting nation but who remained in power for so many years by offering a particular 'tacit compromise' for consolidation afterwards.

4. Péter Vince, 'Az önállósuló egészségbiztosítás dilemmái: a gyógyszerár-támogatási rendszer funkciózavarai' (The dilemmas of health care insurance as it becomes independent: obstacles to the functioning of drug price subsidization), in *Az államtalanítás dilemmái: szociálpolitikai kényszerek és választások* (The dilemmas of state desertion: social policy constraints and choices), ed. Edit Landau *et al.*, Budapest: ATA, 1995, pp.94–113.

5. One of the first steps taken by the new coalition which came to power as a result of the 1998 parliamentary elections was to take the two social security funds once again under direct government supervision, while they cast the two self-governments to the winds. The return to government control was, according to the rhetoric of the time, intended to be only for the short term, and its aim was the proper, centrally directed and technically well-prepared transformation of the social security system and the 'neutral' privatization of its assets. Almost two years have passed in the meantime, but the picture has still not changed: the funds are in central hands, but as far as the marketization of their assets is concerned – beyond slogans and general reform statements – we hear virtually nothing. In this way there is not the smallest chance that at least the relevant experts will be able to properly debate procedures – which in this case are far from clear-cut – for the best use of these assets, as well as the connection of these marketization concepts with the fundamental functions of social security. Without this kind of debate and more thorough practical work, we may scarcely hope that comprehensive and dynamic reform plans will be introduced in the foreseeable future. In the absence of alternative concepts, in the final analysis we have every reason to expect the further drifting and erosion of the system in the coming years.

6. It is true that at least the most vehement demands for asset transfers made by the trade union leaders of the self-governments were to some extent curtailed by the so-called Bokros package, i.e. by the shock therapy-like intervention of the then ruling socialist–liberal coalition government to halt the dangerously rapid debt-increase of the state budget. (The package of cuts and other stringent interventions was named after the Minister of Finance, Lajos Bokros, who bravely took personal responsibility for those unpopular measures in all his public appearances.)

7. Above all, the demographic restructuring which is increasingly breaking apart the old pension system; the unstoppable growth of social security expenditure; the enormous deficit which, as each year passes, poses more of a threat to the balance of the state budget; and the hopeless race – which has been going on for years – between the compulsion to increase benefits and the need to stimulate economic growth.

8. 'A Kormány javaslata az új nyugdíjrendszerre' (Government proposal concerning the new pension system), Budapest, 19 December 1996.

9. 1997. évi LXXXII. törvény a magánnyugdíjról és a magánnyugdíjpénztárakról (Law 82 of 1997 on private pensions and private pension funds).

14. Latin American and East European pension reforms: accounting for a paradigm shift

Katharina Müller

INTRODUCTION

Twenty years after the iconoclastic Chilean reform, half of all Latin American countries had introduced compulsory individually fully funded (IFF) schemes that either compete with, replace or complement the existing public pay-as-you-go (PAYGO) schemes.[1] Another wave of pension privatizations has been taking shape in Eastern Europe and the Former Soviet Union.[2] This move, that has been referred to as 'structural' or 'systemic' pension reform, implies a fundamental paradigmatic departure from the previous pension system. It amounts to a shift from an intergenerational contract to individual provision for old age, as well as from the state to the market as the main supplier of retirement pensions. The paradigm change inherent in radical pension reform therefore amounts to a substantial rewrite of the underlying social contract, which is particularly remarkable as pension systems were long thought difficult to reform.[3] This puzzle has triggered multidisciplinary research over the past few years.[4] Interestingly, however, the similarity of pension reform approaches in Latin America and Eastern Europe has prompted little cross-regional analysis so far. In this chapter, pension privatization in both regions will be analysed comparatively, in an attempt to explore the similarities and differences in Latin American and East European pension policy.

FROM BISMARCK TO FRIEDMAN: STRUCTURAL PENSION REFORM IN LATIN AMERICA

The origins of Bismarckian-style pension schemes in Latin America can be traced back to the first decades of the twentieth century.[5] Coverage and benefits in the pioneer countries were gradually extended from powerful groups such as the military, state employees and well-paid private sector

workers to weaker groups, notably agricultural workers and domestic servants. The expansion of pension programmes reached its peak in the 1950s and 1960s (Mesa-Lago, 1978). The favourable age structure of the insured population as well as the progressive integration of new contribution groups into the pension schemes provided for a comfortable financial basis. In a context of mounting inflation, however, investment of social security funds in public bonds led to a decapitalization of pension reserves. At the same time, pension programmes matured and reached the limits of coverage expansion. In the 1980s, economic crisis, followed by stabilization and adjustment plans, diminished public resources for social policy.

Pension programmes in Latin America also suffered from a weak contribution–benefit link that coincided with generous entitlement conditions and replacement rates, even for early retirement and invalidity benefits. Furthermore, the existing old age security systems were highly fragmented and consisted of multiple funds, each with different legislation and management, benefits and contribution rates. This situation generated high costs and problems of equity between different groups of insured. Last but not least, the most vulnerable groups of the population, particularly the informal sector workers, were generally excluded from Bismarckian-style social insurance.

Chile was the first country in Latin America to implement a radical privatization of its pension system.[6] In 1981, in the context of a liberal ideology and extraordinary powers of the Pinochet regime, the existing public PAYGO system was replaced by a compulsory IFF scheme administrated by private pension funds (*Administradoras de Fondos de Pensiones*, or AFPs). At first, the Chilean reform seemed to remain the bold experiment of an autocratic regime, with little attraction for democratic policy makers elsewhere. Only after a democratic government had taken over in Chile did it evolve as a reform paradigm for Latin America and beyond. In recent years, a number of Latin American countries have implemented variations of the so-called 'Chilean model', most of them under democratic regimes (see Table 14.1).[7]

The reforms in the region can be divided into three main groups: substitutive, parallel and mixed (Mesa-Lago, 1998). Under the substitutive model, the former public system is closed down, being replaced by a privately run IFF system, such as in Chile (1981), Bolivia (1997), El Salvador (1997) and Mexico (1997). The mixed model implies that a newly created IFF component on a mandatory basis complements the reformed public system, such as in Argentina (1994), Uruguay (1996) and Costa Rica (2001). Under the parallel model, a private IFF scheme is introduced as an alternative to public pension insurance, resulting in two coexisting, competing pension systems, such as in Peru (1993) and Colombia (1994). Recently, Nicaragua and the Dominican Republic have also legislated a substitutive pension reform.

Table 14.1   A comparison of Latin American pension privatizations

	Implemented			
	Chile	Peru	Argentina	Colombia
Reform type	substitutive	parallel	mixed	parallel
Starting date	1981	1993	1994	1994
Public mandatory tier	Phased out	Traditional PAYGO scheme; alternative to private tier	Traditional PAYGO scheme; private tier complementary	Traditional PAYGO scheme alternative to private tier
Private mandatory tier**	IFF Mandatory for new entrants to labour market. Other workers may opt to switch from the public tier	IFF Membership in either the private or the public tier is mandatory for all workers	IFF All workers may redirect their contribution to the private tier	IFF Membership in either the private or the public tier is mandatory for all workers
	Individual contribution rate: 10%	Individual contribution rate: 8%	Individual contribution rate: 7.14%*	Individual contribution rate: 2.5%+ employers' contribution rate: 7.5%

Notes:
 * Recently, a temporary reduction of withholdings to 5% has been decreed (this includes commissions and insurance premia).
** It should be noted that, although the IFF tier is dominated by private pension administrators, some countries also admit publicly run pension funds. No information was available on the reform in the Dominican Republic.

	Implemented				Legislated
Uruguay	Bolivia	Mexico	El Salvador	Costa Rica	Nicaragua
mixed	substitutive	substitutive	substitutive	mixed	substitutive
1996	1997	1997	1998	2001	2002
Traditional PAYGO scheme; private tier complementary	Closed down	Closed down	Phased out	Traditional PAYGO scheme; private tier complementary	Phased out
IFF Mandatory for workers earning over US$800 per month, optional for lower earning groups and workers above age 39 to redirect part of their contribution to the private tier	IFF Mandatory for all workers	IFF Mandatory for all workers	IFF Mandatory for new entrants to labour market and affiliates up to age 35. Older workers (up to age 50 for women and age 55 for men) may opt to switch from the public tier	IFF Mandatory for all workers	IFF Mandatory for all workers up to age 43
Individual contribution rate: 12.27%	Individual contribution rate: 10%	Individual contribution 1.125% + employers' contribution rate: 5.2% + state subsidy: 2.2%	Individual contribution rate: 3.25% + employers' contribution rate: 6.75%	Individual contribution rate: 1% + employers' contribution rate: 3.25%	Individual contribution rate: 4% + employers' contribution rate: 6.5%

FROM STATE TO MARKET: STRUCTURAL PENSION REFORM IN EASTERN EUROPE

In a number of South-eastern and Central European countries, stratified Bismarckian-style pension insurance preceded the socialist era. During the decades of socialist rule, a unified pension scheme was set up that was integrated into the state budget. Employees' contributions were largely abolished, making employers' contributions the only source of financing. A major achievement of the postwar years was the gradual expansion of coverage, rendering it universal by the 1960s or 1970s. Overall, there was little benefit differentiation, yet pension privileges granted to occupations of strategic importance marked an important departure from universalism. The insufficient adjustment of current pensions to price or wage dynamics gave rise to problems of inter-cohort fairness and of benefit adequacy (Müller, 2000a).

Economic transformation affected the existing PAYGO systems in the post-socialist countries in several ways. At the onset of market-oriented reforms, price liberalization and the curtailment of subsidies on basic goods and services required a shift from indirect to direct transfers, resulting in rising expenditures for old age security. At a later stage, the restructuring of the state-owned enterprises had an effect on both the revenue and the expenditure side of public pension schemes. The privatization, 'downsizing' and closing down of enterprises was accompanied by a mounting number of disability pensions and by early retirement policies. By leading to an increased number of pensioners and a falling number of contributors to the public pension schemes, this policy resulted in a significant destabilization of public pension finances. By the mid-1990s, system dependency ratios had deteriorated dramatically: in all post-socialist countries but Armenia, Belarus and Macedonia, there were fewer than two contributors per pensioner. The declining revenue base and the erosion of social security are further illustrated by a dramatic drop in coverage ratios, notably in Albania, where coverage plunged to 32 per cent. Whereas public pension spending was on the rise in the region, only Poland and Slovenia surpassed the West European average, with pension expenditures amounting to 14.4 and 13.6 per cent of GDP (Müller, 2002a).

In the course of the 1990s, it became clear that the old age security systems inherited from the socialist past were in dire need of reform. As far as parametric changes to the existing retirement schemes are concerned, it was relatively undisputed among social security experts that essential pension reform measures included the separation of pension schemes from other social insurance plans and from the state budget, the introduction of an employees' contribution, the raising of the retirement age, the abolition of branch privileges, the restriction of early retirement and the tightening of eligibility to invalidity pensions. Moreover, in many countries, benefits were linked more closely to lifetime earnings to improve contribution incentives, most notably by the introduction of notional defined contribution plans, or NDC for short.[8]

A first change in the public–private mix was brought about by introducing supplementary private fully funded schemes, but the amount of voluntary funds collected fell short of expectations. Subsequently, a number of transition countries opted for a more radical approach, as Latin American-style pension privatization gained considerable momentum (Rutkowski, 2001; Müller, 2002b). Explicitly modelled on the Chilean precedent (Andrews, 2001), Kazakhstan has been the only case of a substitutive reform so far (1998). The mixed reform path was implemented in Hungary (1998), Poland (1999), Latvia (2001), Bulgaria, Croatia and Estonia (2002) and legislated in Macedonia (see Table 14.2).

COMPARING STRUCTURAL PENSION REFORMS: PARALLELS AND DIFFERENCES

There are important parallels in the recent waves of pension reform in Latin America and Eastern Europe. In both regions, the public–private mix in the provision for old age has been changed significantly. Before structural pension reform was implemented, most countries in both regions used to have a monolithic public pension system. By now, policy makers have introduced private old age provision on a mandatory basis, while at the same time 'downsizing' or closing down the public tier. The recent move towards pension privatization implied the adoption of a 'worker-choice model' (Lindeman et al., p.32), a system of individual retirement savings accounts, managed by competing pension funds. Fund administrators are exclusively or predominantly private, although in some countries public entities also play a significant role, notably in Uruguay and Kazakhstan, where they dominate the market.

Originally, individual accounts were only fed by employees' contributions to make people save for their own retirement, there being no role for employers. In the words of the architect of the 'Chilean model', this type of pension reform 'sets up impenetrable barriers against communism. . . . By converting all workers into owners, the reform commits them actively to a responsible management of the economy, as well as to political stability and social peace' (Piñera, 1991, p.171).[9] However, in some of the more recent reforms, contributions to the new mandatory private pension tiers are split between employee and employer, as in Colombia, Costa Rica, El

Table 14.2 A comparison of post-socialist pension privatizations

	Implemented							Legislated
	Kazakhstan	Hungary	Poland	Latvia	Bulgaria	Croatia	Estonia	Macedonia
Type of reform	substitutive	mixed	mixed	mixed	mixed	mixed	mixed	mixed
Starting date	1998	1998	1999	2001	2002	2002	2002	*
Public mandatory tier	Closed down	Traditional PAYGO scheme; private tier complementary	NDC scheme; private tier complementary	NDC scheme; private tier complementary	PAYGO scheme with pension points; private tier complementary	PAYGO scheme partly with pension points; private tier complementary	Traditional PAYGO scheme; private tier complementary	Traditional PAYGO scheme; private tier complementary
Private mandatory tier**	IFF Mandatory for all workers	IFF Mandatory for new entrants to labour market, optional for other workers to redirect part of their contribution to the private tier	IFF Mandatory for workers below age 30, optional between ages 30 and 49 to redirect part of their contribution to the private tier	IFF Mandatory for workers below 30 years of age, optional between ages 30 and 49 to redirect part of their contribution to the private tier	IFF Mandatory for all workers up to 42 years of age to redirect part of their contribution to the private tier	IFF Mandatory for workers below age 40, optional between ages 40 and 49 to redirect their contribution to the private tier	IFF Mandatory for workers below age 18, optional for other workers to redirect their contribution to the private tier	IFF Mandatory for new entrants to labour market, optional for other workers to redirect part of their contribution to the private tier

Individual contribution rate: 10%	Individual contribution rate: 6%	Individual contribution rate: 9%	Individual contribution rate to be gradually increased to 10%	Individual contribution rate yet to be defined (2–5%); to be paid in equal shares by employers and employees	Individual contribution rate: 2.5% + employer's contribution rate: 2.5%	Individual contribution rate: 2% + employer's contribution rate: 4%	Individual contribution rate: 7%

Notes:

*In Macedonia, the implementation date has been postponed repeatedly.

**It should be noted that although the IFF tier is dominated by private pension administrators, some countries also admit publicly run pension funds.

379

Salvador, Mexico, Nicaragua, Bulgaria, Croatia and Estonia. Moreover, some countries have complemented the IFF tier with voluntary occupational schemes.

The simultaneous adoption of similar blueprints across countries and regions suggests that there is a common international transmission mechanism of ideas (Stallings, 1994). In the area of old age security, a dominant epistemic community can clearly be identified.[10] While originally not contained in the so-called 'Washington Consensus', systemic reform of old age security schemes has become part and parcel of the neoliberal reform package by now. A research report of the World Bank (1994), intended to establish the guiding criteria of the organization's pension policy, attracted global attention. It may be considered to be the best-known exemplification of what has become the new pension orthodoxy, as well as its major propagating mechanism.[11]

Conservative critics of the welfare state had long prepared the ground for a paradigm change in old age security, as described by Hirschman (1991). It was in the wake of the cold war that the terms of the prevailing discourse in old age protection shifted, interacting with the rise of neoliberalism as the dominant paradigm, particularly in Latin America and Eastern Europe. Today, the mainstream within economic scholarship advocates a shift to funding.[12] This 'new pension orthodoxy' (Lo Vuolo, 1996) has been giving major impulses to pension privatization in Latin America and Eastern Europe, arguing that such a paradigm change in old age security would lead to a rise in saving and efficiency improvements on both the financial and labour markets, thereby resulting in an increase in long-term growth.

An increasing amount of contemporary policy change is affected by policy transfer and the global diffusion of models (Dolowitz and Marsh, 2000; Weyland, 2000). In old age security reform, it was only after the Chilean precedent that pension privatization had turned from a theoretical concept into political reality. It is obvious that the Bank's report could not influence pension privatization in Chile (1980); on the contrary, it was the Chilean reform that had an impact on the World Bank's pension reform blueprint. Yet in the case of those structural pension reforms that started in the 1990s, the impact of the pension orthodoxy has been considerable, both in Latin America and in Eastern Europe. Radical agenda shifting was frequently connected to World Bank involvement, given the prominence of its advice, technical assistance and loans. In recent years other international financial institutions (IFIs) and government agencies, such as the IMF and USAID, the Inter-American Development Bank and the Asian Development Bank, have followed suit.

While structural pension reforms in Latin America and Eastern Europe show striking similarities in their basic design, each of these reforms is unique in its features. The most important difference between the Latin American and East European pension privatizations concerns the size of the private IFF tier, that is, the scope of the paradigm shift.[13] So far, structural pension reform in Latin America has predominantly implied closing down the public tier or phasing it out, while mixed and parallel reform paths were adopted less frequently. In the transition countries, only one post-socialist country (Kazakhstan) replicated the 'Chilean model'. The other transition countries that embarked on pension privatization decided to retain a reduced public pillar under a mixed reform strategy. Those East European countries that have opted for pension privatization exhibit far more diversity in terms of first-tier design than their Latin American counterparts: besides 'traditional' PAYGO pillars, the Swedish concept of notional defined contributions (NDC)[14] or German-style pension points[15] have been introduced in some transition countries to strengthen the contribution–benefit link in public old age provision.

The predominance of the substitutive reform type in Latin America is clearly linked to strong demonstration effects from the 'Chilean model'. When Latin American policy makers compared their countries' economic performance to the Chilean success story, they identified pension privatization as one of the ingredients. The promotional activities of the Chilean pension funds and prominent reformers, such as José Piñera, also contributed to the diffusion of the precedent all over the subcontinent. It seems that, in Latin America, autonomous policy learning by the recipient countries tended to be more important than direct influence of the IFIs as agenda setters, even though virtually all reform teams were effectively financed by the latter (Nelson, 2000).

In the post-socialist pension reforms, Latin American role models were also influential, particularly the mixed 'Argentine model'. Latin American-style pension privatization was recommended as a major reform option by the IFIs.[16] To provide first-hand information on Latin American pension reforms, the World Bank and USAID sponsored trips to Argentina and Chile for Polish MPs, social security experts and journalists. Hence, in Eastern Europe, where the connotations of the 'Chilean model' were more likely to refer to the Pinochet regime than to a regional example of economic success, the IFIs played an important though mostly low-key role as agents of transmission, helping to enhance the low status of the Latin American precedents (Nelson, 2000; Müller, 2001a).

Although individual Latin American reformers passed their experiences on to East European policy makers, in person or via their writing,[17] direct diffusion effects from Chile and other Latin American reform precedents were rather weak in Eastern Europe. Latin America carried the stigma of being a less developed region (Orenstein, 2000) and seemed unsuitable as a benchmark case. Moreover, policy makers were more prone to look to the West than to the South in search of models, given their EU accession plans. However, there is no mainstream pension model in Western Europe. Still, individual EU member states have been sending experts to the transition countries in the past decade. The Swedish reform blueprint – a multi-pillar system combining NDC and full funding – has had an impact on some East European countries, notably those bordering the Baltic Sea. German and Italian design features (pension points and demographic factors) have been adopted by pension reformers in South-eastern Europe.

However, the differences in the public–private mix in the Latin American and East European pension reforms cannot be explained by the impact of role models alone. It seems useful to consider the importance of existing institutional arrangements – policy feedback or path dependency (Pierson and Weaver, 1993). In Bismarckian-style PAYGO schemes, lock-in effects and opportunity costs may result from the entitlements earned by the insured, engendering high transition costs (Mesa-Lago, 2000). The size of this implicit pension debt, that translates into high fiscal costs when made explicit, is determined by a number of factors, notably the percentage of the population covered, the generosity and the maturity of the public scheme, three factors that differ substantially between Latin America and Eastern Europe.

It has been argued elsewhere that, the larger the implicit pension debt, the smaller the likelihood of radical pension privatization (Fox and Palmer 1999; James and Brooks, 2001). The fact that most East European countries – in a region where coverage approached 100 per cent in the past – have opted for the mixed reform path seems to support this hypothesis. Similarly, intraregional conclusions may be drawn from the cases of Argentina and Uruguay, where pre-reform coverage was high, and reformers opted for a mixed scheme. Contrary to this, Bolivian reformers faced a much smaller implicit pension debt and a considerably younger population, hence they considered that radical pension privatization was economically feasible.[18]

While public confidence in the pre-reform pension schemes was shaken by the financial difficulties of the public PAYGO schemes in both regions, this effect was particularly pronounced in Latin America and translated into an earlier move to IFF schemes, as well as a more radical privatization of old age security. Contrary to the East European countries, Latin American countries had a private financial sector in the past decades, ready to administer large quantities of private pension capital. Capital markets, however shaky, had also been in place for a longer period of time. The political viability of full pension privatization is likely to have been increased by a lack of social cohesion and poorly spread values of social justice in Latin America. The fact that Argentina, Uruguay and Costa Rica are the only

Latin American countries that have opted for the mixed model seems indicative in this respect.

POLITICAL ACTORS AND THE POLICY CONTEXT IN PENSION PRIVATIZATION

Although pension privatization in Latin America and Eastern Europe is closely connected with the emergence of the new pension orthodoxy, it was the domestic political process that eventually resulted in the adoption of radical pension reform. The following analysis aims at the identification of the most important political actors in the pension reform arena in both Latin America and Eastern Europe and the consideration of the policy context that shaped their room for manoeuvre, influenced by political factors and economic conditions.

Scholars of the political economy of policy reform[19] have stressed the importance of political leadership by committed individuals, often market-oriented economists. Recent case studies have shown that pension privatization amounts to a paradigm shift that may be greatly facilitated by such committed policy makers. Carlos Menem and Domingo Cavallo (Argentina), Gonzalo Sánchez de Lozada (Bolivia) and Lájos Bokros (Hungary) are famous for the radical reform packages they pushed through. In Argentina and Poland, respectively, there is unanimity that pension privatization would have been impossible without Walter Schulthess and Andrzej Bączkowski, who set up the respective reform teams. Interestingly, in several cases the governing parties implementing the neoliberal agenda had previously been known for their left-wing or populist leanings. This is true of the Peronists in Argentina and the MNR in Bolivia, as well as of the post-socialist governments in Poland and Hungary that had been the driving forces of pension privatization. Old age security is not the only policy area where radical reforms may be more successful when tackled by 'unlikely' administrations, a phenomenon called 'Nixon-in-China syndrome' (Rodrik, 1994).[20]

In most cases the radical paradigm change in old age security was mainly advocated by the Ministries of Finance and Economy, staffed by neoliberal economists. Pension privatization perfectly matched their overall efforts to decrease the role of the state in the economy. They were supported both by local interest groups, such as business organizations and the financial sector, and the IFIs. But there was also opposition to these radical plans, both within and outside government. More often than not, the Ministries of Labour, Welfare or Health, responsible for the existing old age security schemes, were reluctant to engage in structural pension reform, thus reflecting the existing Bismarckian traditions in both Latin America and Eastern

Europe. In several countries these ministries initially objected to the radical paradigm shift, but – given the predominance of the Finance Ministry in the Cabinet – proved too weak to prevent it. Typically, the opposing port-folios' influence on reform design was limited by the setting up of small task forces, mostly attached to the Ministry of Finance. These special pension reform committees worked out the draft legislation and clearly served to bypass the Labour Ministry's pension-related competences.

Other groups that opposed pension privatization included trade unions, social security employees, and – last but not least – pensioners' associations and special interest groups with privileged pension schemes. Clearly, the specific policy context may provide reformers or reform opponents with resources for action (Kay, 1999). The executive's degree of control of the legislature amounts to a relevant institutional variable: in Bolivia and Hungary, the large parliamentary majority of the governing coalitions allowed for a swift passing of structural pension reform. In Argentina, Hungary and Poland, trade unions had traditional ties with the governing parties that were used to ease resistance, pointing to one of the ingredients of the 'Nixon-in-China syndrome'.

On the other side of the coin, these ties implied that reform opponents were in a political position that forced the pension reformers to negotiate with them and to make concessions. In some countries, such as Argentina and Poland, this even implied granting trade unions the right to run their own pension funds. A broader look at both regions shows that, in some countries with an autocratic regime and/or a weak civil society, for example Chile, Peru and El Salvador, there was very little or no public debate about the government's plans to privatize old age security. In the first two cases, pension privatization was not even passed by Congress, but was legislated by the executive via emergency decrees. By contrast, the Uruguayan and Latvian cases illustrate that elements of direct democracy (referenda, pleb-iscites) may even give reform opponents a chance to reverse pension reform laws that have already been passed.

The paradigm choice in Latin American and East European old age security appears to have been substantially influenced by economic factors and considerations. Pension privatization has been primarily proposed for macroeconomic motives, seeking to embark on a virtuous circle towards economic growth. Madrid (1999) and James and Brooks (2001) have pointed to the recent experiences of capital market crises, that may have induced policy makers to seek to reduce vulnerability to capital outflows by boosting domestic savings and the local capital market. Yet the Chilean evi-dence suggests that pension privatization actually had a negative impact on national saving (Mesa-Lago, 1998). Moreover, given that the investment of funds abroad tends to be severely limited, it is surprising that the pre-reform situation of the local capital market, however poor, rarely seems to have been perceived as a constraint on pension privatization.

Scholars of the political economy of policy reform argue that a preceding crisis may induce radical change: the so-called 'benefit of crises' hypothesis (Drazen and Grilli, 1993). Fiscal crises turn the Ministry of Finance into a potential actor in the pension reform arena. More specifically, when pension finances display a deficit, the resulting dependence on budgetary subsidies grant this likely advocate of the 'new pension orthodoxy' an important stake in reforming old age security (Müller, 1999). In most countries that have opted for pension privatization there was an overall deficit in government finance prior to the reform. Hence it may come as no surprise that the finance and/or economics ministries often played a key role in triggering the process of pension privatization. The financial difficulties changed the relevant constellation of actors in such a way that the local privatization faction was reinforced decisively.

Yet another economic factor had an impact on the cases of pension reform reviewed above. When external debt is high, the announcement of pension privatization can be interpreted as a 'signalling' strategy (Rodrik, 1998). And indeed, by the mid-1990s, rating agencies had included radical pension reform as a point in favour in their country-risk assessments. Critical indebtedness also increases the likelihood of the IFIs' involvement in the local pension reform arena (Brooks, 1998). The World Bank amounts to a powerful external actor in a number of highly indebted Latin American and East European countries. Together with other IFIs and government agencies, it exerted its influence first and foremost as an agenda shifter in the local pension debate, engaging in an expert-based knowledge transfer. Moreover, lending activities are a central instrument to support pension privatization in Latin America and Eastern Europe (Holzmann, 2000). As noted by Kay (1999), policy makers were well aware that financial and/or technical support was only available for a pension reform that included a privatization component.[21]

CONCLUDING REMARKS

In spite of being geographically and culturally distant, Eastern Europe and Latin America show interesting parallels as far as the privatization of old age security is concerned. The similarities extend largely to the basic design of structural pension reform in both regions: the almost simultaneous introduction of systems of individual retirement savings accounts managed by predominantly private pension funds, that either compete with, replace or complement the public PAYGO scheme. By pointing to the impact of the new pension orthodoxy, the importance of an international policy transfer mechanism in old age security reform was highlighted. On the other hand, direct diffusion of the 'Chilean model' was much stronger in Latin America than in Eastern Europe. The most important differences between the Latin American and East European pension privatizations concern the size of the private IFF tier; that is, the scope of the paradigm shift, and the diversity in terms of first-tier design. The state retains a greater role in post-socialist old age security than in Latin America and fulfils its first-tier functions in a variety of ways. Overall, the Latin American and East European pension privatizations indicate that, contrary to conventional wisdom in social policy research, a radical paradigm shift in the area of old age security can be politically feasible.

NOTES

1. This chapter was written in the context of the research project, 'The Political Economy of Pension Reform: Eastern Europe and Latin America in Comparison', conducted at the European University Viadrina, Frankfurt (Oder). Funding by the Volkswagen Foundation is gratefully acknowledged. See also Müller (2002c).
2. It should be noted that, even in the case of full pension privatization, the state continues to play an important role. For a more detailed discussion, see Müller (2002d).
3. See Pierson (1998, p.553): 'pay-as-you-go schemes may face incremental cutbacks and adjustments, but they are highly resistant to radical reform'.
4. Studies on the political economy of pension privatization in Latin America include Huber and Stephens (2000), Kay (1998; 1999), Madrid (1999; 2002), Mesa-Lago (1999) and Mesa-Lago and Müller (2002). The making of pension privatization in post-socialist countries was analysed by Müller (1999; 2001b), Nelson (2001) and Orenstein (2000), while Chłoń-Dominczak and Mora (2001) and James and Brooks (2001) aimed at a broader explanatory framework.
5. Mesa-Lago (1991, p.XI) refers to Chile, Uruguay, Argentina, Cuba and Brazil as 'pioneer countries' in establishing pension schemes. The 'intermediate countries', such as Peru, Bolivia, Mexico and Colombia, introduced their first pension programmes in the 1930s and 1940s, while the 'latecomer countries', the Central American and Caribbean countries, set up the first pension plans in the 1950s and 1960s.
6. For a recent account on the Chilean reform see Uthoff (2001).
7. For the 'second-generation reforms', see Queisser (1998), Müller (2000b; 2002a), Devesa-Carpio and Vidal-Meliá (2001), and Mesa-Lago (2001).
8. For a discussion of notional defined contribution plans, see Cichon (1999) and Disney (1999).
9. Translation from the Spanish original by K.M.
10. Following the definition by Haas (1992, p.3), an epistemic community is a network of professionals in a particular domain and with a common policy enterprise, who may come from different professional backgrounds. They share faith in specific truths and in a set of normative and causal beliefs, have shared patterns of reasoning and use shared discursive practices (Adler and Haas, 1992).
11. For critiques, see Kotlikoff (1999), Barr (2000) and Orszag and Stiglitz (2001).
12. Some 'heterodoxy' remains, however. See Mesa-Lago (1996) and Ney (2000) for a comparative analysis of different policy prescriptions by international organizations in old-age security.
13. An overall look at both regions reveals that every second Latin American country has

opted for one or another variant of pension privatization, while the majority of post-socialist transition countries still stick to PAYGO-only reforms.

14. In NDC schemes, all contribution payments are recorded on individualized accounts in the public pension scheme, yet capital accumulation is only virtual. Individual benefit levels depend mainly on past contributions and their notional rate of return, an indexation of the virtual pension capital to the growth of the contributions base. Moreover, future benefit amounts are closely linked to the development of mortality and the chosen retirement age. NDC plans, that introduce a quasi-actuarial pension formula to the public tier, have been developed by Swedish experts, but were pioneered by Latvia in 1996 (see Cichon, 1999; Disney, 1999).

15. The German point system for benefit calculation implies a relatively strict contribution–benefit link: with their contribution payments, the insured acquire pension entitlements assessed in relation to nationwide average earnings in the same period of time. One earnings point is acquired for each calendar year in which individual earnings are exactly equal to the average gross earnings of all employees. As the total of earnings points provides the basis for benefit calculation, pension levels are closely related to the entire contribution history.

16. See World Bank (1994) and Vittas (1997). For similar recommendations, see also Holzmann (1994) and Fougerolles (1996).

17. An example of the latter is the Polish edition (1996) of José Piñera's prominent book (1991) with a preface entitled 'Let's learn from the Chileans!' (Wilczyński, 1996). See Piñera (2000; 2001) for appeals to Russians and Romanians.

18. Yet estimates on the implicit pension debt should not be taken as given, as this potential lock-in may be reduced in size by reform design.

19. For an overview on the political economy of policy reform, see Rodrik (1996), Tommasi and Velasco (1996), Sturzenegger and Tommasi (1998).

20. See also Cukierman and Tommasi (1998a; 1998b).

21. Whereas in some countries, such as Hungary, the IFIs' involvement was kept low-key, in others, such as Argentina, local policy makers explicitly asked to include pension privatization in an IMF accord as a form of 'blame avoidance' (Weaver, 1986). In Poland, the special task force for old age reform was headed by a World Bank economist on leave, granting the Bank a pivotal channel to support the local reform efforts, apart from its overall leverage in the Polish context of high external debt (Müller, 1999).

REFERENCES

Adler, Emanuel and Peter M. Haas (1992), 'Conclusion: epistemic communities, world order, and the creation of a reflective research program', *International Organization*, 46 (1), 367–90.

Andrews, Emily S. (2001), 'Kazakhstan: An Ambitious Pension Reform', SP Discussion Paper no. 0104, World Bank, Washington, DC.

Barr, Nicholas (2000), 'Reforming Pensions: Myths, Truths, and Policy Choices', IMF Working Paper WP/007139, IMF, Washington, DC.

Brooks, Sarah (1998), 'Social Protection in a Global Economy: The Case of Pension Reform in Latin America', Durham NC, mimeo.

Chłoń-Dominczak, Agnieszka and Marek Mora (2001), 'Commitment and Consensus in Pension Reforms', paper prepared for the joint IIASA World Bank Workshop 'The Political Economy of Pension Reform', Laxenburg, 5 April.

Cichon, Michael (1999), 'Notional defined-contribution schemes: Old wine in new bottles?', *International Social Security Review*, 52 (4), 87–105.

Cukierman, Alex and Mariano Tommasi (1998a), 'Credibility of Policymakers and of Economic Reforms', in Federico Sturzenegger and Mariano Tommasi (eds),

The Political Economy of Reform, Cambridge, MA and London: MIT Press, pp.329–47.

Cukierman, Alex and Mariano Tommasi (1998b), 'When Does It Take a Nixon to Go to China?', *American Economic Review*, 88 (1), 180–97.

Devesa-Carpio, José Enrique and Carlos Vidal-Meliá (2001), 'The Reformed Pension Systems in Latin America', World Bank Social Protection Discussion Paper, Washington, DC, mimeo.

Disney, Richard (1999), 'Notional accounts as a pension reform strategy: An evaluation', World Bank Pension Reform Primer, Washington, DC.

Dolowitz, David P. and David Marsh (2000), 'Learning from Abroad: The Role of Policy Transfer in Contemporary Policy-Making', *Governance: An International Journal of Policy and Administration*, 13 (1), 5–24.

Drazen, Allan and Vittorio Grilli (1993), 'The Benefit of Crises for Economic Reforms', *American Economic Review*, 83 (3), 598–607.

Fougerolles, Jean de (1996), 'Pension Privatization in Latin America – Lessons for Central and Eastern Europe', *Russian and East-European Finance and Trade*, 32 (3), 86–104.

Fox, Louise and Edward Palmer (1999), 'Latvian Pension Reform', Social Protection Discussion Paper no. 9922. World Bank, Washington, DC.

Haas, Peter M. (1992), 'Introduction: epistemic communities and international policy coordination', *International Organization*, 46 (1), 1–35.

Hirschman, Albert O. (1991), *The Rhetoric of Reaction: Perversity, Futility, Jeopardy*, Cambridge, MA: Harvard University Press.

Holzmann, Robert (1994), 'Funded and private pensions for Eastern European countries in transition?', *Revista de Análisis Económico*, 9 (1), 183–210.

Holzmann, Robert (2000), 'The World Bank approach to pension reform', *International Social Security Review*, 53 (1), 11–34.

Huber, Evelyne and John D. Stephens (2000), 'The Political Economy of Pension Reform: Latin America in Comparative Perspective', UNRISD Occasional Paper no. 7, UNRISD, Geneva.

James, Estelle and Sarah Brooks (2001), 'The Political Economy of Structural Pension Reform', in Robert Holzmann and Joseph E. Stiglitz (eds), *New Ideas about Old Age Security. Toward Sustainable Pension Systems in the 21st Century*, Washington, DC: World Bank, pp.133–70.

Kay, Stephen J. (1998), 'Politics and Social Security Reform in the Southern Cone and Brazil', PhD dissertation, University of California at Los Angeles, mimeo.

Kay, Stephen J. (1999), 'Unexpected Privatizations. Politics and Social Security Reforms in the Southern Cone', *Comparative Politics*, 31 (4), 403–22.

Kotlikoff, Laurence J. (1999), 'The World Bank's Approach and the Right Approach to Pension Reform', Boston, MA, mimeo.

Lindeman, David, Michał Rutkowski and Oleksiy Sluchynskyy (2000), 'The Evolution of Pension Systems in Eastern Europe and Central Asia: Opportunities, Constraints, Dilemmas and Emerging Practices', World Bank, Washington, DC.

Lo Vuolo, Rubén M. (1996), 'Reformas previsionales en América Latina: el caso argentino', *comercio exterior*, 46 (9), 692–702.

Madrid, Raúl (1999), 'The New Logic of Social Security Reform: Politics and Pension Privatization in Latin America', PhD dissertation, Stanford University, mimeo.

Madrid, Raúl (2002), 'The Politics and Economics of Pension Privatization in Latin America', *Latin American Research Review*, 37 (2), Spring, 159–82.

Mesa-Lago, Carmelo (1978), *Social Security in Latin America. Pressure Groups, Stratification and Inequality*, Pittsburgh, PA: University of Pittsburgh Press.

Mesa-Lago, Carmelo (1991), 'Social Security and Prospects for Equity in Latin America', World Bank Discussion Paper no. 140, Washington, DC.

Mesa-Lago, Carmelo (1996), 'Pension system reforms in Latin America: the position of the international organizations', *CEPAL Review*, (60), 73–98.

Mesa-Lago, Carmelo (1998), 'Comparative Features and Performance of Structural Pension Reforms in Latin America', *Brooklyn Law Review*, 64 (3), 771–93.

Mesa-Lago, Carmelo (1999), 'Política y reforma de la seguridad social en América Latina', *Nueva Sociedad*, (160), 133–50.

Mesa-Lago, Carmelo (2000), 'Estudio comparativo de los costos fiscales en la transición de ocho reformas de pensiones en America Latina', CEPAL, Serie Financiamiento del Dessarrollo no. 93, Santiago de Chile.

Mesa-Lago, Carmelo (2001), 'Structural reform of social security pensions in Latin America: Models, characteristics, results and conclusions', *International Social Security Review*, 54 (4), 67–92.

Mesa-Lago, Carmelo and Katharina Müller (2002), 'The Politics of Pension Reform in Latin America', *Journal of Latin American Studies*, 34 (2), 687–715.

Müller, Katharina (1999), *The Political Economy of Pension Reform in Central–Eastern Europe*, Cheltenham, UK, and Northampton, MA, USA: Edward Elgar.

Müller, Katharina (2000a), 'Die Reform der Alterssicherung in den östlichen Transformationsländern: Eine Zwischenbilanz', *Deutsche Rentenversicherung*, (5), 139–52.

Müller, Katharina (2000b), 'Pension Privatization in Latin America', *Journal of International Development*, (12), 507–18.

Müller, Katharina (2001a), 'Conquistando el Este: los modelos previsionales latinoamericanos en los países ex socialistas', *Socialis. Revista Latinoamericana de Políticas Sociales*, (4), 39–52.

Müller, Katharina (2001b), 'The political economy of pension reform in eastern Europe', *International Social Security Review*, 54 (2–3), 57–79.

Müller, Katharina (2002a), 'Las reformas de pensiones en América Latina y Europa Oriental: contexto, conceptos, experiencias prácticas y enseñanzas', paper presented at the RECAL Workshop on 'Inequality and Social Inclusion', Barcelona, 14–15 March.

Müller, Katharina (2002b), 'Pension Reform Paths in Central–Eastern Europe and the Former Soviet Union', *Social Policy and Administration*, 36 (2), 156–75.

Müller, Katharina (2002c), *Privatising Old-Age Security: Latin America and Eastern Europe Compared*, Frankfurt (Oder): Frankfurt Institute for Transformation Studies.

Müller, Katharina (2002d), 'Public–private Interaction in Structural Pension Reform', in OECD (ed.), *Regulating Private Pension Schemes. Trends and Challenges*, Paris: OECD, pp.105–16.

Nelson, Joan M. (2000), 'External Models, International Influence, and the Politics of Social Sector Reforms', Washington, DC, mimeo.

Nelson, Joan M. (2001), 'The Politics of Pension and Health-Care Reforms in Hungary and Poland', in János Kornai, Stephan Haggard and Robert R. Kaufman (eds), *Reforming the State. Fiscal and Welfare Reform in Post-Socialist Countries*, Cambridge: Cambridge University Press, pp.235–66.

Ney, Steven (2000), 'Are You Sitting Comfortably . . . Then We'll Begin: Three

Gripping Policy Stories About Pension Reform', *Innovation: The European Journal of Social Sciences*, 13 (4), 341–71.

Orenstein, Mitchell (2000), 'How Politics and Institutions Affect Pension Reform in Three Postcommunist Countries', World Bank Policy Research Working Paper 2310, Washington, DC.

Orszag, Peter R. and Joseph E. Stiglitz (2001), 'Rethinking Pension Reform: Ten Myths About Social Security Systems', in Robert Holzmann and Joseph E. Stiglitz (eds), *New Ideas about Old Age Security. Toward Sustainable Pension Systems in the 21st Century*, Washington, DC: World Bank, pp.17–62.

Pensions International, various issues (*http://www.pensionsinternational.co.uk*).

Pierson, Paul (1998), 'Irresistible forces, immovable objects: post-industrial welfare states confront permanent austerity', *Journal of European Public Policy*, 5 (4), 639–60.

Pierson, Paul and R. Kent Weaver (1993), 'Imposing Losses in Pension Policy', in R. Kent Weaver and Bert A. Rockman (eds), *Do Institutions Matter? Government Capabilities in the United States and Abroad*, Washington, DC: The Brookings Institution, pp.110–50.

Piñera, José (1991), *El cascabel al gato. La batalla por la Reforma Previsional*, Santiago de Chile: Zig-Zag.

Piñera, José (1996), *Bez obawy o przyszłość*, Warsaw: Centrum im. Adama Smitha & Fundacja im. Hugona Kołłątaja.

Piñera, José (2000), 'A Chilean Model for Russia', *Foreign Affairs*, 79 (5), 62–73.

Piñera, José (2001), 'Puterea muncitorilor: privatizarea sistemului de asigurari sociale in Chile', *Cato Letter*, no. 10 (*http://www.pensionreform.org/europe.html*).

Queisser, Monika (1998), *The Second-Generation Pension Reforms in Latin America*, OECD: Paris.

Rodrik, Dani (1994), 'Comment', in John Williamson (ed.), *The Political Economy of Policy Reform*, Washington, DC: Institute for International Economics, pp.212–15.

Rodrik, Dani (1996), 'Understanding Economic Policy Reform', *Journal of Economic Literature*, XXXIV (March), 9–41.

Rodrik, Dani (1998), 'Promises, Promises: Credible Policy Reform via Signalling', in Federico Sturzenegger and Mariano Tommasi (eds), *The Political Economy of Reform*, Cambridge, MA and London: MIT Press, pp.307–27.

Rutkowski, Michał (2001), 'Restoring hope, rewarding work: pension reforms in post-communist economies', in Lucjan T. Orlowski (ed.), *Transition and Growth in Post-Communist Countries*, Cheltenham, UK and Northampton, MA, USA: Edward Elgar, pp.243–69.

Stallings, Barbara (1994), 'Discussion', in John Williamson (ed.), *The Political Economy of Policy Reform*, Washington, DC: Institute for International Economics, p.46.

Sturzenegger, Federico and Mariano Tommasi (eds), *The Political Economy of Reform*, Cambridge, MA and London: MIT Press.

Tommasi, Mariano and Andrés Velasco (1996), 'Where Are We in the Political Economy of Reform?', *Journal of Policy Reform*, 1, 187–238.

Uthoff, Andras (2001), 'La reforma del sistema de pensiones en Chile: desafios pendientes', Serie Financiamiento del Desarrollo no. 112, CEPAL, Santiago de Chile.

Vittas, Dimitri (1997), 'The Argentine pension reform and its relevance for Eastern Europe', World Bank, Financial Sector Development Department, Policy Research Working Paper no. 1819, Washington, DC.

Weaver, R. Kent (1986), 'The Politics of Blame Avoidance', *Journal of Public Policy*, 6 (October–December), 371–98.
Weyland, Kurt (2000), 'Learning from Foreign Models in Latin American Policy Reform', Nashville, TN, mimeo.
Wilczyński, Wacław (1996), 'Uczymy się od Chilijczyków!', in José Piñera, *Bez obawy o przyszłość*, Warsaw: Centrum im. Adama Smitha & Fundacja im. Hugona Kollątaja, pp.5–7.
World Bank (1994), *Averting the Old Age Crisis. Policies to Protect the Old and Promote Growth*, Washington, DC: Oxford University Press.

PART III

The public–private mix and wellbeing in aged households

15. The public–private mix of retirement income in nine OECD countries: some evidence from micro data and an exploration of its implications

Bernard H. Casey and Atsuhiro Yamada

Over the past three decades, the wellbeing of people over retirement age has improved, not only absolutely but also relatively.[1] Being old is no longer synonymous with being poor. This improvement has occurred across almost all of the main OECD countries, and has occurred almost regardless of the type of pension system that is operating in the country concerned. This chapter seeks to illustrate the importance or otherwise of the nature of the public–private mix in incomes in old age both in producing this improvement in wellbeing and in leading to differences in the level of wellbeing enjoyed by different types of person. It draws from a number of studies undertaken at the Social Policy Division of the OECD in the course of 2000 and 2001, many of which have been reported upon in OECD (2001) and Yamada and Casey (2002).

The findings presented and discussed here are drawn, largely, from special analyses of the 'Luxembourg Income Study' (LIS). This brings together, on a standardized basis, the income and expenditure surveys of some 25 countries. The OECD's study was limited to nine countries: Canada, Finland, Germany, Italy, the Netherlands, Sweden, the United Kingdom, the United States and Japan. All bar the last of these participate in LIS. Data protection laws prevent Japan contributing, but it was possible to gain access to special tabulations from an equivalent Japanese data set.[2] The LIS and other data were used to provide descriptions of the situation at a moment in time (usually 1994 or 1995) – the most recent available years. Although LIS can provide information for earlier years, it cannot do so in a way that allows a detailed comparison with the information used here. Thus, for the purposes of analysis across time, special analysis was made of a second dataset, the 'OECD income distribution data set'. This had been collected to study changes in the income levels and equality over time and allows comparisons between the mid-1990s and the mid-1980s and, in some cases, between the mid-1980s and the mid-1970s (see Förster, 2000). Lastly, the OECD had put together data on wealth and assets of older people, mainly from the mid 1990s (updating Disney and Mira D'Ercole, 1998). This information, coupled with that obtainable on age-related public spending for older people, was used to complement the income data.

The chapter is organized as follows. In succession, the relative improvement in older people's wellbeing over the period since the mid-1970s and the changing make-up of their incomes are considered. The section concerned shows the growing importance of private provision. The next section looks at recipients of private pensions within the income distribution. It shows that it is largely the better-off older people who are in receipt of private pensions. The next two sections tackle less frequently studied aspects of the public–private mix. One looks at the contribution of private pensions to facilitating early retirement. That section shows they can be important, but so, too, are public pensions and, equally, other public benefits. The other section looks at the impact of private pension receipt on the situation of women. It is well known that women are less frequently covered by private pension systems. The section illustrates what can occur when the death of a husband results in the loss to the surviving wife of his pension. Having looked at transfer payments, the chapter turns to two further determinants of the public–private mix. One section shows how labour incomes are still an important part of the income package of older people in some countries. The older person him or herself might still be working or he or she might be living in a household where other people, especially adult children, are. A further section considers how 'in-kind' benefits provided by the state also have an impact on the overall public–private mix. Whether or not a universal health care system operates can have a major impact on the effective wellbeing of older people. A final section draws some conclusions and discusses how the study of the public–private mix with respect to retirement might be further pursued.

THE RELATIVE IMPROVEMENT IN OLDER PEOPLE'S WELLBEING

Time series data show the relative improvement of older people's wellbeing. Equivalizing to take account of differences in household size, the income of people over retirement age relative to that of people in their late forties and early fifties – a 'quasi-replacement rate' – rose from about two-thirds to about three-quarters across the nine countries (Table 15.1). With the

Table 15.1   *Quasi-replacement rates over time (disposable income of people 65 and over as percentage of disposable incomes of people aged 18–64)*

	Mid-1970s	Mid-1980s	Mid-1990s
Canada	51	87	87
Finland	68	69	72
Germany	n/a	76	78
Italy	n/a	78	78
Japan	n/a	85	82
Netherlands	86	85	79
Sweden	65	74	80
UK	62	60	65
USA	77	84	84
Unweighted average	68	78	78

Source: Own calculations from OECD income distribution data set.

exception of the United Kingdom, much of the improvement seems to have occurred between the mid-1970s and the mid-1980s: relative wellbeing was much more stable over the subsequent decade.

It was not only that relative incomes rose; the composition of incomes of people over retirement age also changed over time. In all nine countries, the proportion of income derived from work – be it the work of the older individual or his/her spouse or of any adult living in the same household – fell. This reflects the continued fall in effective retirement ages and the fact that fewer and fewer people over retirement age still work. This meant that the proportion made up by transfers increased. However, depending on the country in question, the type of transfer that grew in relative importance differed. In almost all countries, income from capital – which is, to a very large extent, income from an individual or company pension – grew in importance. In four countries, it not only grew substantially, it constituted a substantial part of incomes in retirement. The four countries concerned are Canada, the Netherlands, the United States and the United Kingdom. This can be seen in Figure 15.1.

These four countries stand out as the countries in which private or company pensions are particularly important. The difference can be seen in four ways: the proportion of the current workforce that is enrolled in a private pension plan, the proportion of retirement age people who have income from a private pension, the relative importance of private pensions for those who receive them, and the relative importance of private pension income for all older people. Table 15.2 seeks to capture this.

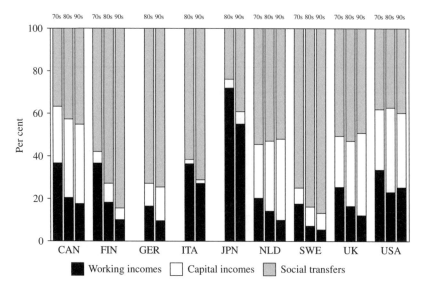

Source: Calculations from the OECD questionnaire on distribution of household incomes.

Figure 15.1   *Composition of gross income over time for people aged 65 and above (percentages, mid-70s, mid-80s and mid-90s)*

The first column of Table 15.2 shows that private pension arrangements are relatively widespread in more than four countries. Germany and Japan have to be added to the list, so too does Sweden, where almost all employees are covered by one of the four collectively agreed private pension arrangements. Amongst current retirees, however, column two shows that only in Sweden do a substantial number have some private pension income. Indeed, the nature of arrangements in that country means that the proportion is the highest in any of the nine countries. However, as far as the importance of private pensions to those who receive them is concerned, column three shows that it is in the original four countries that private pensions are important, followed by Italy and, further behind, by Sweden. The last column sums up the previous three since it takes into account the share of retired people receiving pensions when assessing the importance of private pensions for the income of all retired people. On this basis, and despite their high value for those that do have them, private pensions are relatively unimportant in Italy. Canada, the Netherlands, the United Kingdom and the United States are the countries in which private pensions are an important source of income in old age. Sweden occupies an intermediate position. Finland, Germany, Italy and Japan are countries in which private pensions are relatively unimportant.

Table 15.2   The importance of private pensions

	% of employees in private plans	% of retirement age people with private pensions	% of beneficiaries' disposable income	% of retired men's gross income[a]
Canada	33	58	38	44
Finland	15	*	*	*
Germany	46	16	18	6
Italy	5	3	33	7
Japan	50	5	10	4
Netherlands	91	75	54	53
Sweden	90	86	26	25
UK	46	76	40	55
USA	45	50	36	41

Note: [a] Men aged 65–74.

Source: OECD (2001); own calculations from LIS and equivalent data.

PRIVATE PENSIONERS IN THE INCOME DISTRIBUTION

Although a substantial share of the retired population has some private pension income, it is well known that private pensions, other than in Sweden, tend to cover employees in the primary sector of the economy rather than employees across the whole economy. Thus men are more likely to be covered than women, employees in large enterprises more likely to be covered than those in small enterprises, higher-paid workers are more likely to be covered than low-paid workers, and full-time workers are more likely to be covered than part-time workers. Of course, many of these categories overlap. It is not surprising, therefore, indeed it is almost inevitable, that private pensions reproduce inequalities in working life. Unlike public pensions, they do not normally contain any redistributive provisions,[3] either in the form of thresholds or ceilings, or in the form of crediting times spent not in employment for reasons such as childcare or long-term sickness.

Amongst pensioners themselves, private pensions are important only for the better off. As Figure 15.2 shows, in all of the countries bar the United Kingdom, capital income makes up only about 10 per cent – or less – of the gross income of low-income pensioners. On the other hand, it makes up about half of income for the best off pensioners in Canada, the

Netherlands, the United Kingdom and the United States. Equally, for low-income pensioners, public pensions make up well over 80 per cent of income in all countries bar Japan, but for the best off of pensioners, it is only in Finland, Germany, Italy and Sweden that public pensions make up half or more of gross income.

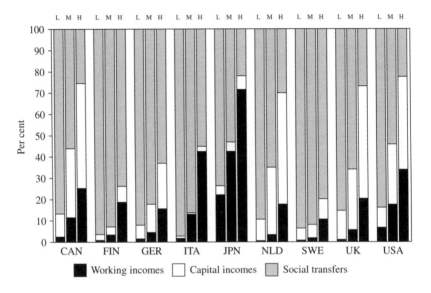

Note: L = low, M = middle, H = high.

Source: Calculations from the OECD questionnaire on distribution of household incomes.

*Figure 15.2   Income source, by income group, people aged 65 and above
(percentages, mid-1990s)*

Lastly, the role of labour income is to be noted. This is a further form of market income, but it is important for people over retirement age only in Japan. There, despite the fall in its importance, labour income still makes up nearly a quarter of income for the least well-off people over pension age, and over two-thirds for the best-off ones.

The relative wellbeing of private pension recipients is further illustrated when they are compared with the generality of pensioners. This is done in Figure 15.3, which shows that recipients of private pensions are least likely to be found at the bottom of the income distribution and more likely to be found towards the middle or even the top. This is particularly the case in Finland, Italy, Japan and Germany, countries in which, for the majority of people, private pensions are relatively unimportant.

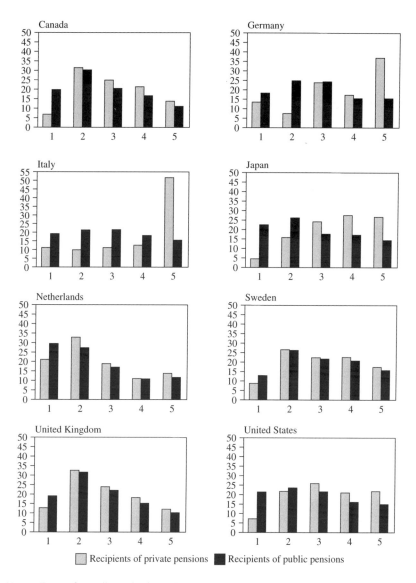

Note: Data refer to disposable incomes.

Source: Own calculations from LIS and equivalent data.

Figure 15.3 *Position of recipients of private pension recipients and all recipients of public pensions in the income distribution, age 65–9 (population of quintiles as a percentage of each category)*

PRIVATE BENEFITS AND EARLY RETIREMENT

Much of the concern of policy makers in the last decade has been with the high incidence of early retirement shown in the industrialized countries. Early retirement can be facilitated in many ways: people can be offered early public age pensions, disability benefits or extended unemployment benefits, often coupled with a lifting of the requirement to register as job seekers. Private pensions can also play an important part. Given the relatively small number of women who can be identified as early retired,[4] it is only with respect to men that cross-sectional data sets allow any detailed study of early retirees.

Early retirees can be broken into two groups, those in their late fifties and those in their early sixties. Table 15.3 shows that private pensions are a considerably more important means by which early retirement is facilitated in the countries where private regular old age pensions are most prevalent, Canada, the Netherlands, the United Kingdom and the United States, and to a lesser extent, Sweden, than elsewhere. In the case of the Netherlands, the private pensions are private early pensions regulated by collective agreements and payable to those reaching 60, 61 or 62. These private benefits are separate from those granted under private age pension schemes, since the latter do not allow pensions to be drawn until age 65 is reached. In the case of Sweden, special bridging payments are likely to be included alongside regular private pensions drawn early. Also to be noted in this respect is the case of Germany, where, as in Sweden, collectively agreed 'social plans' regulating redundancies include private benefits that top up extended unemployment compensation or early public age pensions. In the case of Canada, the United Kingdom and the United States, private pensions may or may not be reduced when they are drawn before 65. They are less likely to be reduced when retirement is 'at the request of the employer' (that is, part of a redundancy settlement). They can also not be reduced simply because some private pension schemes have a normal retirement age that is lower than that which applies under the public age pension system.

With respect to those countries for which the appropriate data were available, it can be seen that private pensions are a much more important facilitator of retirement for people in their late fifties in Canada and the United States than in the United Kingdom and the Netherlands. In the first two countries, disability pension systems are relatively strict in defining eligibility, and there are no provisions extending unemployment benefits for older unemployed people. In the United Kingdom and the Netherlands, eligibility for a public disability pension has been less strict, in so far as 'social' as well as 'medical' criteria can be, or are, taken into account. Moreover, in the Netherlands, although the collectively agreed early retirement provisions

Table 15.3   The public–private mix of early retirement benefits

	Prop. with any private pension	Prop. with any public pension	Prop. with unemployment benefit	Prop. with any other public benefit (max)	Prop. of all households[a] with means-tested benefits
			Non-working men aged 55–59		
Canada	32	18	18	38	15
Finland	1	64	20	16	23
Germany	2	39	25	17	9
Italy	2	72	4	22	n/a
Japan	—	23	13	65	n/a
Netherlands	—	19	11	70	13
Sweden	49	64	14	6	n/a
United Kingdom	46	31	1	34	18
United States	34	28	5	39	12
			Non-working men aged 60–64		
Canada	44	60	5	26	18
Finland	4	95	4	2	18
Germany	15	77	6	8	10
Italy	4	84	1	14	n/a
Japan	12	78	1	20	n/a
Netherlands	48	4	9	13	12
Sweden	66	71	8	2	n/a
United Kingdom	66	34	0	18	20
United States	48	61	2	19	12

Note: [a] households containing someone in the relevant age range.

Source: Own calculations from LIS and equivalent data.

have had a minimum age of eligibility of 60 or higher, the unemployment insurance system can grant benefits to retirement age for those losing their jobs from the age of 57.5 years.

However, it is not only the relative importance of private and public pensions that determines the total public–private mix of early retirement provision. Also important are such public benefits as unemployment compensation and means-tested assistance. Early retirement through receipt of some kind of unemployment benefit is more important for people in their late fifties than for those in their early sixties, and is especially important in Canada, Finland and Germany. Data on receipt of means-tested assistance are more difficult to analyse, since the term is used to describe something other than what is normally understood in some countries and sample numbers are also too small in these or other cases. Also means-tested benefits are awarded to households rather than individuals. Thus the proportions in the final column in Table 15.3 cannot simply be added on to those in the other columns. However, the final column does indicate that, in some countries, means-tested benefits are important. They are particularly so in Finland, where some older job losers fail to qualify for the extended unemployment benefits and early pensions available to many. They are also important in the United Kingdom and to a lesser extent Canada, where some older job losers benefit from early private pensions but where others have little to fall back upon once – or, in the case of the United Kingdom, even before – unemployment benefit is exhausted.[5] Once all public benefits are taken into account, even in those countries where private benefits are important, the public–private mix of early retirement support weighs heavily towards the public.

THE GENDER IMBALANCE OF PRIVATE PENSIONS

An important feature of private pension arrangements that has already been noted is the way in which, amongst current employees, they are more likely to cover men than women. This has its impact on the relative importance they make up in the retirement income package of men and women. A simple illustration of this is provided in Table 15.4. In most countries, private pensions make up only half as much of the pension income of older women than of older men; in Germany, even less. Only in Sweden is the difference rather smaller.

It is reasonable to assume that, in most households, income is shared. However, the death of one partner leads to the loss of that person's contribution to the household account. In so far as a man's private pension income is, on average, larger than that of his wife, widowhood can substan-

*Table 15.4   The public–private mix of age pensions for men and women
(own private pension as percentage of own gross income)*

	Men	Women	Women as % of Men
Canada	44	21	48
Finland	—	—	
Germany	6	1	15
Italy	7	3	46
Japan	4	2	45
Netherlands	53	10	18
Sweden	25	17	68
United Kingdom	55	21	39
United States	41	22	53

Note: Data refer to married men and married women aged 65–74; the ratio used is the share of own private pensions within total own pensions.

Source: Own calculations from LIS and equivalent data.

tially lower her wellbeing. This is over and above the diminution of individual wellbeing resulting from the loss of economies of scale that two-person households enjoy. It is possible to make an estimate of the size of the diminution by comparing women living in couples with those who are widows. Table 15.5 shows that, in three of the countries where private pensions are particularly important, widowhood results in a substantial loss of wellbeing due to a decline in the private pension income coming into the household. This decline is a consequence either of the total loss of the husband's pension or, at best, of its reversion to a lower survivor's pension. On the other hand, in these same three countries, the public pension system, to a greater or lesser extent, compensates for the fall in private pension income.

THE IMPACT OF INCOME FROM WORK

Studies of the role of the public and private contributors to wellbeing in old age have tended to concentrate upon pensions and the extent to which these are provided by the state or by company or individual savings plans. Private pensions can be regarded as a form of market income, public pensions as a form of non-market income. Another form of non-market income that should not be ignored, and that has been of some importance in the past for older people, is income from work. This, too, needs to be taken account of when assessing the nature of the pubic–private mix.

Table 15.5   The impact of widowhood on wellbeing

| | Percentage point fall in wellbeing that is attributable to loss of: | | | |
	Public pensions	Private pensions	Net pension result	Total fall in wellbeing
	Women aged 65–74			
Canada[a]	12	−13	−6	−32
United Kingdom	13	−11	2	−29
United States	5	−7	−3	−33
	Women aged 75 and over			
Canada[a]	12	−14	−2	−29
United Kingdom	8	−13	−4	−22
United States	3	−9	−6	−37

Notes:
[a] Includes divorced and never married.
In each case, the loss of economies of scale due to a move from a two-person household to a one-person household results in a fall in wellbeing of 29%.
Source: Own calculations from LIS and equivalent data.

Table 15.6   The relative importance of labour income (labour income as percentage of gross income)

	Canada	Finland	Germany	Italy	Japan	N'lands	Sweden	UK	USA
Household income (65–74)	23	15	16	21	62	9	12	17	35
Own income (men 65–74)	14	4	6	5	38	7	8	10	28

Source: Own calculations from LIS and equivalent data.

In Figure 15.1, some indications of the declining importance of labour incomes over the past quarter of a century were given. A fuller picture, for the mid-1990s, is given in Table 15.6. The very high contribution made by labour income to household income in Japan can be explained, in part, by the fact that, there, households 'demerge' late – children stay with their parents until, and sometimes even after, marriage – and sometimes even 'remerge': older people go back to live with their children, as subordinates in their households. However, as the second row of the table shows, the contribution of the older person's own labour income is also important. The high contribution made by labour income to own income in the United States, and to a lesser extent in Canada, can be explained by a tendency for older people to continue in some kind of paid employment, perhaps only part-time, after reaching normal retirement age and drawing a pension. Late 'demerging' is common in Italy.

THE IMPACT OF INCOME IN KIND

Studies of the role of the public and private contributors to wellbeing in old age have not only tended to concentrate upon pensions rather than earnings, they have also largely ignored the importance of in-kind benefits. Such benefits are largely, indeed almost exclusively, provided by the state and, thus, are public. One reason for their being ignored is that micro-data sets seldom contain any relevant information. Even if they do record enjoyment of in-kind benefits, they do not do so in a consistent manner. An even greater hindrance to taking in-kind benefits into account is that it is difficult to place a value upon them.

Nevertheless, such benefits are important. Their importance can be seen by referring to macro data on expenditure on publicly provided services to the elderly and disabled (primarily day centres, sheltered accommodation and domestic help services) and health care services: visits to doctors, medicines and hospital stays. Table 15.7 shows the size of such expenditures relative to expenditures on public age, disability and survivors benefits, cash

Table 15.7   Relative importance of public 'in-kind' benefits for older people

	Cash benefits	Social services	Medical care	Total benefits (cash and in-kind)
Canada	100	n/a	90	n/a
Finland	100	13	35	148
Germany	100	5	48	153
Italy	100	1	n/a	n/a
Japan	100	4	70	174
Netherlands	100	6	45	151
Sweden	100	30	46	176
United Kingdom	100	8	45	153
United States	100	1	70	n/a

Source: Own calculations from OECD Public Expenditure and Health data sets.

benefits primarily for older people. Results, particularly those for health care, are at best approximations and should be treated with care. However, in those countries for which full information is available, in-kind benefits seem to be worth between a half and three-quarters of public cash benefits. Of course, this is an average across all older people and all years of old age. Actual health care utilization will be much more 'lumpy' and concentrated in the last years, or even months, of life.

The value of in-kind benefits is highest in Japan and Sweden, although it is the consequence of extensive health care provision in the former and extensive housing and home-help provision in the latter.[6] Differences in the service mix are also apparent for the other countries and reflect very different cultures and institutions.

One further institutional difference that has to be taken into account when considering in-kind health services is how medical expenses are covered. It is well known that, unlike the other eight countries considered here, the United States does not have a universal health insurance system. Health insurance coverage is dependent upon whether an employer offers it or, in the absence of this, whether a person has purchased his or her own individual policy. The exception is people aged over 65 or in receipt of public disability benefits. However, whilst such people are covered by a form of public health insurance, the system concerned, Medicare, reimburses doctors' fees and hospitalization costs, but it does not reimburse the costs of prescription medicines, which can be high. Figure 15.4 shows that, amongst the oldest Americans, expenditure on health-related items accounts for an average of 16 per cent of all expenditures, compared with little over 2 per cent amongst the oldest Germans and Swedes. Thus, if the provision of in-kind benefits swings the public–private balance in one direction in most countries, in the United Sates, the nature of the health insurance system swings it somewhat in the other direction.

CONCLUSIONS AND MATTERS ARISING

By the mid-1990s, older people had, on average achieved a reasonable level of wellbeing. However, in the last decade, many governments have made reforms to their retirement income systems that have sought to reduce the generosity of public pensions and encourage a greater reliance on private pensions. Other reforms, which have restricted access to early retirement and, in some cases, even raised the age at which regular age pensions can be drawn, mean, if successful, that labour incomes will increase in importance.

Such reforms may result in higher levels of wellbeing, if diversified packages bring the benefits often suggested. They may, however, bring lower

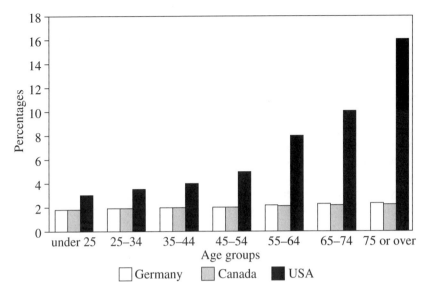

Source: Smeeding (1997).

*Figure 15.4   Share of household consumption accounted for by health
                spending*

levels of wellbeing, if people are left without access to one income source,
an early pension, and no opportunity to take advantage of another – a paid
job. Such people may be forced back onto means-tested benefits. In this
respect, a key to ensuring that reforms to pension systems do go hand-in-
hand with increased wellbeing is an improvement in macroeconomic performance. Only then are there likely to be sufficient employment opportunities
for older people and, thus, for labour income to play a more important role
in the income package of older people.

Private pension schemes are not, by definition, defined contribution
pension schemes. The new public pension systems in Italy and Sweden have
this characteristic, too. However, many private pensions do operate on a
money purchase basis and, in those countries where employers sponsor
pension plans, private, defined benefit schemes are being closed to new
entrants and replaced by defined contribution schemes. Moreover, the
sectors where defined contribution schemes tended to prevail are sectors
that are shrinking, whilst new employers, if they offer pension plans at all,
offer defined contribution plans. Money purchase or defined contribution
schemes leave more people faced with planning how to use their accumulated savings. If people underestimate their remaining length of life, they

could find their retirement income depleted prematurely. In this case, they will become dependent upon some form of public assistance. In addition, and in so far as defined contribution schemes establish a closer link between contributions and benefits, they tend to disadvantage women and they tend to increase the level of inequality in incomes amongst the retirement age population. They do this even if they do not lead to a greater proportion of the old having 'low' incomes.

Having considered some of the policy implications of the changing public–private mix, this chapter concludes with a few suggestions about how the mix itself should be studied in the future. It has argued that to concentrate upon pensions alone is insufficient. First, it is insufficient for a study of incomes in retirement either because labour incomes are still important in some countries, or because, if proposed reforms of pension systems are successful, they might become important. Labour income can be considered a further element within the private part of the income package. Second, it is insufficient for a study of incomes in early retirement because, at least in some countries, unemployment benefits, and even means-tested assistance, are the functional equivalent of early pensions. Such benefits are a further component of the public part of the income package.

Third, such a concentration is insufficient because the size of the public component is determined, in part, by the way benefits are provided. Some countries, particularly some of the Scandinavian ones, make considerable provision of benefits in kind. These take the form of social care services for which no or little charge is made. Taking such benefits into account is important in assessing the overall contribution of the state to the wellbeing of people in old age. Last, it is insufficient because consumption as well as income has to be considered when assessing the public–private mix. The impact of a health insurance system that places considerable emphasis on co-payments or that excludes critical items from reimbursement can be seen with reference to the United States. It might also be noted that, where private pension provision is voluntary rather than obligatory, contributions are not normally taken into account when disposable income is being assessed. Rather, they are only identifiable, if at all, through an analysis of consumption. A full assessment of the size of the public element within the public–private mix needs to take this into account.

NOTES

1. This chapter draws upon work undertaken while the authors were working in the Social Policy Division of the OECD. However, views expressed are those of the authors and should not be taken to represent the position of the OECD.

2. This is the 'Income Redistribution Survey'.
3. Except in so far as defined benefit systems tend to redistribute from members who leave before retirement age to those who stay.
4. This is because, whilst most older non-working men can be presumed to have been in work during most of their previous adult lives, this is not the case with respect to women. Many of those who are currently in old age might have stopped working once they started to have children, and many of these did not return to work later, or, if they did, did so on a part-time, casual or intermittent basis.
5. The level of unemployment benefit in the UK is so low that most recipients, particularly those with dependants, are eligible for complementary means-tested assistance.
6. In the case of Japan, some of the 'health' expenditure might actually relate to services closer to long-term care. In this case, it should be counted in column two rather than column three. The introduction of a mandatory long-term care insurance system in Japan in 2000 seems to have resulted in some shift of the care of the frail elderly from the health service to social services.

REFERENCES

Disney, R. and M. Mira D'Ercole (1998), 'Resources during Retirement', *OECD Ageing Working Papers*, 4 (3), Paris.
Förster, M. (2000), 'Trends and Driving Factors in Income distribution and Poverty in the OECD Area', Occasional Paper DEELSA/ELSDA/WD(2000)X, OECD, Paris.
OECD (2001), *Ageing and Income: financial resources and retirement in nine OECD countries*: Paris: OECD.
Smeeding, T. (1997), 'Reshuffling Responsibilities in Old Age: The United States in a comparative perspective.', Luxembourg Income Study, working paper 153 (*www.lisproject.org/publications/liswps/153.pdf*).
Yamada A. and B. Casey (2002), 'Getting Older, Getting Poorer? A study of the earnings, pensions, assets and living arrangements of older people in nine countries', Occasional Paper DEELSA/ELSDA/WD(2002), OECD, Paris.

16. Income packaging and economic wellbeing in the last stage of the working career

Martin Rein and Heinz Stapf-Finé

INTRODUCTION

The main purpose of this study is to identify the changing composition of income in the last stage of the working career. As a first step, we identify cross-national differences in the income mix among households with a head over the age of 55, with a special focus on the age groups 60–64 and 65–9, which are the transitional ages towards retirement. Second, we compare the income package of households at the top and the bottom end of the income distribution. Third, we investigate how the income package of the 65–9 age group changed between the mid-1980s and the mid-1990s. Finally, we examine the impact of these developments on the economic wellbeing of older people.

Luxembourg Income Study (LIS) data are used to analyse the experience of ten countries: Australia, Canada, Finland, Germany, Netherlands, Norway, Sweden, Switzerland, United Kingdom and United States. LIS provides detailed data on income sources of most of the industrialized countries. The intention of the LIS project is to make income data internationally comparable, by introducing a common system of classification.

HOW TO MEASURE INCOME PACKAGES

In this section we address the following methodological questions: what are the sources of income and what are useful categories for grouping these different sources of income; what is the unit of analysis, and what are the different approaches for measuring the income package?

Income Sources

The first methodological issue is to identify the income sources that need to be observed. We make use of nine different sources: wages (without the spouse), wages of the spouse, self-employment income, property income (assets), social retirement (statutory public pensions), means-tested income, pathways to retirement (primarily unemployment and disability transfers), occupational pensions (employer provided), other income.

The concept of pathways as an income source needs some clarification. Where there is a fixed chronological point of entry into the public social retirement system, a practice emerges to use other programmes for the younger age groups to serve the same purpose as pensions, namely labour force withdrawal. These programmes are found in all countries and are the functional equivalents to pensions, but have other programmatic names: disability, unemployment, sickness and accident insurance. We call these programmes, 'retirement pathways' because, when they are received by older household heads, they lead to exit from the labour force. These programmes regulate the exit from the labour market before age 65.

We have introduced a residual category of 'other income.' which includes public benefits, such as family allowances and also inter-family transfers. For a study of the last stage of the working career, this seems to be an acceptable procedure. However, this procedure does introduce some anomalies since, in some countries and in certain age groups, 'other income' is about 4 per cent of the gross household income. In our summary tables we pay special attention to four sources: (a) earnings (wages of all household members), (b) income from assets (identical with property income), (c) public or state transfer benefits (including social retirement, means-tested income and pathways to retirement), and (d) occupational pensions (individual personal accounts cannot be separated).

In the analysis that follows, we further simplify the income package and reduce the varied income sources into two types: income from transfers, including both state and occupational pensions, and market income from earnings and personal assets. The reason for combining occupational pensions and state transfers (social insurance, means-tested income and pathways) is that these sources are either substitutes or complements for each other. In recent pension reforms in Germany and Sweden, we see further confirmation that public policies regard private pensions and public pensions as substitutable. In both countries a portion of the former public pension is designated for use in creating personal accounts. We think that it is not the source of financing that is important, but its use. Moreover, in both forms of transfer the income is redistributed either over time or among individuals in the sense that the active generation is financing the pensions. In an increasing number of countries, means-tested programmes, and public and occupational pensions are tightly coupled by introducing the idea of transfer testing. Not total income, but only the transfer income is subject to a test of need in determining an individual's eligibility for benefits, as in the case of UK and Denmark.

Unit of Analysis

We use the household as the unit of analysis on the assumption that there is a pooling of resources and therefore economies of scales need to be taken into account, whereas other studies have focused on individuals or the family. To make households of different sizes comparable, we make use of an equivalence scale. We are using the OECD equivalence scale giving a weight of 1 to the household head, of 0.5 to the spouse and 0.3 to each of the other household members.[1] We group the households in five-year age groups, depending on the age of the household head. This is our measure of the stage in the life course.

Measurement Approaches

The issue is whether to construct income packages by weighting each source in terms of 'the share of total income' or by computing the share of each household's income first and then taking 'the mean percentage of the shares'.

A simple example helps to illustrate these different approaches. Consider one income source, namely, public transfer income. In the first approach, household A has $10000 in gross income and $2000 in public transfer income; household B has $100000 in gross income and $5000 in public transfer income. If we compute the shares first of household A, we get 20 per cent of its income from transfers while household B has 5 per cent. If we then take the mean of the shares of the two households, we get 12.5 per cent of their income coming from public transfers. This method effectively weights by household. Each household gets the same weight in the calculation of the mean. This approach might be called the 'mean of the shares'.

The second approach starts by taking account of the amount of gross and public transfer incomes of the two households together. If we add the gross incomes we get $110000. If we add the transfer incomes, we get $7000. Dividing $7000 by $110000 gives us a mean of 6.4 per cent. This approach effectively weights each household by its gross income. This might be called the 'mean share of total income' approach.

The choice of whether to compute an income package by using the 'mean of the shares' or the 'mean share of total income' depends on the question that we are trying to answer. If the question is the relative income source of the typical household, the weighting by household is the appropriate procedure. The 'mean of the shares' measure is therefore called for. In using this approach, it is necessary to exclude all the cases where the gross income was zero because it is not possible to divide by zero to calculate a share for each household. If the question is what percentage of the total income for different groups comes from each source, the appropriate measure is the 'mean share of total income'. We are inquiring into the question of what is the share of income of households for each five-year age group. It is for this reason that the mean of the shares is the appropriate measure.

It is interesting to note that in the United States the report prepared by Susan Grad and published by the Social Security Administration Office of Research and Statistics makes use primarily of the shares of aggregate income of aged units.[2] In many analyses of income sources using LIS data, the reverse situation is the case:[3] the mean of the shares approach is preferred.

The mean of the shares almost uniformly shows a larger role of the state than does the share of the total income approach. In the United States, almost a third of the income in the age group 62–4 comes from the state, following the share of the total income approach, compared to 42 per cent when using the mean of the shares approach (see Table 16.1).

Table 16.1 The mean of the shares and the share of total income of aged units in the USA, 1992

Income sources USA 1992	Mean of the shares			Share of total income		
	55–61	62–64	65+	55–61	62–64	65+
Retirement benefits	15	42	73	9.5	28.7	59.1
Social security	7	27	58	2.2	13.5	39.5
Gov't worker pensions	4	6	6	3.6	6.6	—
Private pension & annuity	5	9	8	3.6	8.2	10.2
Earnings	69	42	9	78.7	56.4	17.1
Public assistance	4	3	3	0.6	0.7	0.9
Income from assets	7	9	13	8.6	11.1	20.6

Source: Income of the Population 55 or Older, 1992, Social Security Administration, May 1994, Table VI A1 and Table VII 1, pp.89, 109.

These results are not at all surprising, since higher income groups have lower reliance on state income and more reliance on other income sources than do lower income groups. Results are sensitive to outliers. The share of total income is dominated by the sources of income that the wealthy receive. Therefore weighting by income reduces the role of the state as compared to weighting by household units.

INCOME PACKAGE AT DIFFERENT STAGES IN THE LIFE COURSE

In Table 16.2 we can observe the changing composition of income in the last stage of the working career. As expected, it can be seen that earnings decline with age. As we would also expect, in households with heads under the age of 55 the income from earnings is very high. At age 60–64, we can already observe the effect of early retirement as the income from pathways rises. And then, moving towards the retirement years, the role of earnings starts to decline. At the beginning of the retirement (age 65–9), earnings decline sharply, but they are still important in Australia, Canada, Norway[4] and the United States. In the Netherlands, earnings in this age group are dramatically lower. And the other countries lie in between these two extremes. In the United States, earnings continue to play a visible role even at age 70 and above.

Turning to property income, we see that households with a head below 55 years of age are still in the process of cumulating their assets. As a result, in most of the countries the income share from assets is low, at 3 per cent or less, Switzerland being the exception. With increasing age, however, the households have accumulated more assets and the role that these assets play in the income package is significant larger. In most countries we observe that assets in the income package increase with age. And, at age 70 plus, assets play a visible important role in Australia, Switzerland and the United States, possibly because of the influence of home ownership.

Occupational pensions play virtually no role for households headed by a person under 55. At age 60–64, they become increasingly more important as part of the early retirement package in the Netherlands, Sweden, the UK, Switzerland, the United States and Canada. In the case of Finland, LIS classifies the social security pension scheme as a private occupational pension, which is an error, and must be corrected so as not to come to misleading conclusions. Most Finnish experts agree that they are part of the statutory public system even if they are managed by the private sector. The importance of occupational pensions increases with age. After age 70, their importance seems to decline somewhat.

Public transfers below the age of 55 are important in Sweden, Finland, the Netherlands and the UK, but in other countries they only play a significant role at age 60–64, gaining in importance when social security becomes the major source of income.

To better explain cross-national differences, we use the market transfer dichotomy as the empirical framework to develop a typology of country differences (Table 16.3). As a first step in this analysis, we divided the countries into three ordinal categories (high, medium and low), depending on their

Table 16.2　Income packages at different stages in the life course in ten countries

	<55	60–64	65–69	70+
Earnings				
Australia	75.4	48.8	24.1	8.3
Canada	86.8	52.1	22.4	7.7
Finland	75.5	32.6	12.6	4.7
Germany	89.4	51.6	17.2	4.9
Netherlands	85.5	21.7	7.9	4.6
Norway	86.1	65.4	33.5	8.6
Sweden	75.9	49.9	16.1	3.6
Switzerland	91.3	66.3	15.1	7.3
UK	81.6	41.6	15.6	6.6
USA	91.0	61.4	28.8	11.6
Assets				
Australia	1.8	8.5	17.9	18.0
Canada	1.4	5.1	6.5	9.1
Finland	1.6	2.9	3.1	2.9
Germany	1.4	2.6	3.3	3.8
Netherlands	1.2	3.6	5.3	6.0
Norway	1.8	4.4	5.5	6.2
Sweden	1.9	4.5	5.0	7.0
Switzerland	4.7	13.1	19.2	19.6
UK	2.0	9.3	10.0	10.1
USA	2.5	8.3	12.2	12.7
Employer-provided pensions				
Australia	0.4	5.8	11.0	9.8
Canada	0.7	16.0	20.2	22.0
Finland	1.3	48.1	64.1	56.5
Germany	0.0	4.4	9.5	11.5
Netherlands	0.0	36.8	28.6	24.6
Norway	0.3	7.1	16.2	14.0
Sweden	0.5	13.9	16.4	13.3
Switzerland	0.3	10.2	21.8	17.4
UK	1.2	25.2	27.3	21.2
USA	0.4	12.4	17.4	9.5
Government transfers				
Australia	6.0	34.9	44.5	60.1
Canada	5.5	20.2	46.6	57.5
Finland	14.1	15.5	19.7	35.3
Germany	5.5	41.3	70.0	79.3
Netherlands	8.1	36.7	57.5	64.2
Norway	6.9	22.3	43.8	70.1
Sweden	12.5	31.0	62.0	74.9
Switzerland	2.8	10.1	43.1	55.0
UK	9.3	22.4	46.3	61.6
USA	5.2	17.4	41.3	58.1

Table 16.3   Transfer–market mix for ten countries, by age

Market	60–64	65–69	70+
High			
Australia	57.3	**42.0**	26.3
USA	69.7	**41.0**	24.3
Norway	69.8	**39.0**	14.8
Medium			
Switzerland	79.4	**34.3**	26.9
Canada	57.2	**28.9**	16.8
UK	50.9	**25.6**	16.7
Low			
Sweden	54.4	**21.1**	10.6
Germany	54.2	**20.5**	8.7
Finland	35.5	**15.7**	7.6
Netherlands	25.3	**13.2**	10.6
Transfer	60–64	65–69	70+
High			
Netherlands	73.5	**86.1**	88.8
Finland	63.6	**83.8**	91.8
Germany	45.7	**79.5**	90.8
Sweden	44.9	**78.4**	88.2
Medium			
UK	47.6	**73.6**	82.8
Canada	36.2	**66.8**	79.5
Switzerland	20.3	**64.9**	72.4
Low			
Norway	29.4	**60.0**	84.1
USA	29.8	**58.7**	67.6
Australia	40.7	**55.5**	69.9

share of each component of the public–private mix. This procedure was repeated for three age groups: 60–64, 65–9 and 70 plus. We did not include the 55–9 age group, since the earnings for this group are still quite substantial.

Other attempts at classification based on constructed types did not prove helpful, for several reasons. Models based on three pillars proved inadequate because they neglected to include the role of earnings of other members of households headed by an older person. Earnings turned out to be important, not only in the stage before retirement, but at virtually every stage thereafter. In the Smeeding *et al.*[5] study of private income sources, earnings, assets and occupational pensions are grouped together. This is a reasonable approach to the task of classifying income sources. We believe,

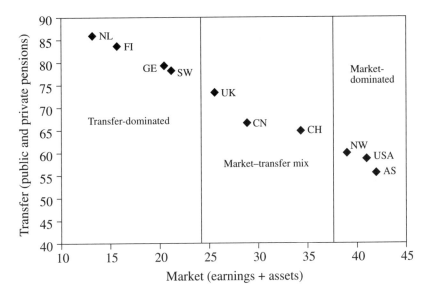

Figure 16.1   Transfer–market welfare mix (as a share of total income)

however, that it is conceptually more meaningful to group all forms of pension income together, since, as explained earlier, they perform a similar function. Obviously, this is an important point of disagreement and clearly requires further discussion and argumentation. Second, we expected that the income package might change at each stage of the working career; therefore a single classification of types was likely to be unsatisfactory. To sidestep this problem we focus on the 65–9 age group.

In Table 16.3 we examined whether there were natural cut-off points to distinguish the extent to which a country relied on market and on transfers. We found a uniform pattern starting at the age group 65–9. For this age group and for the 70 plus group, three categories of countries with high, medium and low reliance on earnings can be distinguished. This pattern is presented in Figure 16.1 for the 65–9 age group. The chart clearly depicts which source of income is dominant.

What emerges from this analysis of 10 countries is the three ideal types. The types are interesting in their own right and quite different from the conventional grouping in the literature.

Type 1: Transfer-dominated

Transfer domination occurs when a country is high on occupational pension and state transfers and low on earnings and cash property income.

The low market income shares range from 13 per cent to 21 per cent and the high transfer shares range from 78 per cent to 86 per cent as shown in Figure 16.1. The Netherlands represent the strongest prototype of this idealized pattern of transfer domination. This ideal type of transfer dominance is quite clear and unambiguous.

Type 2: Market–transfer Mix

This is a complementary pattern where transfers and market income complement each other. In other words, the elements of the package are nested and combined into a cumulative pattern, characterized by a medium-level position for each component of the package. The countries that fall into this pattern include two Anglo-American countries (Canada and UK) and one continental country (Switzerland). Had we decided on a dichotomy instead of three types, we would have drawn the line differently and included Switzerland as embracing a high market-dominated pattern.

Type 3: Market-dominated

The market-dominated pattern includes three countries where earnings and cash property income accounts for about 40 per cent of the household income at age 65 to 69. This is a very striking pattern especially since so much attention has been given to early retirement. But what we see is that earnings account for 39 per cent of total income in Norway, 41 per cent in the USA and 42 per cent in Australia. It seems likely that this pattern will increase, for two reasons: the better educated aging will want to continue their jobs since they are less physically stressful than blue-collar work, and many countries, as a matter of public policy, are encouraging the employment of older workers. In the summer of 2000, the USA removed any economic penalty for those working at age 65. Thus the social security programme was converted from a retirement programme into an age pension. In the case of Norway, one must take into consideration the later official retirement age of 67, and therefore the importance of earnings in this age group is greater than in other countries.

These three patterns appear to be quite robust. We are confident that we have identified, for households headed by those who are 65–9 years of age, two reasonably strong reciprocal patterns: one characterized by a strong reliance on earnings and assets, and the other by dominant pattern of transfers, occupational and state pensions. In addition there is a clear pattern which draws on the middle range of the market and transfer income components.

INCOME PACKAGE BY AGE AND POSITION IN THE INCOME DISTRIBUTION

We next analyse the income package of the top 60 per cent and bottom 40 per cent of the income distribution, not over time, but across the stage of the life cycle for the most recent year available at LIS. We know that the income package varies, not only by the life course, but by a household's position in the income distribution. The data are presented in Table 16.4.

The conventional way of dealing with this question is to create income deciles or quintiles, but, since we want to examine the role of both age and income, we believed this would make the results less robust, since the number of observations in each cell would be small. Instead we use a much cruder measure of the top 60 per cent and bottom 40 per cent of the household income distribution. The story that emerges is both complicated and interesting.

What we see, as expected, in all countries and in all age groups, is that the top of the income distribution receives a considerably larger share of their income from earnings as compared to the bottom of the distribution. And these differences are quite dramatic. Particularly striking is the case of Australia where half of the income package of the well-off end of the distribution at age 65–9 comes from earnings, compared to only 10 per cent for the bottom 40 per cent of the distribution. The reason for this discrepancy in Australia is self-evident, since the main source of public income in this age group is a national state-administered means-tested transfer age pension which penalizes earnings. But assets, by contrast, have a much higher income disregard. Thus the Australian assets at the bottom end of the income distribution are among the highest of the ten countries, with only those of Switzerland being higher. So the lesson from the Australian experience is that policy matters. A country can shape the income package by the way in which it designs the rules that guide its public transfer system.[6]

At the upper end of the income distribution, as compared to the bottom end, we find a greater reliance not only on earnings but also on property income that is convertible into a cash income flow which we call 'assets'. These assets become increasingly important over the life course for the well-off, but less so for the bottom end of the distribution, where they are more or less stable. The exceptions are Switzerland and Australia. So it appears that households in the upper end of the distribution accumulate resources that are later convertible into an income stream and that they are more able to do this than the bottom end of the income distribution. We cannot disaggregate the property income with LIS data and therefore cannot distinguish between savings, home ownership, equities and personal pensions accounts.

Table 16.4 Mean of the shares of income packages for the top 60 per cent and the bottom 40 per cent of the income distribution

	Top 60% of income distribution					Bottom 40% of income distribution				
Country	<55	55–59	60–64	65–69	70+	<55	55–59	60–64	65–69	70+
Netherlands 1994										
Earnings	92.3	69.7	23.9	16.1	5.5	73.0	31.8	19.4	2.1	4.2
Assets	1.3	3.3	4.2	8.9	12.3	1.1	5.2	2.9	2.8	2.7
State transfers	4.1	17.1	19.1	36.0	37.2	15.5	58.1	54.7	72.7	78.3
Private pensions	—	8.6	50.7	37.9	44.0	—	4.0	22.5	22.2	14.4
Finland 1995										
Earnings	85.2	67.0	44.5	19.7	8.2	59.6	28.0	14.9	6.5	2.5
Assets	2.0	3.2	3.2	4.7	5.2	1.0	1.8	2.5	1.7	1.4
State transfers	6.4	12.0	8.7	9.1	24.6	26.5	33.0	25.4	28.7	42.2
Private pensions	1.3	8.8	20.0	33.6	30.4	1.3	25.9	41.1	51.3	39.4
Germany 1994										
Earnings	94.1	87.4	62.2	17.6	6.8	82.0	72.1	39.2	16.6	2.8
Assets	1.9	3.2	3.7	4.1	4.8	0.6	1.2	1.3	2.5	2.7
State transfers	2.3	7.5	27.7	61.9	70.5	10.7	26.0	57.1	78.5	89.5
*Private pensions	0.2	1.4	6.4	16.2	17.5	—	—	2.0	2.2	4.4
Sweden 1995										
Earnings	85.2	79.3	55.9	21.9	8.7	60.0	55.8	34.3	8.1	1.4
Assets	2.0	3.6	4.3	5.4	8.9	1.8	5.1	4.9	4.4	6.2
State transfers	7.0	12.9	23.8	51.8	61.6	21.7	31.8	49.5	75.5	80.7
Private pensions	0.5	3.8	15.4	20.4	20.3	0.4	3.4	10.1	11.0	10.2

UK 1995										
Earnings	92.7	72.9	53.1	25.0	14.2	59.5	36.2	26.9	7.3	3.1
Assets	1.8	5.6	10.3	14.2	18.3	2.4	6.7	8.1	6.3	6.4
State transfers	1.6	6.1	12.8	26.6	31.0	24.5	35.7	34.5	63.6	75.6
Private pensions	1.3	14.5	22.8	33.6	35.9	1.0	15.9	28.3	21.8	14.5
Canada 1997										
Earnings	93.6	84.0	66.1	33.1	12.7	75.0	57.8	33.6	12.3	3.7
Assets	1.4	3.2	5.6	8.8	13.3	1.3	4.4	4.5	4.4	5.5
State transfers	2.3	3.2	8.7	28.4	37.5	11.3	18.9	35.4	63.7	74.2
Private pensions	0.7	6.9	16.2	26.1	33.3	0.7	8.7	15.7	14.6	12.7
Switzerland 1992										
Earnings	92.2	84.2	67.7	19.5	9.7	90.2	84.4	61.0	8.6	4.8
Assets	5.5	9.6	13.9	21.6	26.7	3.6	3.7	10.3	15.6	12.9
State transfers	1.3	4.4	7.8	30.2	36.7	4.5	9.5	18.2	62.1	72.2
Private pensions	0.3	1.3	10.3	28.1	26.2	0.3	0.8	9.8	12.5	9.2
Norway 1995										
Earnings	90.5	85.3	74.5	46.1	20.3	77.0	69.5	49.4	20.3	4.5
Assets	2.2	3.8	4.2	6.5	8.6	1.1	2.6	4.8	4.5	5.3
State transfers	3.7	8.7	14.5	28.4	46.7	13.0	24.6	36.1	59.9	78.7
Private pensions	0.3	1.3	6.3	18.4	23.8	0.2	1.3	8.5	14.0	10.4
USA 1997										
Earnings	93.9	83.2	68.6	34.7	17.9	86.4	70.9	47.4	20.2	6.4
Assets	3.4	7.3	9.6	16.3	20.2	1.2	5.5	5.9	6.4	6.4
State transfers	1.5	3.1	8.3	26.1	37.2	11.0	16.3	35.2	63.1	75.6
*Private pensions	0.9	5.9	13.1	12.6	22.4	0.6	7.1	10.9	10.0	11.3
Australia 1994										
Earnings	95.2	91.2	76.1	49.8	25.2	69.6	44.4	27.6	9.1	3.9
Assets	1.9	5.5	10.1	24.9	27.3	1.7	8.2	7.2	13.9	15.6
State transfers	1.3	1.8	6.3	7.4	21.1	16.4	40.6	57.2	66.0	70.3
Private pensions	0.4	0.9	6.7	17.2	23.0	0.4	4.4	5.1	7.4	6.3

Note: *Includes public and private occupational pensions.

Turning next to the transfer system, what we find is that employer-provided pensions over the life course are, as expected, uniformly higher for the top compared to the bottom end of the distribution. This pattern of greater importance of the private pensions at the top end of the distribution holds uniformly after the conventional retirement age of 65. Finland, at first sight, seems to be an exception, but this is not really the case, because state and private pensions must be added together since, in constructing Table 16.4, we use the LIS definition which misspecified private pensions which are really part of the public statutory programme. Virtually the entire private sector is covered by a mandatory earnings-related pension, that is partially funded and administered by pension funds and life insurance companies.[7] In some countries, such as the Netherlands and the UK, private pensions are even more important than all the state transfers for the top end of the income distribution, but, for the bottom end of the distribution, state transfers dominate.

However, this pattern is somewhat different for the period immediately before the entry into the normal social retirement programmes of the state at age 60–64. What we see is that, in countries such as the UK, Switzerland, Norway, Canada and Australia, private pensions are broadly similar at both ends of the income distribution. The reason appears to be that the structure of the pathway programmes (unemployment insurance, sickness and disability) has a different public–private mix in these countries as compared with the normal retirement age.

But the most striking transfer pattern that emerges from these data is that income packages exist only at the top end of the income distribution. Income diversification appears to be strongly skewed in the income distribution. And this pattern of discrepancy between reliance on the state at the bottom end of the distribution compared to the top is not only true in Anglo-American countries, but it is also found in Social Democratic welfares states like Sweden and the Netherlands. Consider the case of Sweden. After reaching the retirement age, 75 per cent of the income share comes from the state in the low end of the distribution, compared to only about 50 per cent at the top of the distribution. Even more striking is the Dutch pattern, where the bottom end of the distribution gets almost three-quarters of its income from state transfers and the top gets about a third. However, this pattern should not be overstated, because, at both ends of the income distribution, the state becomes increasingly more important with age.

INCOME PACKAGING AND WELLBEING

In summary, then, we find that for the years before retirement there are many ways of combining the elements of an income package. What is crucial for our concerns is whether the pattern makes any difference in terms of its effect on wellbeing. We have chosen to measure wellbeing in terms of three indexes: the poverty rate set at half of the mean of adjusted household income, the gini coefficient as a measure of inequality, and relative net adjusted disposable income,[8] where the adjustments take family size into account. In the measure of net adjusted disposable income the comparison is with the household headed by a person under 55 years of age. This is a measure of how well-off households in the last stage of the life course are relative to those at an earlier stage, rather than in comparison to all households.

Does the market–transfer mix provide a clue about its impact on our three measures of economic wellbeing? The data in Table 16.5 show that some effects are clear. If a country has high market and low transfer income, the poverty rates are substantially higher and the inequality much greater than when the situation is reversed, as in the Netherlands. However, Norway is an exception, because it shows that a country can have low poverty and inequality, even if it is market-dominated. The Norwegian market domination arises mainly because of its heavy reliance on earnings, largely because the retirement age is 67. However, a third of the household income in Norway comes from work, where the spouse contributes slightly

Table 16.5   The market–transfer mix and wellbeing of households

Pattern	Country	Poverty rate[1]		Gini		Relative net dpi[2]	
		60–64	65–69	60–64	65–69	60–64	65–69
Transfer-	Netherlands	7.2	8.2	0.2833	0.2568	0.94	0.83
dominated	Finland	5.7	8.9	0.2237	0.2281	1.01	0.91
	Germany	12.9	7.8	0.2872	0.2645	0.94	0.94
	Sweden	4.1	2.2	0.1999	0.1934	1.07	0.98
Market–	UK	14.6	17.0	0.2978	0.2911	0.86	0.81
transfer mix	Canada	21.3	8.5	0.3309	0.2678	0.92	0.88
	Switzerland	6.9	6.8	0.3009	0.3487	1.22	1.11
Market-	Norway	7.6	6.6	0.2260	0.2718	1.02	1.00
dominated	USA	23.3	24.7	0.4024	0.3881	1.08	0.97
	Australia	32.4	29.6	0.3831	0.2973	0.78	0.66

Notes:
[1] Equivalence scale = 1/0.5/0.3; as a percentage of mean income.
[2] Relative net disposable income: ratio of net adjusted income of the given age group divided by the disposable income of the age group under 55.

more to the household income at age 65–9 than does the male head from his wages. The same pattern of the importance of the spouse's income occurs for the other age groups under consideration (60–64, 70 plus) (see appendix). This reliance on the income of the spouse is found also in some other Nordic countries, but not to the same extent.

But by the measure of relative net disposable income we find the extremes lie within a type, rather than across types. Switzerland has the highest net disposable income for households headed by a person aged 65–9, while UK and Canada, with almost the same type, have a relative low disposable income. A similar discrepancy is found for Australia as compared to Norway and the United States. By this measure similar types yield different outcomes, and similar outcomes can be found with different types.

On the other hand, different types can also produce similar outcomes using the measure of poverty and inequality. Norway and Holland have similar poverty and ginis, even though Norway is market-dominated and the Netherlands are transfer-dominated. The USA and Australia also seem to produce similar outcomes of high poverty and inequality when compared to the UK.

If we start with the outcome rather than the input, it would seem to be the case that poverty and inequality are greatest in countries where pensions, both occupational and public, are low and earning and assets are high or medium. The other combinations seem to have a less decisive impact on wellbeing. On the other hand, low poverty and inequality can also be achieved through different types of mixes, as the comparison of Norway and Holland suggests. However, the transfer-dominated pattern uniformly produces the best poverty results, but not necessarily the best relative net disposable income. These data confirm how different measures of wellbeing affect our results.

The finding that outcomes vary within a type and across types is important. It suggests that the same types can lead to different results and that different types can yield similar outcomes. In brief, there are different ways to achieve low poverty and inequality. Occupational and public pensions can be complementary and not merely substitutes for each other – a pattern which holds for Sweden as well as Holland. Similarly, market income and pensions can combine in different ways.

These data, with modification, support the Smeeding, Torrey and Rainwater[9] findings that, the smaller the role of public sources, the higher the level of income inequality and poverty. There are two important qualifications to this thesis: what the transfer domination pattern does can also be achieved by the market–transfer mix (Switzerland) and also by the market-dominated pattern (Norway).

In a more recent paper, Tim Smeeding also qualifies this hypothesis: 'At higher income levels one finds a more balanced portfolio in almost all nations.'[10] Thus he seems to agree that the income composition also matters.

ANALYSIS OF TRENDS IN THE INCOME PACKAGE OF EIGHT COUNTRIES BETWEEN 1980 AND 1995

In the rest of this chapter we proceed by examining the different income packages at the top 60 per cent and the bottom 40 per cent of the income distribution, measuring the income shares in terms of the mean of the individual share of each household. We start with a portrait of four main income sources for eight countries over time, using only the earliest and latest year for which we have data. We separate earnings from assets in market income and occupational pensions and state social security in transfer income, creating four main income sources, and consider trends over time for each of the two income classes. We present the main findings and consider their implications for theory and practice.

Table 16.6 summarizes our findings. The data confirm the expected variations across countries and show as well how this pattern varies by a household's position in the income distribution. Reaching the age of 65 to 69, households work less and rely more on state transfers in all countries. In this table we focus on the conventional age of retirement and uncover some surprises, or at least observations that are not self-evident.

The first most striking finding in Table 16.6 is how substantial is the share of earnings in the last stage of the working career, how strong is the difference between the top 60 per cent and the bottom 40 per cent of the income distribution, and how varied is the experience of different countries. In 1980, at age 65–9, high-income households' earnings account for between 28 and 45 per cent of household income in all countries except the Netherlands and Germany. In 1995, the overall situation remained the same, but in four countries we actually see a rather sharp decline in the earnings share of the well-off, which is not offset by an increase in asset income.

Considering the income distribution as a whole at age 65–9, a clear pattern can be found over time: there is an observable retreat of the state in almost all countries, Germany being the only exception. The reduction of state transfers is offset by increases in employer-provided pensions, but not by increases in earnings and cash property income. Only in Australia is the share of earnings significantly rising. A paper by Scherer using OECD data reports that in the 'top three deciles, the share of income provided by social security transfers has been growing in almost all countries'.[11] Note that the difference in findings is due to the different definitions of the public sector. We have a broader definition of the public sphere which includes means

Table 16.6 *Trends in state transfers, employer-provided pensions, earnings and property income at age 65–9 as the mean of the shares of gross income*

Country	1980			1995		
	Total sample (%)	Top 60% (%)	Bottom 40% (%)	Total sample (%)	Top 60% (%)	Bottom 40% (%)
Netherlands (1983, 1994)						
State transfers	64.1	46.2	88.1	57.7	36.0	72.7
Emp.-provided	22.9	35.1	6.8	28.6	37.9	22.2
Earnings	10.5	15.0	4.6	7.9	16.1	2.1
Property inc.	1.5	2.6	0.1	5.3	8.9	2.8
Germany (1987, 1994)						
State transfers	62.4	50.4	79.8	70.0	61.9	78.5
Emp.-provided	15.9	22.4	4.0	9.5	16.2	2.2
Earnings	15.4	19.8	9.1	17.2	17.6	16.6
Property inc.	6.5	7.2	5.5	3.3	4.1	2.5
UK (1979, 1995)						
State transfers	63.0	30.1	79.3	46.3	26.6	63.6
Emp.-provided	12.6	20.7	8.5	27.3	33.6	21.8
Earnings	16.4	38.3	5.3	15.6	25.0	7.3
Property inc.	6.7	9.5	5.4	10.0	14.2	6.3
Canada (1981, 1997)						
State transfers	49.1	22.0	70.4	46.6	28.4	63.7
Emp.-provided	9.3	14.7	5.2	20.2	26.1	14.6
Earnings	20.6	36.4	8.2	22.4	33.1	12.3
Property inc.	17.1	23.4	12.1	6.5	8.8	4.4

Switzerland (1982, 1992)						
State transfers	51.4	31.1	67.1	43.1	30.2	62.1
Emp.-provided	12.5	18.5	7.9	21.8	28.1	12.5
Earnings	17.5	27.9	9.5	15.1	19.5	8.6
Property inc	17.7	21.6	14.6	19.2	21.6	15.6
Norway (1979, 1995)						
State transfers	49.5	29.3	72.6	43.8	28.4	59.9
Emp.-provided	5.3	6.8	3.5	16.2	18.4	14.0
Earnings	38.2	56.7	17.2	33.5	46.1	20.3
Property inc	5.6	5.8	5.4	5.5	6.5	4.5
USA (1979, 1997)						
State transfers	51.7	29.2	72.9	41.3	26.1	63.1
Emp.-provided	10.7	15.6	6.0	17.4	22.6	10.0
Earnings	24.3	35.4	13.5	28.8	34.7	20.2
Property inc	12.6	18.6	6.7	12.2	16.3	6.4
Australia (1981, 1994)						
State transfers	57.9	16.1	76.5	44.5	7.4	66.0
Emp.-provided	4.4	9.7	2.0	11.0	17.2	7.4
Earnings	16.8	44.6	4.4	24.1	49.8	9.1
Property inc	16.4	26.7	11.7	17.9	24.9	13.9

testing and pathways. In addition Scherer's study uses net income, a decile distribution and a different data set. Another OECD study by Casey and Yamada using mainly LIS data confirms, however, the growth of private or company pensions and reconfirms our findings that, in four countries (Canada, the Netherlands, the UK and the USA), and employer-provided pension 'constitutes a substantial part of incomes in retirement'.[12]

One would expect the upper 60 per cent of the income distribution over time to rely less on the state. But what we observe is that there is only a slight decline of their reliance on state transfers. However, what is remarkable is that it is the lower part of the income distribution that gets less from the state. And this is a uniform pattern over all the countries. Employer-provided pensions increase uniformly, with two exceptions: the USA and Germany. In these countries the decline appears also to be met by a stronger work commitment at the bottom end of the income distribution. We did not expect that the role of earnings in the income package of households would increase after age 65. And we would not have expected the rich to work less over time and the poor to work more. But this appears to be the pattern we find, with the share of the income of the bottom being higher, with the exceptions of the Netherlands and Switzerland.

CONCLUSION

Since the poverty rates are higher in the Anglo-American countries where the state benefits are lower, and the poverty rates are lower in the European countries where the state benefit share of household income is larger, Smeeding, Torrey and Rainwater reached the following important conclusion: 'The smaller the role of public sources of income the higher the level of income inequality.' They argue that the reason for this outcome is that 'private sources are less stable across age and over time than public sources. These public transfer sources of income are those which are systematically adjusted for price change and which provide fail-safe sources of income among the aged'. As reported earlier, in their study private sources are defined as earnings, income from assets and occupational pensions. We tell a very different story, because we believe that occupational pensions cannot readily be separated into public and private components in most countries. The state accounts in most countries for less than half of the gross household income of the more affluent 60 per cent of the income distribution and between 60 and 70 per cent of the less affluent bottom 40 per cent of the distribution.

Consider in more detail the situation in the United Kingdom. Data from the Goode report show the trends in the composition of gross income of pensioner units. In 1979, the state pension accounted for 61 per cent of aged household income, occupational pension 16 per cent, savings and earnings 12 per cent each. By 1990–91, state pension declined to 50 per cent, occupational pensions grew to 22 per cent, savings to 20 per cent, while earnings declined to 10 per cent.[13] In the Smeeding, Torrey and Rainwater paper, covering roughly the same period of time, the percentage of low-income people over 60 years of age declined from 17 per cent to 6.7 per cent. Even the Gini for heads aged 65–74 declined slightly, from 0.251 to 0.235. These data are very striking: poverty and inequality decline in the face of declining state pensions and a growing occupational and personal pillar. So something else must be at play other than the mix itself.

We report that countries like the Netherlands and the UK all have high occupational pensions. The Dutch data on public pensions are imputed and are therefore probably an overestimate, since there are undoubtedly many households that qualify for lower benefits since they do not meet the eligibility requirement for years of coverage. But we know that in these countries occupational pensions are large. Yet only in the UK are poverty relatively high and state pensions relatively low and declining, as discussed above. An effective public transfer system can be combined with a substantial occupational system, as appears to be the case in the Netherlands. The main difference is the level of coverage. In the Netherlands, despite low union membership, the Dutch have in effect created a hybrid system; contracts are voluntary, but once agreed upon are mandatory under certain conditions. The result appears to be a public mandatory occupational system covering 90 per cent or more of all workers, whereas the UK system of occupational pensions covers perhaps half of wage and salary workers. Yet the Netherlands has one of the lowest poverty and inequality measures among Western economies. What accounts for the parallel expansion of occupational pensions and low inequality? One interpretation is that inequality depends on three main factors: the level of coverage and the height of the income ceiling that is protected and the value of the benefits received.

Consider another feature in the design of the mix that positively affects the wellbeing of the aged. Before the current pension reform in Sweden, some analysts predicted that, with continued economic growth, the ATP in Sweden's earnings-related scheme would simply become a new, higher, basic-level pension as most of the full-time working population would earn above this income ceiling. Occupational pensions in Sweden are the outcome of national collective bargaining agreements covering virtually the whole working population. Occupational pensions in this context had an important distributional effect. They stabilized the present distribution of income and prevented the further narrowing of the distribution of income by continually raising the ceiling of protection. Greater income equality was being achieved by this silent strategy of raising the floor while keeping the same ceiling. Occupational pensions acted to offset this equalizing trend and stabilized the income distribution.

The British, Dutch and Swedish examples would seem to suggest that the hypothesis that 'the smaller the role of public sources the higher the level of inequality' needs to be qualified. The proposition holds under certain conditions, namely, when coverage of the occupational pension is limited to a small segment of the population and when public pensions have a low and declining replacement rate. The issue of the relative role of public and private pensions is very much on the political agenda of many countries, hence understanding under what conditions occupational pensions can reinforce rather than threaten objectives to equalize income and reduce poverty.

All countries seem to be moving towards a public–private mix. Our analysis shows that it is not the mix per se that affects the wellbeing of the aged, but how the mix is designed.

NOTES

1. On the sensitivity of the results according to the use of different equivalent scales, see Michael Förster, 'Comparing poverty in 13 OECD countries: traditional and synthetic approaches', LIS working paper 100, 1993.
2. Susan Grad, *Income of the Population 55 or Older, 1992* (Washington, DC: U.S. Department of Health and Human Services, Social Security Administration Office of Research and Statistics, May 1994, SSA publication No. 13-11981).
3. These comments are based on a personal conversation of Martin Rein with Susan Grad. Europeans have also noticed the issue, but reached different conclusions about how to handle the matter. See, for example, Juergen K. Kohl, 'The Public/Private Mix in the Income Package of the Elderly. A Comparative Study', a paper prepared for the conference, 'Social Security Fifty Years After Beveridge', University of York, England, September 1992. Kohl identifies the two approaches to measure income shares and concludes that what we have called 'the mean of the shares' approach 'gives a more realistic view of the income structure typical for the majority of the households. For this reason, preference is given to this variant in the following analysis'. Susan Grad's report for the USA Social Security Administration followed the opposite convention, weighting by income rather than household.
4. In the case of Norway, this is due to a later official retirement age of 67 years.
5. Tim Smeeding, Barbara Torrey and Lee Rainwater, 'Going to Extremes: An International Perspective on the Economic Status of the US Aged', LIS working paper 87, February, 1993.
6. See Whiteford, Chapter 3 in this volume.
7. Tryggi Thor Herbertsson, Michael Orzag and Peter Orgag, 'Retirement in the Nordic Countries', prepared for the Nordic Council, May 2000, pp.72–84
8. We are using the OECD equivalence scale (1.0/0.5/0.3). On the sensitivity of the results according to the use of different equivalent scales, see Michael Förster, 'Comparing poverty in 13 OECD countries: traditional and synthetic approaches', LIS working paper 100, 1993. We opted for measuring poverty as a percentage of households below

half of the mean income, since we get a more pronounced picture compared to using the median income, because our interest was to relate the poverty measures to different public–private mixes.

9. Tim Smeeding, Barbara Torrey and Lee Rainwater, 'Going to Extremes: An International Perspective on the Economic Status of the US Aged', LIS working paper 87, February, 1993.
10. Tim Smeeding, 'Income Maintenance in Old Age: What can be learned from cross-national comparisons', paper prepared for the Third Annual Conference of the Retirement Research Consortium, 17–18 May 2001, Washington, DC, p.20.
11. Peter Scherer, 'Financial resources in retirement: the roles of pensions and other sources', paper presented at the Ninth International Research Seminar on 'Issues in Social Security', 15–18 June 2002, Sigtunahojden, Sigtuna, Sweden, p.7
12. See Casey and Yamada, Chapter 15 in this volume.
13. *The Goode Report on Pension Law Reform* (1994, pp.152–3).

APPENDIX

Table 16A.1 *Income source of household as a percentage of gross income by age (total of the income distribution)*

Australia 1994	Total	<55	55–59	60–64	65–69	70+
Wages without spouse	46.4	56.5	49.0	28.6	14.7	5.7
Self-employed	8.3	8.9	10.6	11.1	4.9	1.8
Spouse % gross wage	17.3	21.8	15.8	9.1	4.5	0.8
Total earnings	72.0	87.2	75.4	48.8	24.1	8.3
Property income	5.2	1.8	6.4	8.5	17.9	18.0
Social retirement	6.3	0.2	0.8	4.9	37.1	35.4
Means-tested	0.3	0.3	0.3	0.3	—	—
Pathways	9.8	5.5	13.8	29.7	7.4	24.7
Total state	16.4	6.0	14.9	34.9	44.5	60.1
Private pensions	2.5	0.4	2.1	5.8	11.0	9.8
Other income	3.9	4.6	1.2	2.0	2.5	3.8

Canada 1997	Total	<55	55–59	60–64	65–69	70+
Wages without spouse	45.0	54.8	48.1	31.7	11.9	4.1
Self-employed	6.6	7.3	8.4	7.0	4.0	1.8
Spouse % gross wage	20.0	24.7	18.7	13.4	6.5	1.8
Total earnings	71.6	86.8	75.2	52.1	22.4	7.7
Property income	2.9	1.4	3.6	5.1	6.5	9.1
Social retirement	10.1	0.8	3.1	12.7	44.9	56.5
Means-tested	2.3	2.2	3.0	5.7	0.9	0.8
Pathways	2.1	2.5	2.4	1.8	0.8	0.2
Total state	14.5	5.5	8.5	20.2	46.6	57.5
Private pensions	5.6	0.7	7.5	16.0	20.2	22.0
Other income	5.4	5.6	5.2	6.7	4.4	3.6

Finland 1995	Total	<55	55–59	60–64	65–69	70+
Wages without spouse	31.2	40.4	23.6	9.4	1.4	1.0
Self-employed	7.4	8.0	9.7	8.1	5.1	2.2
Spouse % gross wage	22.5	27.1	23.8	15.1	6.1	1.5
Total earnings	61.1	75.5	57.1	32.6	12.6	4.7
Property income	2.0	1.6	2.9	2.9	3.1	2.9
Social retirement	4.3	0.5	3.2	6.8	16.5	25.0
Means-tested	5.0	6.4	2.5	1.7	1.3	0.8
Pathways	7.4	7.2	11.6	7.0	1.9	9.5
Total state	16.7	14.1	17.3	15.5	19.7	35.3
Private pensions	9.6	1.3	13.1	28.5	43.1	35.8
Public sector pensions	5.5	0.7	8.5	19.6	21.0	20.7
Other income	5.0	6.8	1.2	1.0	0.5	0.6

Germany 1994	Total	<55	55–59	60–64	65–69	70+
Wages without spouse	48.9	61.5	62.2	32.7	10.0	2.7
Self-employed	4.9	6.3	2.8	4.9	2.2	0.8
Spouse % gross wage	17.1	21.6	17.5	14.0	5.0	1.4
Total earnings	70.9	89.4	82.5	51.6	17.2	4.9
Property income	2.0	1.4	2.5	2.6	3.3	3.8
Social retirement	17.8	0.8	7.3	36.1	67.4	77.3
Means-tested	2.2	2.6	1.5	2.2	1.5	0.5
Pathways	2.3	2.1	4.7	3.0	1.1	1.5
Total state	22.3	5.5	13.5	41.3	70.0	79.3
Private pensions	0.7	—	0.4	1.1	2.7	3.0
Public sector pensions	1.8	0.1	0.5	3.3	6.8	8.5
Other income	2.3	3.6	0.5	0.2	0.2	0.4

Netherlands 1994	Total	<55	55–59	60–64	65–69	70+
Wages without spouse	46.8	59.7	44.4	13.1	3.9	3.6
Self-employed	3.7	4.2	5.3	2.5	2.2	0.5
Spouse % gross wage	16.5	21.6	8.7	6.1	1.8	0.5
Total earnings	67.0	85.5	58.4	21.7	7.9	4.6
Property income	2.3	1.2	3.8	3.6	5.3	6.0
Social retirement	8.8	0.3	1.0	3.4	46.8	63.4
Means-tested	2.1	2.2	3.3	2.2	1.0	0.5
Pathways	8.8	5.6	24.9	31.1	9.7	0.3
Total state	19.7	8.1	29.2	36.7	57.5	64.2
Private pensions	7.2	—	7.2	36.8	28.6	24.6
Other income	3.9	5.1	1.3	1.3	0.8	0.6

Norway 1995	Total	<55	55–59	60–64	65–69	70+
Wages without spouse	40.4	51.2	45.8	36.4	13.0	3.4
Self-employed	7.8	8.6	13.0	9.3	6.0	1.8
Spouse % gross wage	21.5	26.3	22.8	19.7	14.5	3.4
Total earnings	69.7	86.1	81.6	65.4	33.5	8.6
Property income	3.0	1.8	3.5	4.4	5.5	6.2
Social retirement	12.7	1.4	1.6	3.0	27.5	68.1
Means-tested	1.2	1.6	0.8	0.3	0.3	0.1
Pathways	5.9	3.9	10.2	19.0	16.0	1.9
Total state	19.8	6.9	12.6	22.3	43.8	70.1
Private pensions	3.9	0.3	1.3	7.1	16.2	14.0
Other income	3.6	5.0	1.0	0.8	0.9	1.0

Sweden 1995	Total	<55	55–59	60–64	65–69	70+
Gross wages						
without spouse	34.1	45.8	42.3	24.7	3.2	0.5
Self-employed	2.6	2.9	3.5	3.5	1.3	0.7
Spouse % gross wage	22.1	27.2	29.1	21.7	11.6	2.4
Total earnings	58.8	75.9	74.9	49.9	16.1	3.6
Property income	3.3	1.9	3.9	4.5	5.0	7.0
Social retirement	18.4	1.3	7.9	22.0	58.7	73.4
Means-tested	2.5	3.4	0.6	1.2	0.9	1.2
Pathways	6.3	7.8	7.8	7.8	2.4	0.3
Total state	27.2	12.5	16.3	31.0	62.0	74.9
Private pensions	4.8	0.5	3.7	13.9	16.4	13.3
Other income	6.0	9.1	1.1	0.8	0.6	1.1

Switzerland 1992	Total	<55	55–59	60–64	65–69	70+
Gross wages	53.7	65.8	64.9	49.2	7.7	3.5
Self-employed	8.2	9.6	9.7	7.8	3.5	2.1
Spouse % gross wage	12.5	15.9	9.7	9.3	3.9	1.7
Total earnings	74.4	91.3	84.3	66.3	15.1	7.3
Property income	8.2	4.7	8.4	13.1	19.2	19.6
Social retirement	10.0	0.8	3.4	8.3	42.1	52.3
Means-tested	0.8	0.7	0.7	0.5	0.7	1.8
Pathways	1.2	1.3	1.4	1.3	0.3	0.9
Total state	12.0	2.8	5.5	10.1	43.1	55.0
Private pensions	4.5	0.3	1.2	10.2	21.8	17.4
Other income	0.9	1.0	0.7	0.3	0.9	0.8

United Kingdom 1995	Total	<55	55–59	60–64	65–69	70+
Gross wages						
without spouse	37.2	48.2	36.4	23.5	6.1	3.5
Self-employed	9.6	12.0	10.0	6.8	4.1	1.4
Spouse % gross wage	16.6	21.4	14.2	11.3	5.4	1.7
Total earnings	63.4	81.6	60.6	41.6	15.6	6.6
Property income	4.4	2.0	6.0	9.3	10.0	10.1
Social retirement	9.3	0.2	0.8	3.3	35.8	54.6
Means-tested	5.7	6.1	6.5	5.8	2.4	4.8
Pathways	4.5	3.0	8.7	13.3	8.1	2.2
Total state	19.5	9.3	16.0	22.4	46.3	61.6
Private pensions	8.3	1.2	15.0	25.2	27.3	21.2
Other income	4.3	5.9	2.4	1.4	0.9	0.5

United States 1997	Total	<55	55–59	60–64	65–69	70+
Gross wages						
without spouse	49.0	59.8	49.8	35.8	15.3	6.9
Self-employed	5.2	5.5	7.6	6.8	3.2	1.6
Spouse % gross wage	21.6	25.7	22.3	18.8	10.3	3.1
Total earnings	75.8	91.0	79.7	61.4	28.8	11.6
Property income	4.9	2.5	6.8	8.3	12.2	12.7
Social retirement	10.4	1.2	3.7	13.3	39.0	55.5
Means-tested	2.5	3.0	1.6	2.4	1.2	1.1
Pathways	1.2	1.0	1.5	1.7	1.1	1.5
Total state	14.1	5.2	6.8	17.4	41.3	58.1
Private pensions	2.7	0.4	3.4	7.7	9.8	9.5
Public sector pensions	2.1	0.4	2.8	4.7	7.6	7.8
Other income	0.5	0.6	0.4	0.5	0.4	0.2

Index